Tenoy
Feel the LOVE

David Chelsea
2011

David Chelsea
in Love

David Chelsea

DAVID CHELSEA

In Love

Reed
Graphica

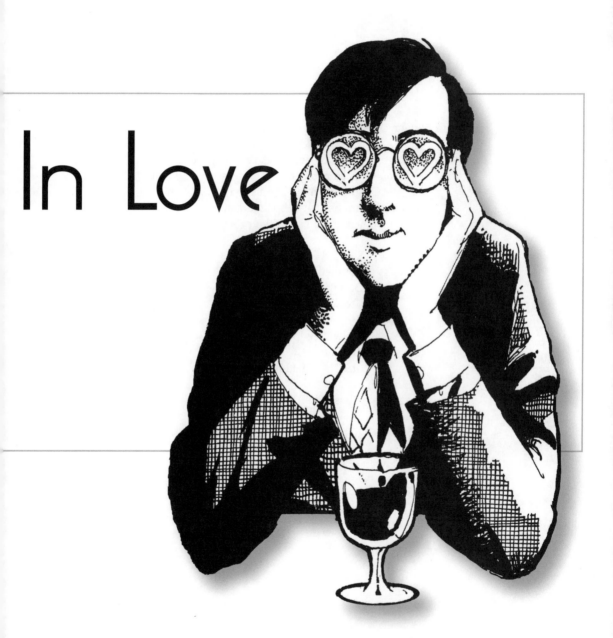

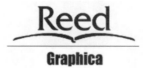

DAVID CHELSEA IN LOVE ™

Copyright © 1991, 1992, 1993, 2003 by David Chelsea

A Reed Graphica Book
Published by Reed Press™
360 Park Avenue South
New York, NY 10010

www.reedpress.com

ISBN: 1-59429-004-0

Originally published in 1993 by Eclipse Books.

Book design by John Reinhardt Book Design

Printed in the United States of America

10 9 8 7 6 5 4 3 2 1

BIO

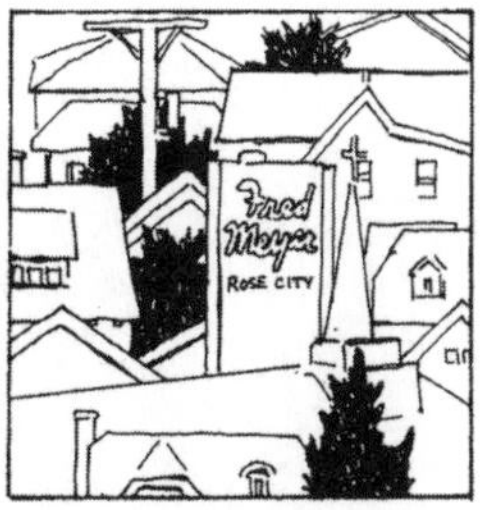

Fred Meyer
ROSE CITY

I was born in Portland, Oregon, in 1954.

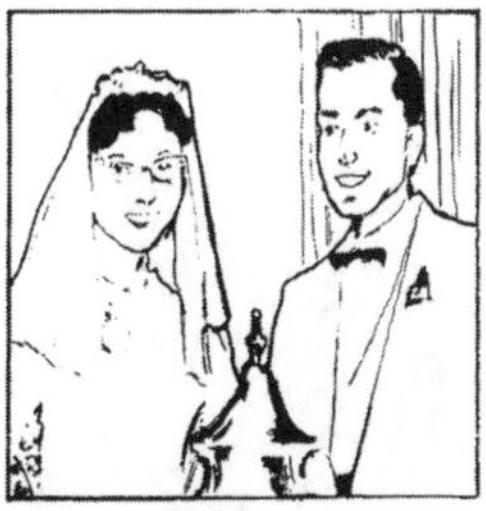
I come from the penniless intellectuals. My father was a schoolteacher and my mother a graphic designer.

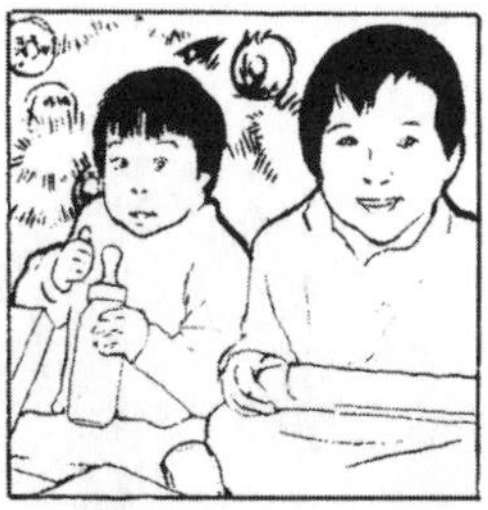
I have two sisters. Anny was born in 1960 and Teresa in 1962.

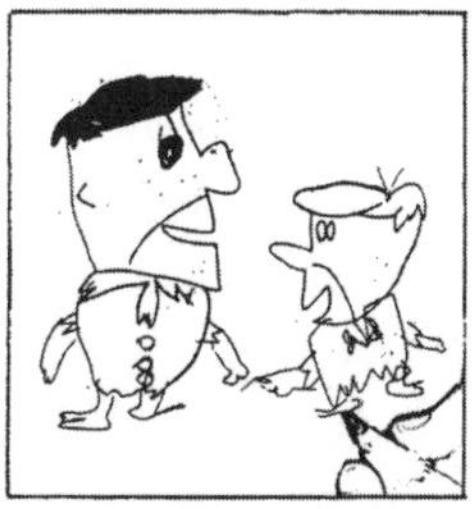
From the very beginning I drew what I saw.

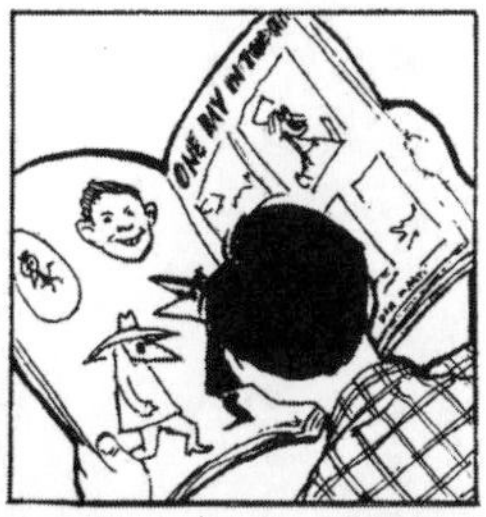
I was introduced to satire when my father brought home a copy of MAD he'd seized from a kid in his class.

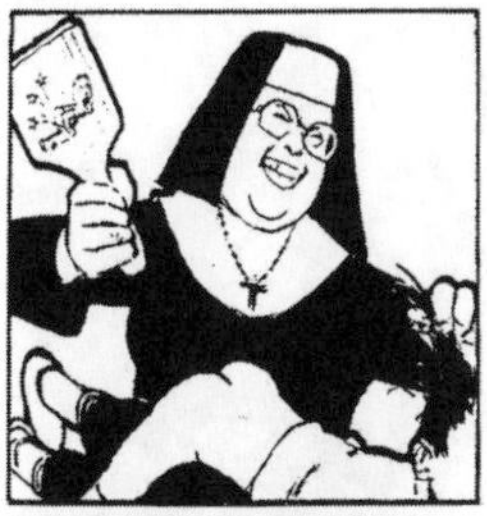
In third grade at Immaculate Heart I began drawing Paul Revere and the Raiders into a Nativity scene. I have been an enemy of religion ever since.

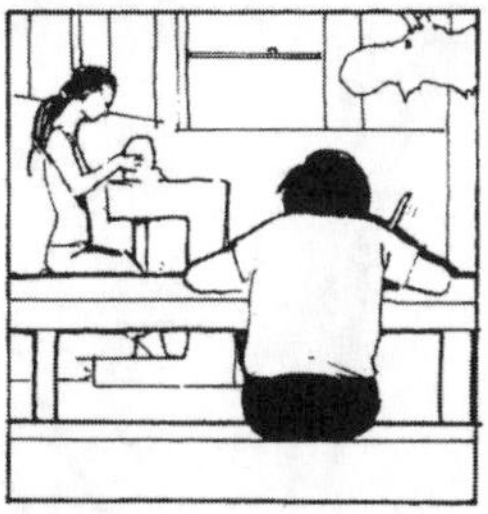
In fifth grade I switched to a local "alternative" school and spent most of the next eight years drawing comics.

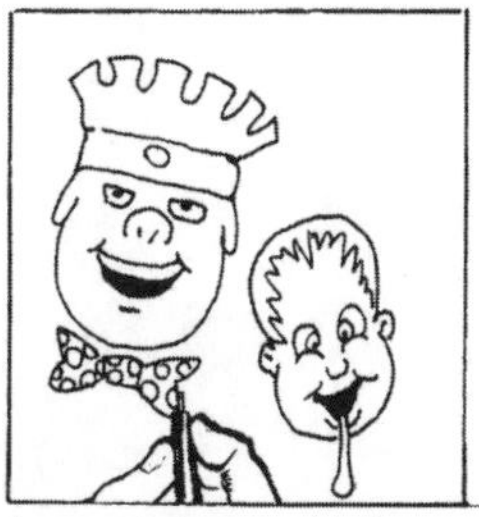
Among my early characters were Piggola, a raunchy pig, and Seanso, a moronic, drooling, baby.

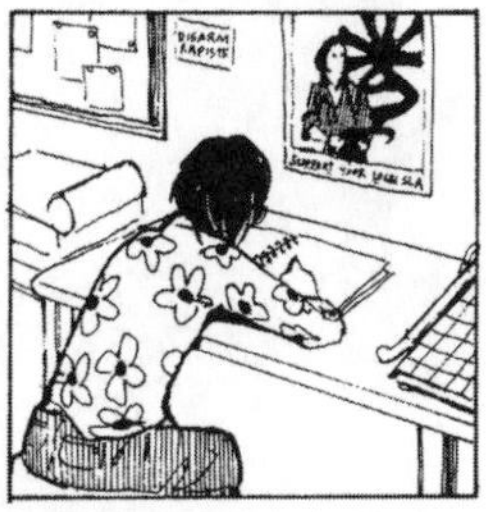
Even before I graduated high school I found work doing illustrations for the local underground weekly for $5 each.

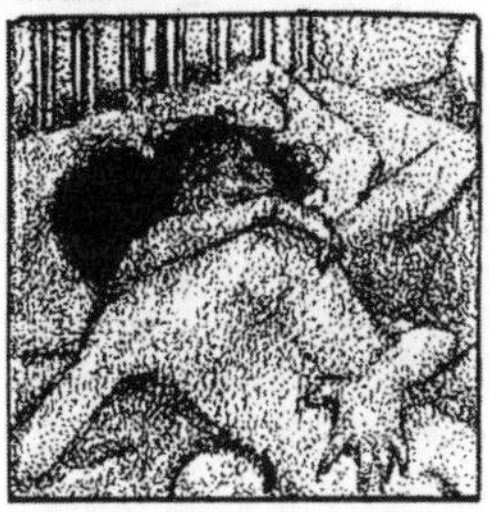
After high school I hung around for a year, acting in theater and dating older actresses. Sometime around then I lost my virginity.

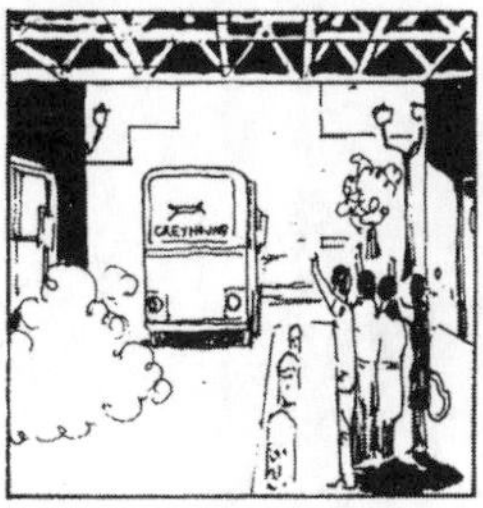

GREYHOUND

Eventually I was accepted at the School of Visual Arts in New York. I left town around the time my parents split up.

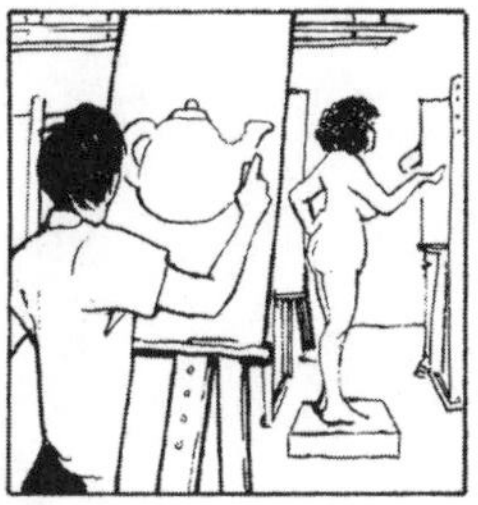
Art school bored me, and I dropped out after one semester.

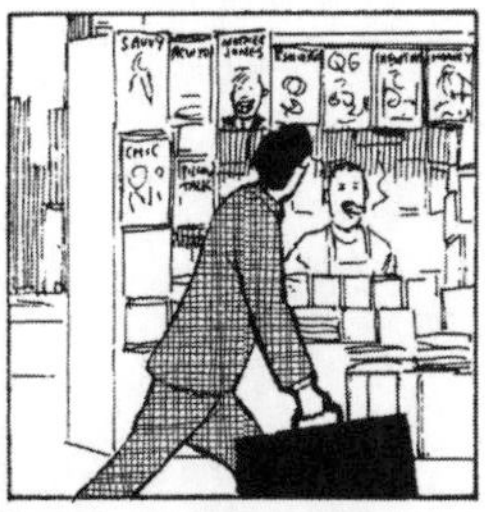
I began taking my illustration portfolio around and soon saw my work appear in major magazines like *New York* and *The National Lampoon.*

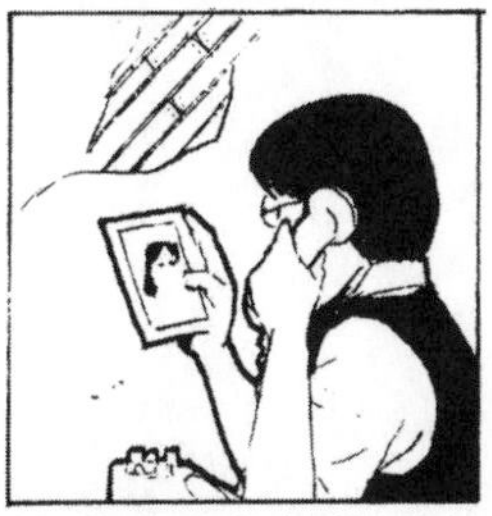
My love life suffered in New York. I had a brief affair with a woman in New York and two long-distance romances with women in Portland, which were short-lived.

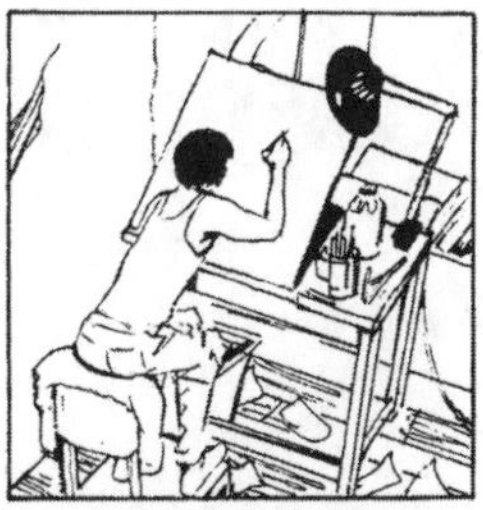
I had made few friends in college and virtually none after I dropped out. I busied myself in work and took frequent bus trips home.

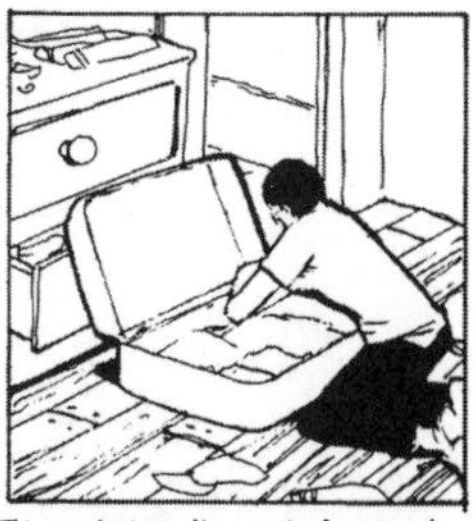
This story begins as I'm preparing for yet another trip home in late spring of 1980.

DAVID CHELSEA IN LOVE

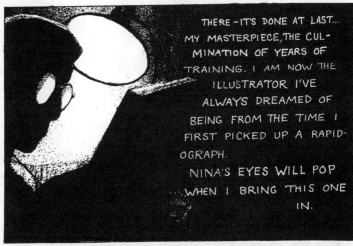

THERE – IT'S DONE AT LAST... MY MASTERPIECE, THE CULMINATION OF YEARS OF TRAINING. I AM NOW THE ILLUSTRATOR I'VE ALWAYS DREAMED OF BEING FROM THE TIME I FIRST PICKED UP A RAPIDOGRAPH.

NINA'S EYES WILL POP WHEN I BRING THIS ONE IN.

AAH... NEW YORK AT DAWN...THIS TOWN IS MY OYSTER, AND ALL I NEED IS SOMEONE TO SHARE IT WITH ME — A WOMAN WHO CAN SEE THE STUFF OF ROMANCE IN ME – I KNOW SHE'S OUT THERE SOMEWHERE...

MINNIE MAURIER!

WHAT? OH, I'M NEXT?

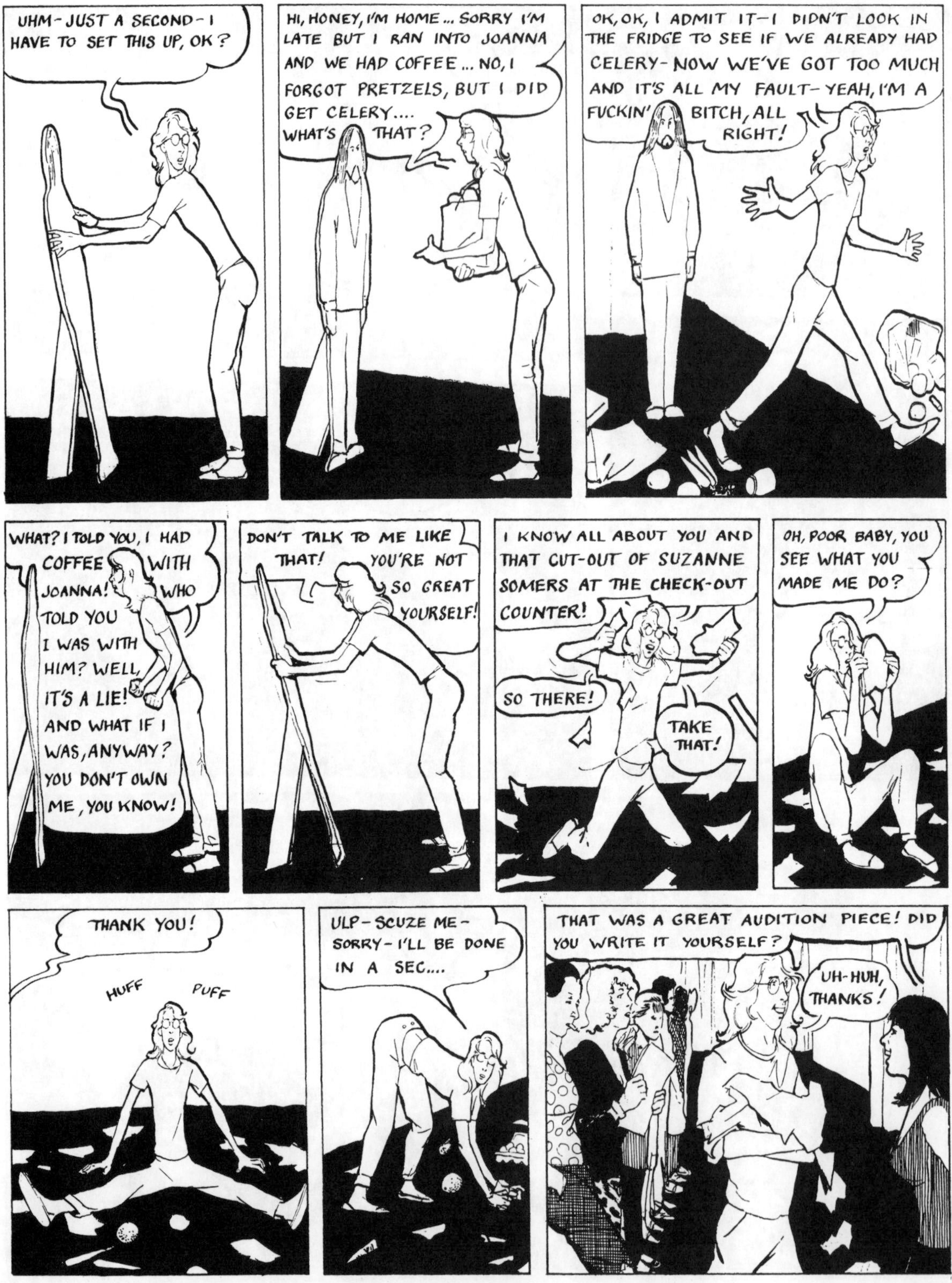
UHM-JUST A SECOND-I HAVE TO SET THIS UP, OK?
HI, HONEY, I'M HOME... SORRY I'M LATE BUT I RAN INTO JOANNA AND WE HAD COFFEE... NO, I FORGOT PRETZELS, BUT I DID GET CELERY.... WHAT'S THAT?
OK, OK, I ADMIT IT-I DIDN'T LOOK IN THE FRIDGE TO SEE IF WE ALREADY HAD CELERY-NOW WE'VE GOT TOO MUCH AND IT'S ALL MY FAULT-YEAH, I'M A FUCKIN' BITCH, ALL RIGHT!
WHAT? I TOLD YOU, I HAD COFFEE WITH JOANNA! WHO TOLD YOU I WAS WITH HIM? WELL, IT'S A LIE! AND WHAT IF I WAS, ANYWAY? YOU DON'T OWN ME, YOU KNOW!
DON'T TALK TO ME LIKE THAT! YOU'RE NOT SO GREAT YOURSELF!
I KNOW ALL ABOUT YOU AND THAT CUT-OUT OF SUZANNE SOMERS AT THE CHECK-OUT COUNTER!
SO THERE!
TAKE THAT!
OH, POOR BABY, YOU SEE WHAT YOU MADE ME DO?
THANK YOU!
HUFF
PUFF
ULP-SCUZE ME-SORRY-I'LL BE DONE IN A SEC....
THAT WAS A GREAT AUDITION PIECE! DID YOU WRITE IT YOURSELF?
UH-HUH, THANKS!

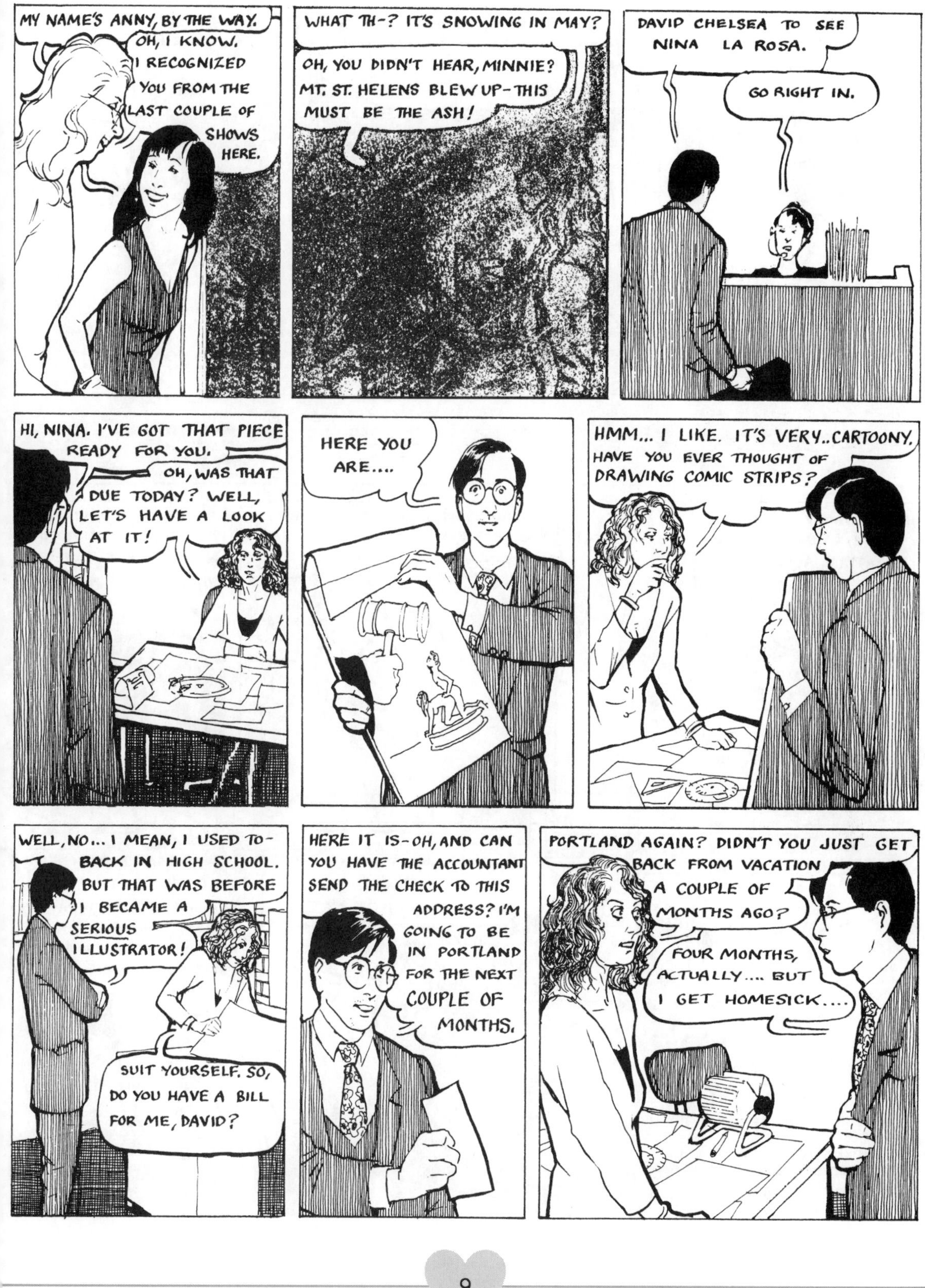
MY NAME'S ANNY, BY THE WAY.
OH, I KNOW. I RECOGNIZED YOU FROM THE LAST COUPLE OF SHOWS HERE.
WHAT TH-? IT'S SNOWING IN MAY?
OH, YOU DIDN'T HEAR, MINNIE? MT. ST. HELENS BLEW UP-THIS MUST BE THE ASH!
DAVID CHELSEA TO SEE NINA LA ROSA.
GO RIGHT IN.
HI, NINA. I'VE GOT THAT PIECE READY FOR YOU.
OH, WAS THAT DUE TODAY? WELL, LET'S HAVE A LOOK AT IT!
HERE YOU ARE....
HMM... I LIKE. IT'S VERY.. CARTOONY. HAVE YOU EVER THOUGHT OF DRAWING COMIC STRIPS?
WELL, NO... I MEAN, I USED TO-BACK IN HIGH SCHOOL. BUT THAT WAS BEFORE I BECAME A SERIOUS ILLUSTRATOR!
SUIT YOURSELF. SO, DO YOU HAVE A BILL FOR ME, DAVID?
HERE IT IS-OH, AND CAN YOU HAVE THE ACCOUNTANT SEND THE CHECK TO THIS ADDRESS? I'M GOING TO BE IN PORTLAND FOR THE NEXT COUPLE OF MONTHS.
PORTLAND AGAIN? DIDN'T YOU JUST GET BACK FROM VACATION A COUPLE OF MONTHS AGO?
FOUR MONTHS, ACTUALLY.... BUT I GET HOMESICK....

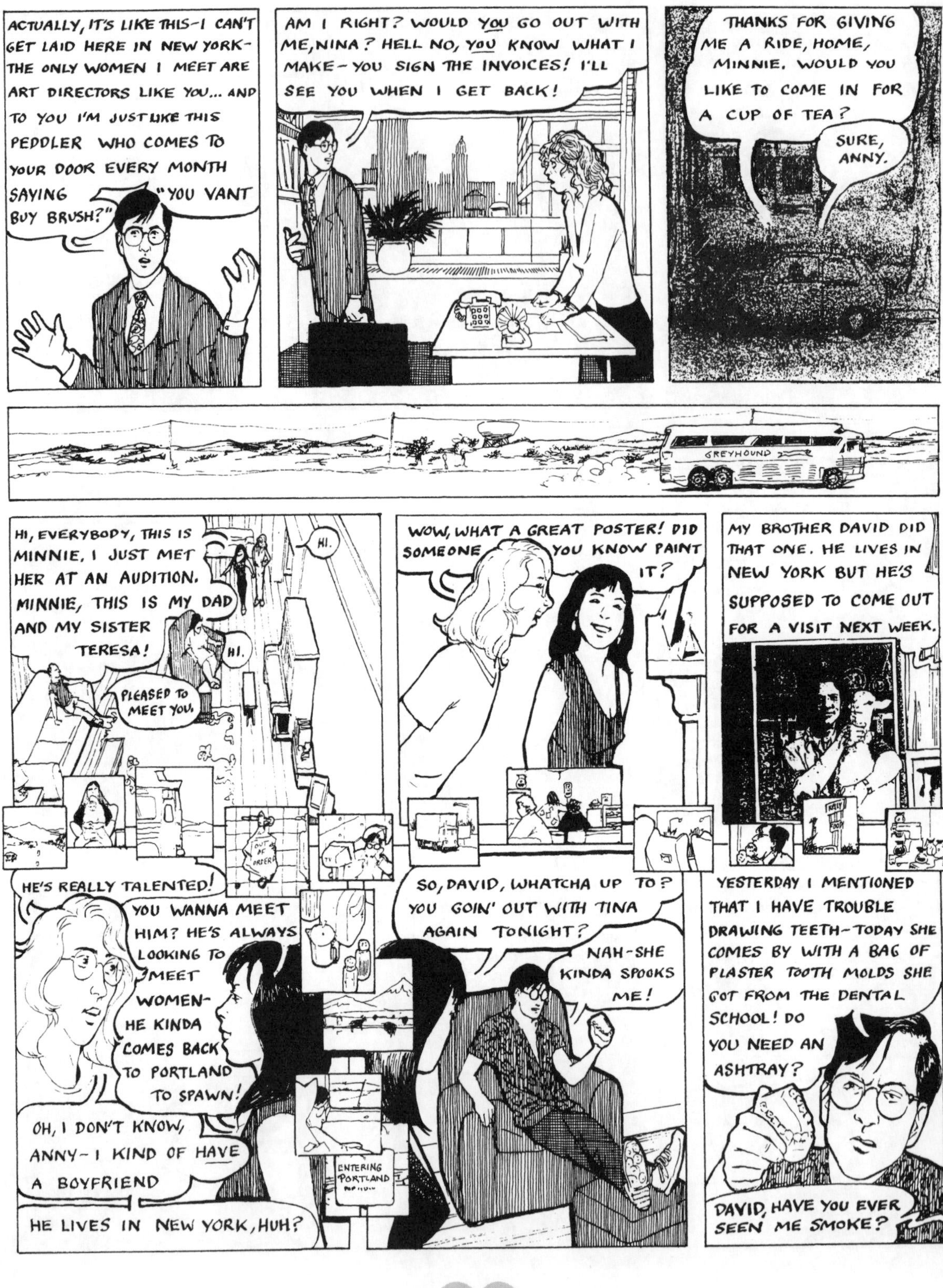
ACTUALLY, IT'S LIKE THIS–I CAN'T GET LAID HERE IN NEW YORK–THE ONLY WOMEN I MEET ARE ART DIRECTORS LIKE YOU... AND TO YOU I'M JUST LIKE THIS PEDDLER WHO COMES TO YOUR DOOR EVERY MONTH SAYING "YOU VANT BUY BRUSH?"
AM I RIGHT? WOULD YOU GO OUT WITH ME, NINA? HELL NO, YOU KNOW WHAT I MAKE–YOU SIGN THE INVOICES! I'LL SEE YOU WHEN I GET BACK!
THANKS FOR GIVING ME A RIDE, HOME, MINNIE. WOULD YOU LIKE TO COME IN FOR A CUP OF TEA?
SURE, ANNY.
GREYHOUND
HI, EVERYBODY, THIS IS MINNIE, I JUST MET HER AT AN AUDITION. MINNIE, THIS IS MY DAD AND MY SISTER TERESA!
HI.
HI.
PLEASED TO MEET YOU.
WOW, WHAT A GREAT POSTER! DID SOMEONE YOU KNOW PAINT IT?
MY BROTHER DAVID DID THAT ONE. HE LIVES IN NEW YORK BUT HE'S SUPPOSED TO COME OUT FOR A VISIT NEXT WEEK.
OUT OF ORDER
HE'S REALLY TALENTED!
YOU WANNA MEET HIM? HE'S ALWAYS LOOKING TO MEET WOMEN–HE KINDA COMES BACK TO PORTLAND TO SPAWN!
OH, I DON'T KNOW, ANNY–I KIND OF HAVE A BOYFRIEND
HE LIVES IN NEW YORK, HUH?
ENTERING PORTLAND
SO, DAVID, WHATCHA UP TO? YOU GOIN' OUT WITH TINA AGAIN TONIGHT?
NAH–SHE KINDA SPOOKS ME!
YESTERDAY I MENTIONED THAT I HAVE TROUBLE DRAWING TEETH–TODAY SHE COMES BY WITH A BAG OF PLASTER TOOTH MOLDS SHE GOT FROM THE DENTAL SCHOOL! DO YOU NEED AN ASHTRAY?
DAVID, HAVE YOU EVER SEEN ME SMOKE?

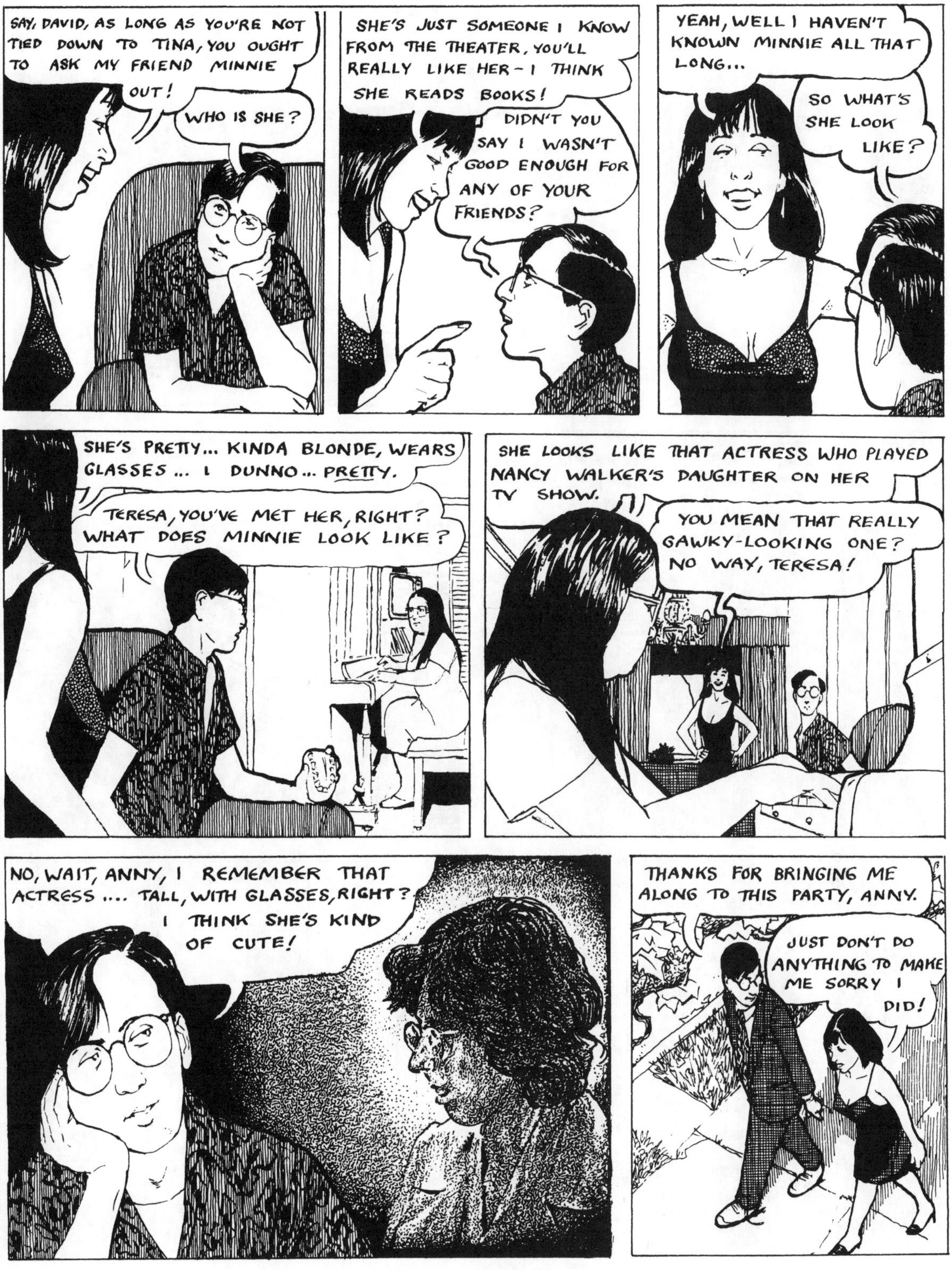
SAY, DAVID, AS LONG AS YOU'RE NOT TIED DOWN TO TINA, YOU OUGHT TO ASK MY FRIEND MINNIE OUT!
WHO IS SHE?
SHE'S JUST SOMEONE I KNOW FROM THE THEATER, YOU'LL REALLY LIKE HER - I THINK SHE READS BOOKS!
DIDN'T YOU SAY I WASN'T GOOD ENOUGH FOR ANY OF YOUR FRIENDS?
YEAH, WELL I HAVEN'T KNOWN MINNIE ALL THAT LONG...
SO WHAT'S SHE LOOK LIKE?
SHE'S PRETTY... KINDA BLONDE, WEARS GLASSES... I DUNNO... PRETTY.
TERESA, YOU'VE MET HER, RIGHT? WHAT DOES MINNIE LOOK LIKE?
SHE LOOKS LIKE THAT ACTRESS WHO PLAYED NANCY WALKER'S DAUGHTER ON HER TV SHOW.
YOU MEAN THAT REALLY GAWKY-LOOKING ONE? NO WAY, TERESA!
NO, WAIT, ANNY, I REMEMBER THAT ACTRESS.... TALL, WITH GLASSES, RIGHT?
I THINK SHE'S KIND OF CUTE!
THANKS FOR BRINGING ME ALONG TO THIS PARTY, ANNY.
JUST DON'T DO ANYTHING TO MAKE ME SORRY I DID!

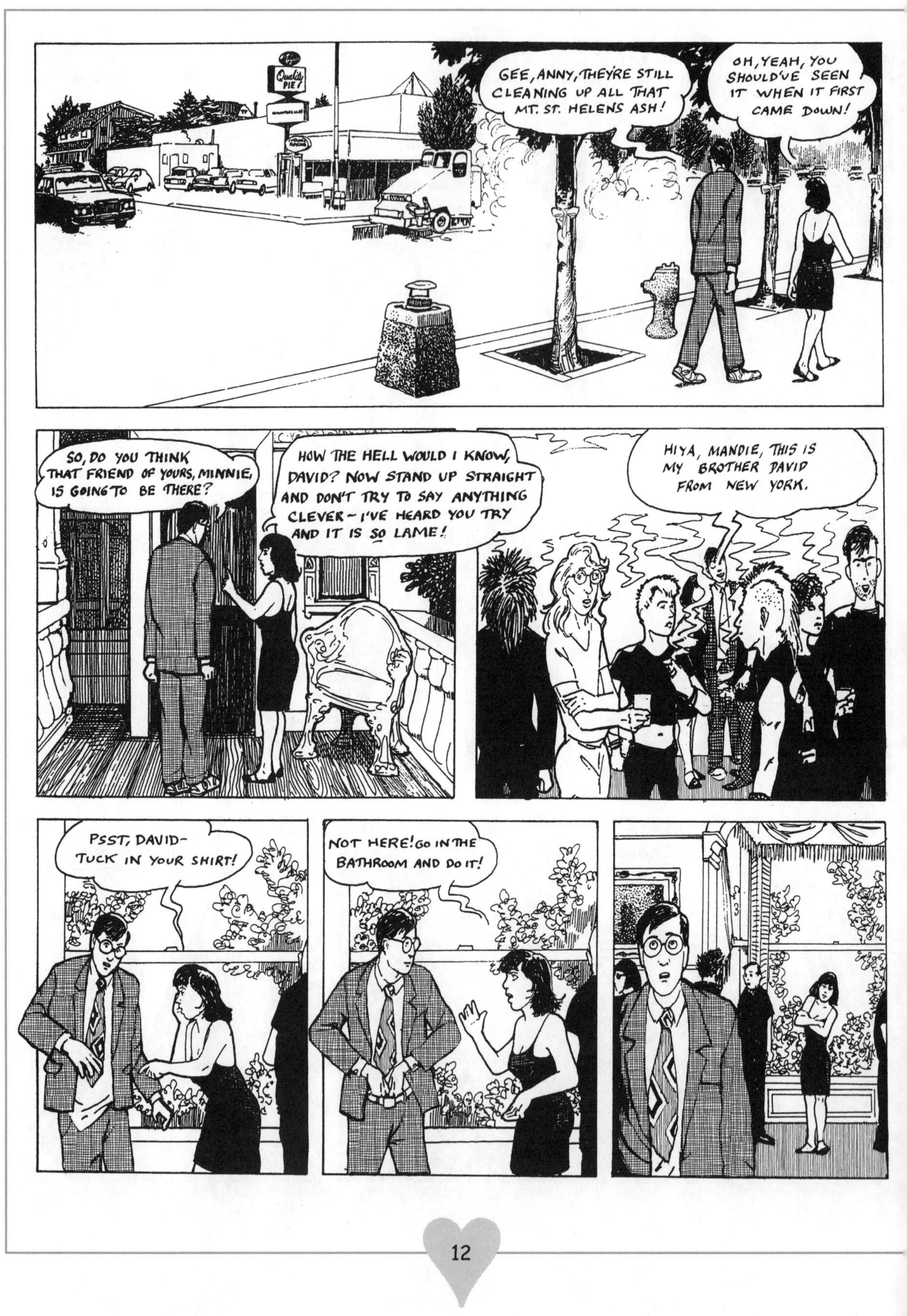
Quality PIE
GEE, ANNY, THEY'RE STILL CLEANING UP ALL THAT MT. ST. HELENS ASH!
OH, YEAH, YOU SHOULD'VE SEEN IT WHEN IT FIRST CAME DOWN!
SO, DO YOU THINK THAT FRIEND OF YOURS, MINNIE, IS GOING TO BE THERE?
HOW THE HELL WOULD I KNOW, DAVID? NOW STAND UP STRAIGHT AND DON'T TRY TO SAY ANYTHING CLEVER - I'VE HEARD YOU TRY AND IT IS SO LAME!
HIYA, MANDIE, THIS IS MY BROTHER DAVID FROM NEW YORK.
PSST, DAVID- TUCK IN YOUR SHIRT!
NOT HERE! GO IN THE BATHROOM AND DO IT!

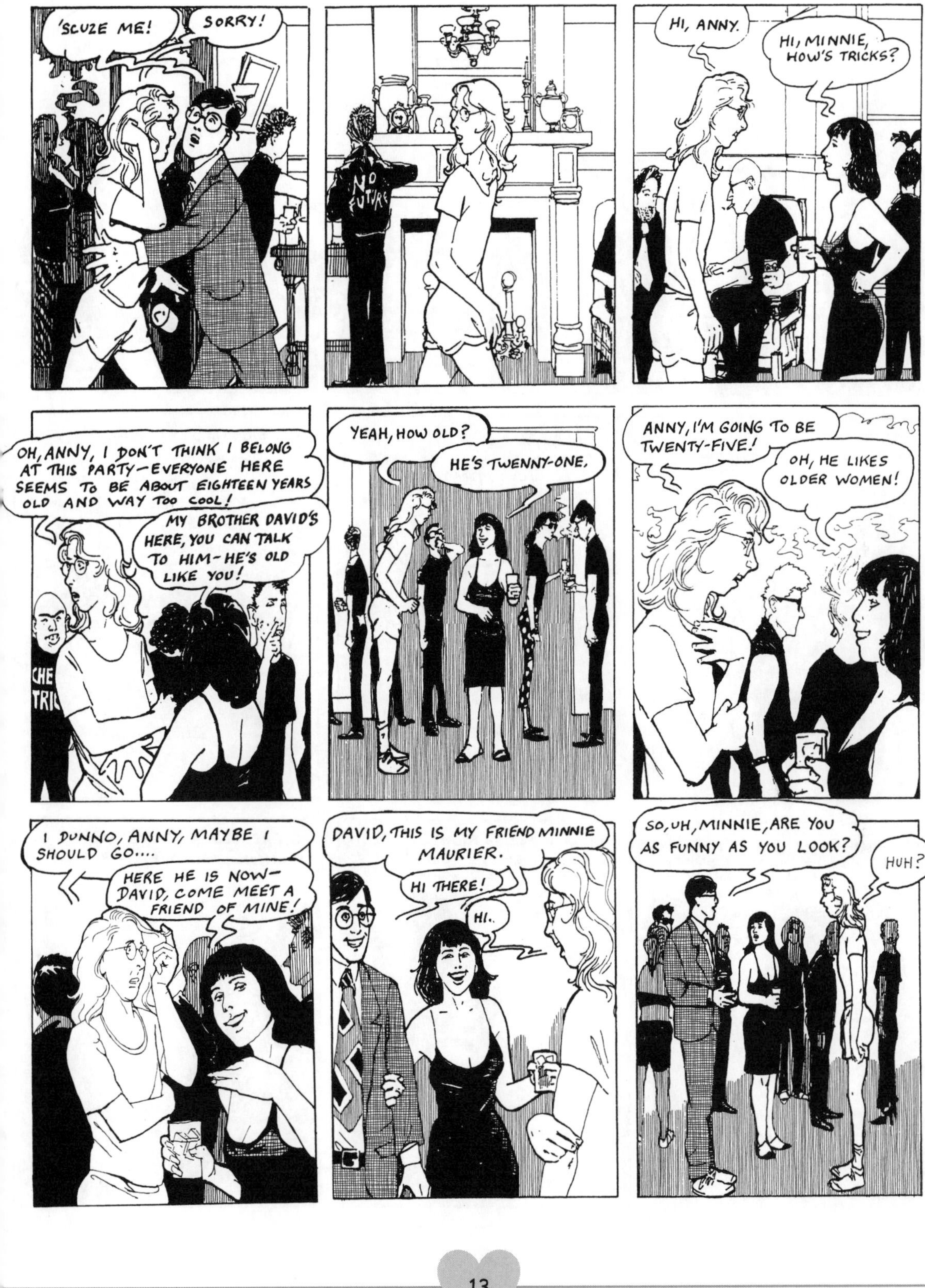
'SCUZE ME!
SORRY!
NO FUTURE
HI, ANNY.
HI, MINNIE, HOW'S TRICKS?
OH, ANNY, I DON'T THINK I BELONG AT THIS PARTY—EVERYONE HERE SEEMS TO BE ABOUT EIGHTEEN YEARS OLD AND WAY TOO COOL!
MY BROTHER DAVID'S HERE, YOU CAN TALK TO HIM—HE'S OLD LIKE YOU!
YEAH, HOW OLD?
HE'S TWENNY-ONE.
ANNY, I'M GOING TO BE TWENTY-FIVE!
OH, HE LIKES OLDER WOMEN!
I DUNNO, ANNY, MAYBE I SHOULD GO....
HERE HE IS NOW—DAVID, COME MEET A FRIEND OF MINE!
DAVID, THIS IS MY FRIEND MINNIE MAURIER.
HI THERE!
HI..
SO, UH, MINNIE, ARE YOU AS FUNNY AS YOU LOOK?
HUH?

I'M SORRY, I....
ASSHOLE!
LOOK, I DIDN'T REALLY MEAN TO SAY THAT YOU WERE FUNNY LOOKING.... ACTUALLY, YOU'RE QUITE BEAUTIFUL IN A KIND OF AN UNUSUAL, SORT OF A...
I THINK THE WORD YOU'RE LOOKING FOR IS "TALL"...
... TALL WAY.
I THINK I'M GONNA GO SOAK MY HEAD IN THE PUNCHBOWL....
NO, DON'T GO - TELL ME, WHAT DO YOU DO IN NEW YORK?
OH, DO YOU REALLY WANT TO KNOW? I'M A COMMERCIAL ILLUSTRATOR!
WHO DO YOU ILLUSTRATE FOR?
OH, BIG-TIME MAGAZINES LIKE...
Fast Service
executive female
AND...
Geriatric Nursing
REALLY!
SO, MINNIE, CAN WE GO OUT SOMETIME?
HMM... COULD BE. HOW LONG ARE YOU GONNA BE IN TOWN?
A WEEK AND A HALF.
AND THEN YOU GO RIGHT BACK TO NEW YORK AND I NEVER SEE YOU AGAIN, RIGHT?
RIGHT- NO, WAIT, I'LL BE BACK AT CHRISTMASTIME, AND IN BETWEEN YOU CAN COME VISIT ME IN NEW YORK....
THERE YOU ARE! I'VE BEEN LOOKING ALL OVER FOR YOU!
MATT!

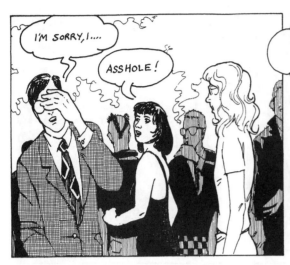

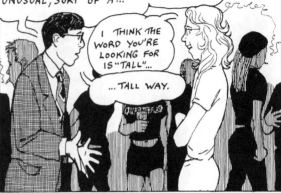

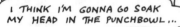

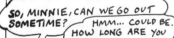

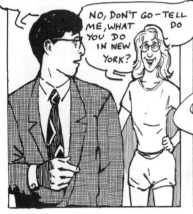

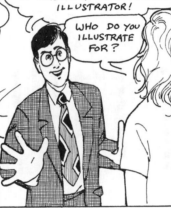

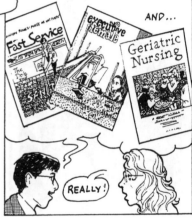

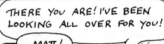

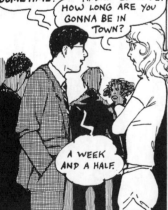

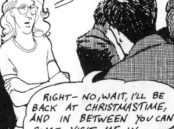

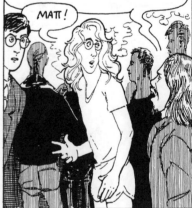

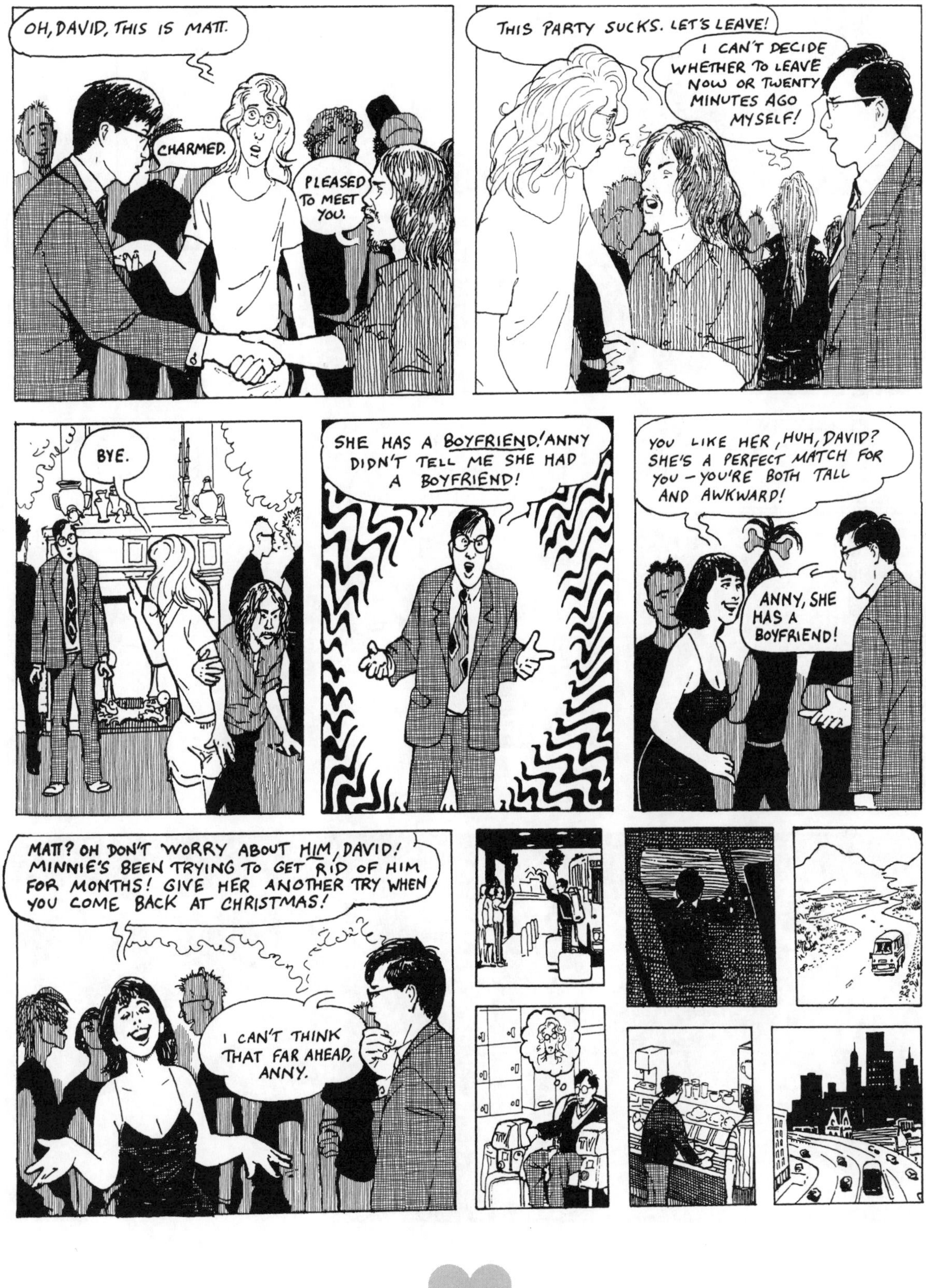
OH, DAVID, THIS IS MATT.
CHARMED.
PLEASED TO MEET YOU.
THIS PARTY SUCKS. LET'S LEAVE!
I CAN'T DECIDE WHETHER TO LEAVE NOW OR TWENTY MINUTES AGO MYSELF!
BYE.
SHE HAS A BOYFRIEND! ANNY DIDN'T TELL ME SHE HAD A BOYFRIEND!
YOU LIKE HER, HUH, DAVID? SHE'S A PERFECT MATCH FOR YOU – YOU'RE BOTH TALL AND AWKWARD!
ANNY, SHE HAS A BOYFRIEND!
MATT? OH DON'T WORRY ABOUT HIM, DAVID! MINNIE'S BEEN TRYING TO GET RID OF HIM FOR MONTHS! GIVE HER ANOTHER TRY WHEN YOU COME BACK AT CHRISTMAS!
I CAN'T THINK THAT FAR AHEAD, ANNY.

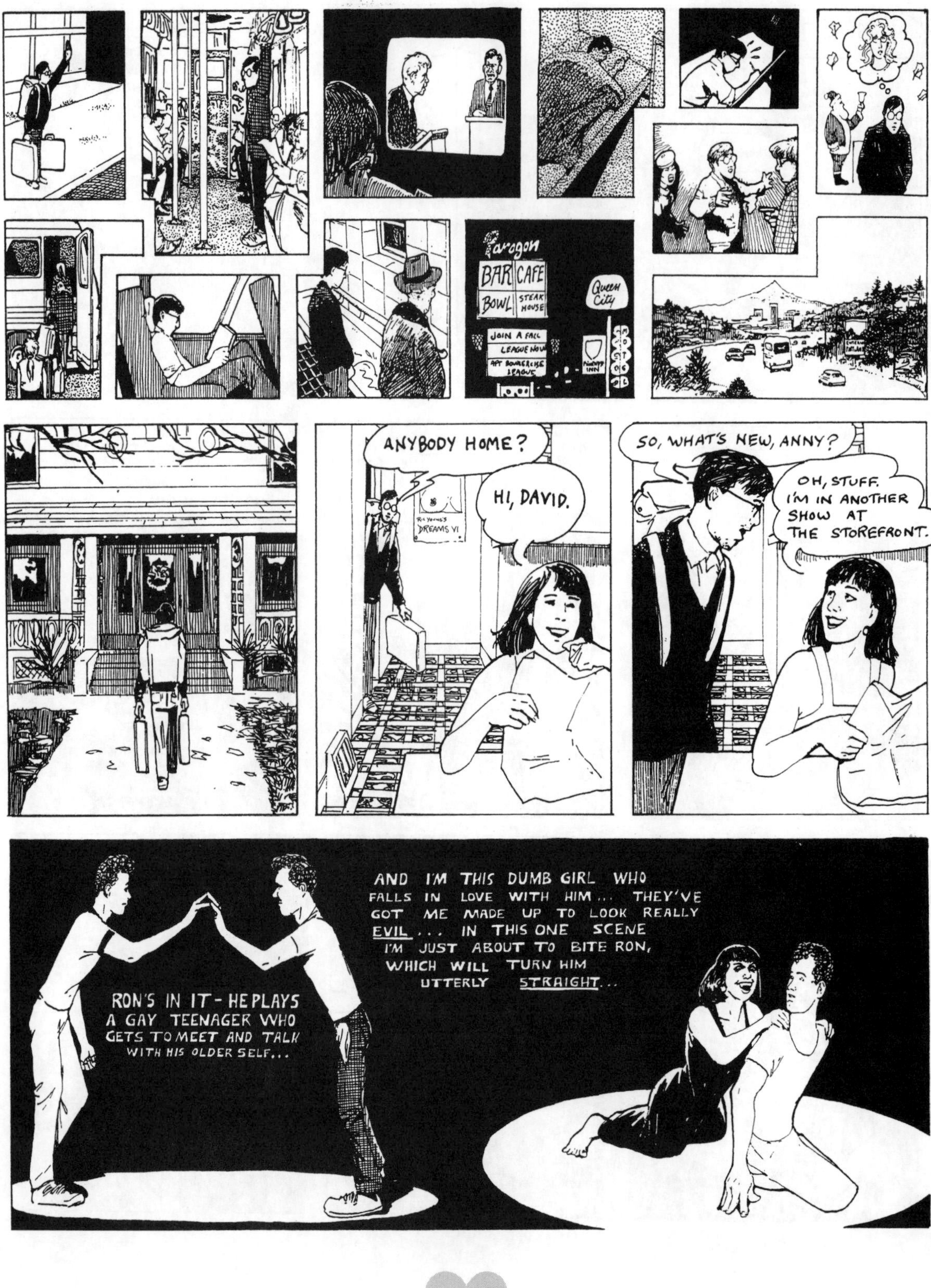
Paragon
BAR CAFE
BOWL STEAK HOUSE
JOIN A FALL
LEAGUE NOW
Queen City
ANYBODY HOME?
DREAMS VI
HI, DAVID.
SO, WHAT'S NEW, ANNY?
OH, STUFF. I'M IN ANOTHER SHOW AT THE STOREFRONT.
RON'S IN IT - HE PLAYS A GAY TEENAGER WHO GETS TO MEET AND TALK WITH HIS OLDER SELF...
AND I'M THIS DUMB GIRL WHO FALLS IN LOVE WITH HIM... THEY'VE GOT ME MADE UP TO LOOK REALLY EVIL... IN THIS ONE SCENE I'M JUST ABOUT TO BITE RON, WHICH WILL TURN HIM UTTERLY STRAIGHT...

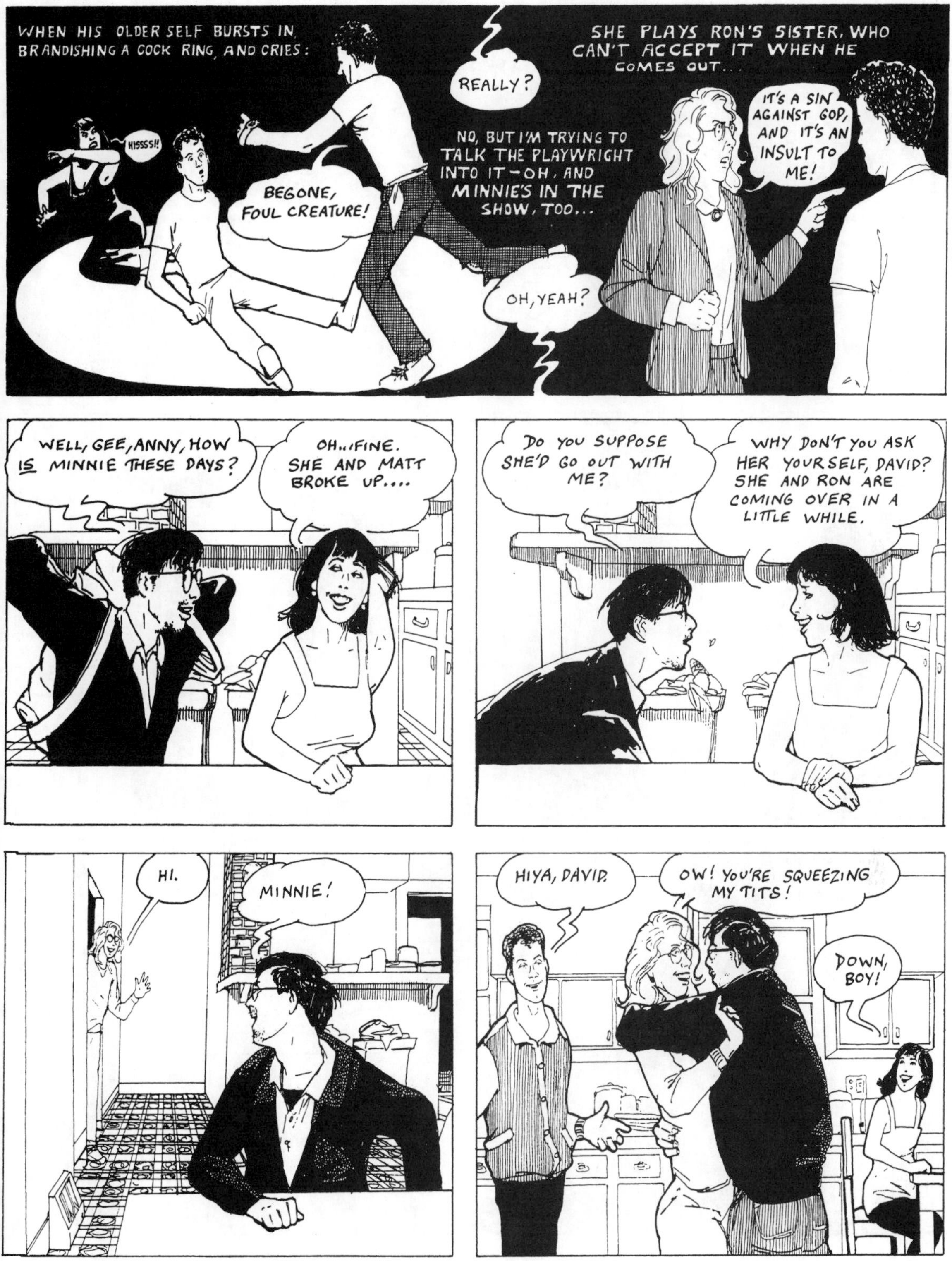
WHEN HIS OLDER SELF BURSTS IN, BRANDISHING A COCK RING, AND CRIES:
HISSSS!
BEGONE, FOUL CREATURE!
REALLY?
NO, BUT I'M TRYING TO TALK THE PLAYWRIGHT INTO IT - OH, AND MINNIE'S IN THE SHOW, TOO...
OH, YEAH?
SHE PLAYS RON'S SISTER, WHO CAN'T ACCEPT IT WHEN HE COMES OUT...
IT'S A SIN AGAINST GOD, AND IT'S AN INSULT TO ME!
WELL, GEE, ANNY, HOW IS MINNIE THESE DAYS?
OH...FINE. SHE AND MATT BROKE UP....
DO YOU SUPPOSE SHE'D GO OUT WITH ME?
WHY DON'T YOU ASK HER YOURSELF, DAVID? SHE AND RON ARE COMING OVER IN A LITTLE WHILE.
HI.
MINNIE!
HIYA, DAVID.
OW! YOU'RE SQUEEZING MY TITS!
DOWN, BOY!

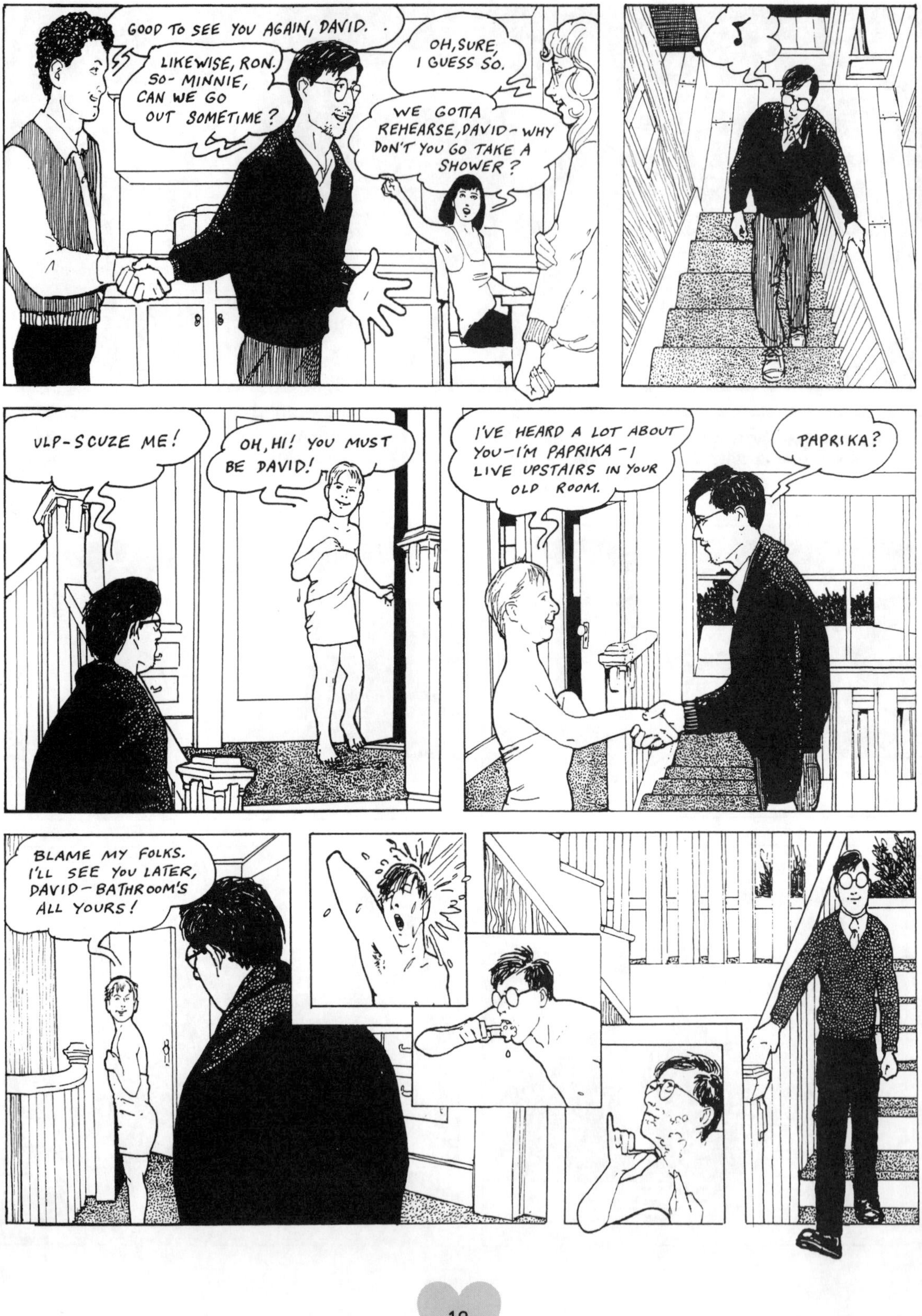
GOOD TO SEE YOU AGAIN, DAVID.
LIKEWISE, RON. SO- MINNIE, CAN WE GO OUT SOMETIME?
OH, SURE, I GUESS SO.
WE GOTTA REHEARSE, DAVID- WHY DON'T YOU GO TAKE A SHOWER?
ULP-SCUZE ME!
OH, HI! YOU MUST BE DAVID!
I'VE HEARD A LOT ABOUT YOU-I'M PAPRIKA-I LIVE UPSTAIRS IN YOUR OLD ROOM.
PAPRIKA?
BLAME MY FOLKS. I'LL SEE YOU LATER, DAVID-BATHROOM'S ALL YOURS!

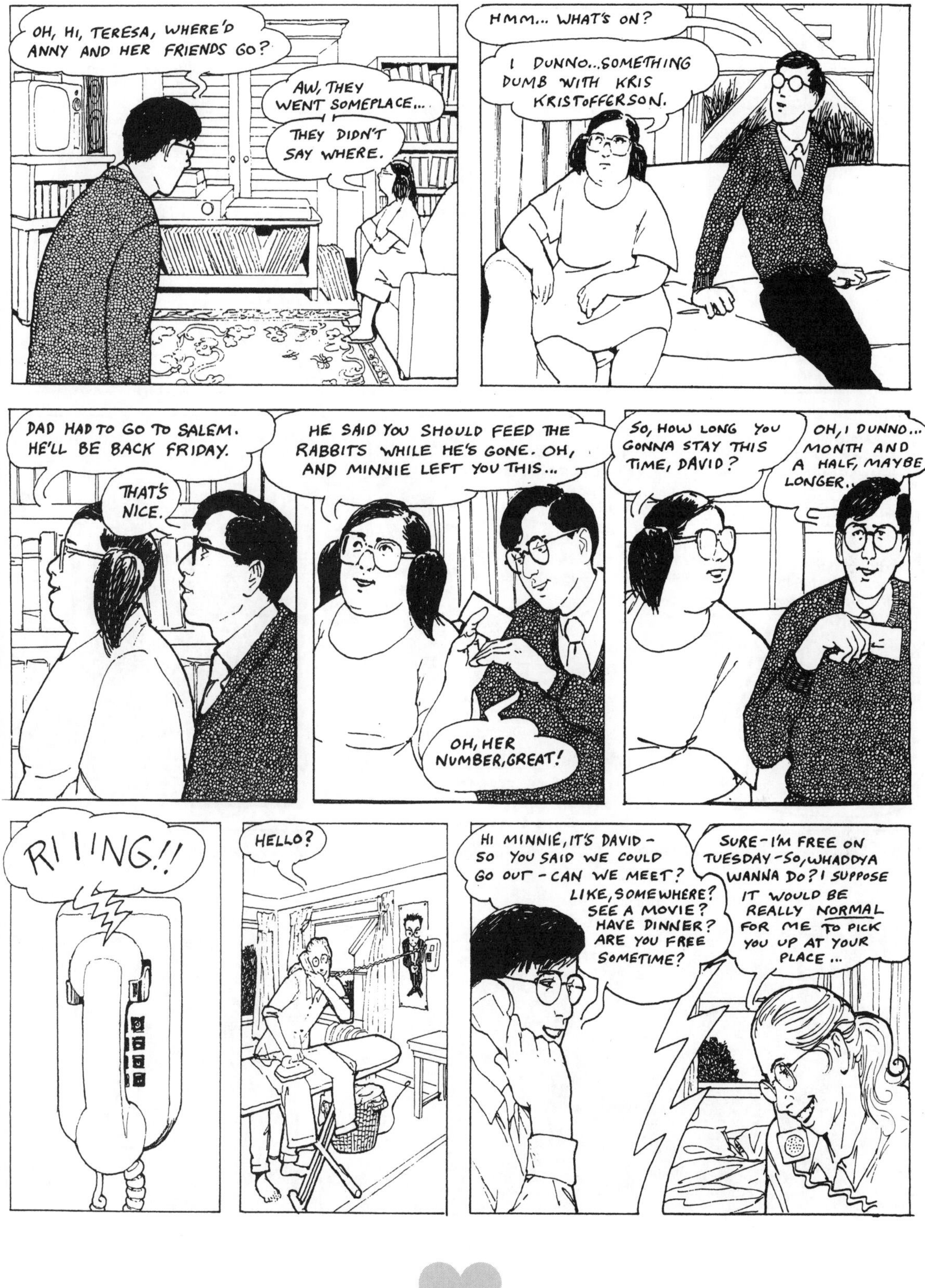
OH, HI, TERESA, WHERE'D ANNY AND HER FRIENDS GO?
AW, THEY WENT SOMEPLACE...
THEY DIDN'T SAY WHERE.
HMM... WHAT'S ON?
I DUNNO...SOMETHING DUMB WITH KRIS KRISTOFFERSON.
DAD HAD TO GO TO SALEM. HE'LL BE BACK FRIDAY.
THAT'S NICE.
HE SAID YOU SHOULD FEED THE RABBITS WHILE HE'S GONE. OH, AND MINNIE LEFT YOU THIS...
OH, HER NUMBER, GREAT!
SO, HOW LONG YOU GONNA STAY THIS TIME, DAVID?
OH, I DUNNO... MONTH AND A HALF, MAYBE LONGER...
RIIING!!
HELLO?
HI MINNIE, IT'S DAVID - SO YOU SAID WE COULD GO OUT - CAN WE MEET? LIKE, SOMEWHERE? SEE A MOVIE? HAVE DINNER? ARE YOU FREE SOMETIME?
SURE - I'M FREE ON TUESDAY - SO, WHADDYA WANNA DO? I SUPPOSE IT WOULD BE REALLY NORMAL FOR ME TO PICK YOU UP AT YOUR PLACE...

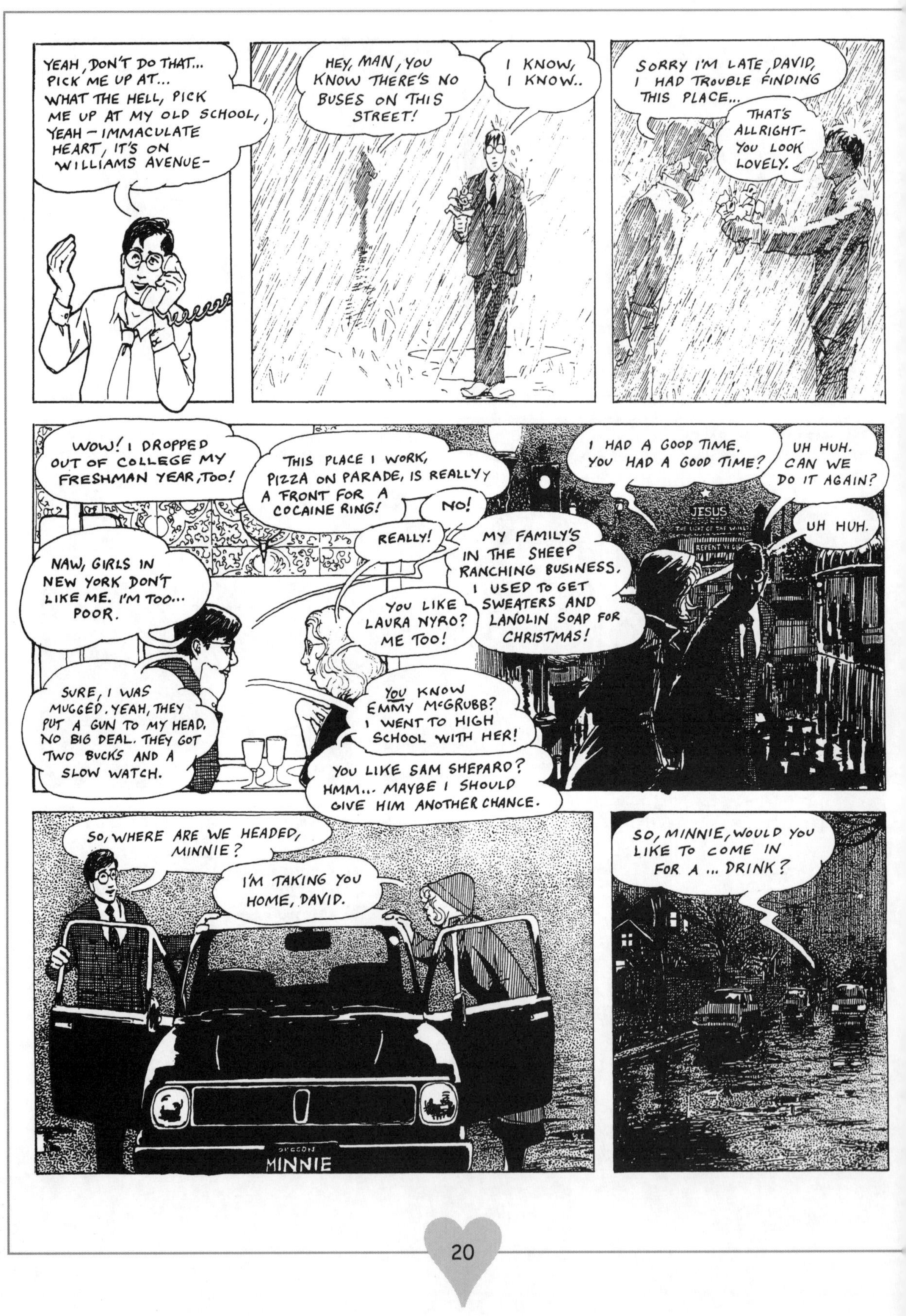
YEAH, DON'T DO THAT... PICK ME UP AT... WHAT THE HELL, PICK ME UP AT MY OLD SCHOOL, YEAH – IMMACULATE HEART, IT'S ON WILLIAMS AVENUE-
HEY, MAN, YOU KNOW THERE'S NO BUSES ON THIS STREET!
I KNOW, I KNOW..
SORRY I'M LATE, DAVID, I HAD TROUBLE FINDING THIS PLACE...
THAT'S ALLRIGHT- YOU LOOK LOVELY.
WOW! I DROPPED OUT OF COLLEGE MY FRESHMAN YEAR, TOO!
THIS PLACE I WORK, PIZZA ON PARADE, IS REALLY A FRONT FOR A COCAINE RING!
NO!
REALLY!
NAW, GIRLS IN NEW YORK DON'T LIKE ME. I'M TOO... POOR.
MY FAMILY'S IN THE SHEEP RANCHING BUSINESS. I USED TO GET SWEATERS AND LANOLIN SOAP FOR CHRISTMAS!
YOU LIKE LAURA NYRO? ME TOO!
SURE, I WAS MUGGED. YEAH, THEY PUT A GUN TO MY HEAD. NO BIG DEAL. THEY GOT TWO BUCKS AND A SLOW WATCH.
YOU KNOW EMMY McGRUBB? I WENT TO HIGH SCHOOL WITH HER!
YOU LIKE SAM SHEPARD? HMM... MAYBE I SHOULD GIVE HIM ANOTHER CHANCE.
JESUS
I HAD A GOOD TIME. YOU HAD A GOOD TIME?
UH HUH. CAN WE DO IT AGAIN?
UH HUH.
SO, WHERE ARE WE HEADED, MINNIE?
I'M TAKING YOU HOME, DAVID.
MINNIE
SO, MINNIE, WOULD YOU LIKE TO COME IN FOR A ... DRINK?

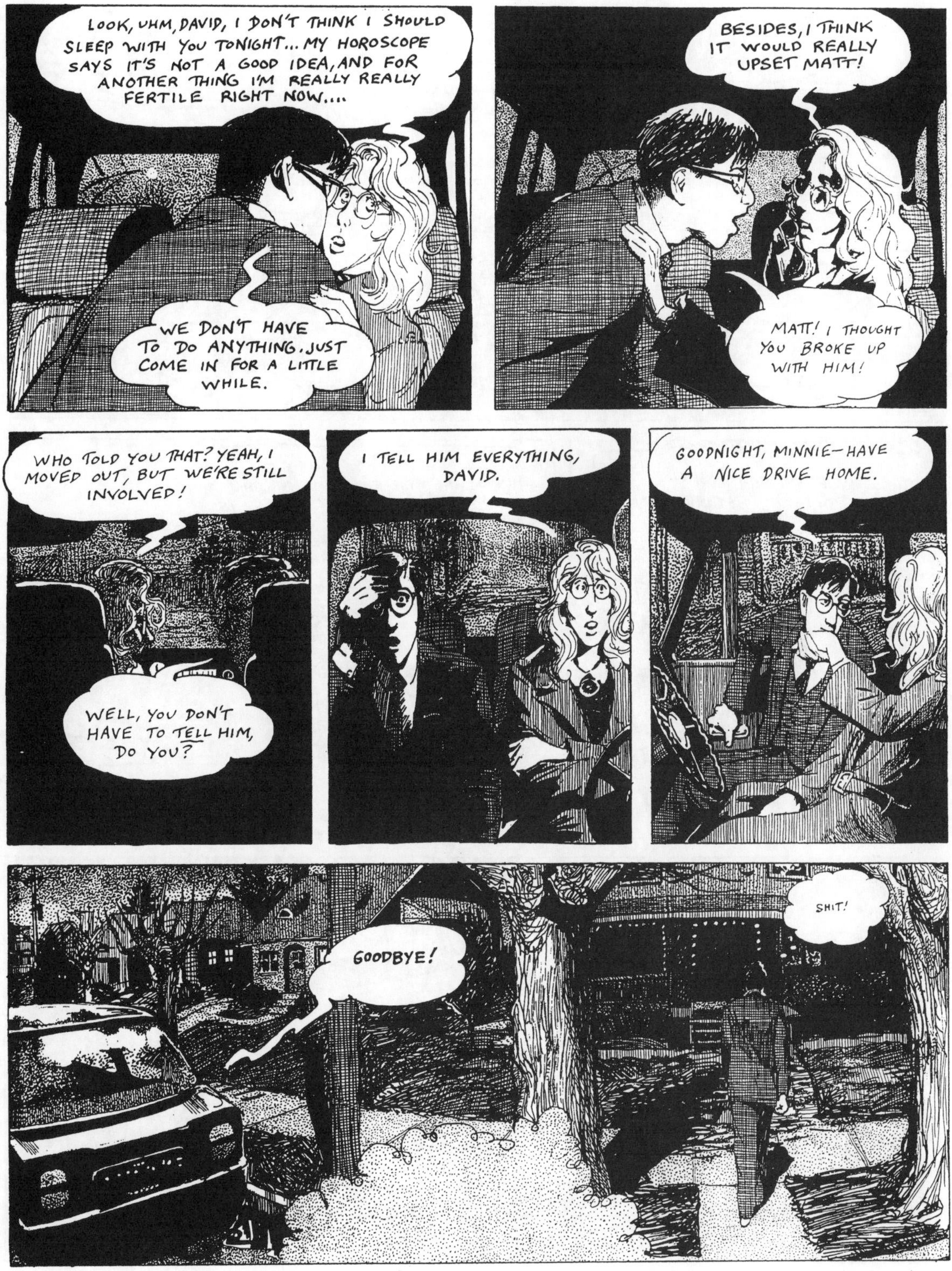
LOOK, UHM, DAVID, I DON'T THINK I SHOULD SLEEP WITH YOU TONIGHT... MY HOROSCOPE SAYS IT'S NOT A GOOD IDEA, AND FOR ANOTHER THING I'M REALLY REALLY FERTILE RIGHT NOW....
WE DON'T HAVE TO DO ANYTHING. JUST COME IN FOR A LITTLE WHILE.
BESIDES, I THINK IT WOULD REALLY UPSET MATT!
MATT! I THOUGHT YOU BROKE UP WITH HIM!
WHO TOLD YOU THAT? YEAH, I MOVED OUT, BUT WE'RE STILL INVOLVED!
WELL, YOU DON'T HAVE TO TELL HIM, DO YOU?
I TELL HIM EVERYTHING, DAVID.
GOODNIGHT, MINNIE—HAVE A NICE DRIVE HOME.
GOODBYE!
SHIT!

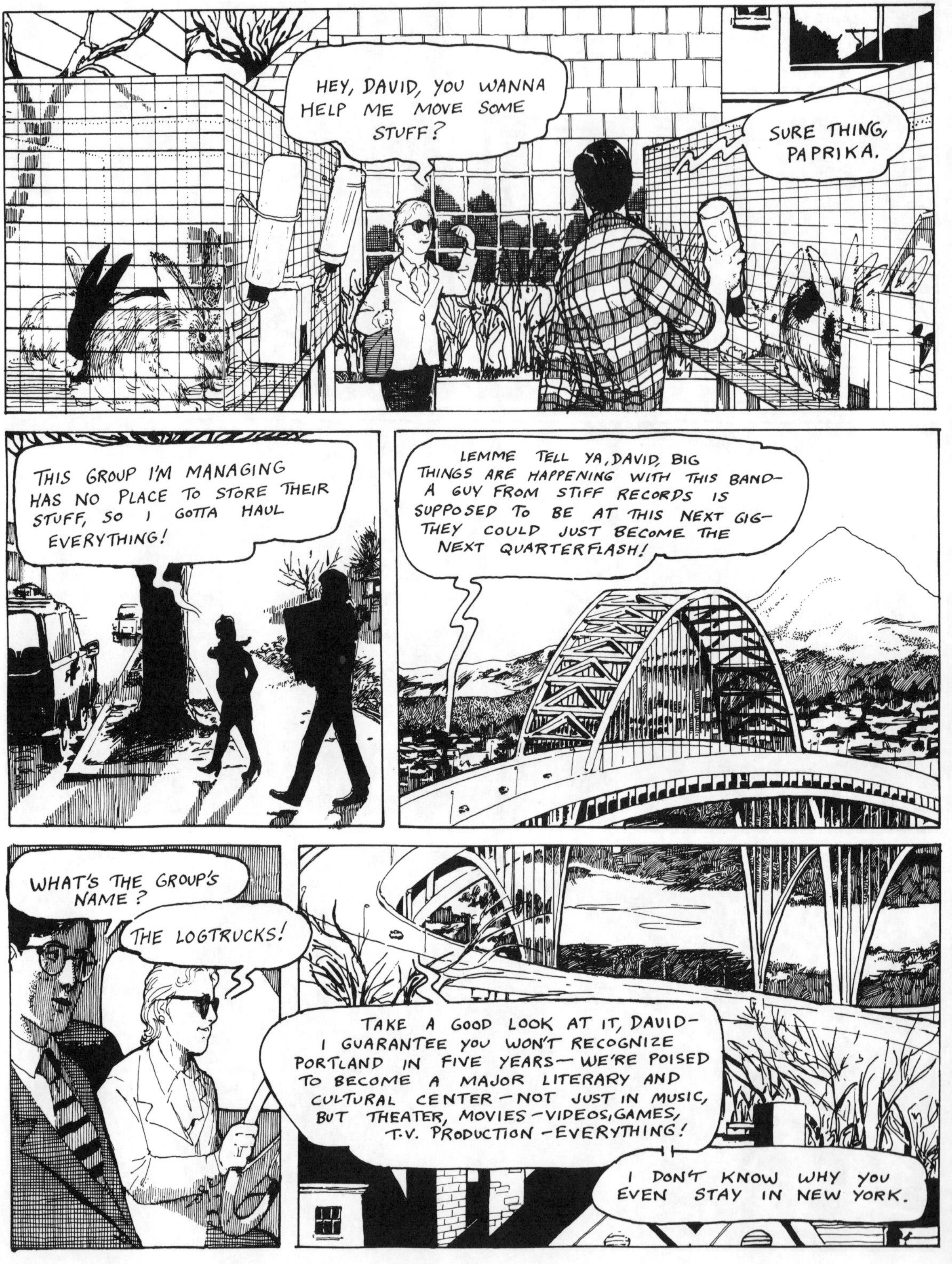
HEY, DAVID, YOU WANNA HELP ME MOVE SOME STUFF?
SURE THING, PAPRIKA.
THIS GROUP I'M MANAGING HAS NO PLACE TO STORE THEIR STUFF, SO I GOTTA HAUL EVERYTHING!
LEMME TELL YA, DAVID, BIG THINGS ARE HAPPENING WITH THIS BAND- A GUY FROM STIFF RECORDS IS SUPPOSED TO BE AT THIS NEXT GIG- THEY COULD JUST BECOME THE NEXT QUARTERFLASH!
WHAT'S THE GROUP'S NAME?
THE LOGTRUCKS!
TAKE A GOOD LOOK AT IT, DAVID- I GUARANTEE YOU WON'T RECOGNIZE PORTLAND IN FIVE YEARS- WE'RE POISED TO BECOME A MAJOR LITERARY AND CULTURAL CENTER- NOT JUST IN MUSIC, BUT THEATER, MOVIES-VIDEOS, GAMES, T.V. PRODUCTION -EVERYTHING!
I DON'T KNOW WHY YOU EVEN STAY IN NEW YORK.

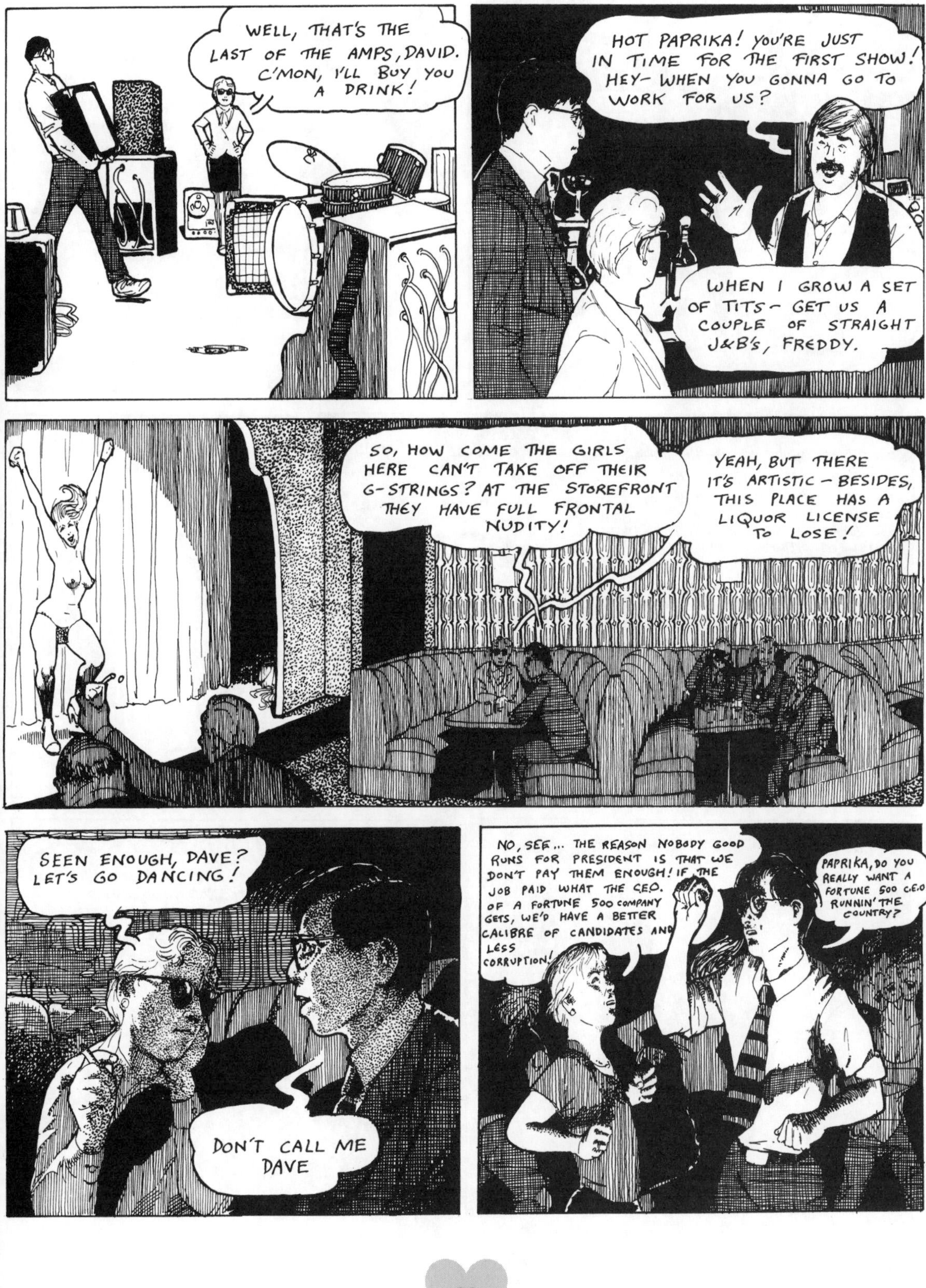
WELL, THAT'S THE LAST OF THE AMPS, DAVID. C'MON, I'LL BUY YOU A DRINK!
HOT PAPRIKA! YOU'RE JUST IN TIME FOR THE FIRST SHOW! HEY- WHEN YOU GONNA GO TO WORK FOR US?
WHEN I GROW A SET OF TITS- GET US A COUPLE OF STRAIGHT J&B'S, FREDDY.
SO, HOW COME THE GIRLS HERE CAN'T TAKE OFF THEIR G-STRINGS? AT THE STOREFRONT THEY HAVE FULL FRONTAL NUDITY!
YEAH, BUT THERE IT'S ARTISTIC - BESIDES, THIS PLACE HAS A LIQUOR LICENSE TO LOSE!
SEEN ENOUGH, DAVE? LET'S GO DANCING!
DON'T CALL ME DAVE
NO, SEE... THE REASON NOBODY GOOD RUNS FOR PRESIDENT IS THAT WE DON'T PAY THEM ENOUGH! IF THE JOB PAID WHAT THE C.E.O. OF A FORTUNE 500 COMPANY GETS, WE'D HAVE A BETTER CALIBRE OF CANDIDATES AND LESS CORRUPTION!
PAPRIKA, DO YOU REALLY WANT A FORTUNE 500 C.E.O. RUNNIN' THE COUNTRY?

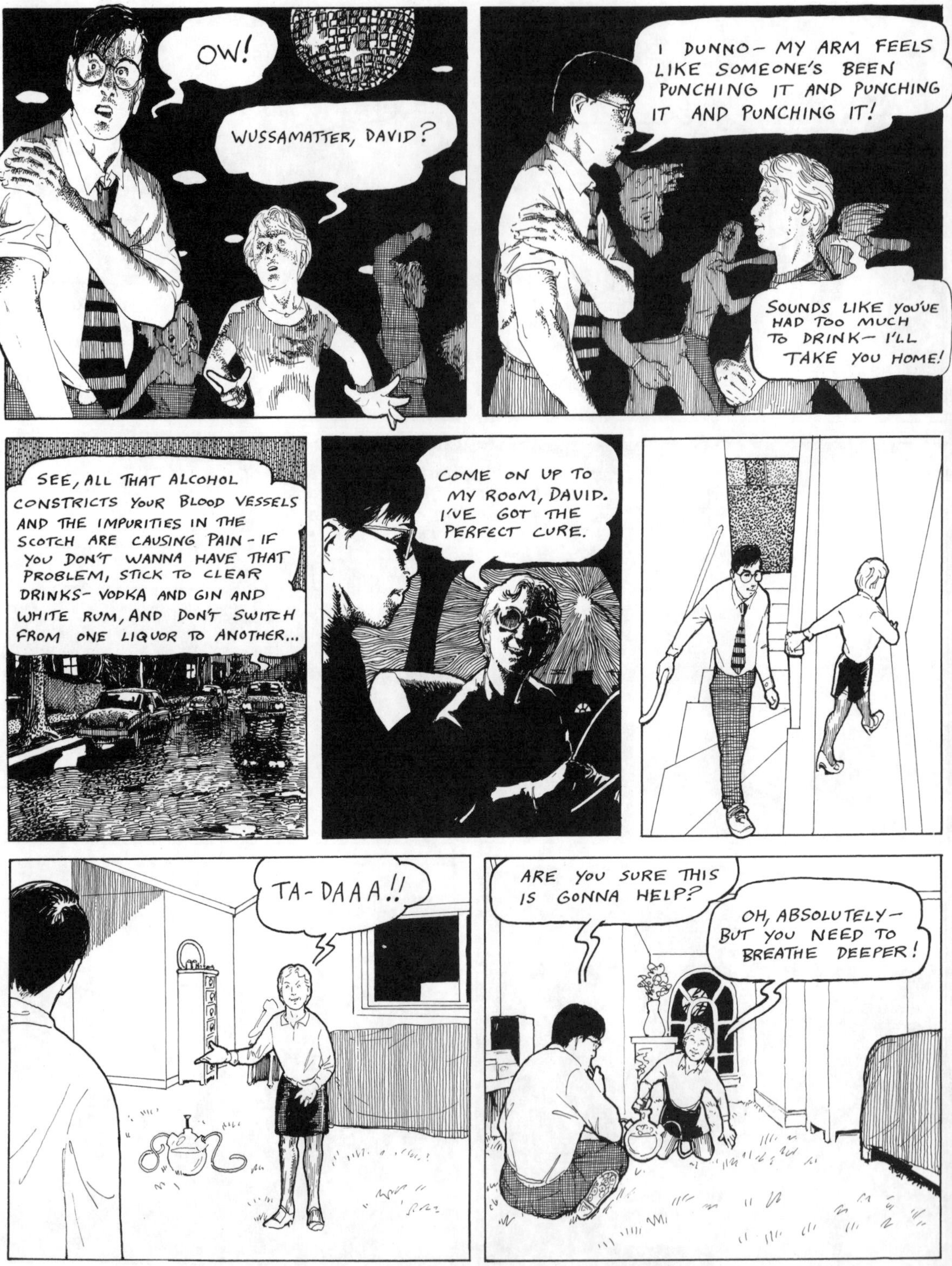
OW!
WUSSAMATTER, DAVID?
I DUNNO— MY ARM FEELS LIKE SOMEONE'S BEEN PUNCHING IT AND PUNCHING IT AND PUNCHING IT!
SOUNDS LIKE YOU'VE HAD TOO MUCH TO DRINK— I'LL TAKE YOU HOME!
SEE, ALL THAT ALCOHOL CONSTRICTS YOUR BLOOD VESSELS AND THE IMPURITIES IN THE SCOTCH ARE CAUSING PAIN - IF YOU DON'T WANNA HAVE THAT PROBLEM, STICK TO CLEAR DRINKS- VODKA AND GIN AND WHITE RUM, AND DON'T SWITCH FROM ONE LIQUOR TO ANOTHER...
COME ON UP TO MY ROOM, DAVID. I'VE GOT THE PERFECT CURE.
TA-DAAA!!
ARE YOU SURE THIS IS GONNA HELP?
OH, ABSOLUTELY— BUT YOU NEED TO BREATHE DEEPER!

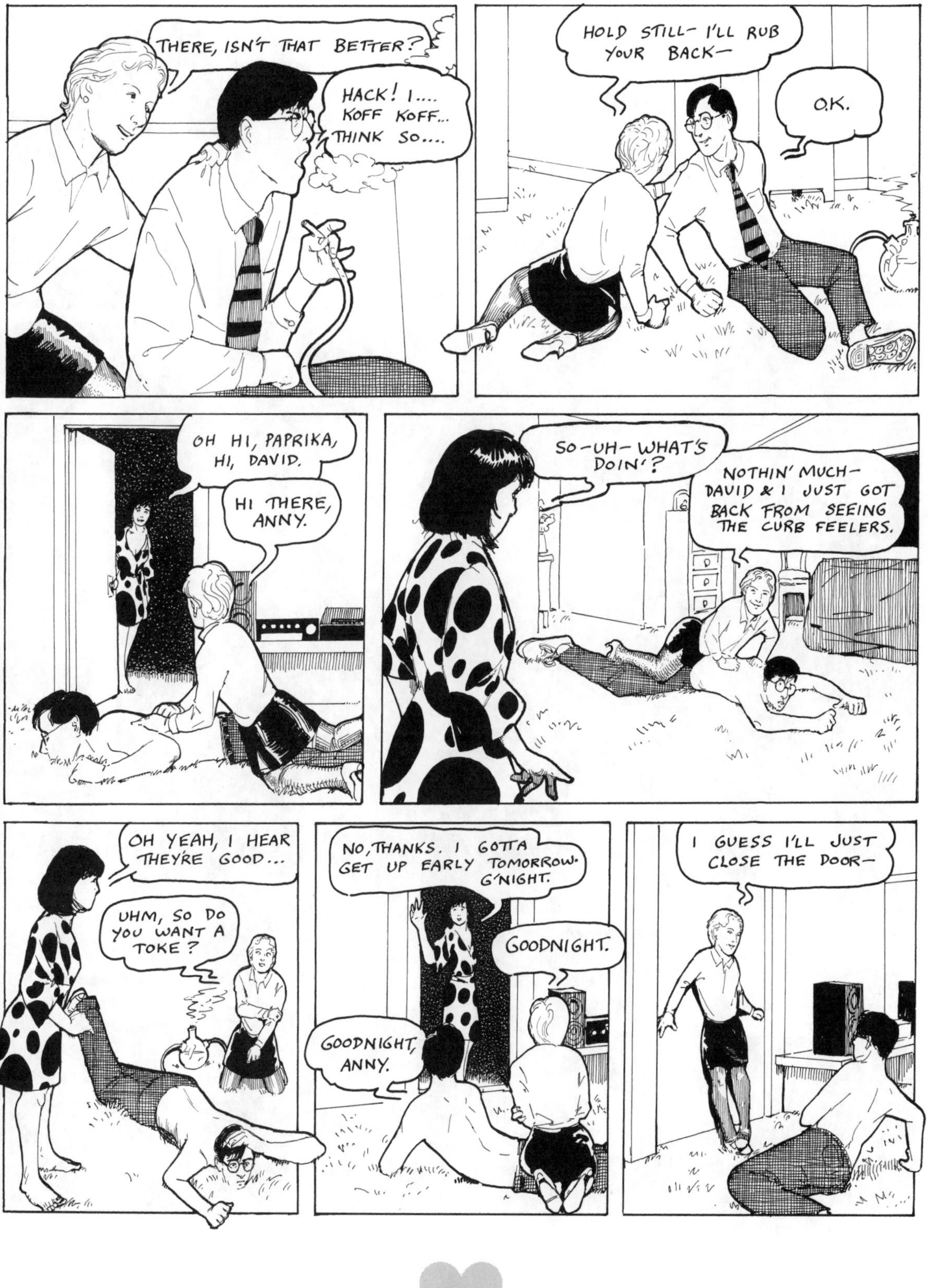
THERE, ISN'T THAT BETTER?
HACK! I.... KOFF KOFF... THINK SO....
HOLD STILL— I'LL RUB YOUR BACK—
O.K.
OH HI, PAPRIKA, HI, DAVID.
HI THERE, ANNY.
SO—UH— WHAT'S DOIN'?
NOTHIN' MUCH— DAVID & I JUST GOT BACK FROM SEEING THE CURB FEELERS.
OH YEAH, I HEAR THEY'RE GOOD...
UHM, SO DO YOU WANT A TOKE?
NO, THANKS. I GOTTA GET UP EARLY TOMORROW. G'NIGHT.
GOODNIGHT.
GOODNIGHT, ANNY.
I GUESS I'LL JUST CLOSE THE DOOR—

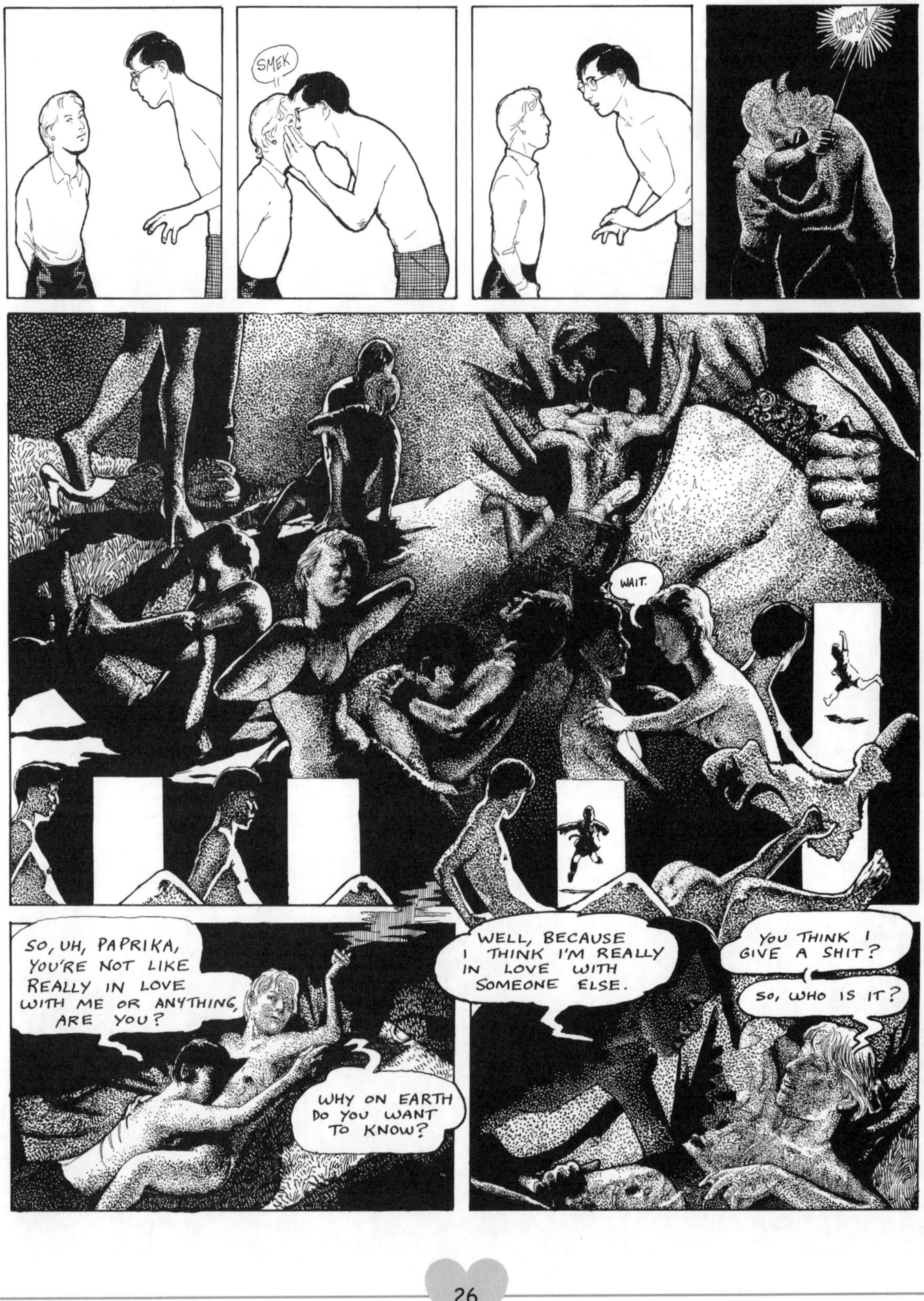
SMEK
KLIK!
WAIT.
SO, UH, PAPRIKA, YOU'RE NOT LIKE REALLY IN LOVE WITH ME OR ANYTHING, ARE YOU?
WHY ON EARTH DO YOU WANT TO KNOW?
WELL, BECAUSE I THINK I'M REALLY IN LOVE WITH SOMEONE ELSE.
YOU THINK I GIVE A SHIT?
SO, WHO IS IT?

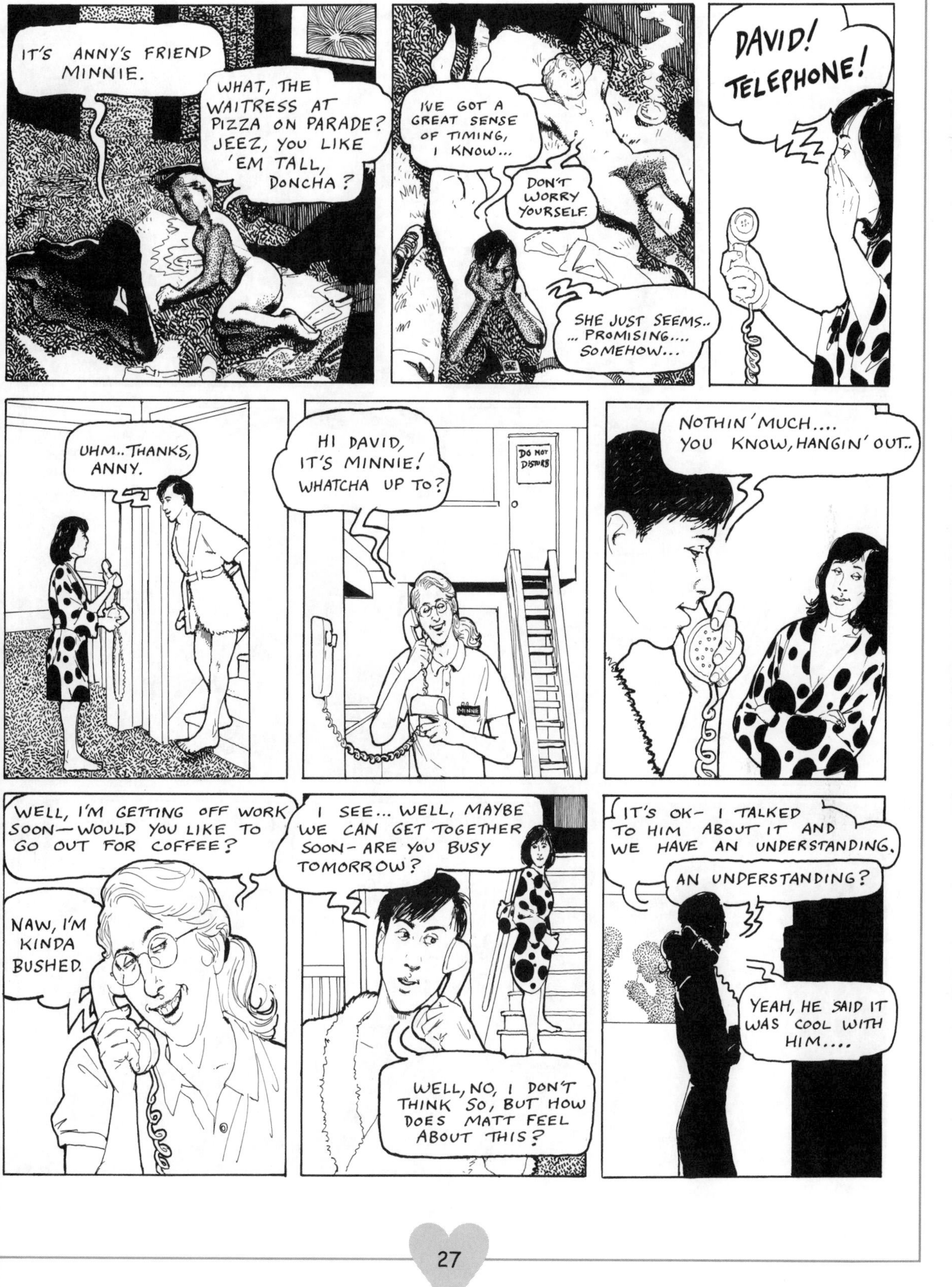

IT'S ANNY'S FRIEND MINNIE.
WHAT, THE WAITRESS AT PIZZA ON PARADE? JEEZ, YOU LIKE 'EM TALL, DONCHA?
I'VE GOT A GREAT SENSE OF TIMING, I KNOW...
DON'T WORRY YOURSELF.
SHE JUST SEEMS.. ...PROMISING.... SOMEHOW...
DAVID! TELEPHONE!
UHM.. THANKS, ANNY.
HI DAVID, IT'S MINNIE! WHATCHA UP TO?
DO NOT DISTURB
MINNIE
NOTHIN' MUCH.... YOU KNOW, HANGIN' OUT..
WELL, I'M GETTING OFF WORK SOON—WOULD YOU LIKE TO GO OUT FOR COFFEE?
NAW, I'M KINDA BUSHED.
I SEE... WELL, MAYBE WE CAN GET TOGETHER SOON- ARE YOU BUSY TOMORROW?
WELL, NO, I DON'T THINK SO, BUT HOW DOES MATT FEEL ABOUT THIS?
IT'S OK- I TALKED TO HIM ABOUT IT AND WE HAVE AN UNDERSTANDING.
AN UNDERSTANDING?
YEAH, HE SAID IT WAS COOL WITH HIM....

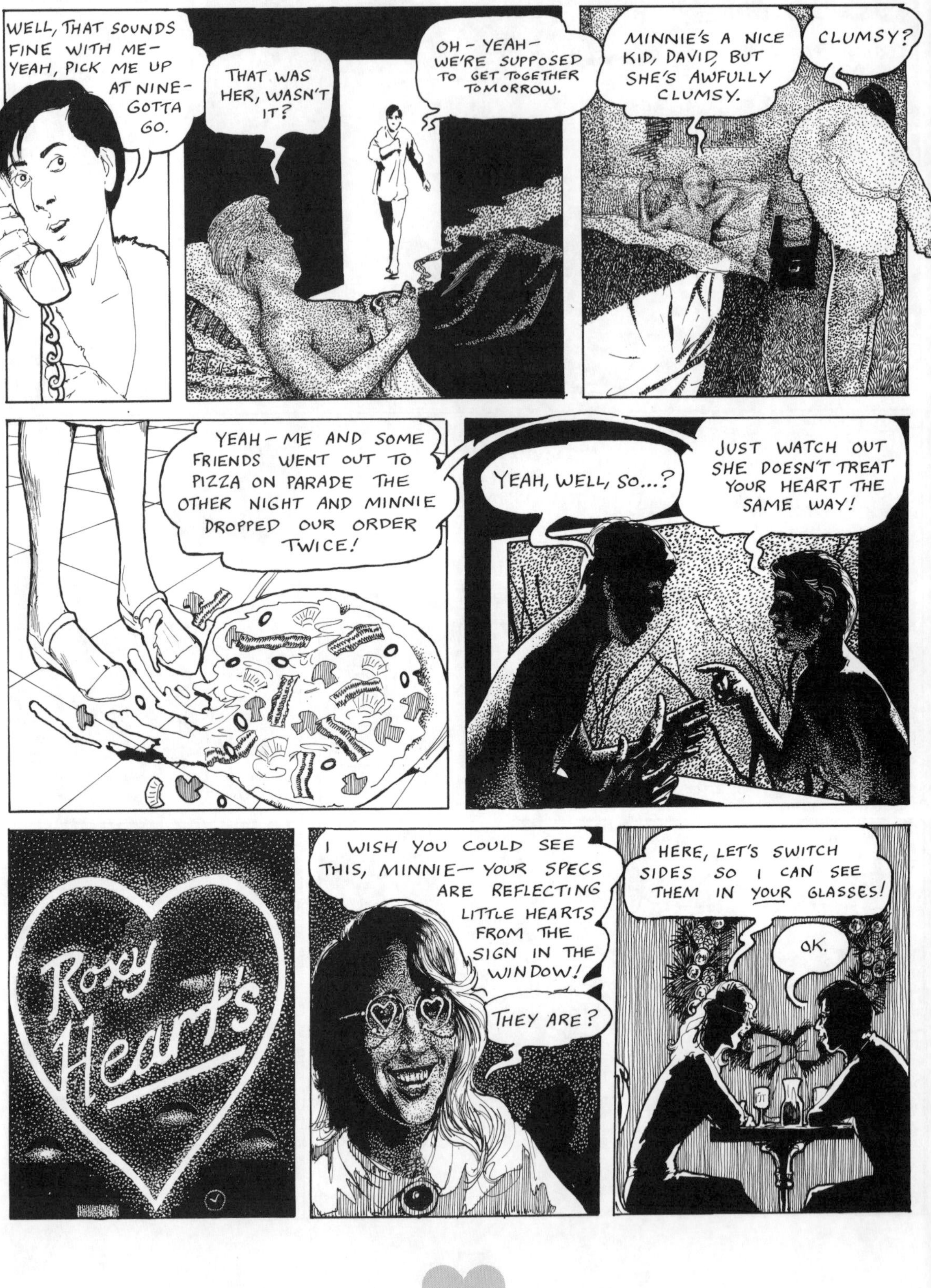
WELL, THAT SOUNDS FINE WITH ME- YEAH, PICK ME UP AT NINE- GOTTA GO.
THAT WAS HER, WASN'T IT?
OH - YEAH- WE'RE SUPPOSED TO GET TOGETHER TOMORROW.
MINNIE'S A NICE KID, DAVID, BUT SHE'S AWFULLY CLUMSY.
CLUMSY?
YEAH - ME AND SOME FRIENDS WENT OUT TO PIZZA ON PARADE THE OTHER NIGHT AND MINNIE DROPPED OUR ORDER TWICE!
YEAH, WELL, SO...?
JUST WATCH OUT SHE DOESN'T TREAT YOUR HEART THE SAME WAY!
Roxy Heart's
I WISH YOU COULD SEE THIS, MINNIE- YOUR SPECS ARE REFLECTING LITTLE HEARTS FROM THE SIGN IN THE WINDOW!
THEY ARE?
HERE, LET'S SWITCH SIDES SO I CAN SEE THEM IN YOUR GLASSES!
O.K.

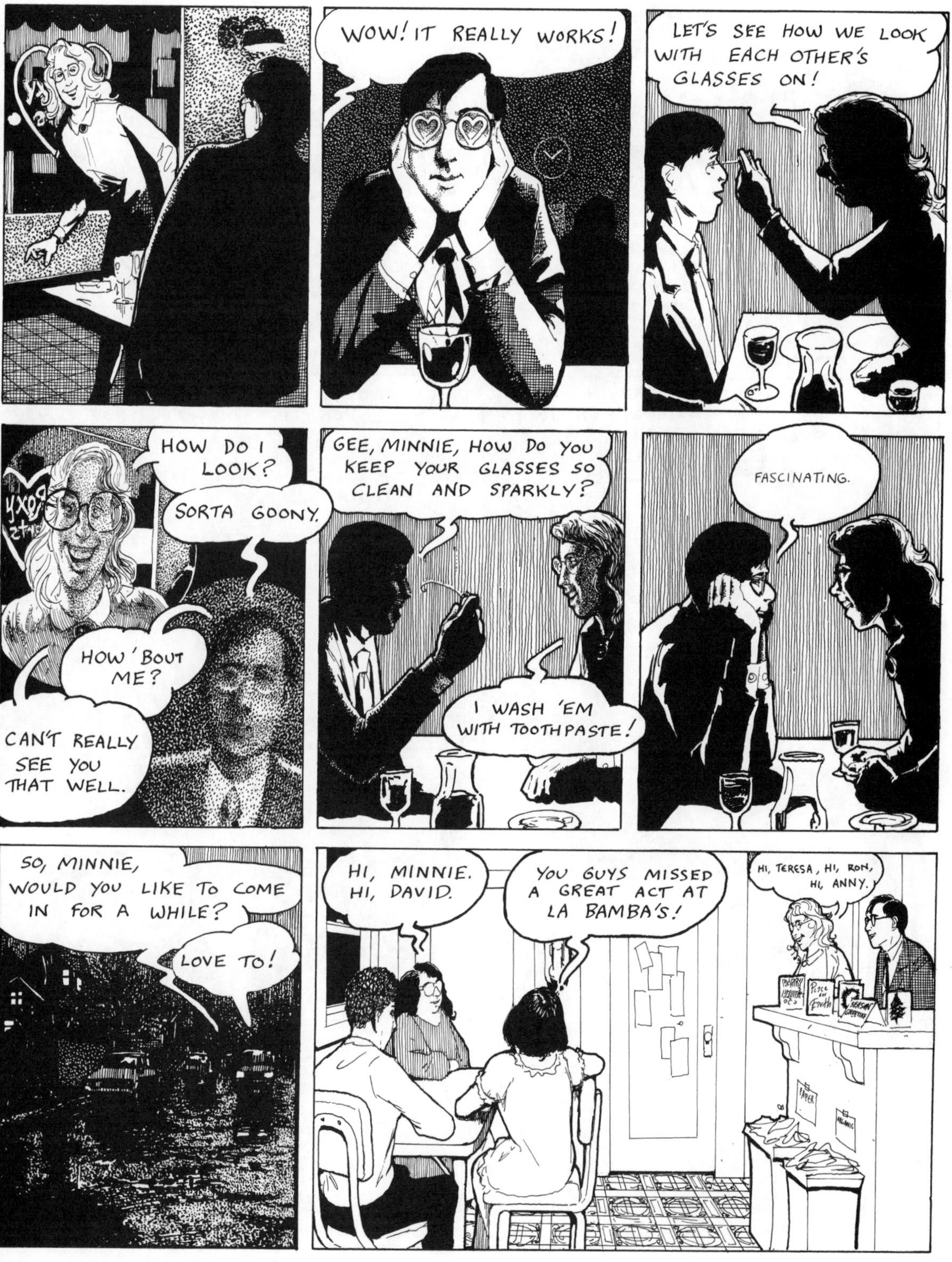
WOW! IT REALLY WORKS!
LET'S SEE HOW WE LOOK WITH EACH OTHER'S GLASSES ON!
HOW DO I LOOK?
SORTA GOONY.
HOW 'BOUT ME?
CAN'T REALLY SEE YOU THAT WELL.
GEE, MINNIE, HOW DO YOU KEEP YOUR GLASSES SO CLEAN AND SPARKLY?
I WASH 'EM WITH TOOTHPASTE!
FASCINATING.
SO, MINNIE, WOULD YOU LIKE TO COME IN FOR A WHILE?
LOVE TO!
HI, MINNIE. HI, DAVID.
YOU GUYS MISSED A GREAT ACT AT LA BAMBA'S!
HI, TERESA, HI, RON, HI, ANNY.

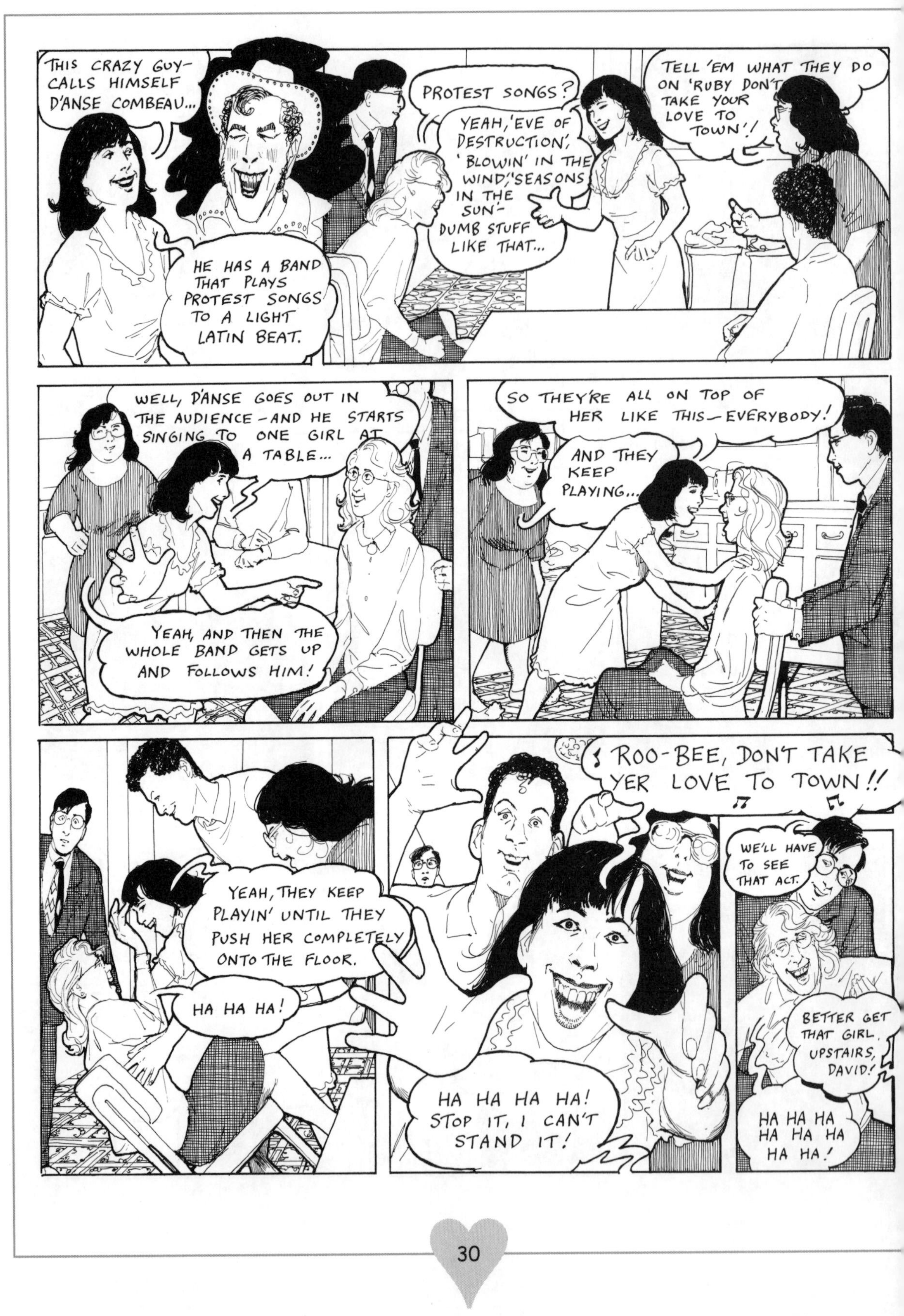
THIS CRAZY GUY- CALLS HIMSELF D'ANSE COMBEAU...
HE HAS A BAND THAT PLAYS PROTEST SONGS TO A LIGHT LATIN BEAT.
PROTEST SONGS?
YEAH, 'EVE OF DESTRUCTION', 'BLOWIN' IN THE WIND', 'SEASONS IN THE SUN'- DUMB STUFF LIKE THAT...
TELL 'EM WHAT THEY DO ON 'RUBY DON'T TAKE YOUR LOVE TO TOWN'!
WELL, D'ANSE GOES OUT IN THE AUDIENCE - AND HE STARTS SINGING TO ONE GIRL AT A TABLE...
YEAH, AND THEN THE WHOLE BAND GETS UP AND FOLLOWS HIM!
SO THEY'RE ALL ON TOP OF HER LIKE THIS - EVERYBODY!
AND THEY KEEP PLAYING...
YEAH, THEY KEEP PLAYIN' UNTIL THEY PUSH HER COMPLETELY ONTO THE FLOOR.
HA HA HA!
ROO-BEE, DON'T TAKE YER LOVE TO TOWN!!
HA HA HA HA! STOP IT, I CAN'T STAND IT!
WE'LL HAVE TO SEE THAT ACT.
BETTER GET THAT GIRL UPSTAIRS, DAVID!
HA HA HA HA HA HA HA HA!

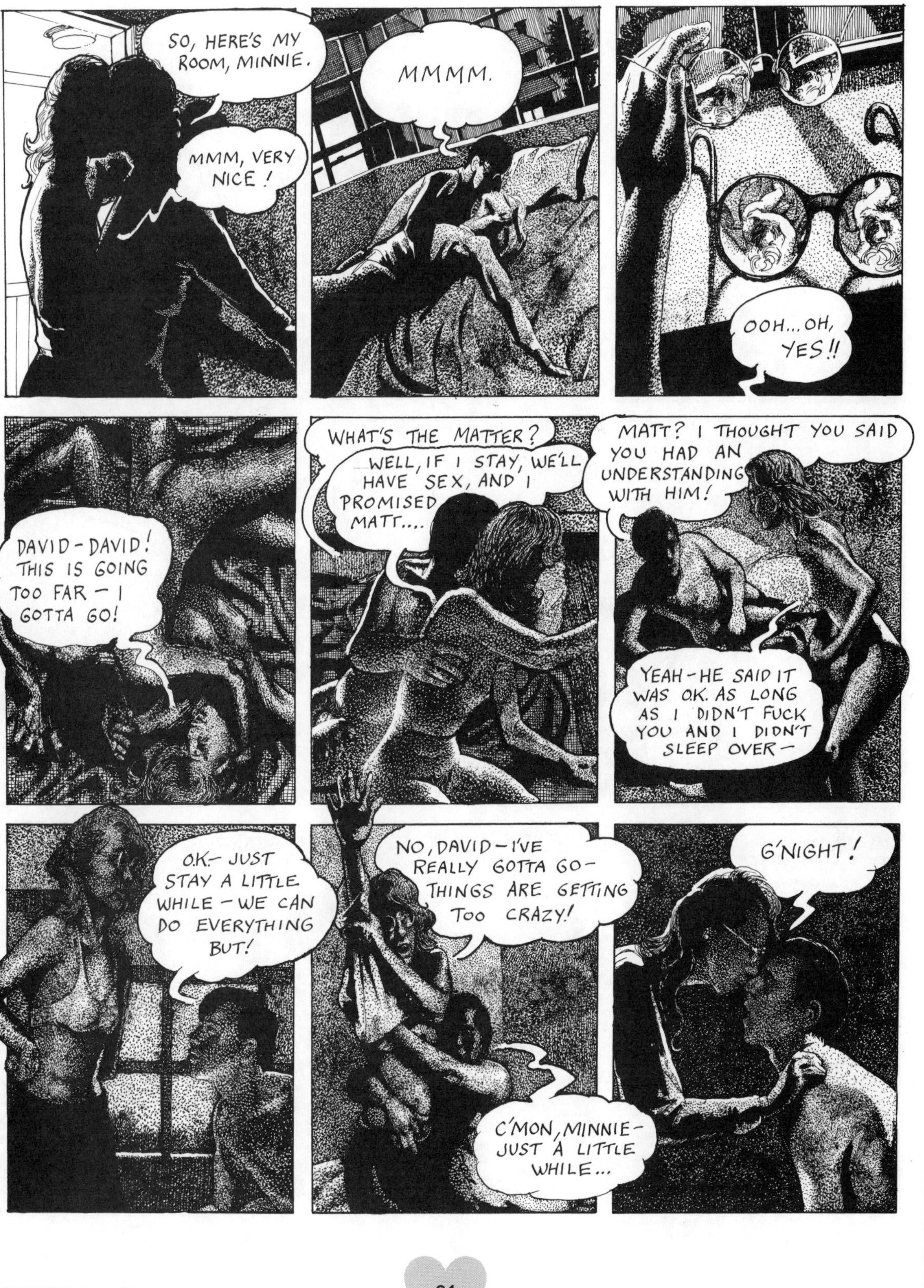
SO, HERE'S MY ROOM, MINNIE.
MMM, VERY NICE!
MMMM.
OOH... OH, YES!!
DAVID-DAVID! THIS IS GOING TOO FAR - I GOTTA GO!
WHAT'S THE MATTER?
WELL, IF I STAY, WE'LL HAVE SEX, AND I PROMISED MATT....
MATT? I THOUGHT YOU SAID YOU HAD AN UNDERSTANDING WITH HIM!
YEAH - HE SAID IT WAS O.K. AS LONG AS I DIDN'T FUCK YOU AND I DIDN'T SLEEP OVER -
O.K.- JUST STAY A LITTLE WHILE - WE CAN DO EVERYTHING BUT!
NO, DAVID - I'VE REALLY GOTTA GO - THINGS ARE GETTING TOO CRAZY!
C'MON, MINNIE - JUST A LITTLE WHILE...
G'NIGHT!

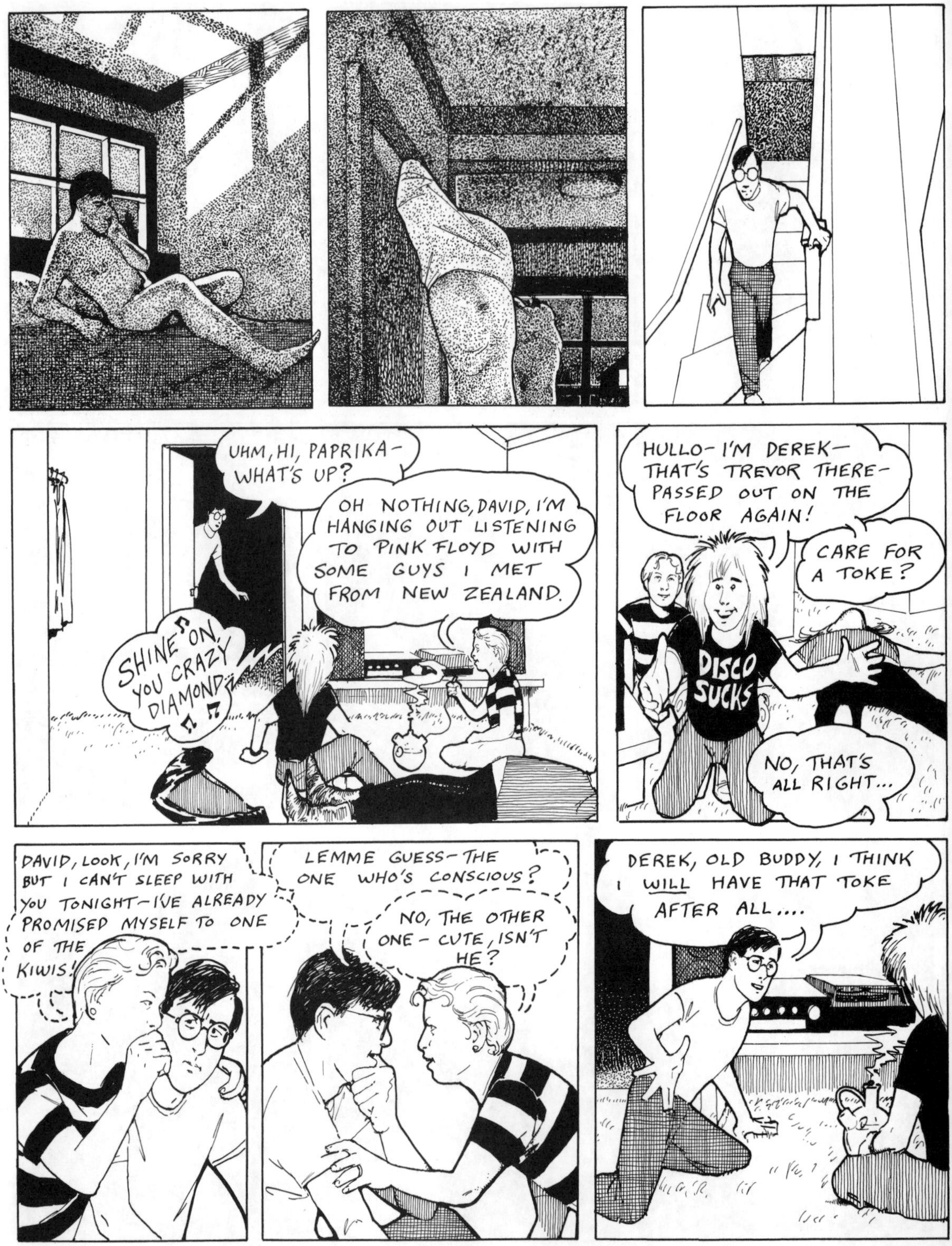
UHM, HI, PAPRIKA- WHAT'S UP?
OH NOTHING, DAVID, I'M HANGING OUT LISTENING TO PINK FLOYD WITH SOME GUYS I MET FROM NEW ZEALAND.
SHINE ON, YOU CRAZY DIAMOND
HULLO- I'M DEREK- THAT'S TREVOR THERE- PASSED OUT ON THE FLOOR AGAIN!
CARE FOR A TOKE?
DISCO SUCKS
NO, THAT'S ALL RIGHT...
DAVID, LOOK, I'M SORRY BUT I CAN'T SLEEP WITH YOU TONIGHT- I'VE ALREADY PROMISED MYSELF TO ONE OF THE KIWIS!
LEMME GUESS- THE ONE WHO'S CONSCIOUS?
NO, THE OTHER ONE- CUTE, ISN'T HE?
DEREK, OLD BUDDY, I THINK I WILL HAVE THAT TOKE AFTER ALL....

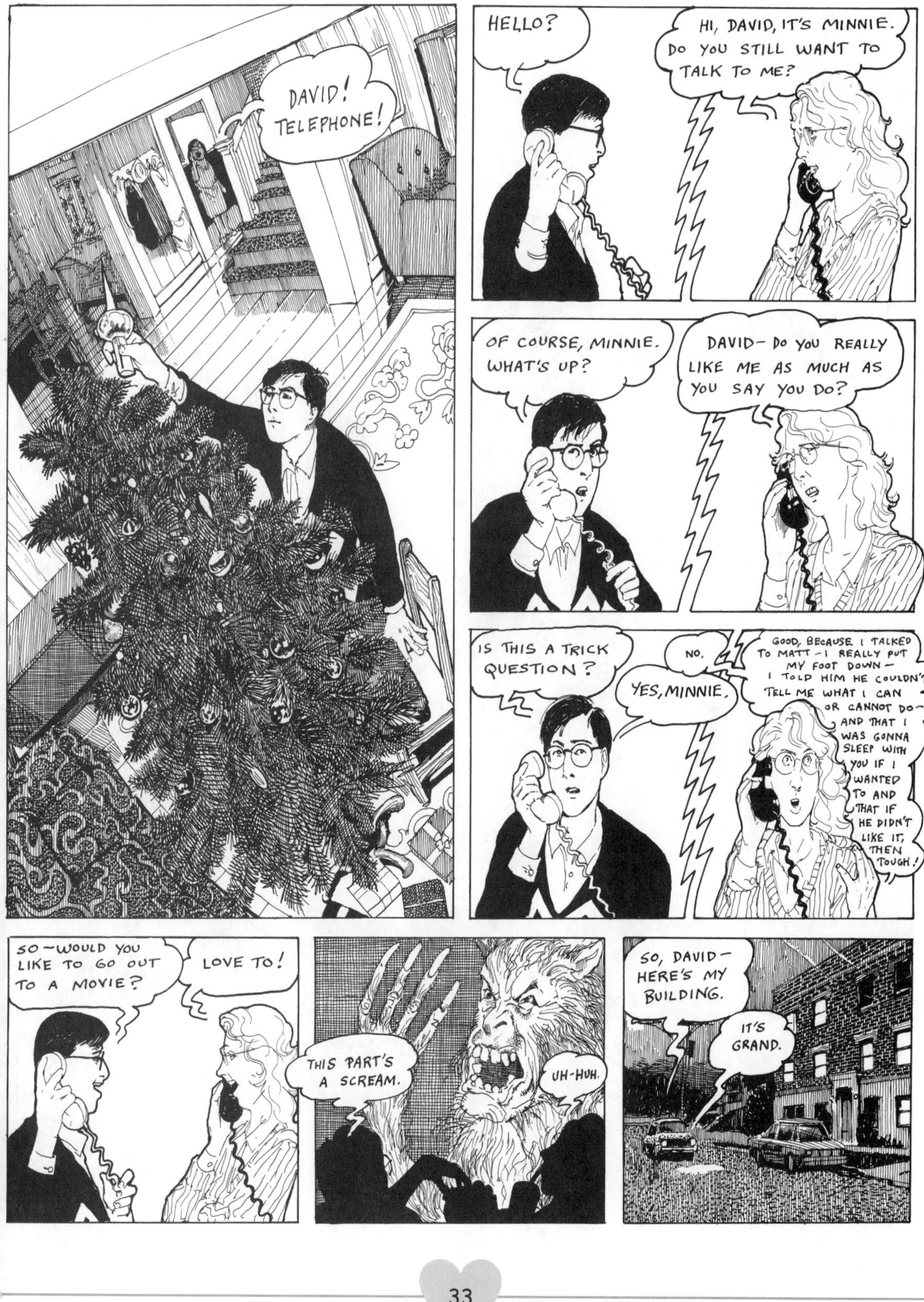
DAVID! TELEPHONE!
HELLO?
HI, DAVID, IT'S MINNIE. DO YOU STILL WANT TO TALK TO ME?
OF COURSE, MINNIE. WHAT'S UP?
DAVID— DO YOU REALLY LIKE ME AS MUCH AS YOU SAY YOU DO?
IS THIS A TRICK QUESTION?
NO.
YES, MINNIE.
GOOD, BECAUSE I TALKED TO MATT— I REALLY PUT MY FOOT DOWN— I TOLD HIM HE COULDN'T TELL ME WHAT I CAN OR CANNOT DO— AND THAT I WAS GONNA SLEEP WITH YOU IF I WANTED TO AND THAT IF HE DIDN'T LIKE IT, THEN TOUGH!
SO— WOULD YOU LIKE TO GO OUT TO A MOVIE?
LOVE TO!
THIS PART'S A SCREAM.
UH-HUH.
SO, DAVID— HERE'S MY BUILDING.
IT'S GRAND.

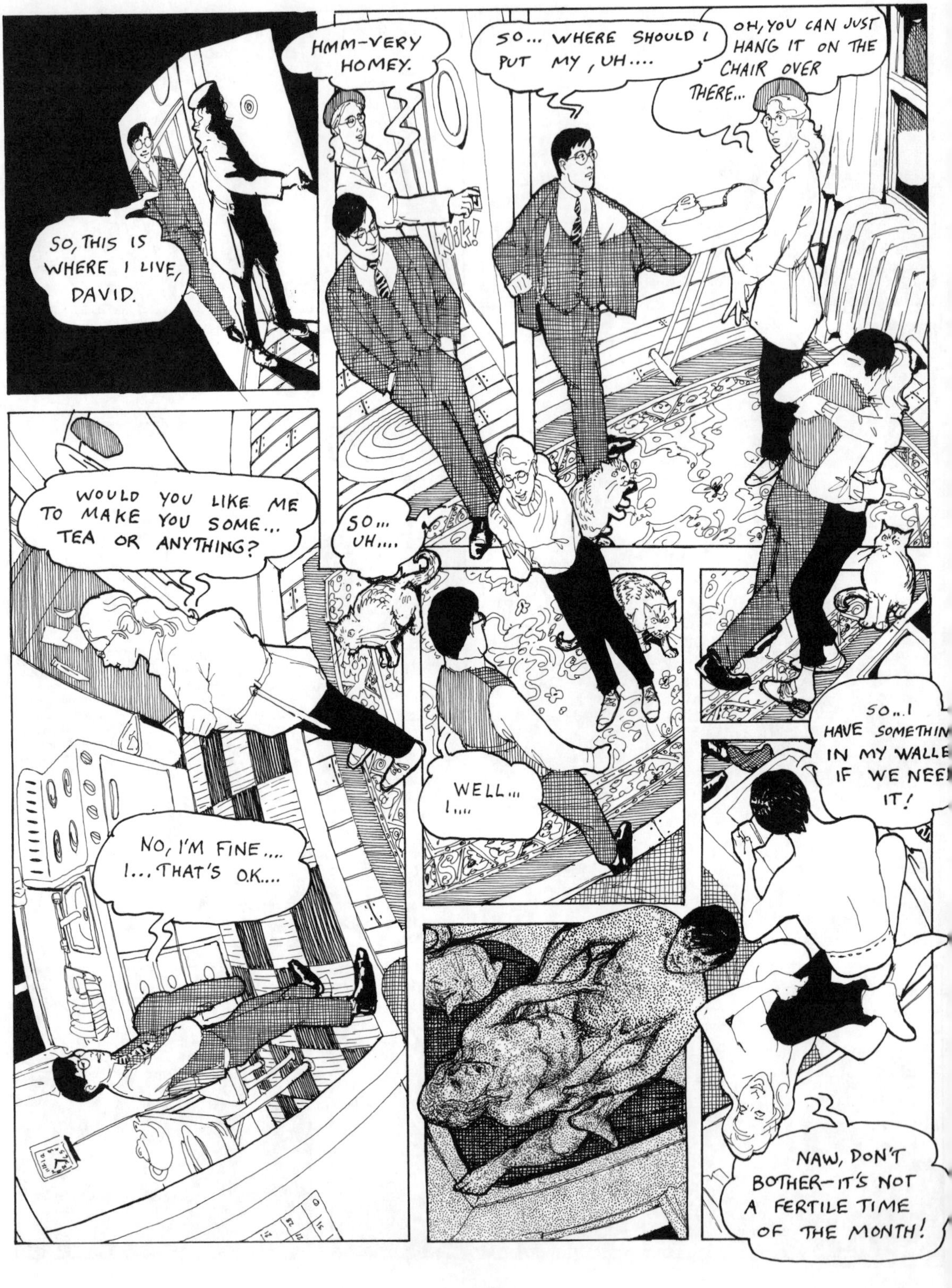
SO, THIS IS WHERE I LIVE, DAVID.
HMM—VERY HOMEY.
KLIK!
SO... WHERE SHOULD I PUT MY, UH....
OH, YOU CAN JUST HANG IT ON THE CHAIR OVER THERE...
WOULD YOU LIKE ME TO MAKE YOU SOME... TEA OR ANYTHING?
SO... UH....
NO, I'M FINE.... I... THAT'S O.K....
WELL... I....
NAW, DON'T BOTHER—IT'S NOT A FERTILE TIME OF THE MONTH!

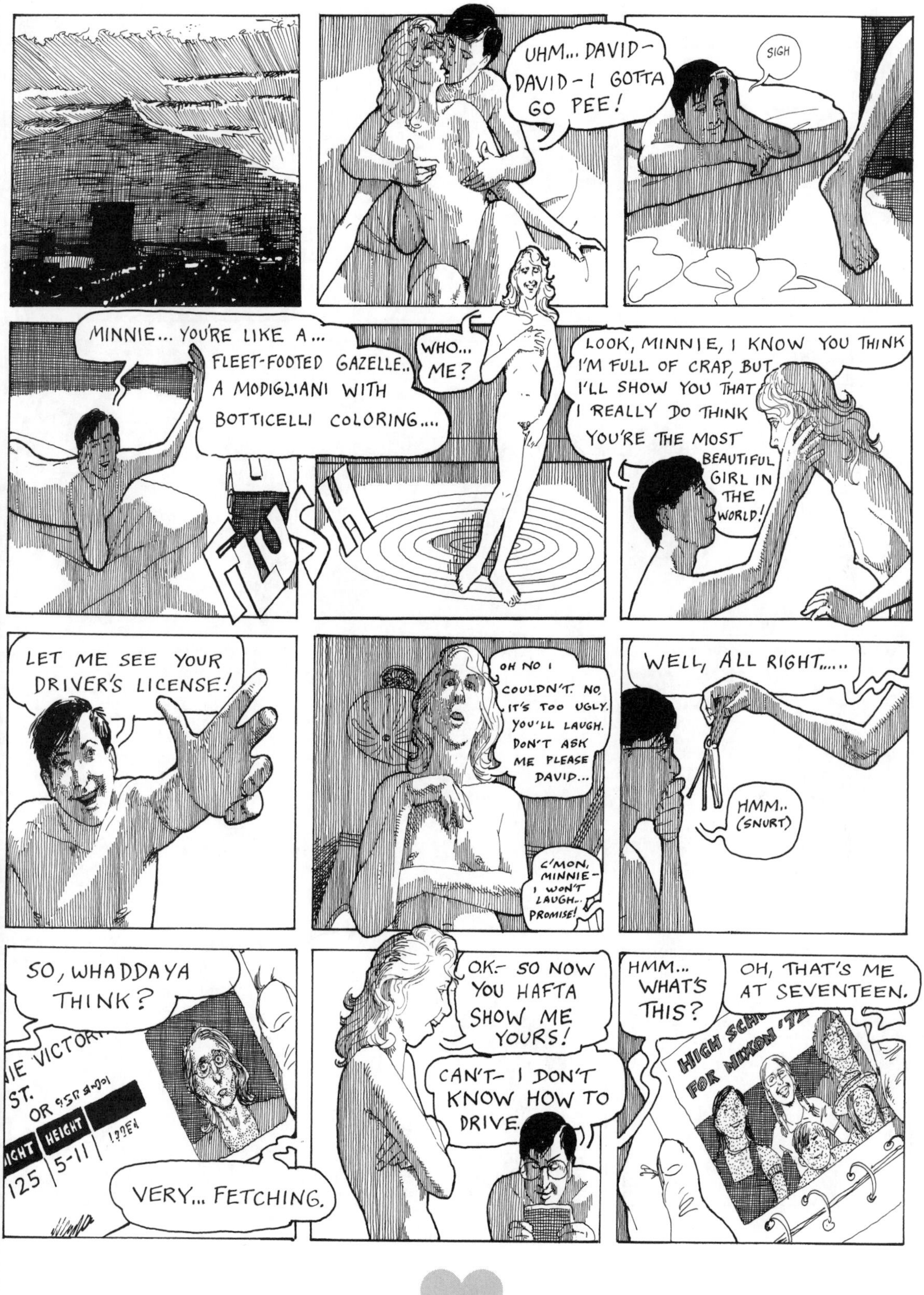
UHM... DAVID- DAVID- I GOTTA GO PEE!
SIGH
MINNIE... YOU'RE LIKE A... FLEET-FOOTED GAZELLE.. A MODIGLIANI WITH BOTTICELLI COLORING....
FLUSH
WHO... ME?
LOOK, MINNIE, I KNOW YOU THINK I'M FULL OF CRAP, BUT I'LL SHOW YOU THAT I REALLY DO THINK YOU'RE THE MOST BEAUTIFUL GIRL IN THE WORLD!
LET ME SEE YOUR DRIVER'S LICENSE!
OH NO I COULDN'T. NO, IT'S TOO UGLY. YOU'LL LAUGH. DON'T ASK ME PLEASE DAVID...
C'MON, MINNIE- I WON'T LAUGH.. PROMISE!
WELL, ALL RIGHT......
HMM.. (SNURT)
SO, WHADDAYA THINK?
ST.
HEIGHT
125
5-11
VERY... FETCHING.
O.K.- SO NOW YOU HAFTA SHOW ME YOURS!
CAN'T- I DON'T KNOW HOW TO DRIVE.
HMM... WHAT'S THIS?
OH, THAT'S ME AT SEVENTEEN.

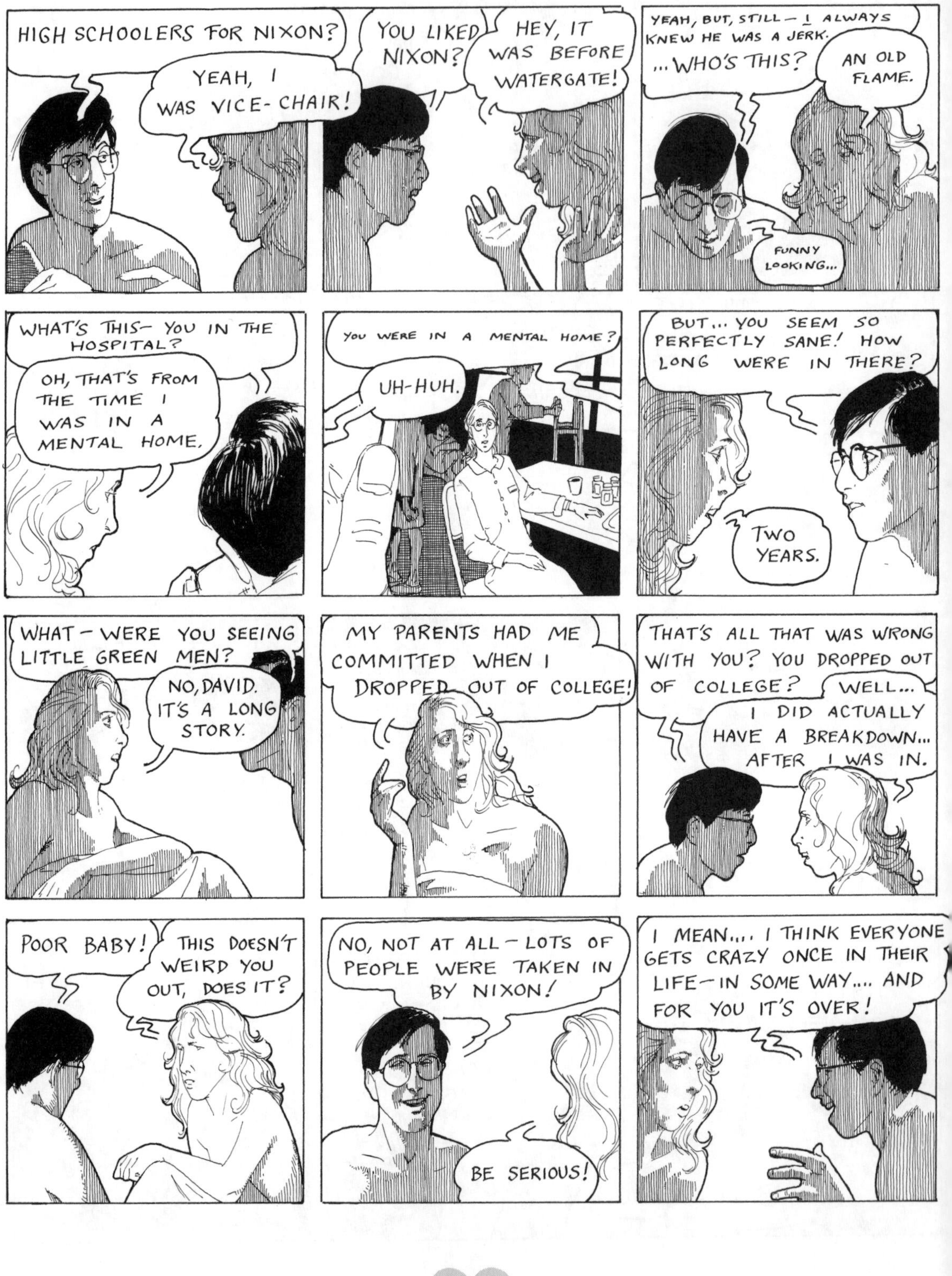
HIGH SCHOOLERS FOR NIXON?
YEAH, I WAS VICE-CHAIR!
YOU LIKED NIXON?
HEY, IT WAS BEFORE WATERGATE!
YEAH, BUT, STILL— I ALWAYS KNEW HE WAS A JERK.
...WHO'S THIS?
AN OLD FLAME.
FUNNY LOOKING...
WHAT'S THIS— YOU IN THE HOSPITAL?
OH, THAT'S FROM THE TIME I WAS IN A MENTAL HOME.
YOU WERE IN A MENTAL HOME?
UH-HUH.
BUT... YOU SEEM SO PERFECTLY SANE! HOW LONG WERE IN THERE?
TWO YEARS.
WHAT— WERE YOU SEEING LITTLE GREEN MEN?
NO, DAVID. IT'S A LONG STORY.
MY PARENTS HAD ME COMMITTED WHEN I DROPPED OUT OF COLLEGE!
THAT'S ALL THAT WAS WRONG WITH YOU? YOU DROPPED OUT OF COLLEGE?
WELL... I DID ACTUALLY HAVE A BREAKDOWN... AFTER I WAS IN.
POOR BABY!
THIS DOESN'T WEIRD YOU OUT, DOES IT?
NO, NOT AT ALL— LOTS OF PEOPLE WERE TAKEN IN BY NIXON!
BE SERIOUS!
I MEAN.... I THINK EVERYONE GETS CRAZY ONCE IN THEIR LIFE— IN SOME WAY.... AND FOR YOU IT'S OVER!

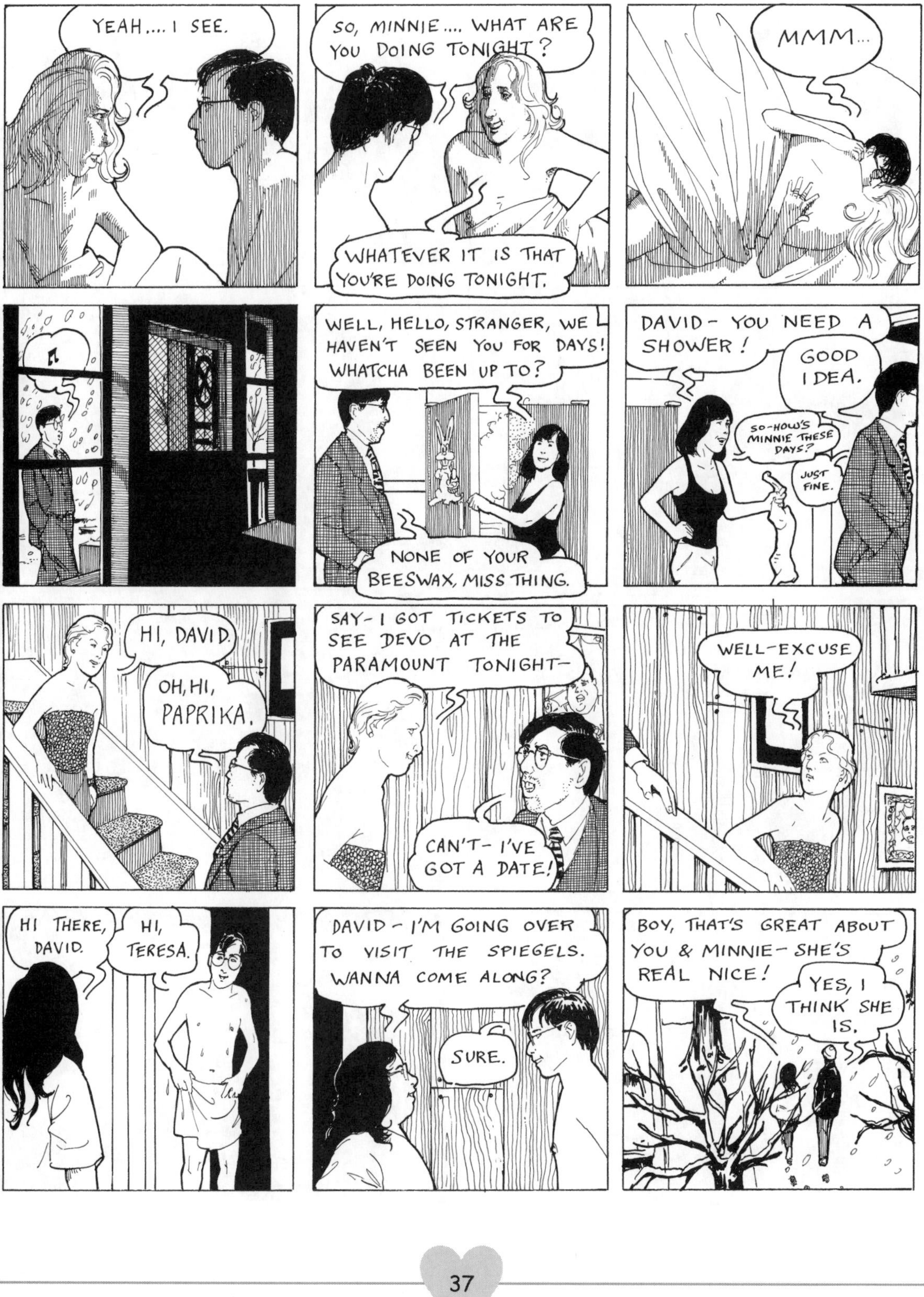
YEAH.... I SEE.
SO, MINNIE.... WHAT ARE YOU DOING TONIGHT?
WHATEVER IT IS THAT YOU'RE DOING TONIGHT.
MMM...
WELL, HELLO, STRANGER, WE HAVEN'T SEEN YOU FOR DAYS! WHATCHA BEEN UP TO?
NONE OF YOUR BEESWAX, MISS THING.
DAVID- YOU NEED A SHOWER!
GOOD IDEA.
SO-HOW'S MINNIE THESE DAYS?
JUST FINE.
HI, DAVID.
OH, HI, PAPRIKA.
SAY- I GOT TICKETS TO SEE DEVO AT THE PARAMOUNT TONIGHT-
CAN'T- I'VE GOT A DATE!
WELL-EXCUSE ME!
HI THERE, DAVID.
HI, TERESA.
DAVID - I'M GOING OVER TO VISIT THE SPIEGELS. WANNA COME ALONG?
SURE.
BOY, THAT'S GREAT ABOUT YOU & MINNIE- SHE'S REAL NICE!
YES, I THINK SHE IS.

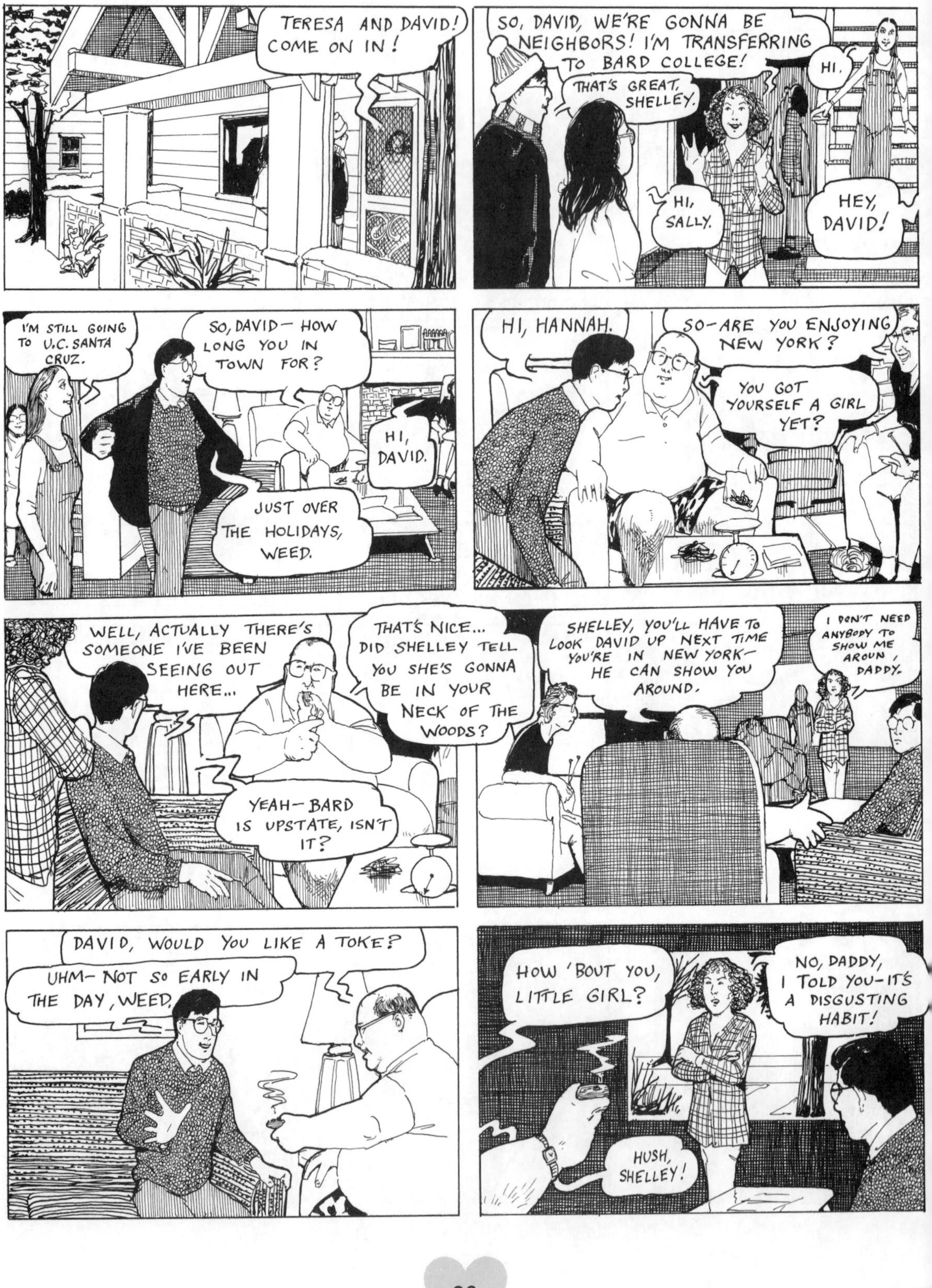
TERESA AND DAVID! COME ON IN!
SO, DAVID, WE'RE GONNA BE NEIGHBORS! I'M TRANSFERRING TO BARD COLLEGE!
THAT'S GREAT, SHELLEY.
HI.
HI, SALLY.
HEY, DAVID!
I'M STILL GOING TO U.C. SANTA CRUZ.
SO, DAVID— HOW LONG YOU IN TOWN FOR?
HI, DAVID.
JUST OVER THE HOLIDAYS, WEED.
HI, HANNAH.
SO—ARE YOU ENJOYING NEW YORK?
YOU GOT YOURSELF A GIRL YET?
WELL, ACTUALLY THERE'S SOMEONE I'VE BEEN SEEING OUT HERE...
THAT'S NICE... DID SHELLEY TELL YOU SHE'S GONNA BE IN YOUR NECK OF THE WOODS?
YEAH— BARD IS UPSTATE, ISN'T IT?
SHELLEY, YOU'LL HAVE TO LOOK DAVID UP NEXT TIME YOU'RE IN NEW YORK— HE CAN SHOW YOU AROUND.
I DON'T NEED ANYBODY TO SHOW ME AROUN , DADDY.
DAVID, WOULD YOU LIKE A TOKE?
UHM— NOT SO EARLY IN THE DAY, WEED.
HOW 'BOUT YOU, LITTLE GIRL?
NO, DADDY, I TOLD YOU—IT'S A DISGUSTING HABIT!
HUSH, SHELLEY!

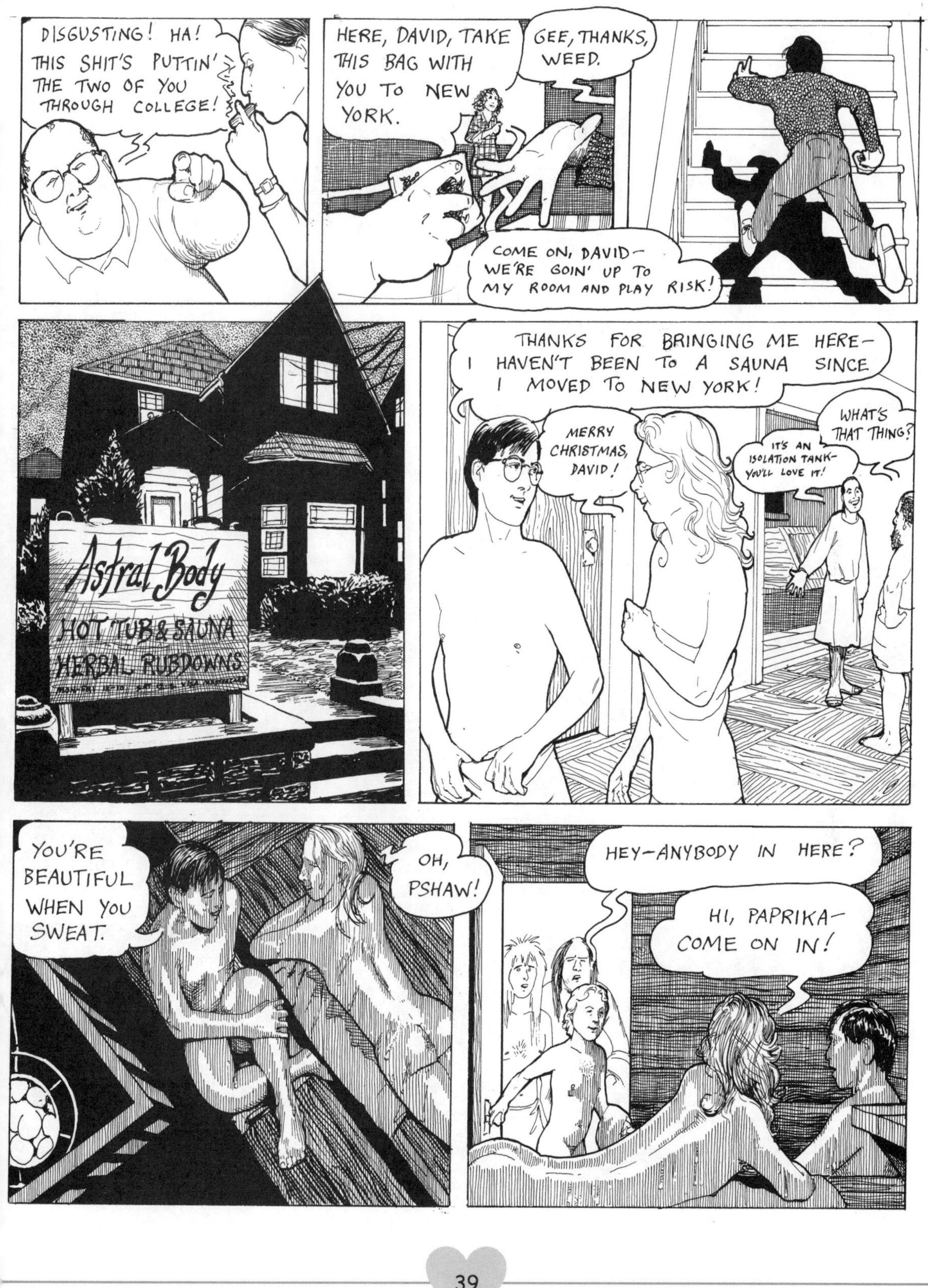

DISGUSTING! HA! THIS SHIT'S PUTTIN' THE TWO OF YOU THROUGH COLLEGE!
HERE, DAVID, TAKE THIS BAG WITH YOU TO NEW YORK.
GEE, THANKS, WEED.
COME ON, DAVID- WE'RE GOIN' UP TO MY ROOM AND PLAY RISK!
Astral Body
HOT TUB & SAUNA
HERBAL RUBDOWNS
THANKS FOR BRINGING ME HERE- I HAVEN'T BEEN TO A SAUNA SINCE I MOVED TO NEW YORK!
MERRY CHRISTMAS, DAVID!
WHAT'S THAT THING?
IT'S AN ISOLATION TANK- YOU'LL LOVE IT!
YOU'RE BEAUTIFUL WHEN YOU SWEAT.
OH, PSHAW!
HEY-ANYBODY IN HERE?
HI, PAPRIKA- COME ON IN!

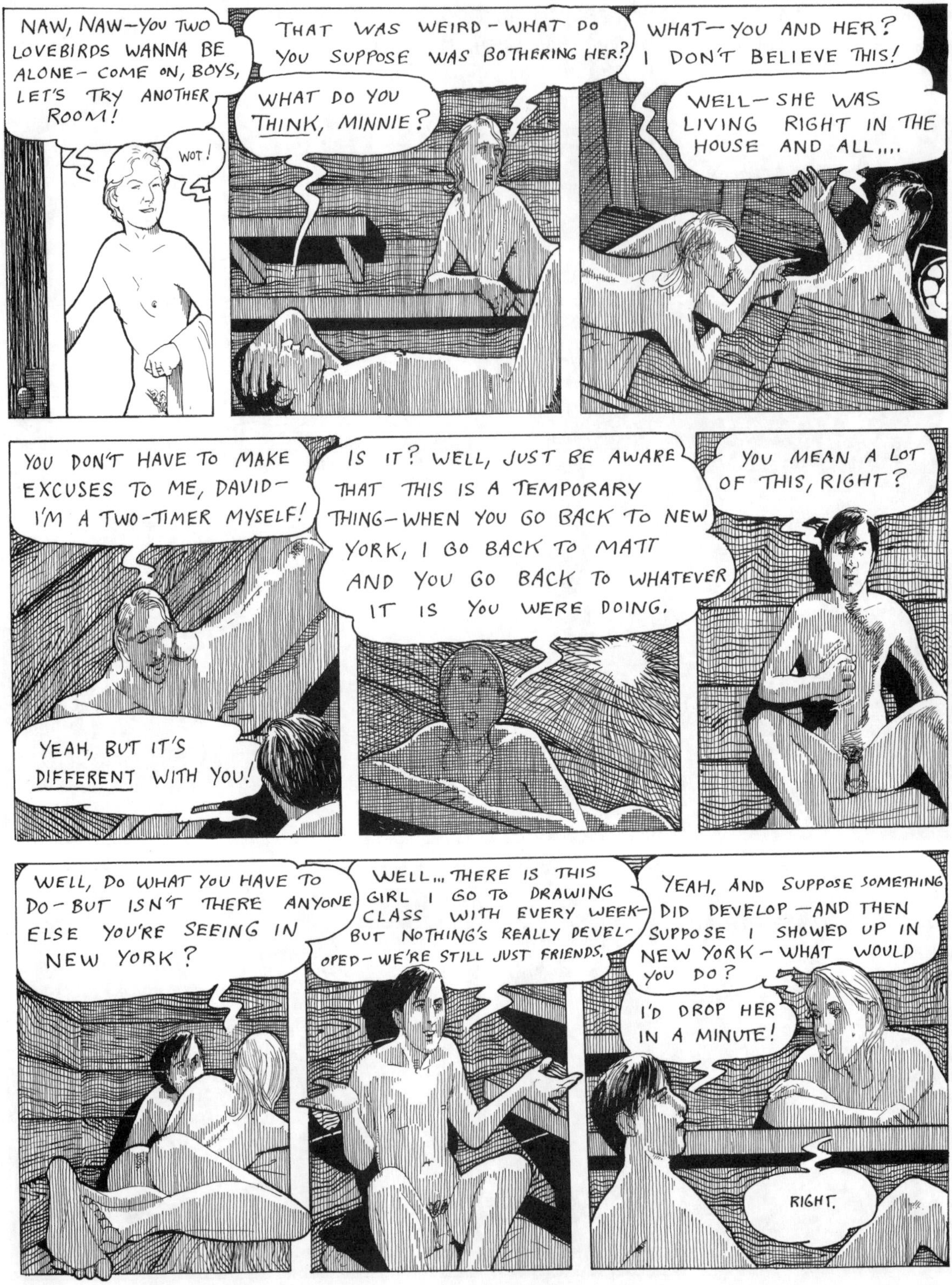
NAW, NAW—YOU TWO LOVEBIRDS WANNA BE ALONE— COME ON, BOYS, LET'S TRY ANOTHER ROOM!
WOT!
THAT WAS WEIRD—WHAT DO YOU SUPPOSE WAS BOTHERING HER?
WHAT DO YOU THINK, MINNIE?
WHAT—YOU AND HER? I DON'T BELIEVE THIS!
WELL—SHE WAS LIVING RIGHT IN THE HOUSE AND ALL....
YOU DON'T HAVE TO MAKE EXCUSES TO ME, DAVID— I'M A TWO-TIMER MYSELF!
YEAH, BUT IT'S DIFFERENT WITH YOU!
IS IT? WELL, JUST BE AWARE THAT THIS IS A TEMPORARY THING—WHEN YOU GO BACK TO NEW YORK, I GO BACK TO MATT AND YOU GO BACK TO WHATEVER IT IS YOU WERE DOING.
YOU MEAN A LOT OF THIS, RIGHT?
WELL, DO WHAT YOU HAVE TO DO—BUT ISN'T THERE ANYONE ELSE YOU'RE SEEING IN NEW YORK?
WELL... THERE IS THIS GIRL I GO TO DRAWING CLASS WITH EVERY WEEK— BUT NOTHING'S REALLY DEVELOPED—WE'RE STILL JUST FRIENDS.
YEAH, AND SUPPOSE SOMETHING DID DEVELOP—AND THEN SUPPOSE I SHOWED UP IN NEW YORK—WHAT WOULD YOU DO?
I'D DROP HER IN A MINUTE!
RIGHT.

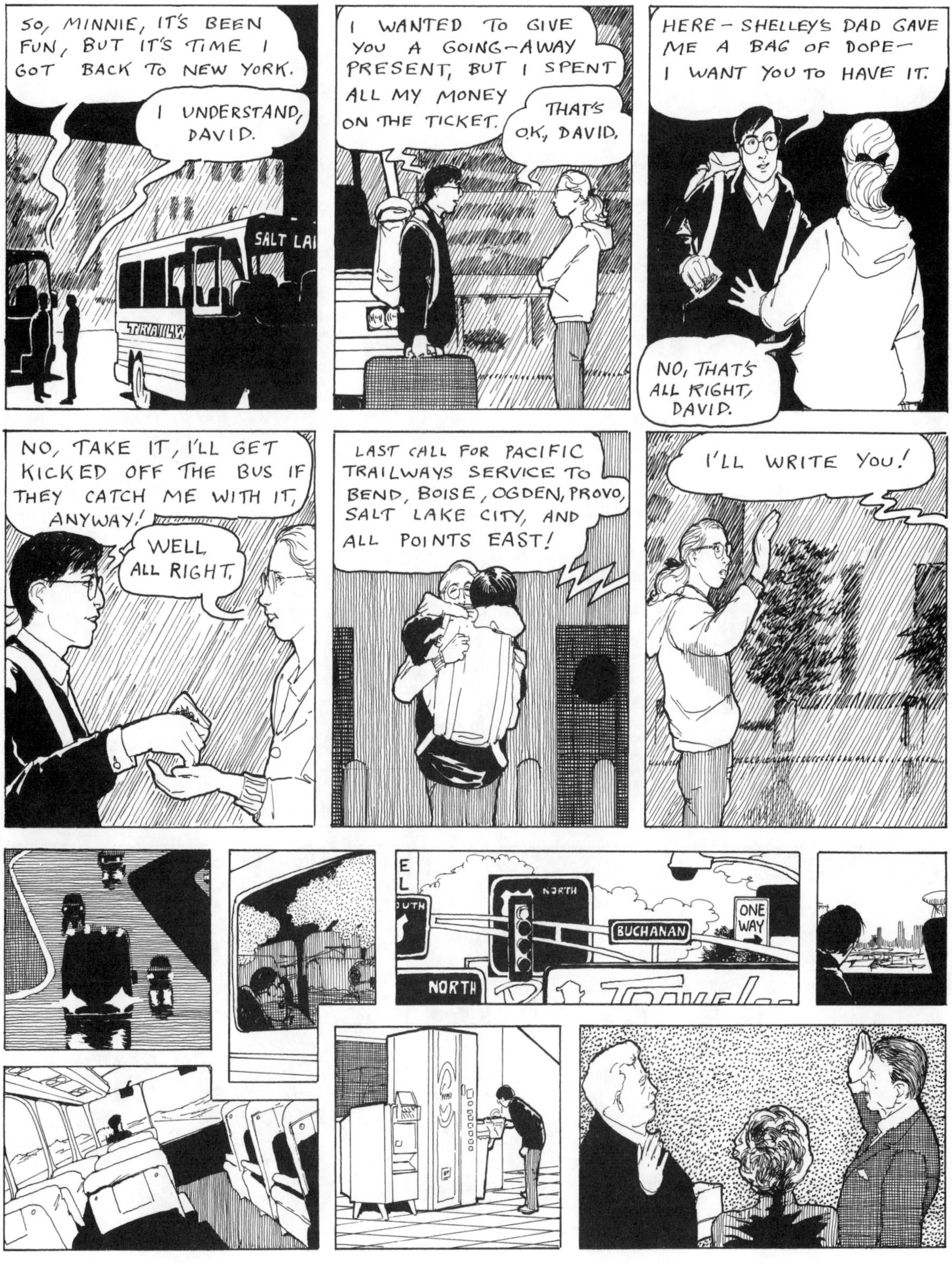
SO, MINNIE, IT'S BEEN FUN, BUT IT'S TIME I GOT BACK TO NEW YORK.
I UNDERSTAND, DAVID.
SALT LA
I WANTED TO GIVE YOU A GOING-AWAY PRESENT, BUT I SPENT ALL MY MONEY ON THE TICKET.
THAT'S O.K., DAVID.
HERE - SHELLEY'S DAD GAVE ME A BAG OF DOPE - I WANT YOU TO HAVE IT.
NO, THAT'S ALL RIGHT, DAVID.
NO, TAKE IT, I'LL GET KICKED OFF THE BUS IF THEY CATCH ME WITH IT, ANYWAY!
WELL, ALL RIGHT.
LAST CALL FOR PACIFIC TRAILWAYS SERVICE TO BEND, BOISE, OGDEN, PROVO, SALT LAKE CITY, AND ALL POINTS EAST!
I'LL WRITE YOU!
NORTH
BUCHANAN
ONE WAY
NORTH

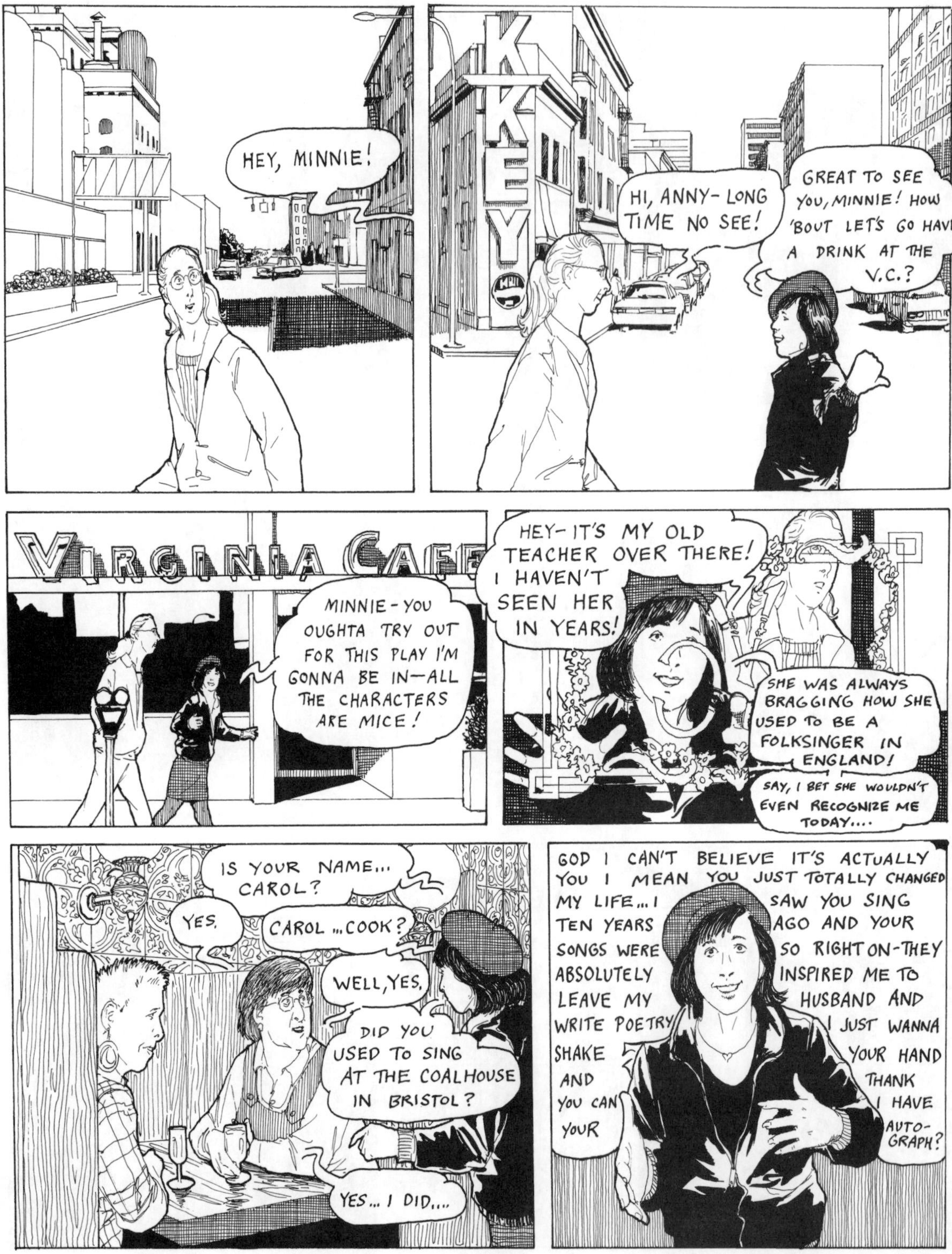
HEY, MINNIE!
KEY
HI, ANNY- LONG TIME NO SEE!
GREAT TO SEE YOU, MINNIE! HOW 'BOUT LET'S GO HAVE A DRINK AT THE V.C.?
VIRGINIA CAFE
MINNIE - YOU OUGHTA TRY OUT FOR THIS PLAY I'M GONNA BE IN—ALL THE CHARACTERS ARE MICE!
HEY- IT'S MY OLD TEACHER OVER THERE! I HAVEN'T SEEN HER IN YEARS!
SHE WAS ALWAYS BRAGGING HOW SHE USED TO BE A FOLKSINGER IN ENGLAND!
SAY, I BET SHE WOULDN'T EVEN RECOGNIZE ME TODAY....
IS YOUR NAME... CAROL?
YES.
CAROL ...COOK?
WELL, YES.
DID YOU USED TO SING AT THE COALHOUSE IN BRISTOL?
YES... I DID....
GOD I CAN'T BELIEVE IT'S ACTUALLY YOU I MEAN YOU JUST TOTALLY CHANGED MY LIFE... I SAW YOU SING TEN YEARS AGO AND YOUR SONGS WERE SO RIGHT ON-THEY ABSOLUTELY INSPIRED ME TO LEAVE MY HUSBAND AND WRITE POETRY I JUST WANNA SHAKE YOUR HAND AND THANK YOU CAN I HAVE YOUR AUTO-GRAPH?

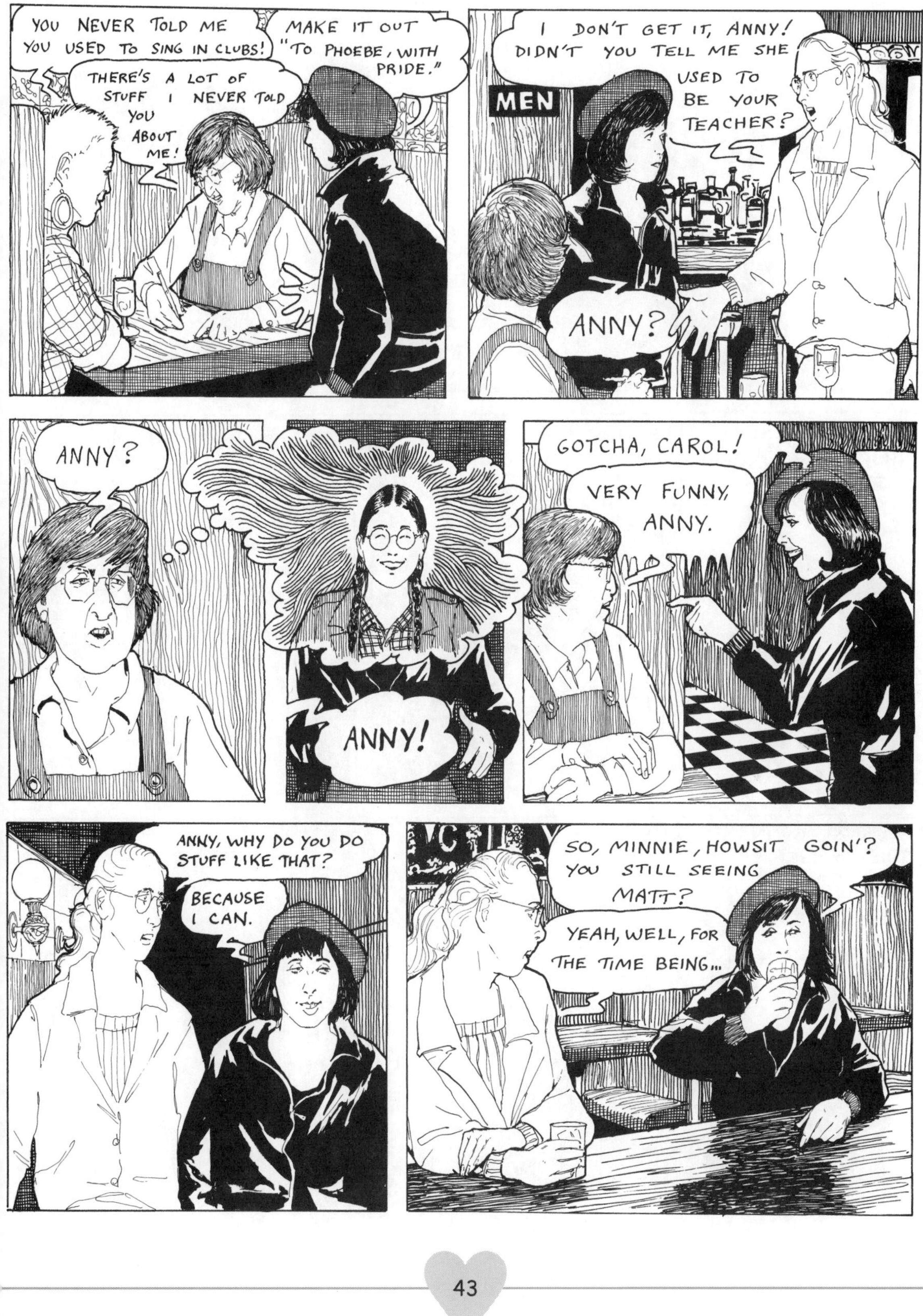
YOU NEVER TOLD ME YOU USED TO SING IN CLUBS!
MAKE IT OUT "TO PHOEBE, WITH PRIDE."
THERE'S A LOT OF STUFF I NEVER TOLD YOU ABOUT ME!
I DON'T GET IT, ANNY! DIDN'T YOU TELL ME SHE USED TO BE YOUR TEACHER?
MEN
ANNY?
ANNY?
ANNY!
GOTCHA, CAROL!
VERY FUNNY, ANNY.
ANNY, WHY DO YOU DO STUFF LIKE THAT?
BECAUSE I CAN.
SO, MINNIE, HOWSIT GOIN'? YOU STILL SEEING MATT?
YEAH, WELL, FOR THE TIME BEING...

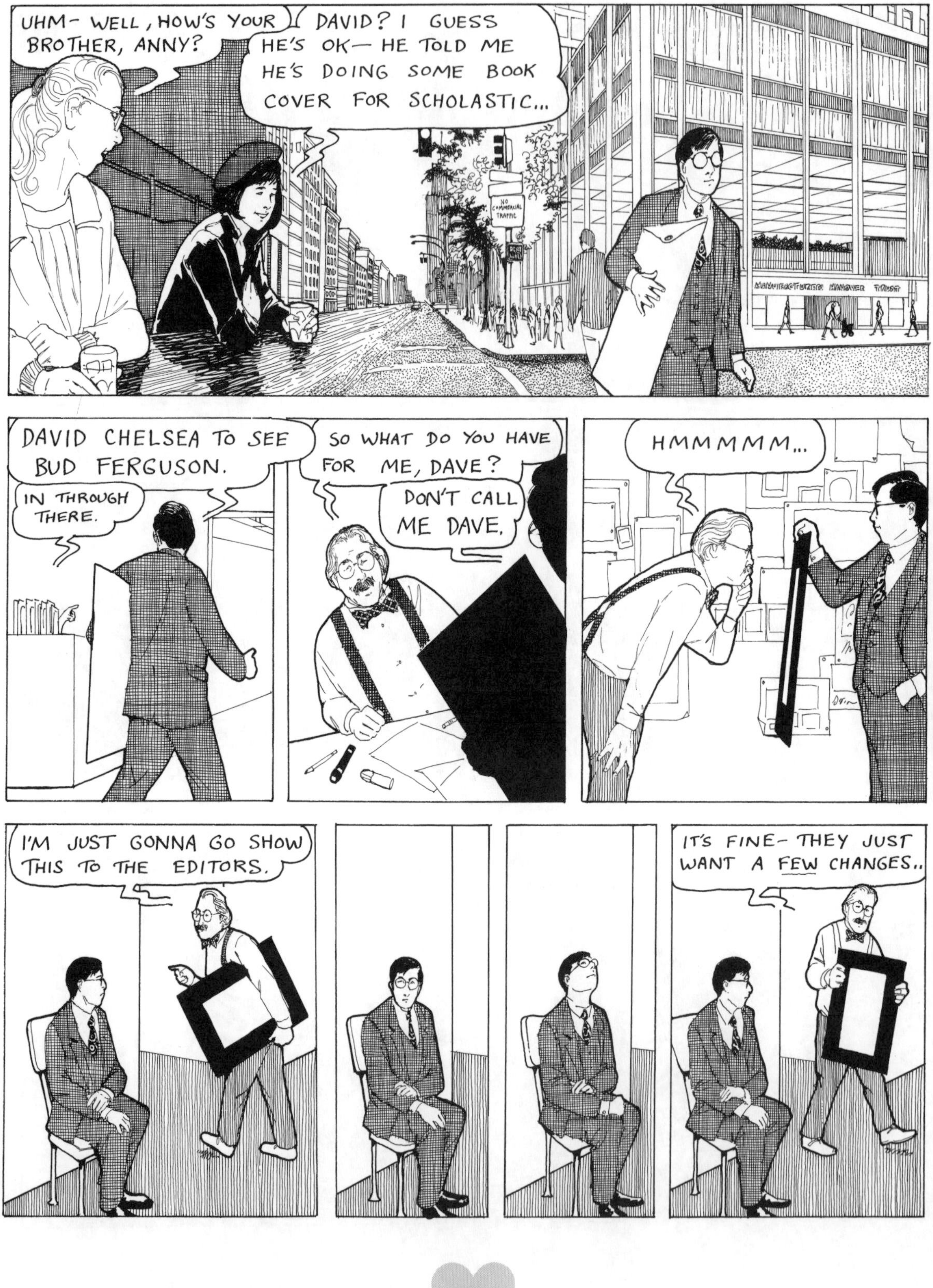
UHM- WELL, HOW'S YOUR BROTHER, ANNY?
DAVID? I GUESS HE'S OK— HE TOLD ME HE'S DOING SOME BOOK COVER FOR SCHOLASTIC...
NO COMMERCIAL TRAFFIC
MANUFACTURERS HANOVER TRUST
DAVID CHELSEA TO SEE BUD FERGUSON.
IN THROUGH THERE.
SO WHAT DO YOU HAVE FOR ME, DAVE?
DON'T CALL ME DAVE.
HMMMMM...
I'M JUST GONNA GO SHOW THIS TO THE EDITORS.
IT'S FINE- THEY JUST WANT A FEW CHANGES..

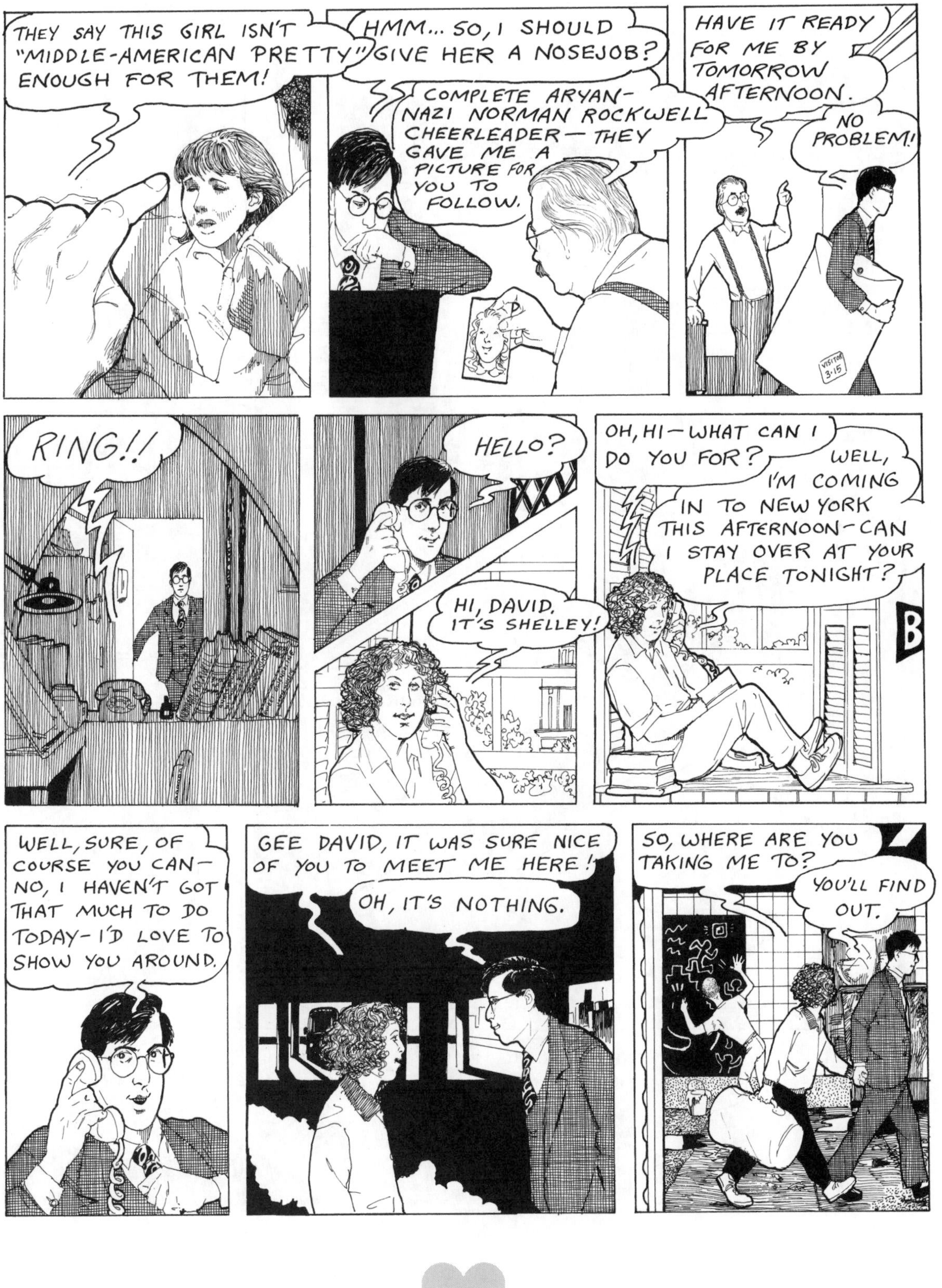
THEY SAY THIS GIRL ISN'T "MIDDLE-AMERICAN PRETTY" ENOUGH FOR THEM!
HMM... SO, I SHOULD GIVE HER A NOSEJOB?
COMPLETE ARYAN-NAZI NORMAN ROCKWELL CHEERLEADER— THEY GAVE ME A PICTURE FOR YOU TO FOLLOW.
HAVE IT READY FOR ME BY TOMORROW AFTERNOON.
NO PROBLEM!
VISITOR 3·15
RING!!
HELLO?
HI, DAVID. IT'S SHELLEY!
OH, HI— WHAT CAN I DO YOU FOR?
WELL, I'M COMING IN TO NEW YORK THIS AFTERNOON- CAN I STAY OVER AT YOUR PLACE TONIGHT?
B
WELL, SURE, OF COURSE YOU CAN— NO, I HAVEN'T GOT THAT MUCH TO DO TODAY- I'D LOVE TO SHOW YOU AROUND.
GEE DAVID, IT WAS SURE NICE OF YOU TO MEET ME HERE!
OH, IT'S NOTHING.
SO, WHERE ARE YOU TAKING ME TO?
YOU'LL FIND OUT.

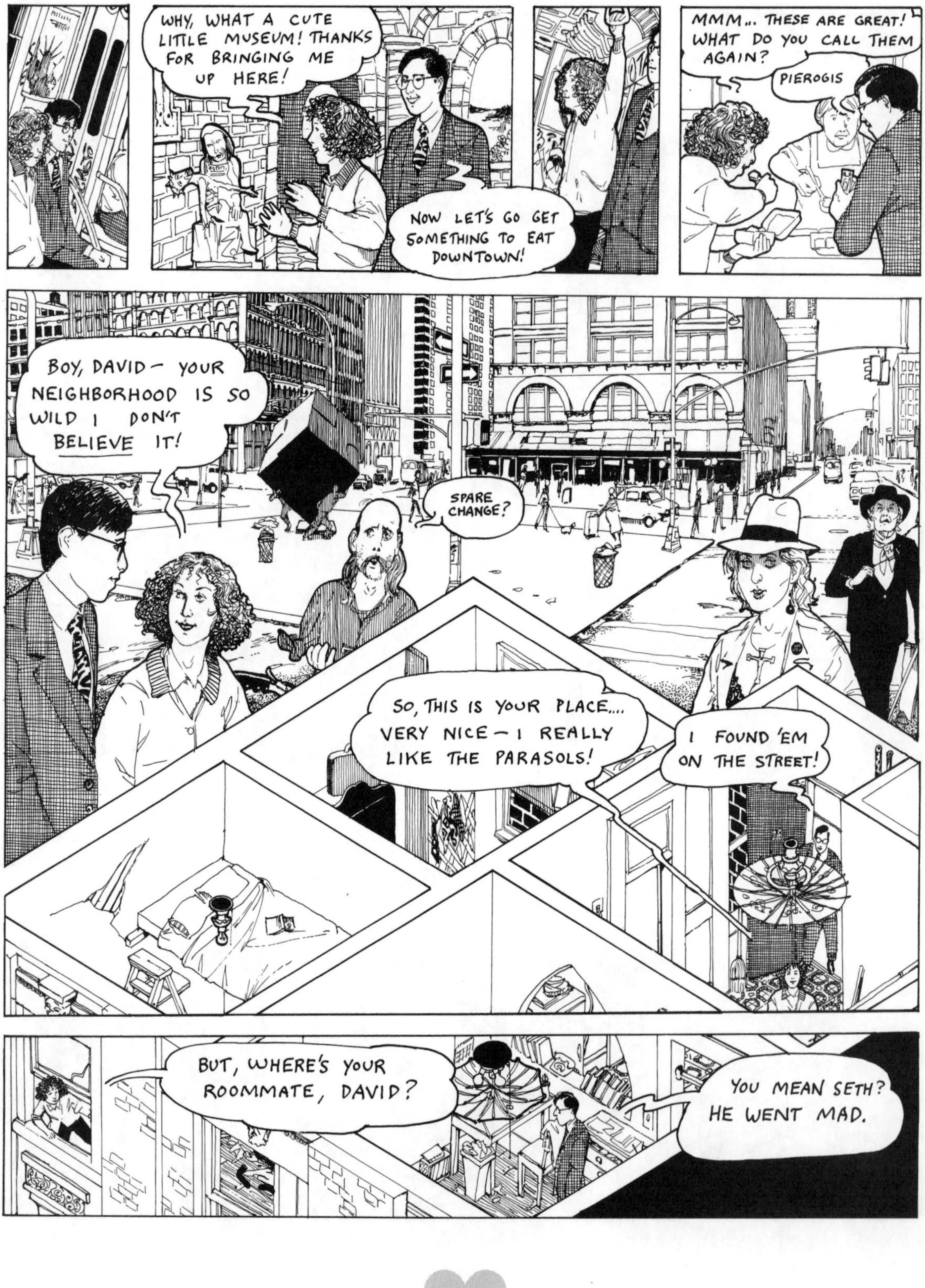
WHY, WHAT A CUTE LITTLE MUSEUM! THANKS FOR BRINGING ME UP HERE!
NOW LET'S GO GET SOMETHING TO EAT DOWNTOWN!
MMM... THESE ARE GREAT! WHAT DO YOU CALL THEM AGAIN?
PIEROGIS
BOY, DAVID— YOUR NEIGHBORHOOD IS SO WILD I DON'T BELIEVE IT!
SPARE CHANGE?
SO, THIS IS YOUR PLACE.... VERY NICE— I REALLY LIKE THE PARASOLS!
I FOUND 'EM ON THE STREET!
BUT, WHERE'S YOUR ROOMMATE, DAVID?
YOU MEAN SETH? HE WENT MAD.

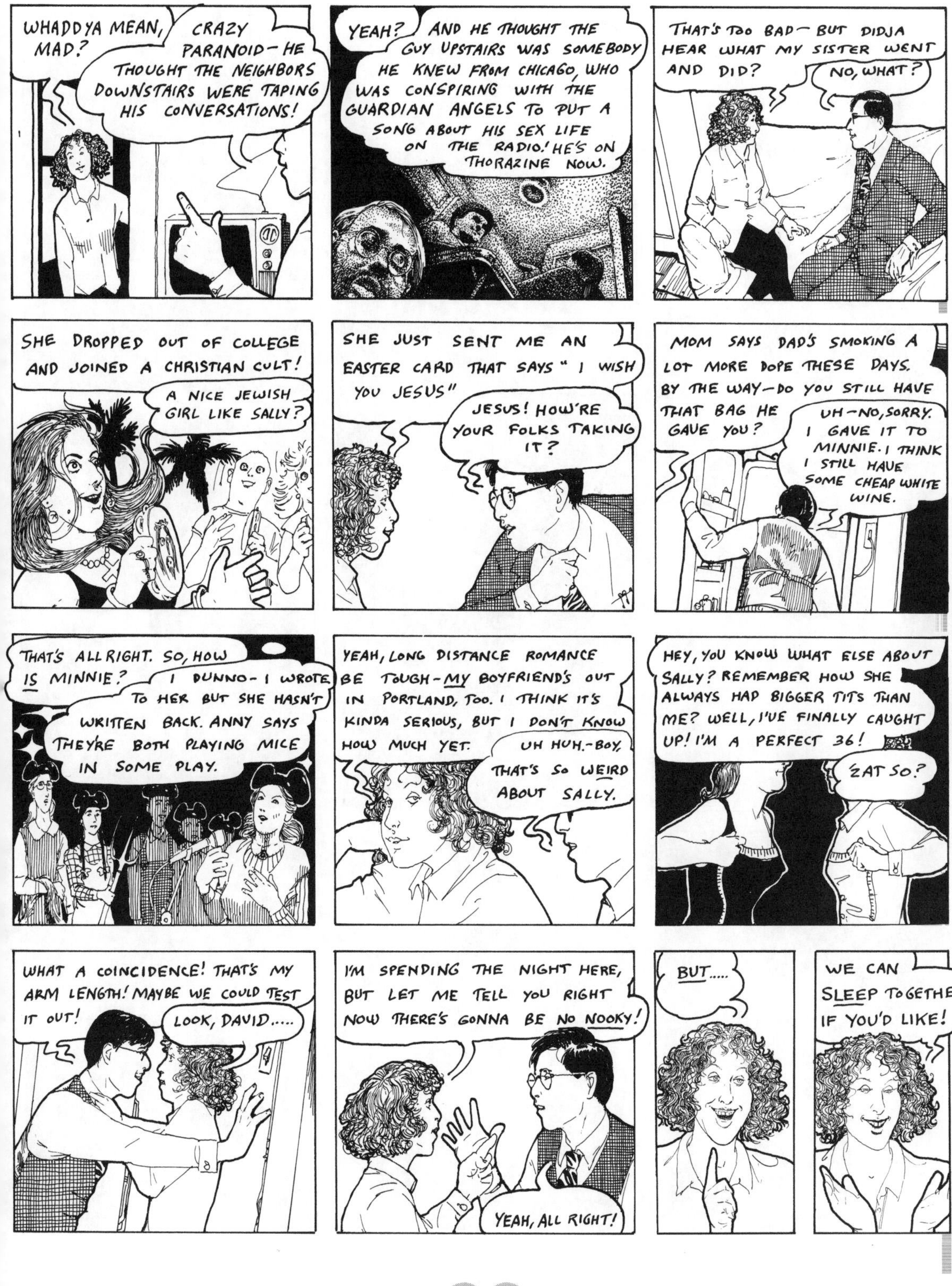
WHADDYA MEAN, MAD?
CRAZY PARANOID—HE THOUGHT THE NEIGHBORS DOWNSTAIRS WERE TAPING HIS CONVERSATIONS!
YEAH?
AND HE THOUGHT THE GUY UPSTAIRS WAS SOMEBODY HE KNEW FROM CHICAGO, WHO WAS CONSPIRING WITH THE GUARDIAN ANGELS TO PUT A SONG ABOUT HIS SEX LIFE ON THE RADIO! HE'S ON THORAZINE NOW.
THAT'S TOO BAD—BUT DIDJA HEAR WHAT MY SISTER WENT AND DID?
NO, WHAT?
SHE DROPPED OUT OF COLLEGE AND JOINED A CHRISTIAN CULT!
A NICE JEWISH GIRL LIKE SALLY?
SHE JUST SENT ME AN EASTER CARD THAT SAYS "I WISH YOU JESUS"
JESUS! HOW'RE YOUR FOLKS TAKING IT?
MOM SAYS DAD'S SMOKING A LOT MORE DOPE THESE DAYS. BY THE WAY—DO YOU STILL HAVE THAT BAG HE GAVE YOU?
UH—NO, SORRY. I GAVE IT TO MINNIE. I THINK I STILL HAVE SOME CHEAP WHITE WINE.
THAT'S ALL RIGHT. SO, HOW IS MINNIE?
I DUNNO—I WROTE TO HER BUT SHE HASN'T WRITTEN BACK. ANNY SAYS THEY'RE BOTH PLAYING MICE IN SOME PLAY.
YEAH, LONG DISTANCE ROMANCE BE TOUGH—MY BOYFRIEND'S OUT IN PORTLAND, TOO. I THINK IT'S KINDA SERIOUS, BUT I DON'T KNOW HOW MUCH YET.
UH HUH.—BOY, THAT'S SO WEIRD ABOUT SALLY.
HEY, YOU KNOW WHAT ELSE ABOUT SALLY? REMEMBER HOW SHE ALWAYS HAD BIGGER TITS THAN ME? WELL, I'VE FINALLY CAUGHT UP! I'M A PERFECT 36!
'ZAT SO?
WHAT A COINCIDENCE! THAT'S MY ARM LENGTH! MAYBE WE COULD TEST IT OUT!
LOOK, DAVID.....
I'M SPENDING THE NIGHT HERE, BUT LET ME TELL YOU RIGHT NOW THERE'S GONNA BE NO NOOKY!
YEAH, ALL RIGHT!
BUT.....
WE CAN SLEEP TOGETHER IF YOU'D LIKE!

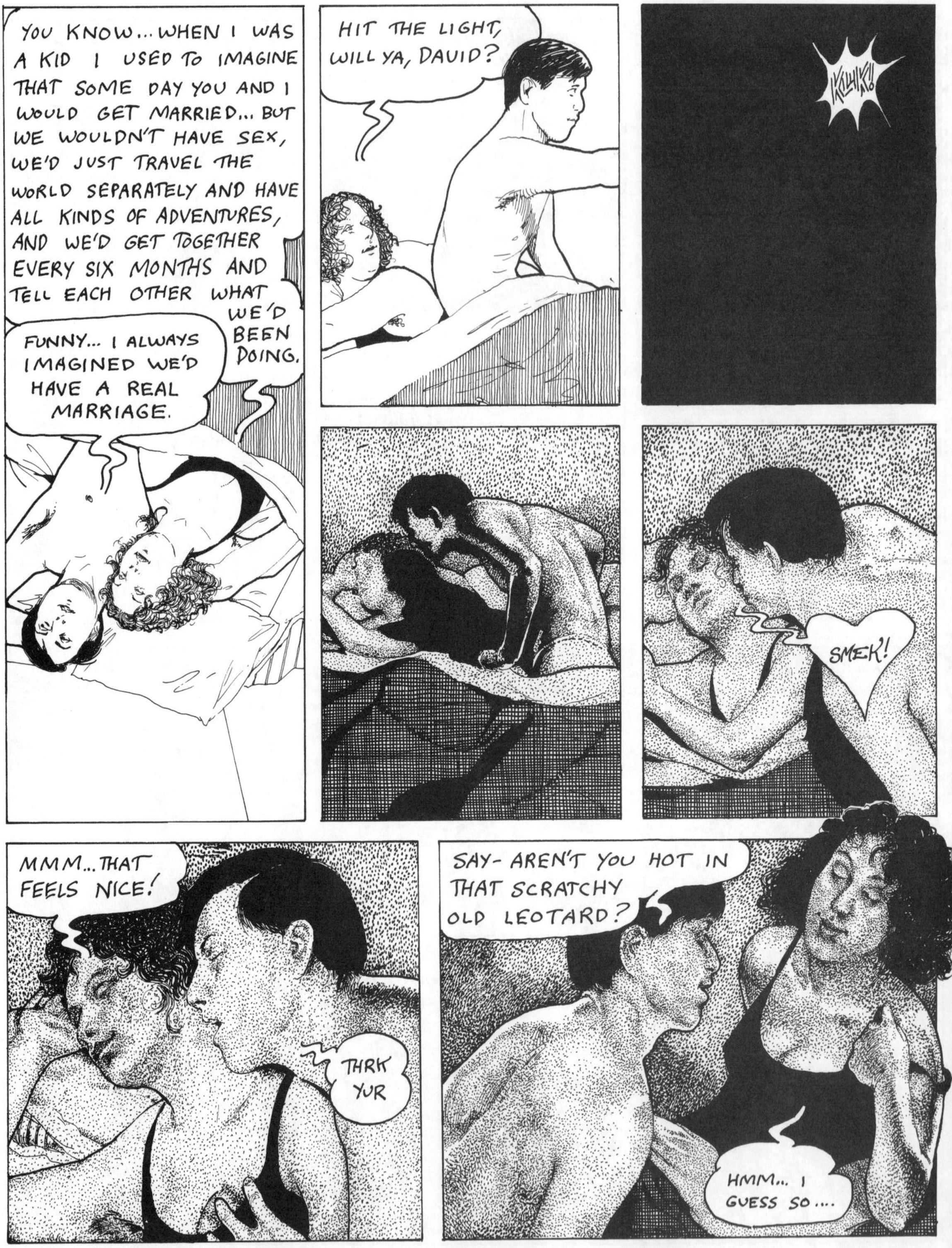
YOU KNOW... WHEN I WAS A KID I USED TO IMAGINE THAT SOME DAY YOU AND I WOULD GET MARRIED... BUT WE WOULDN'T HAVE SEX, WE'D JUST TRAVEL THE WORLD SEPARATELY AND HAVE ALL KINDS OF ADVENTURES, AND WE'D GET TOGETHER EVERY SIX MONTHS AND TELL EACH OTHER WHAT WE'D BEEN DOING.
FUNNY... I ALWAYS IMAGINED WE'D HAVE A REAL MARRIAGE.
HIT THE LIGHT, WILL YA, DAVID?
SMEK!
MMM... THAT FEELS NICE!
THRK YUR
SAY- AREN'T YOU HOT IN THAT SCRATCHY OLD LEOTARD?
HMM... I GUESS SO....

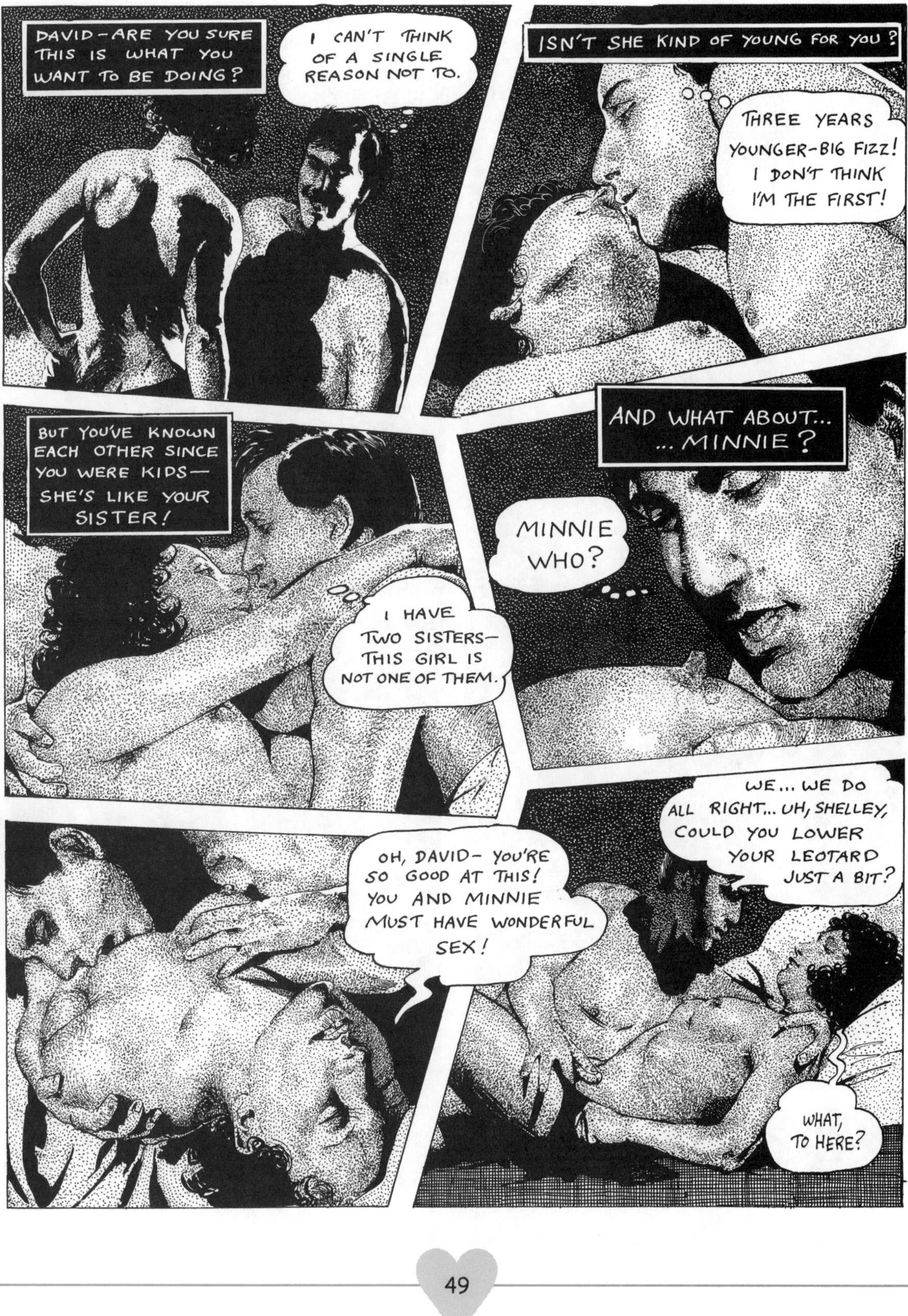
DAVID-ARE YOU SURE THIS IS WHAT YOU WANT TO BE DOING?
I CAN'T THINK OF A SINGLE REASON NOT TO.
ISN'T SHE KIND OF YOUNG FOR YOU?
THREE YEARS YOUNGER-BIG FIZZ! I DON'T THINK I'M THE FIRST!
BUT YOU'VE KNOWN EACH OTHER SINCE YOU WERE KIDS— SHE'S LIKE YOUR SISTER!
I HAVE TWO SISTERS— THIS GIRL IS NOT ONE OF THEM.
AND WHAT ABOUT... ...MINNIE?
MINNIE WHO?
OH, DAVID- YOU'RE SO GOOD AT THIS! YOU AND MINNIE MUST HAVE WONDERFUL SEX!
WE... WE DO ALL RIGHT... UH, SHELLEY, COULD YOU LOWER YOUR LEOTARD JUST A BIT?
WHAT, TO HERE?

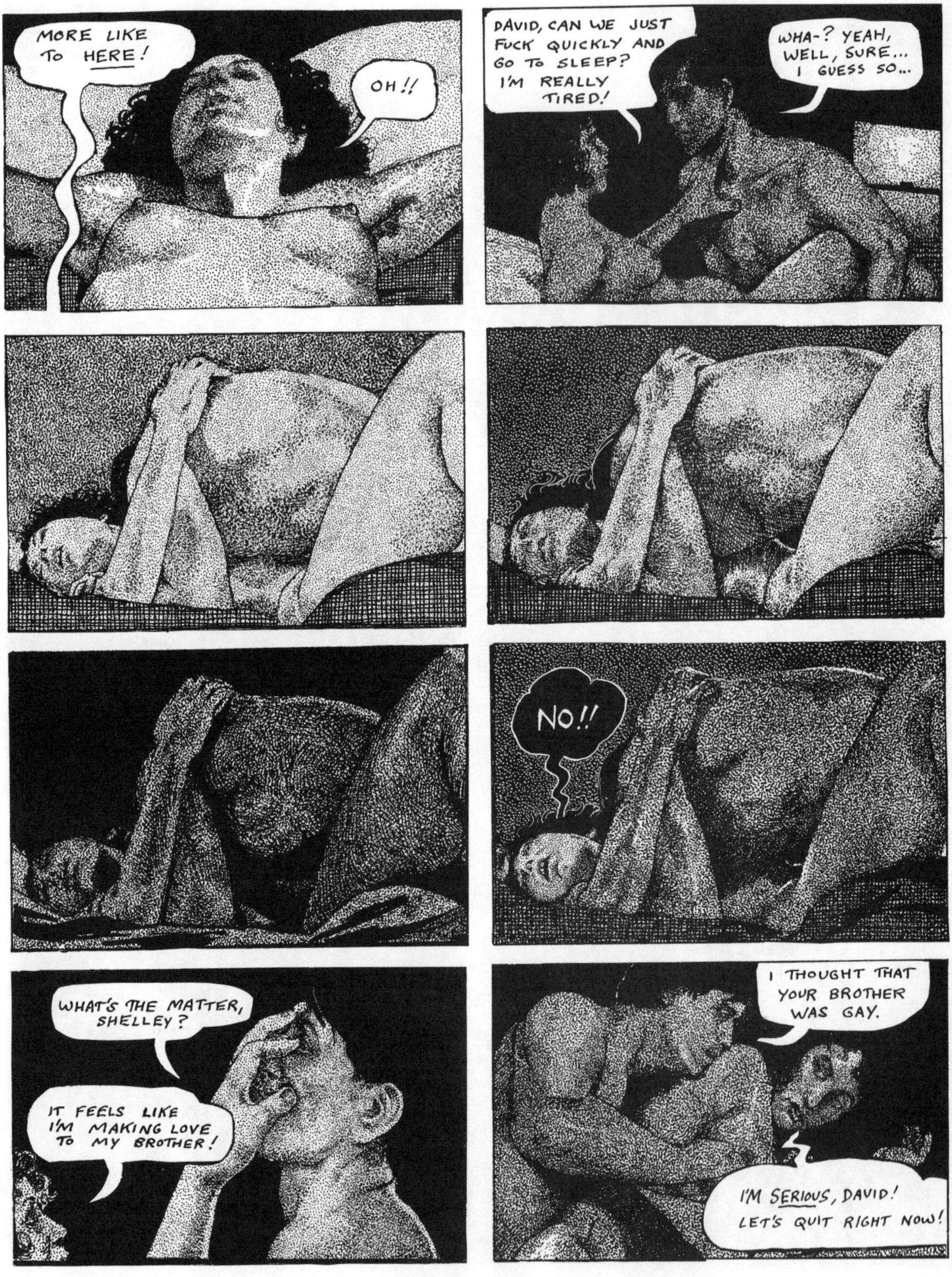
MORE LIKE TO HERE!
OH!!
DAVID, CAN WE JUST FUCK QUICKLY AND GO TO SLEEP? I'M REALLY TIRED!
WHA-? YEAH, WELL, SURE... I GUESS SO...
NO!!
WHAT'S THE MATTER, SHELLEY?
IT FEELS LIKE I'M MAKING LOVE TO MY BROTHER!
I THOUGHT THAT YOUR BROTHER WAS GAY.
I'M SERIOUS, DAVID! LET'S QUIT RIGHT NOW!

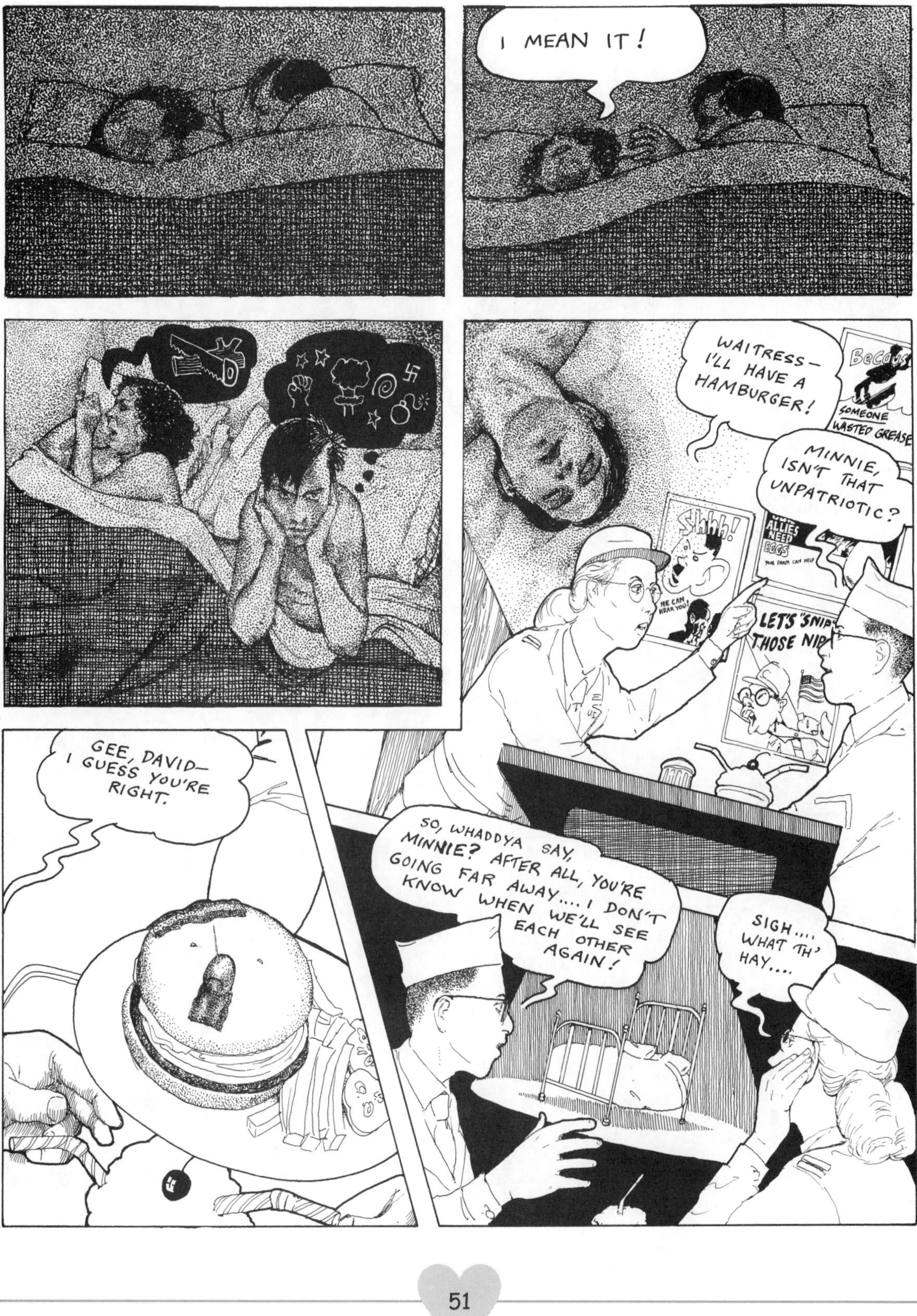

I MEAN IT!
WAITRESS— I'LL HAVE A HAMBURGER!
BECAUSE SOMEONE WASTED GREASE
MINNIE, ISN'T THAT UNPATRIOTIC?
Shhh! HE CAN HEAR YOU!
ALLIES NEED EGGS YOUR FARM CAN HELP
LET'S "SNIP" THOSE NIP
GEE, DAVID— I GUESS YOU'RE RIGHT.
SO, WHADDYA SAY, MINNIE? AFTER ALL, YOU'RE GOING FAR AWAY.... I DON'T KNOW WHEN WE'LL SEE EACH OTHER AGAIN!
SIGH.... WHAT TH' HAY....

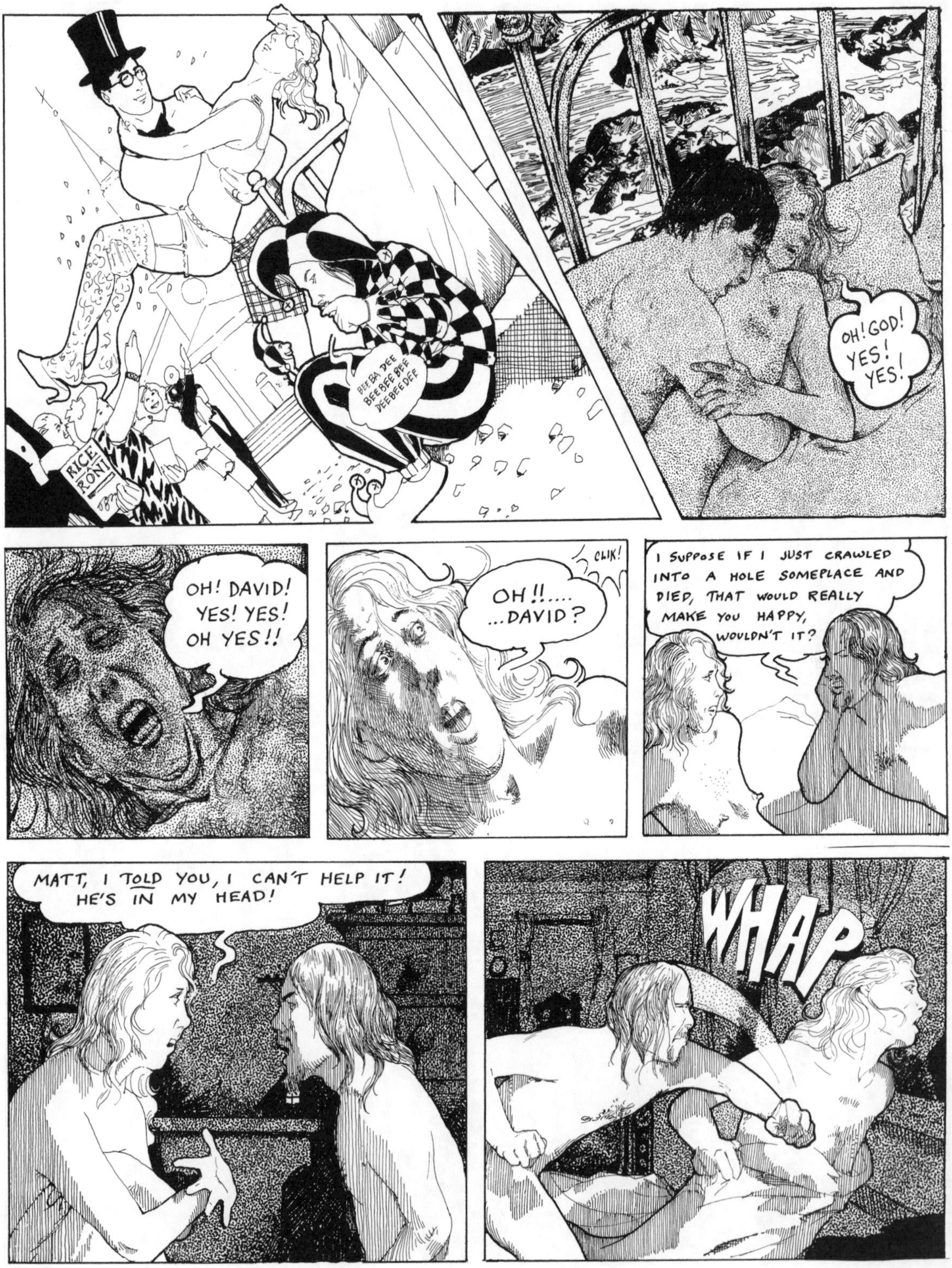
BEEBA DEE BEEBEE BEE DEEBEEDEE
RICE RONI
OH! GOD! YES! YES!
OH! DAVID! YES! YES! OH YES!!
CLIK!
OH!!.... ...DAVID?
I SUPPOSE IF I JUST CRAWLED INTO A HOLE SOMEPLACE AND DIED, THAT WOULD REALLY MAKE YOU HAPPY, WOULDN'T IT?
MATT, I TOLD YOU, I CAN'T HELP IT! HE'S IN MY HEAD!
WHAP

I'M SORRY I'M SORRY I'M SORRY
NO, I'M SORRY!
DON'T EVER LEAVE ME!
HMMM....
YOU KNOW? I THINK I LIKED HER FACE BETTER BEFORE.
DO TELL.
ST. MARKS
PVT. BENJAMIN
PRINCE OF THE CITY
FRI SAT MID ERASERHEAD
I DON'T SEE ANY CABS HERE – MAYBE WE'D DO BETTER OVER ON THIRD AVENUE.
WAIT, DAVID, LET'S GO GET OUR FORTUNES READ AT THAT PLACE OVER THERE!

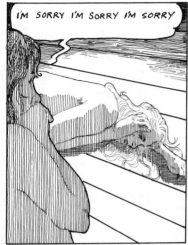

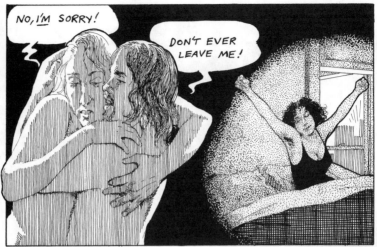

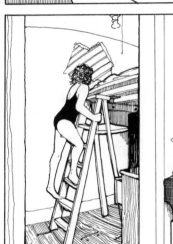

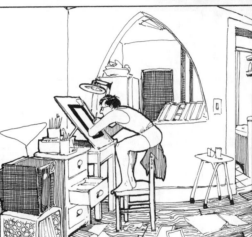

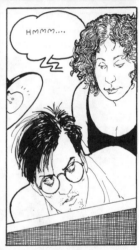

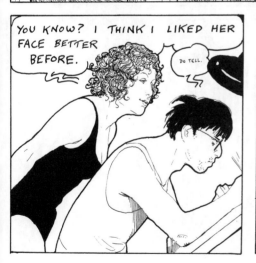

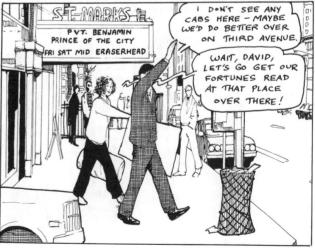

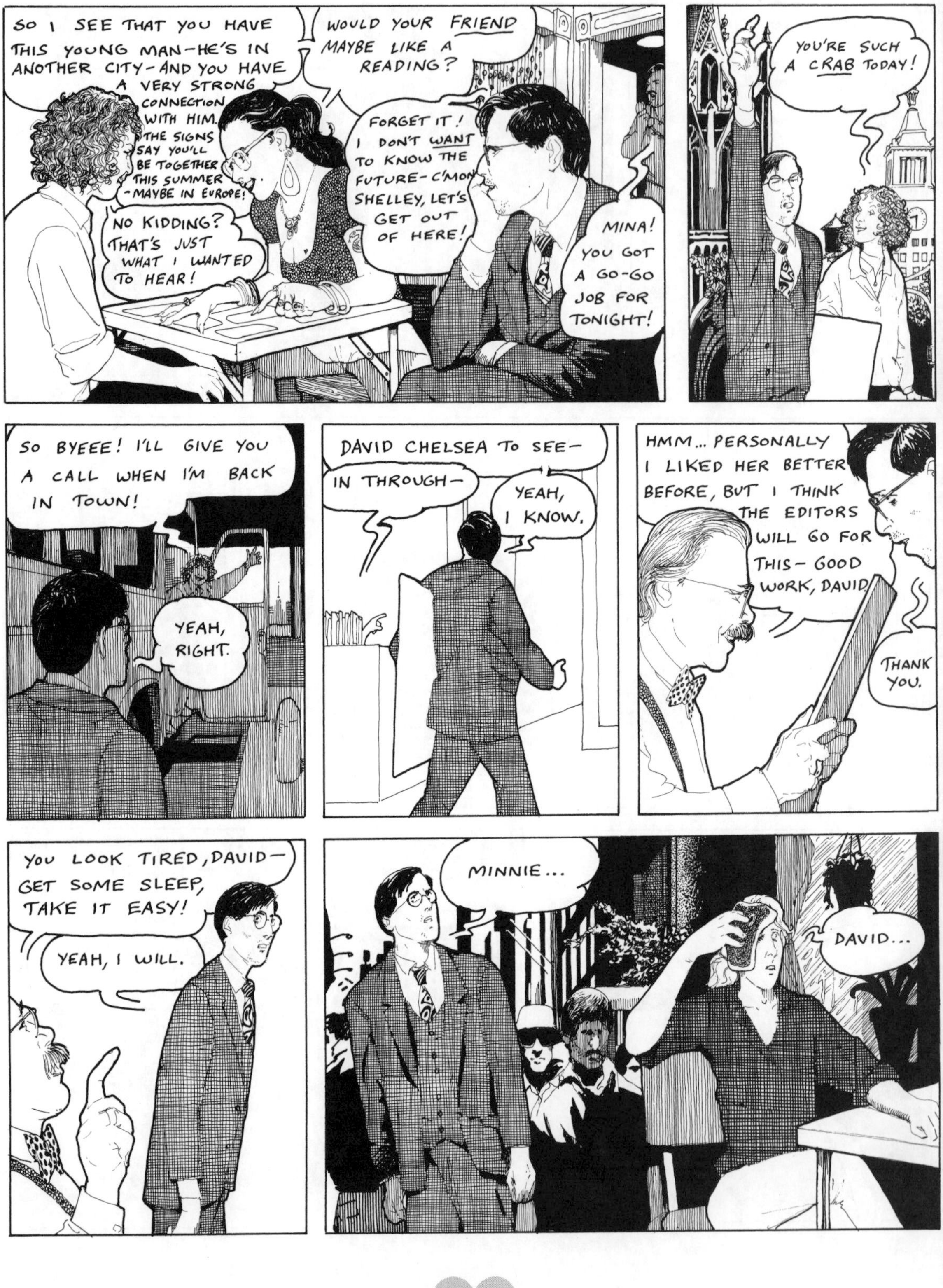
SO I SEE THAT YOU HAVE THIS YOUNG MAN–HE'S IN ANOTHER CITY–AND YOU HAVE A VERY STRONG CONNECTION WITH HIM. THE SIGNS SAY YOU'LL BE TOGETHER THIS SUMMER –MAYBE IN EUROPE!
NO KIDDING? THAT'S JUST WHAT I WANTED TO HEAR!
WOULD YOUR FRIEND MAYBE LIKE A READING?
FORGET IT! I DON'T WANT TO KNOW THE FUTURE–C'MON SHELLEY, LET'S GET OUT OF HERE!
MINA! YOU GOT A GO-GO JOB FOR TONIGHT!
YOU'RE SUCH A CRAB TODAY!
SO BYEEE! I'LL GIVE YOU A CALL WHEN I'M BACK IN TOWN!
YEAH, RIGHT.
DAVID CHELSEA TO SEE–
IN THROUGH–
YEAH, I KNOW.
HMM... PERSONALLY I LIKED HER BETTER BEFORE, BUT I THINK THE EDITORS WILL GO FOR THIS–GOOD WORK, DAVID.
THANK YOU.
YOU LOOK TIRED, DAVID–GET SOME SLEEP, TAKE IT EASY!
YEAH, I WILL.
MINNIE...
DAVID...

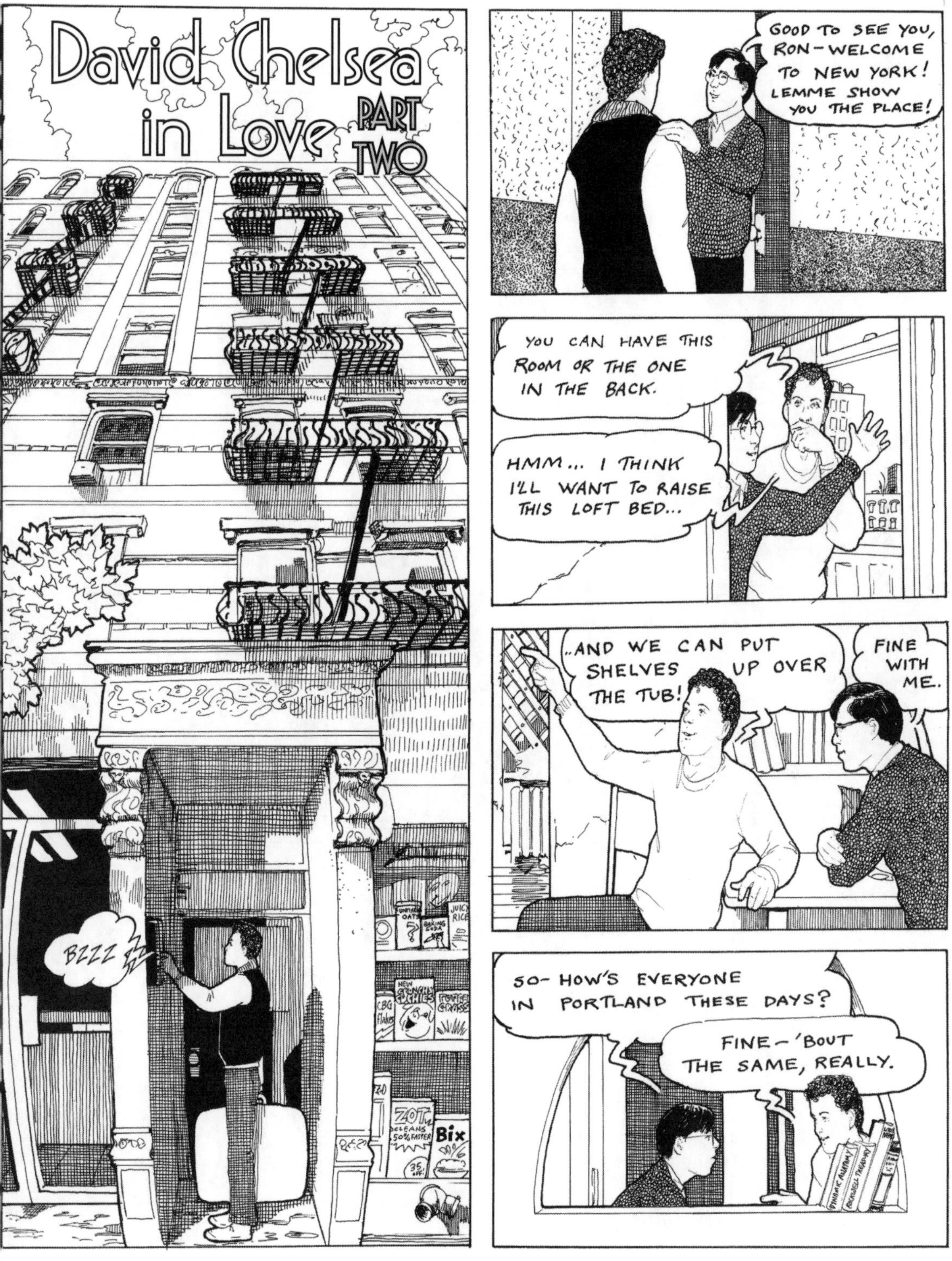
David Chelsea in Love
PART TWO
BZZZ
GOOD TO SEE YOU, RON—WELCOME TO NEW YORK! LEMME SHOW YOU THE PLACE!
YOU CAN HAVE THIS ROOM OR THE ONE IN THE BACK.
HMM... I THINK I'LL WANT TO RAISE THIS LOFT BED...
..AND WE CAN PUT SHELVES UP OVER THE TUB!
FINE WITH ME.
SO—HOW'S EVERYONE IN PORTLAND THESE DAYS?
FINE—'BOUT THE SAME, REALLY.

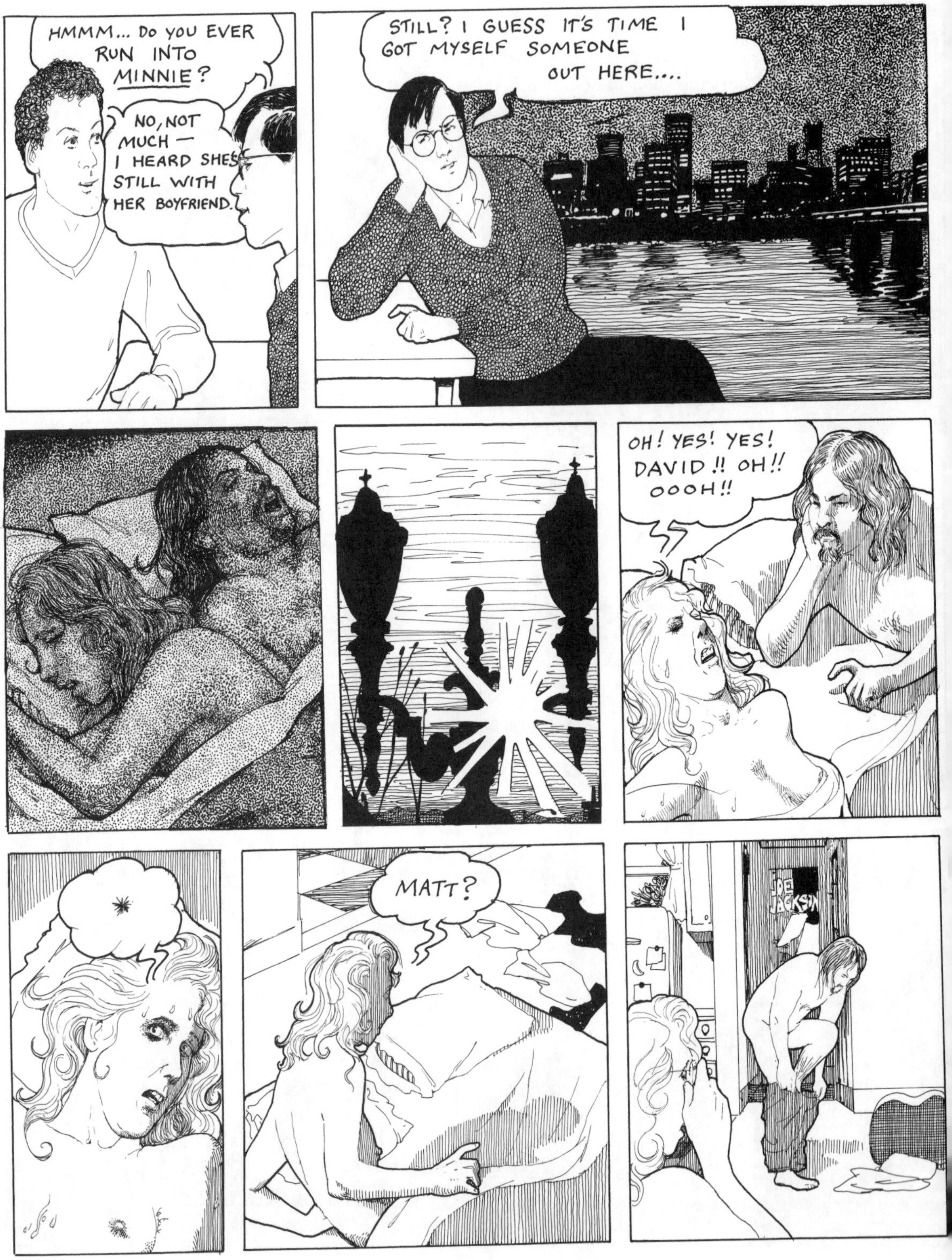
HMMM... DO YOU EVER RUN INTO MINNIE?
NO, NOT MUCH — I HEARD SHE'S STILL WITH HER BOYFRIEND.
STILL? I GUESS IT'S TIME I GOT MYSELF SOMEONE OUT HERE....
OH! YES! YES! DAVID!! OH!! OOOH!!
MATT?
JOE JACKSON

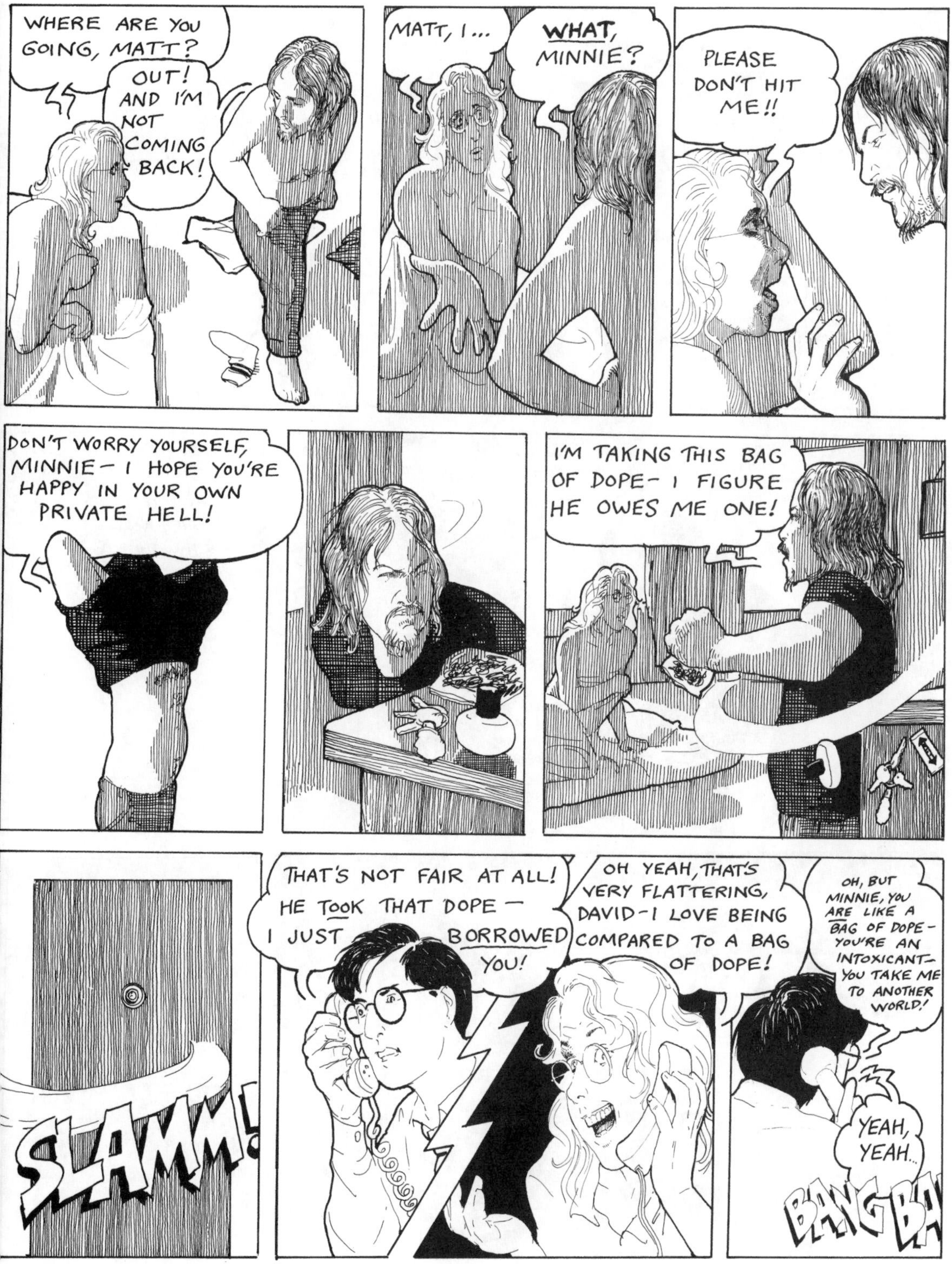
WHERE ARE YOU GOING, MATT?
OUT! AND I'M NOT COMING BACK!
MATT, I...
WHAT, MINNIE?
PLEASE DON'T HIT ME!!
DON'T WORRY YOURSELF, MINNIE- I HOPE YOU'RE HAPPY IN YOUR OWN PRIVATE HELL!
I'M TAKING THIS BAG OF DOPE- I FIGURE HE OWES ME ONE!
SLAMM!
THAT'S NOT FAIR AT ALL! HE TOOK THAT DOPE — I JUST BORROWED YOU!
OH YEAH, THAT'S VERY FLATTERING, DAVID- I LOVE BEING COMPARED TO A BAG OF DOPE!
OH, BUT MINNIE, YOU ARE LIKE A BAG OF DOPE- YOU'RE AN INTOXICANT- YOU TAKE ME TO ANOTHER WORLD!
YEAH, YEAH...
BANG BA

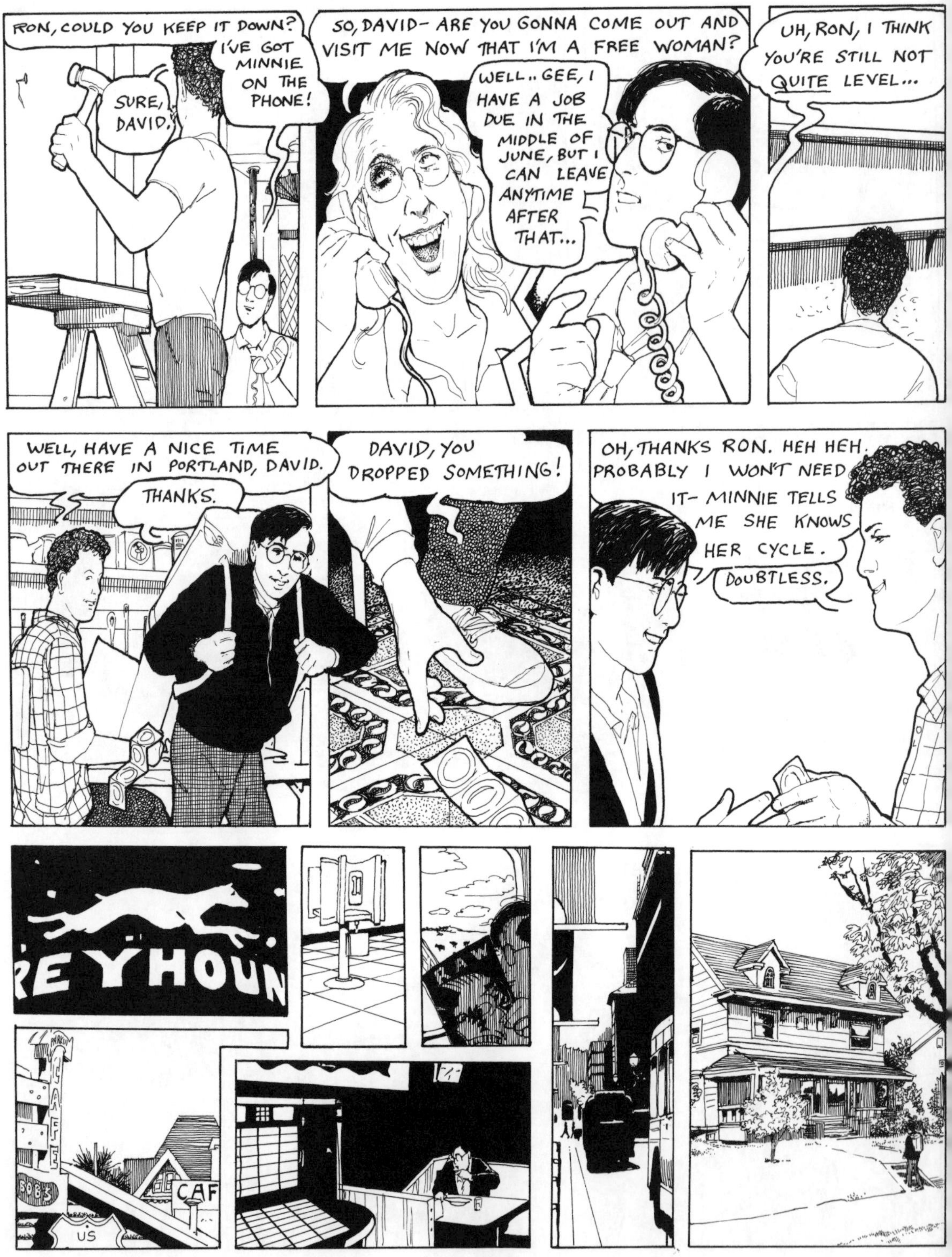
RON, COULD YOU KEEP IT DOWN? I'VE GOT MINNIE ON THE PHONE!
SURE, DAVID.
SO, DAVID- ARE YOU GONNA COME OUT AND VISIT ME NOW THAT I'M A FREE WOMAN?
WELL.. GEE, I HAVE A JOB DUE IN THE MIDDLE OF JUNE, BUT I CAN LEAVE ANYTIME AFTER THAT...
UH, RON, I THINK YOU'RE STILL NOT QUITE LEVEL...
WELL, HAVE A NICE TIME OUT THERE IN PORTLAND, DAVID.
THANKS.
DAVID, YOU DROPPED SOMETHING!
OH, THANKS RON. HEH HEH. PROBABLY I WON'T NEED IT- MINNIE TELLS ME SHE KNOWS HER CYCLE.
DOUBTLESS.
REYHOUN
CAF
BOB'S
US

HEY, TERESA!
OH, HI, DAVID- WHAT ARE YOU DOING IN TOWN?
OH, WELL- THINGS WERE KINDA SLOW IN NEW YORK- SO WHERE ARE YOU GOING WITH THAT SOUP?
UP TO ANNY'S ROOM - SHE JUST HAD HER WISDOM TEETH OUT....
NOW, MITCH, GET A HOLD ON YOURSELF! HOW COULD YOU HAVE THAT NEW GAY CANCER - I MEAN, WHEN'S THE LAST TIME YOU WERE IN SAN FRANCISCO? FIVE YEARS AGO? WELL, WHO EVER HEARD OF A DISEASE THAT'S DORMANT THAT LONG?
YOO-HOO, ANNY! YOU GOT COMPANY!
GOTTA GO, MITCH!
WHY, HI, TERESA- IS THAT- COULD IT BE- BROTHER DAVID WITH YOU?
GOOD TO SEE YOU, ANNY, BUT WHAT HAPPENED? YOU LOOK LIKE A CHIPMUNK!
OH, THANKS, DAVID!
WELL, I HADDA GO AND HAVE ALL FOUR WISDOMS OUT AT ONCE! WHY? IT JUST SEEMED LIKE THE THING TO DO AT THE TIME.
I COULD HEAR WHAT WAS GOING ON- AT FIRST IT WAS KIND OF INTERESTING, LISTENING TO THE TWO DOCTORS TALKING BACK AND FORTH, BUT WHEN I STARTED HEARING THINGS LIKE "OH GOD, AM I NERVOUS!" AND "I DON'T KNOW WHAT I'M DOING." I BEGAN TO WORRY- AS MUCH AS I COULD WITH ALL THAT LIQUID VALIUM IN ME.
IT WASN'T UNTIL I GOT UNDER ANAESTHESIA THAT I FOUND OUT MY SURGEON WAS A STUDENT. UP TILL THEN HE SEEMED REAL MATURE, BUT HE JUST KIND OF CRUMBLED UNDER PRESSURE.

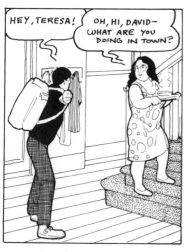

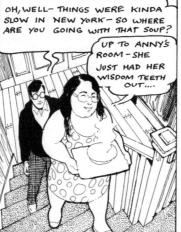

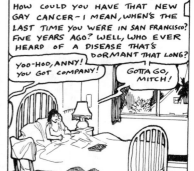

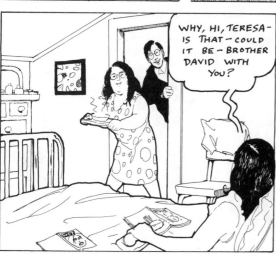

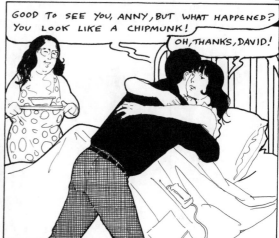

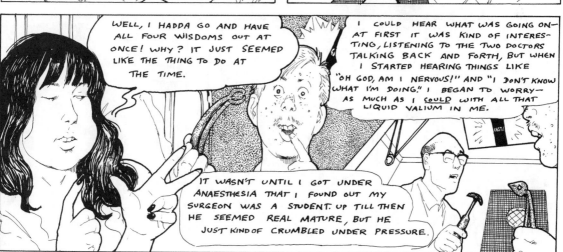

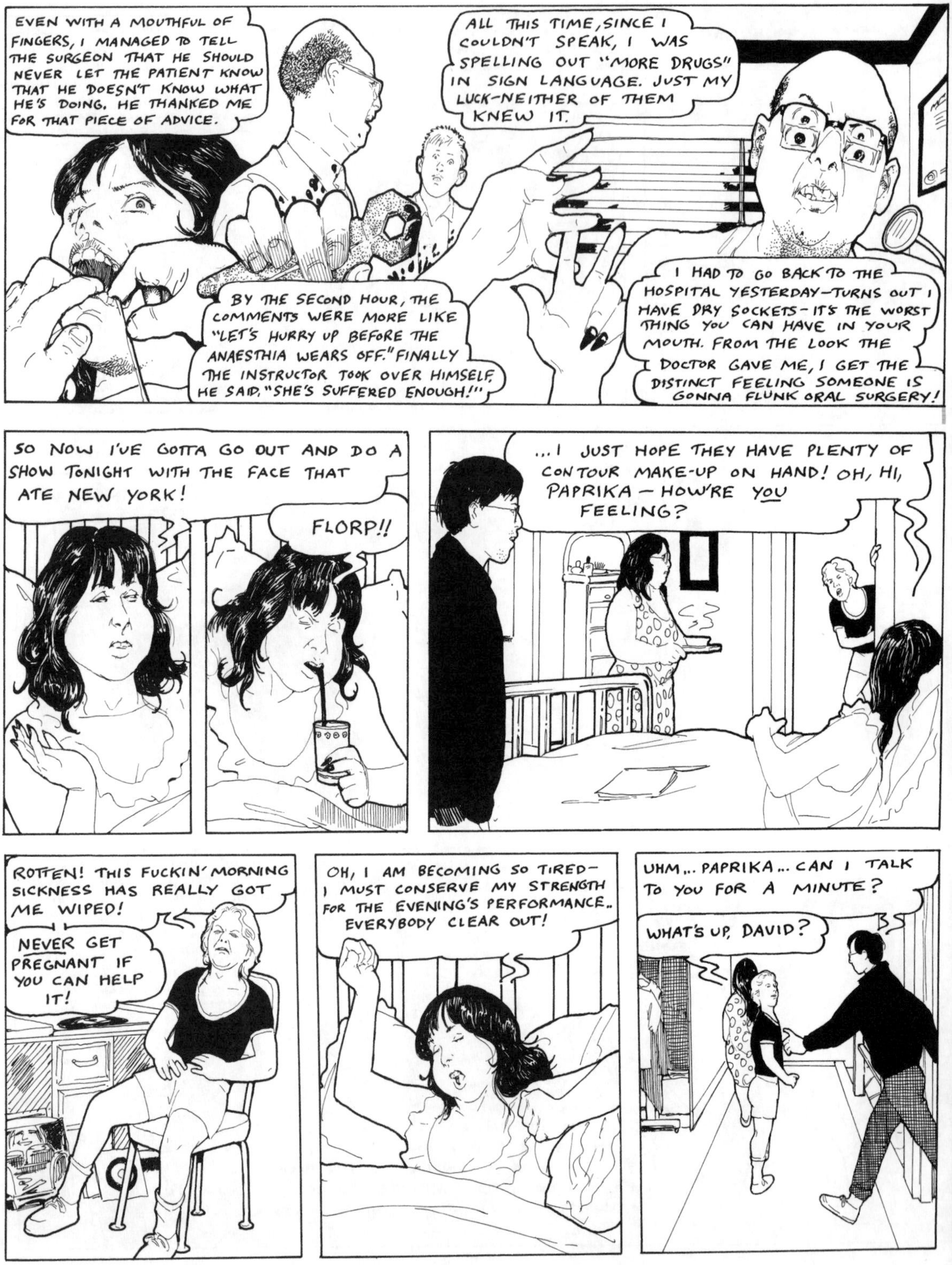
EVEN WITH A MOUTHFUL OF FINGERS, I MANAGED TO TELL THE SURGEON THAT HE SHOULD NEVER LET THE PATIENT KNOW THAT HE DOESN'T KNOW WHAT HE'S DOING. HE THANKED ME FOR THAT PIECE OF ADVICE.
BY THE SECOND HOUR, THE COMMENTS WERE MORE LIKE "LET'S HURRY UP BEFORE THE ANAESTHIA WEARS OFF." FINALLY THE INSTRUCTOR TOOK OVER HIMSELF, HE SAID, "SHE'S SUFFERED ENOUGH!"
ALL THIS TIME, SINCE I COULDN'T SPEAK, I WAS SPELLING OUT "MORE DRUGS" IN SIGN LANGUAGE. JUST MY LUCK-NEITHER OF THEM KNEW IT.
I HAD TO GO BACK TO THE HOSPITAL YESTERDAY—TURNS OUT I HAVE DRY SOCKETS—IT'S THE WORST THING YOU CAN HAVE IN YOUR MOUTH. FROM THE LOOK THE DOCTOR GAVE ME, I GET THE DISTINCT FEELING SOMEONE IS GONNA FLUNK ORAL SURGERY!
SO NOW I'VE GOTTA GO OUT AND DO A SHOW TONIGHT WITH THE FACE THAT ATE NEW YORK!
FLORP!!
...I JUST HOPE THEY HAVE PLENTY OF CONTOUR MAKE-UP ON HAND! OH, HI, PAPRIKA—HOW'RE YOU FEELING?
ROTTEN! THIS FUCKIN' MORNING SICKNESS HAS REALLY GOT ME WIPED!
NEVER GET PREGNANT IF YOU CAN HELP IT!
OH, I AM BECOMING SO TIRED—I MUST CONSERVE MY STRENGTH FOR THE EVENING'S PERFORMANCE.. EVERYBODY CLEAR OUT!
UHM... PAPRIKA... CAN I TALK TO YOU FOR A MINUTE?
WHAT'S UP, DAVID?

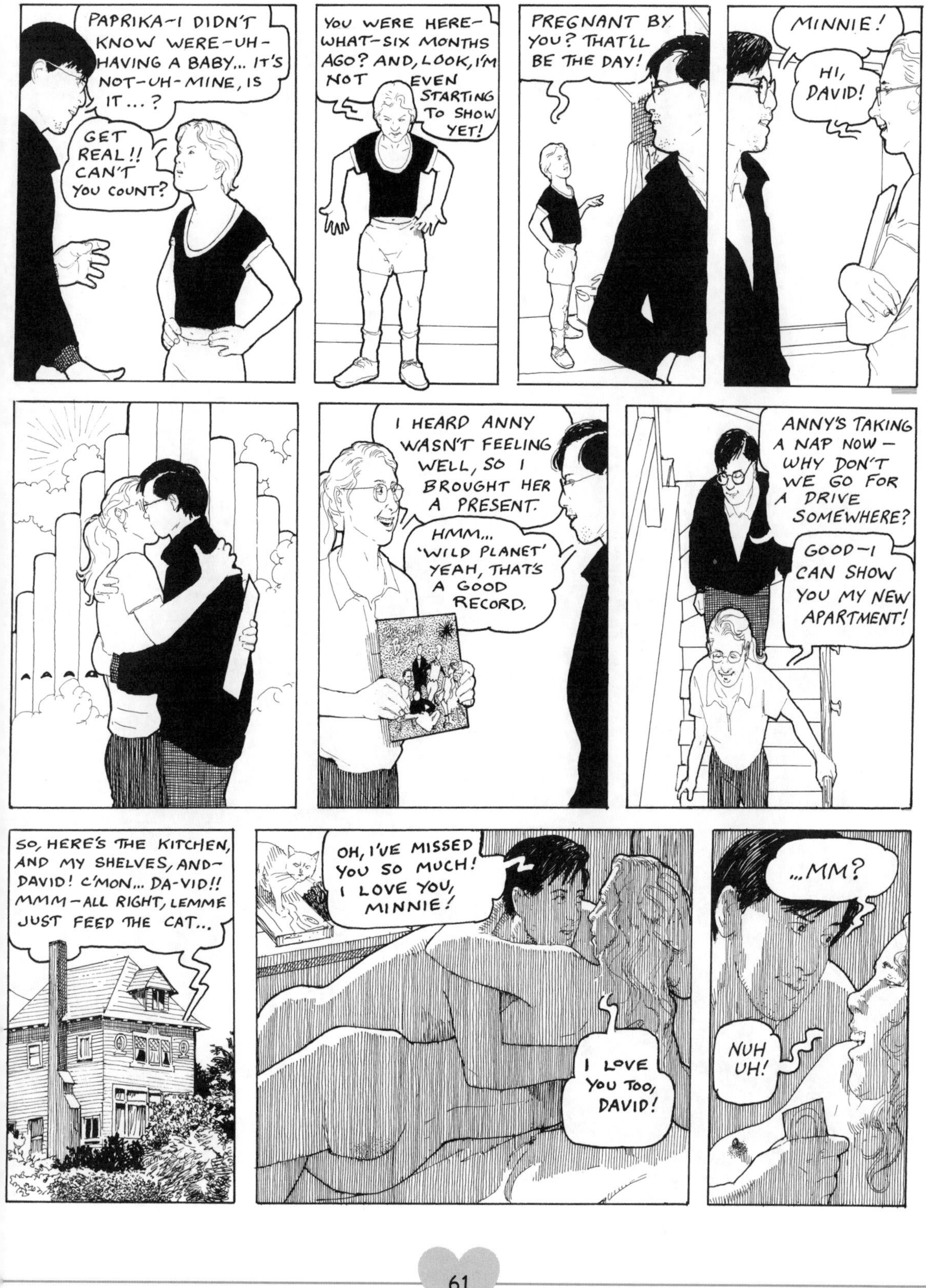
PAPRIKA-I DIDN'T KNOW WERE-UH-HAVING A BABY... IT'S NOT-UH-MINE, IS IT...?
GET REAL!! CAN'T YOU COUNT?
YOU WERE HERE-WHAT-SIX MONTHS AGO? AND, LOOK, I'M NOT EVEN STARTING TO SHOW YET!
PREGNANT BY YOU? THAT'LL BE THE DAY!
MINNIE!
HI, DAVID!
I HEARD ANNY WASN'T FEELING WELL, SO I BROUGHT HER A PRESENT.
HMM... 'WILD PLANET' YEAH, THAT'S A GOOD RECORD.
ANNY'S TAKING A NAP NOW-WHY DON'T WE GO FOR A DRIVE SOMEWHERE?
GOOD-I CAN SHOW YOU MY NEW APARTMENT!
SO, HERE'S THE KITCHEN, AND MY SHELVES, AND-DAVID! C'MON... DA-VID!! MMM-ALL RIGHT, LEMME JUST FEED THE CAT...
OH, I'VE MISSED YOU SO MUCH! I LOVE YOU, MINNIE!
I LOVE YOU TOO, DAVID!
...MM?
NUH UH!

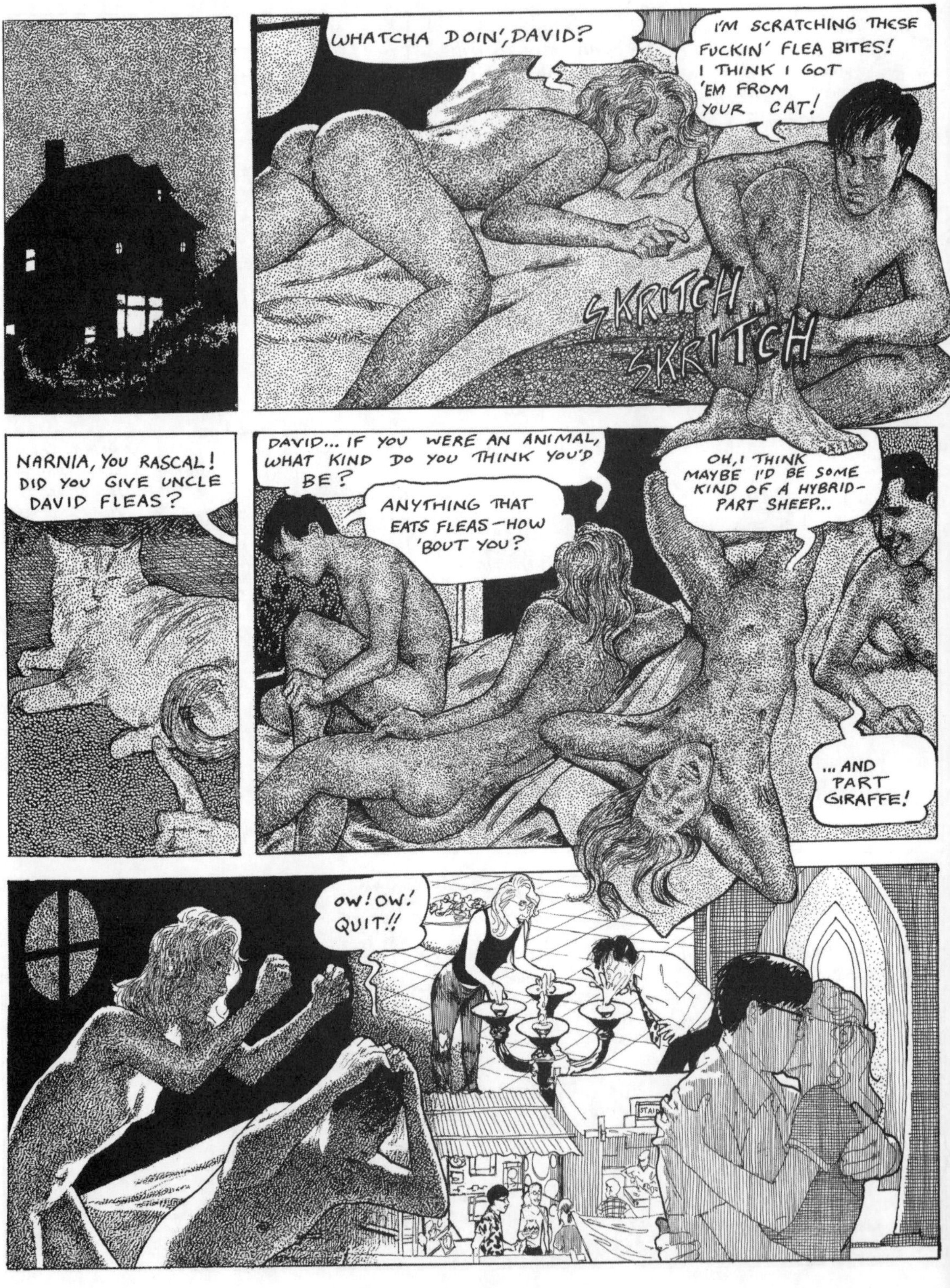
WHATCHA DOIN', DAVID?
I'M SCRATCHING THESE FUCKIN' FLEA BITES! I THINK I GOT 'EM FROM YOUR CAT!
SKRITCH SKRITCH
NARNIA, YOU RASCAL! DID YOU GIVE UNCLE DAVID FLEAS?
DAVID... IF YOU WERE AN ANIMAL, WHAT KIND DO YOU THINK YOU'D BE?
ANYTHING THAT EATS FLEAS—HOW 'BOUT YOU?
OH, I THINK MAYBE I'D BE SOME KIND OF A HYBRID—PART SHEEP...
...AND PART GIRAFFE!
OW! OW! QUIT!!

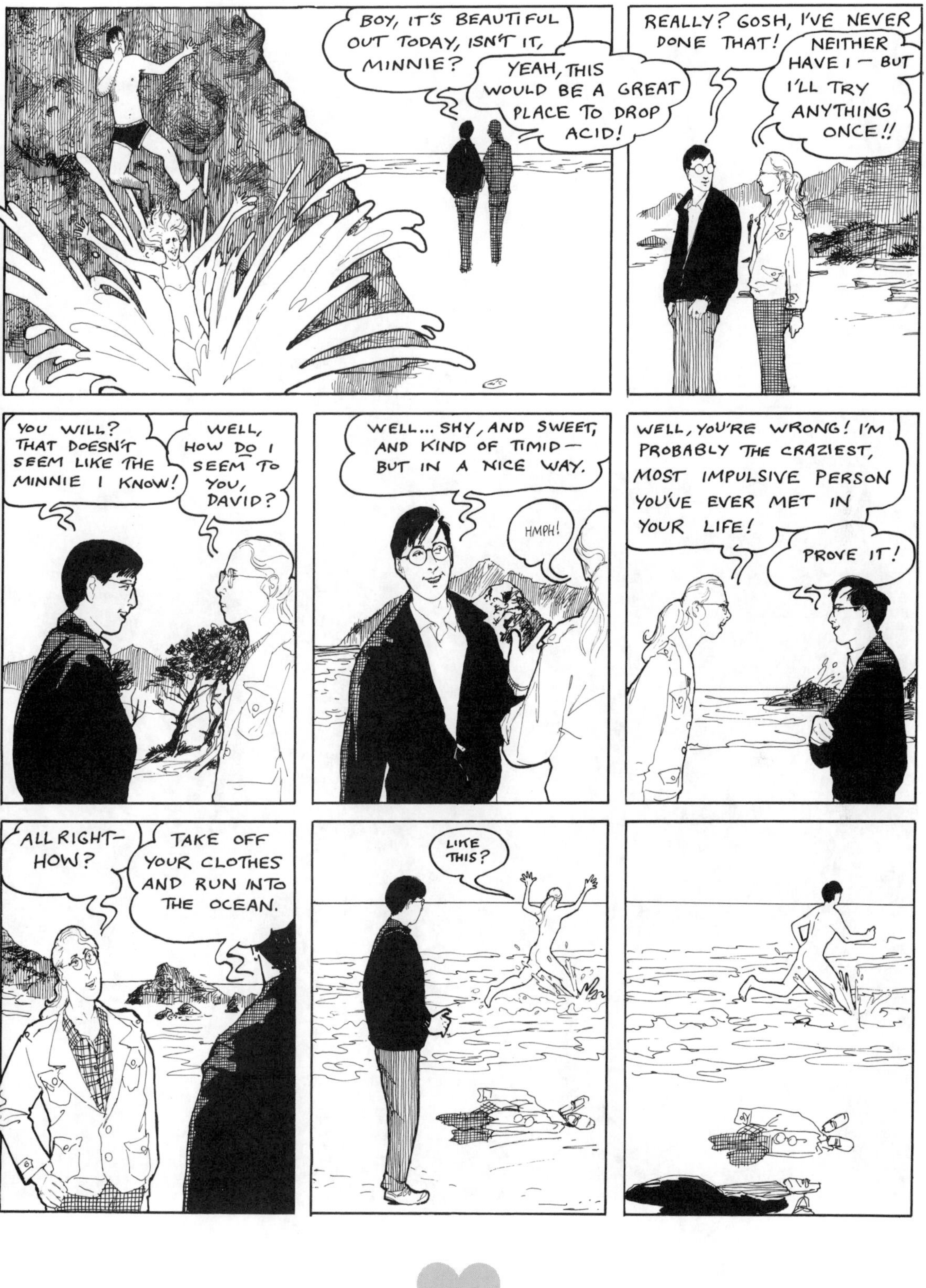
BOY, IT'S BEAUTIFUL OUT TODAY, ISN'T IT, MINNIE?
YEAH, THIS WOULD BE A GREAT PLACE TO DROP ACID!
REALLY? GOSH, I'VE NEVER DONE THAT!
NEITHER HAVE I — BUT I'LL TRY ANYTHING ONCE!!
YOU WILL? THAT DOESN'T SEEM LIKE THE MINNIE I KNOW!
WELL, HOW DO I SEEM TO YOU, DAVID?
WELL... SHY, AND SWEET, AND KIND OF TIMID— BUT IN A NICE WAY.
HMPH!
WELL, YOU'RE WRONG! I'M PROBABLY THE CRAZIEST, MOST IMPULSIVE PERSON YOU'VE EVER MET IN YOUR LIFE!
PROVE IT!
ALL RIGHT— HOW?
TAKE OFF YOUR CLOTHES AND RUN INTO THE OCEAN.
LIKE THIS?

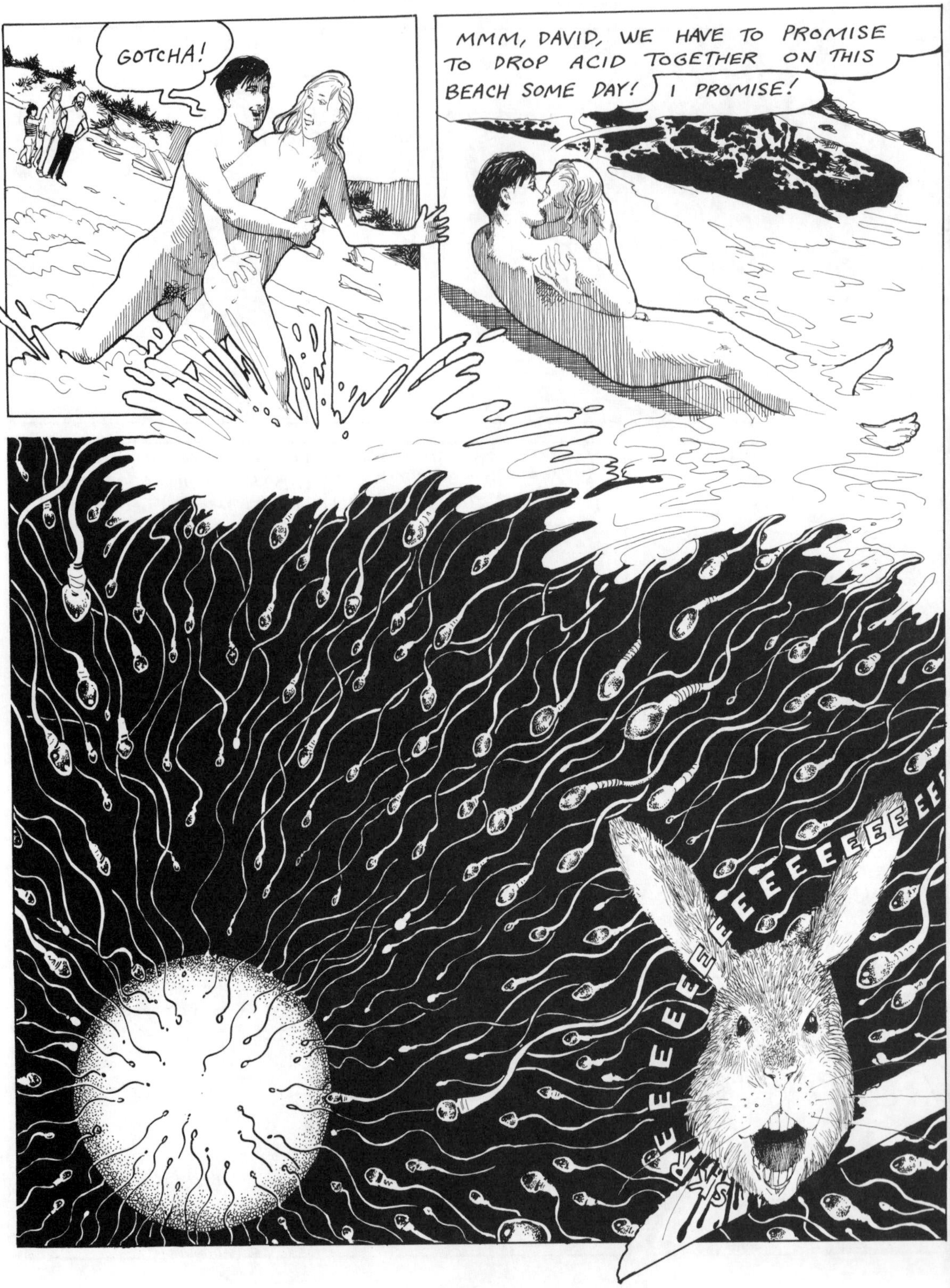
GOTCHA!
MMM, DAVID, WE HAVE TO PROMISE TO DROP ACID TOGETHER ON THIS BEACH SOME DAY!
I PROMISE!
EEEEEEEEEEEEEEEEE

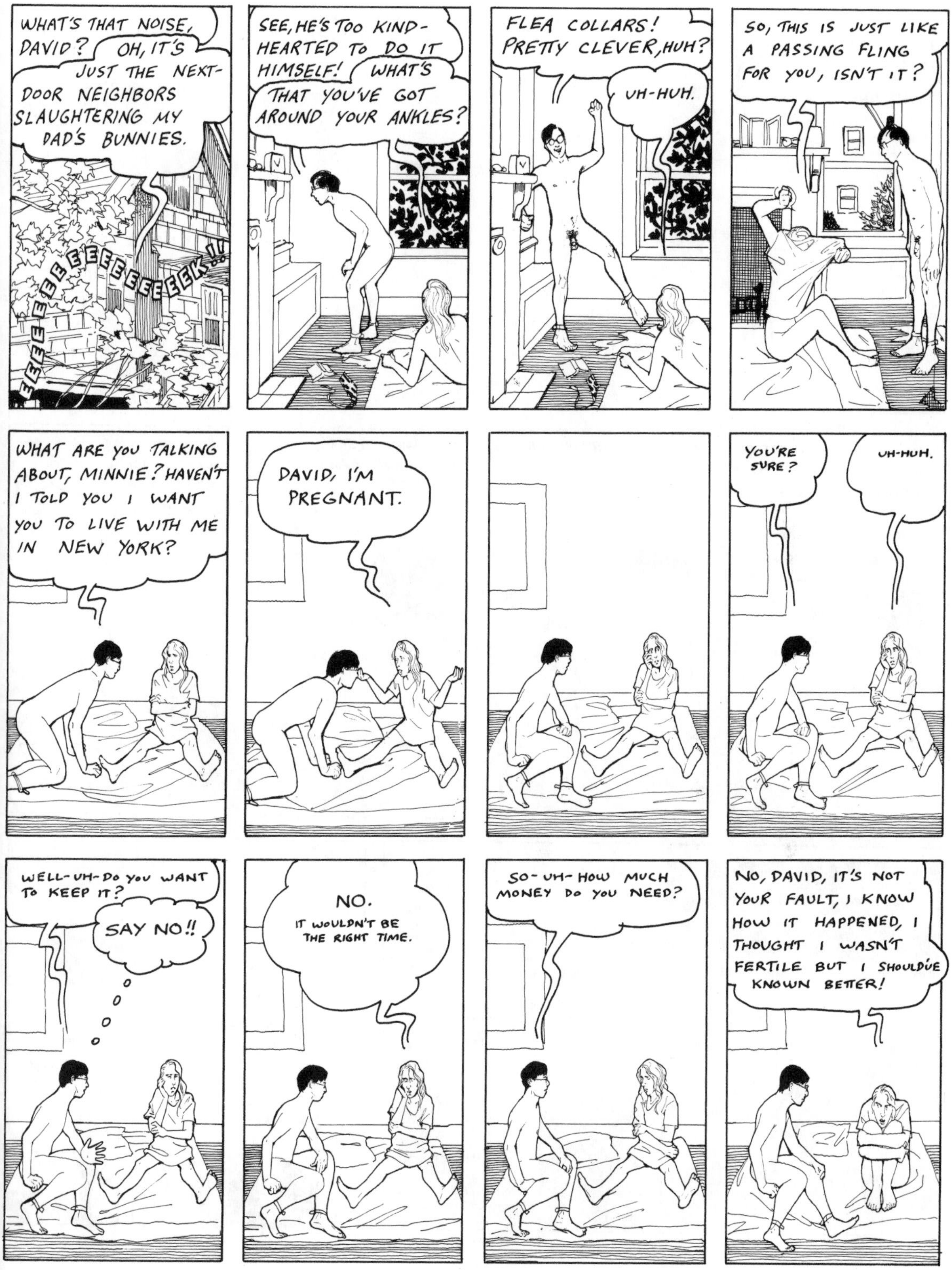
WHAT'S THAT NOISE, DAVID?
OH, IT'S JUST THE NEXT-DOOR NEIGHBORS SLAUGHTERING MY DAD'S BUNNIES.
EEEEEEEEEEEEEEEEK!!
SEE, HE'S TOO KIND-HEARTED TO DO IT HIMSELF!
WHAT'S THAT YOU'VE GOT AROUND YOUR ANKLES?
FLEA COLLARS! PRETTY CLEVER, HUH?
UH-HUH.
SO, THIS IS JUST LIKE A PASSING FLING FOR YOU, ISN'T IT?
WHAT ARE YOU TALKING ABOUT, MINNIE? HAVEN'T I TOLD YOU I WANT YOU TO LIVE WITH ME IN NEW YORK?
DAVID, I'M PREGNANT.
YOU'RE SURE?
UH-HUH.
WELL-UH-DO YOU WANT TO KEEP IT?
SAY NO!!
NO.
IT WOULDN'T BE THE RIGHT TIME.
SO-UH-HOW MUCH MONEY DO YOU NEED?
NO, DAVID, IT'S NOT YOUR FAULT, I KNOW HOW IT HAPPENED, I THOUGHT I WASN'T FERTILE BUT I SHOULD'VE KNOWN BETTER!

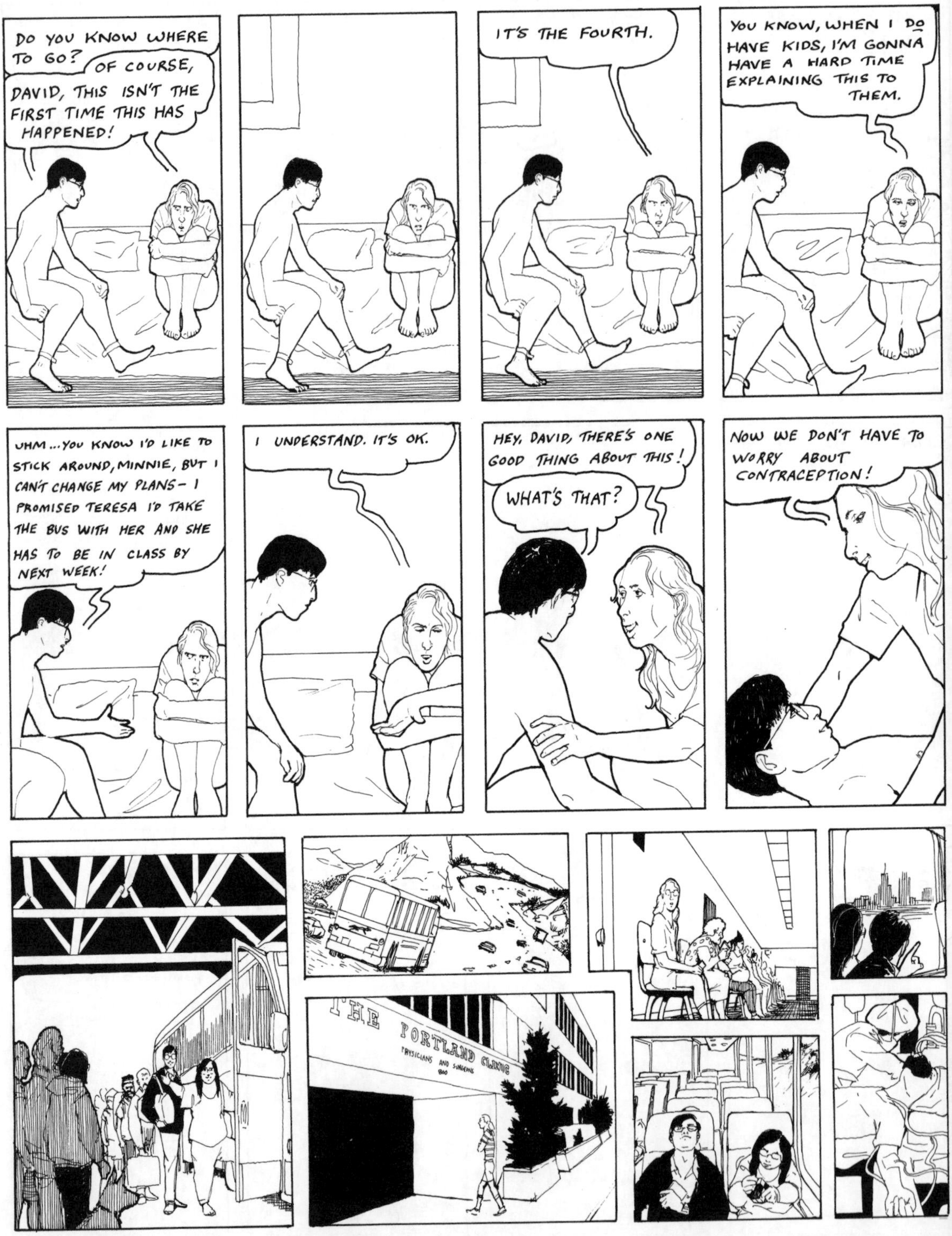
DO YOU KNOW WHERE TO GO?
OF COURSE, DAVID, THIS ISN'T THE FIRST TIME THIS HAS HAPPENED!
IT'S THE FOURTH.
YOU KNOW, WHEN I DO HAVE KIDS, I'M GONNA HAVE A HARD TIME EXPLAINING THIS TO THEM.
UHM...YOU KNOW I'D LIKE TO STICK AROUND, MINNIE, BUT I CAN'T CHANGE MY PLANS— I PROMISED TERESA I'D TAKE THE BUS WITH HER AND SHE HAS TO BE IN CLASS BY NEXT WEEK!
I UNDERSTAND. IT'S OK.
HEY, DAVID, THERE'S ONE GOOD THING ABOUT THIS!
WHAT'S THAT?
NOW WE DON'T HAVE TO WORRY ABOUT CONTRACEPTION!
THE PORTLAND CLINIC
PHYSICIANS AND SURGEONS

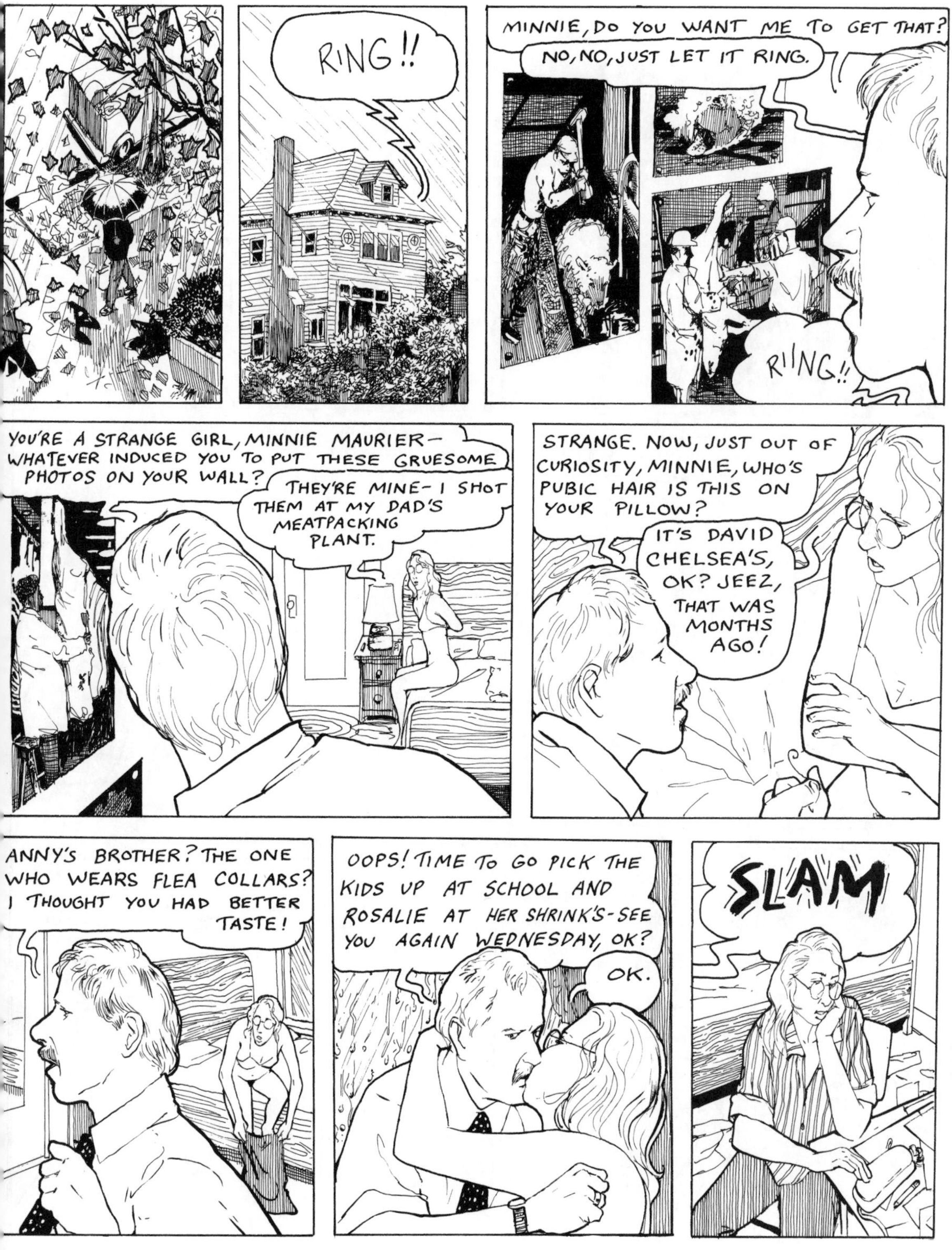
RING!!
MINNIE, DO YOU WANT ME TO GET THAT?
NO, NO, JUST LET IT RING.
RING!!
YOU'RE A STRANGE GIRL, MINNIE MAURIER— WHATEVER INDUCED YOU TO PUT THESE GRUESOME PHOTOS ON YOUR WALL?
THEY'RE MINE- I SHOT THEM AT MY DAD'S MEATPACKING PLANT.
STRANGE. NOW, JUST OUT OF CURIOSITY, MINNIE, WHO'S PUBIC HAIR IS THIS ON YOUR PILLOW?
IT'S DAVID CHELSEA'S, OK? JEEZ, THAT WAS MONTHS AGO!
ANNY'S BROTHER? THE ONE WHO WEARS FLEA COLLARS? I THOUGHT YOU HAD BETTER TASTE!
OOPS! TIME TO GO PICK THE KIDS UP AT SCHOOL AND ROSALIE AT HER SHRINK'S-SEE YOU AGAIN WEDNESDAY, OK?
OK.
SLAM

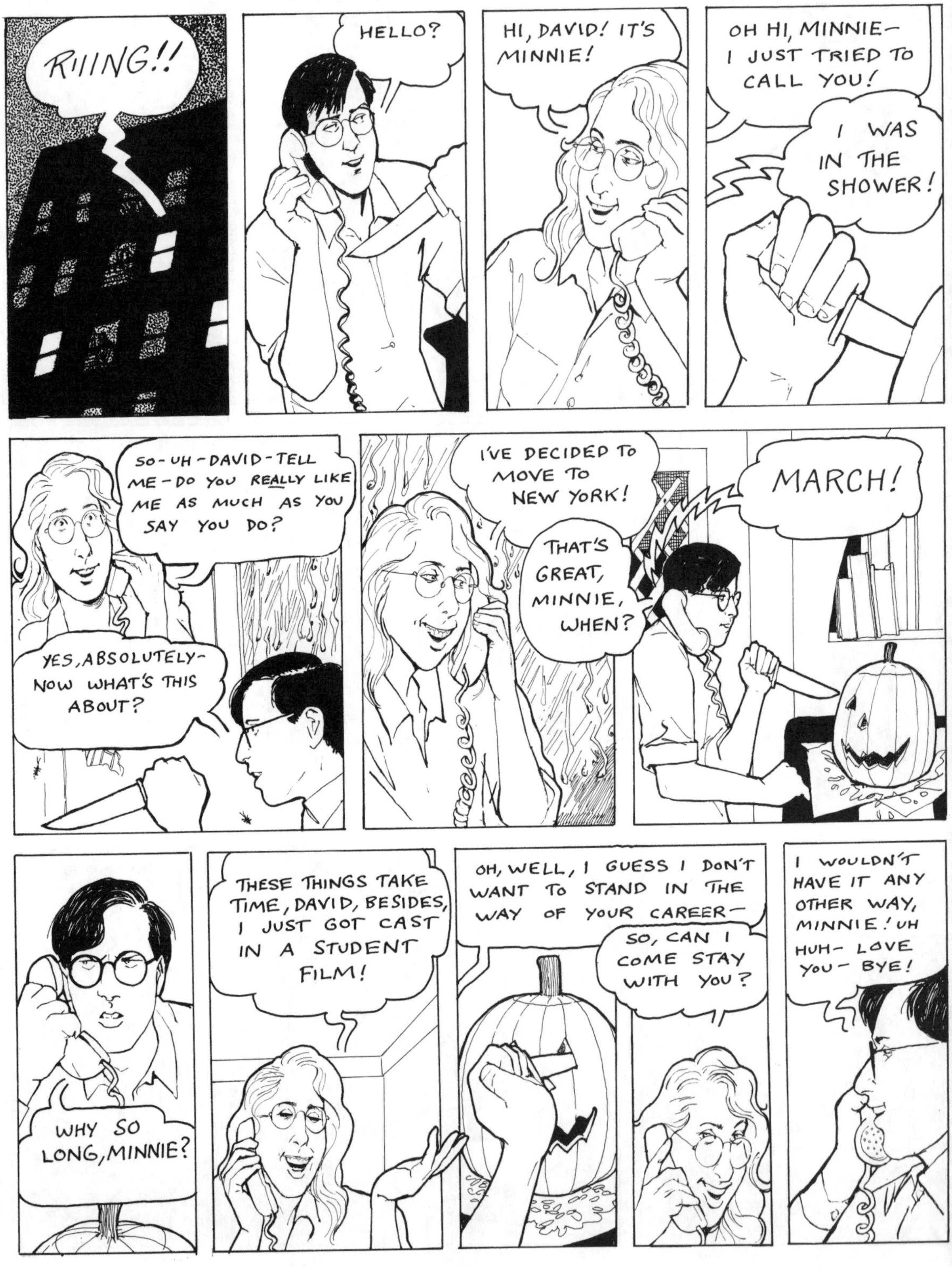
RIIING!!
HELLO?
HI, DAVID! IT'S MINNIE!
OH HI, MINNIE- I JUST TRIED TO CALL YOU!
I WAS IN THE SHOWER!
SO-UH-DAVID-TELL ME-DO YOU REALLY LIKE ME AS MUCH AS YOU SAY YOU DO?
YES, ABSOLUTELY- NOW WHAT'S THIS ABOUT?
I'VE DECIDED TO MOVE TO NEW YORK!
THAT'S GREAT, MINNIE, WHEN?
MARCH!
WHY SO LONG, MINNIE?
THESE THINGS TAKE TIME, DAVID, BESIDES, I JUST GOT CAST IN A STUDENT FILM!
OH, WELL, I GUESS I DON'T WANT TO STAND IN THE WAY OF YOUR CAREER-
SO, CAN I COME STAY WITH YOU?
I WOULDN'T HAVE IT ANY OTHER WAY, MINNIE! UH HUH- LOVE YOU- BYE!

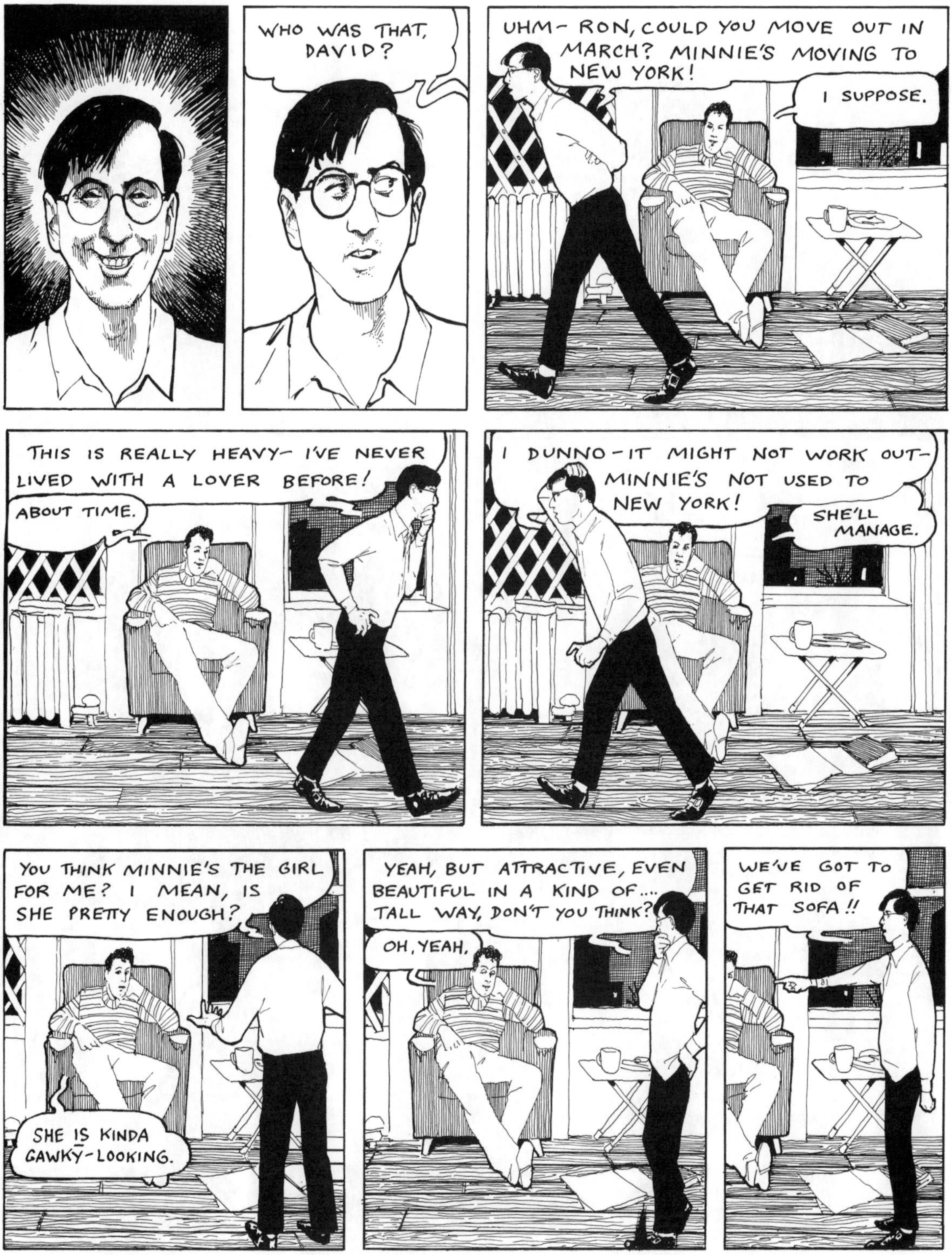
WHO WAS THAT, DAVID?
UHM- RON, COULD YOU MOVE OUT IN MARCH? MINNIE'S MOVING TO NEW YORK!
I SUPPOSE.
THIS IS REALLY HEAVY- I'VE NEVER LIVED WITH A LOVER BEFORE!
ABOUT TIME.
I DUNNO-IT MIGHT NOT WORK OUT- MINNIE'S NOT USED TO NEW YORK!
SHE'LL MANAGE.
YOU THINK MINNIE'S THE GIRL FOR ME? I MEAN, IS SHE PRETTY ENOUGH?
SHE IS KINDA GAWKY-LOOKING.
YEAH, BUT ATTRACTIVE, EVEN BEAUTIFUL IN A KIND OF.... TALL WAY, DON'T YOU THINK?
OH, YEAH.
WE'VE GOT TO GET RID OF THAT SOFA!!

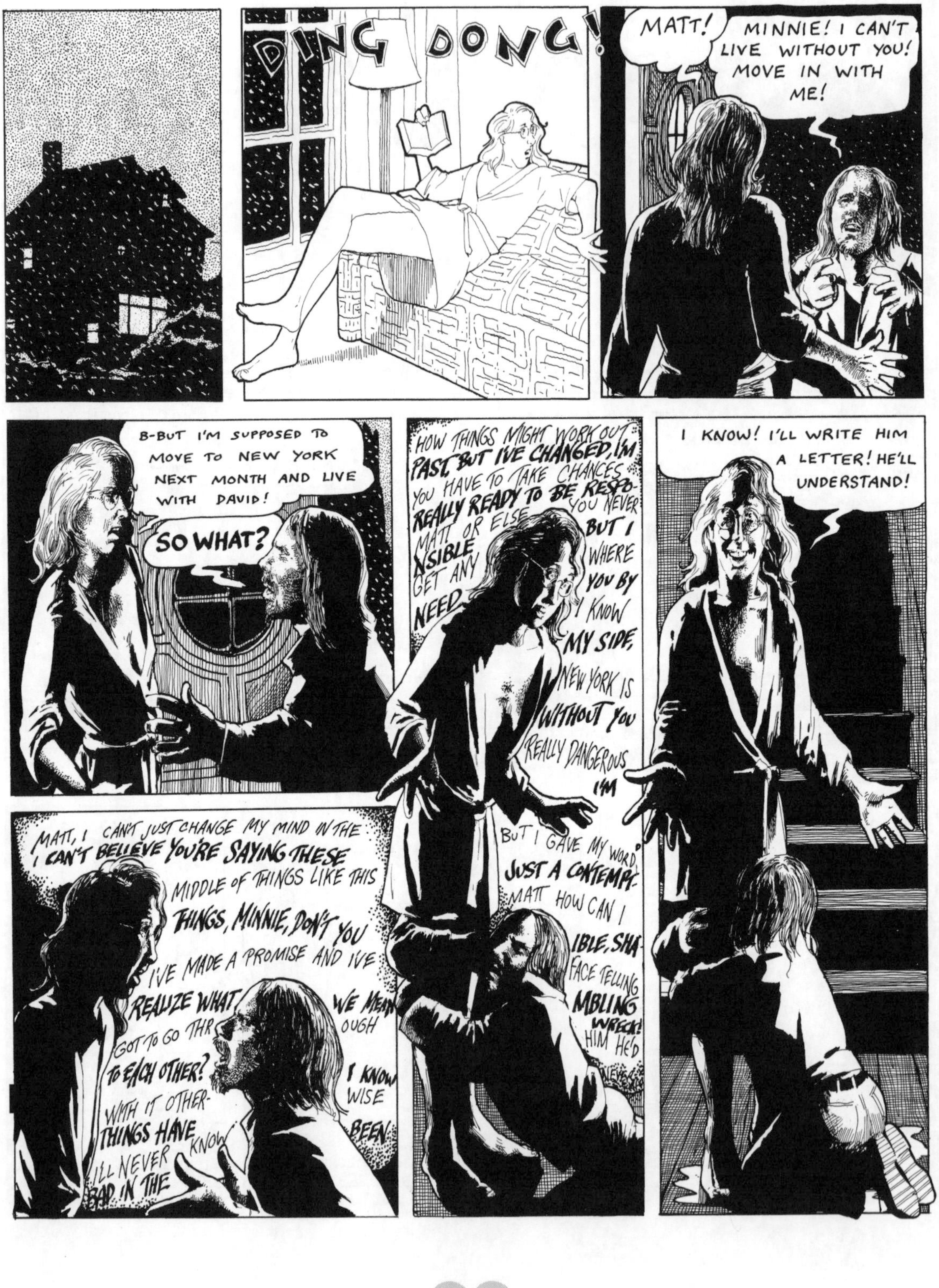
DING DONG!
MATT!
MINNIE! I CAN'T LIVE WITHOUT YOU! MOVE IN WITH ME!
B-BUT I'M SUPPOSED TO MOVE TO NEW YORK NEXT MONTH AND LIVE WITH DAVID!
SO WHAT?
HOW THINGS MIGHT WORK OUT
PAST, BUT I'VE CHANGED, I'M
YOU HAVE TO TAKE CHANCES
REALLY READY TO BE RESPO-
YOU NEVER
MATT OR ELSE
NSIBLE
BUT I
GET ANY
WHERE
NEED
YOU BY
I KNOW
MY SIDE,
NEW YORK IS
WITHOUT YOU
REALLY DANGEROUS
I'M
BUT I GAVE MY WORD,
JUST A CONTEMPT-
MATT HOW CAN I
IBLE, SHA
FACE TELLING
MBLING
WRECK!
HIM HE'D
MATT, I CAN'T JUST CHANGE MY MIND IN THE
I CAN'T BELIEVE YOU'RE SAYING THESE
MIDDLE OF THINGS LIKE THIS
THINGS, MINNIE, DON'T YOU
I'VE MADE A PROMISE AND I'VE
REALIZE WHAT
WE MEAN
GOT TO GO THR
OUGH
TO EACH OTHER?
I KNOW
WITH IT OTHER-
WISE
THINGS HAVE
BEEN
I'LL NEVER
KNOW
BAD IN THE
I KNOW! I'LL WRITE HIM A LETTER! HE'LL UNDERSTAND!

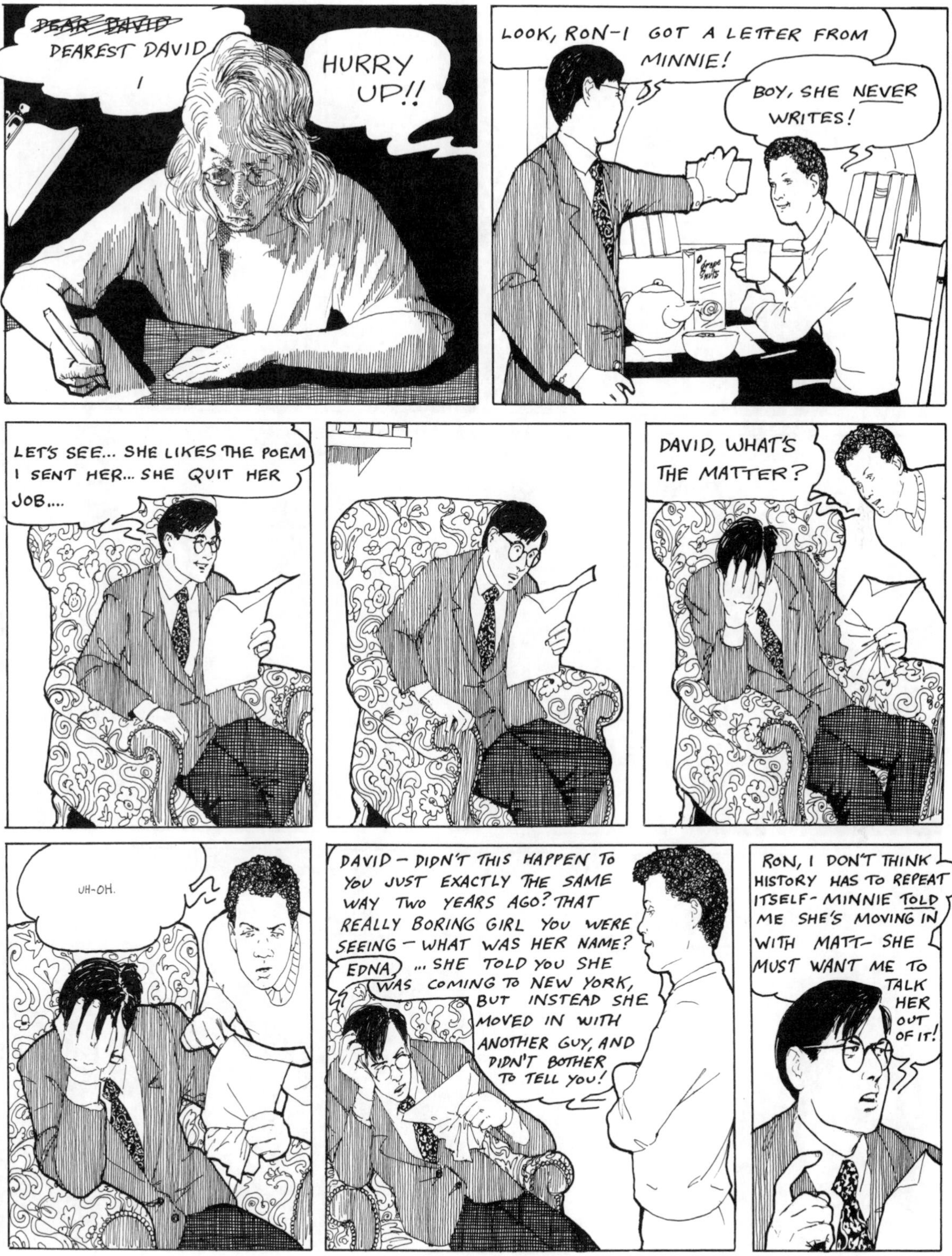
DEAR DAVID
DEAREST DAVID
I
HURRY UP!!
LOOK, RON-I GOT A LETTER FROM MINNIE!
BOY, SHE NEVER WRITES!
LET'S SEE... SHE LIKES THE POEM I SENT HER... SHE QUIT HER JOB....
DAVID, WHAT'S THE MATTER?
UH-OH.
DAVID - DIDN'T THIS HAPPEN TO YOU JUST EXACTLY THE SAME WAY TWO YEARS AGO? THAT REALLY BORING GIRL YOU WERE SEEING - WHAT WAS HER NAME?
EDNA
... SHE TOLD YOU SHE WAS COMING TO NEW YORK, BUT INSTEAD SHE MOVED IN WITH ANOTHER GUY, AND DIDN'T BOTHER TO TELL YOU!
RON, I DON'T THINK HISTORY HAS TO REPEAT ITSELF- MINNIE TOLD ME SHE'S MOVING IN WITH MATT- SHE MUST WANT ME TO TALK HER OUT OF IT!

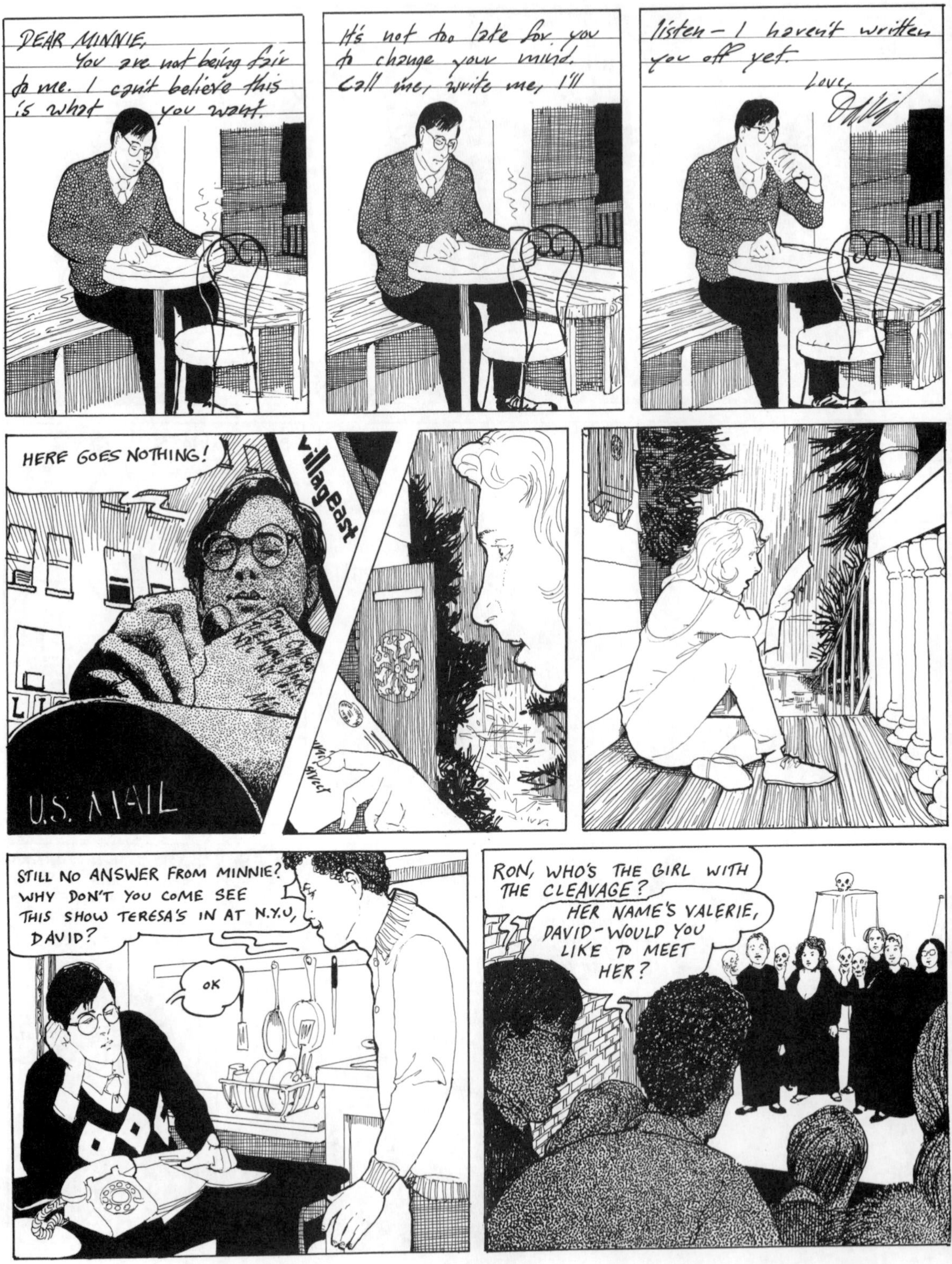
DEAR MINNIE,
You are not being fair to me. I can't believe this is what you want.
It's not too late for you to change your mind. Call me, write me, I'll
listen - I haven't written you off yet.
Love,
HERE GOES NOTHING!
villagEast
U.S. MAIL
STILL NO ANSWER FROM MINNIE? WHY DON'T YOU COME SEE THIS SHOW TERESA'S IN AT N.Y.U, DAVID?
OK
RON, WHO'S THE GIRL WITH THE CLEAVAGE?
HER NAME'S VALERIE, DAVID - WOULD YOU LIKE TO MEET HER?

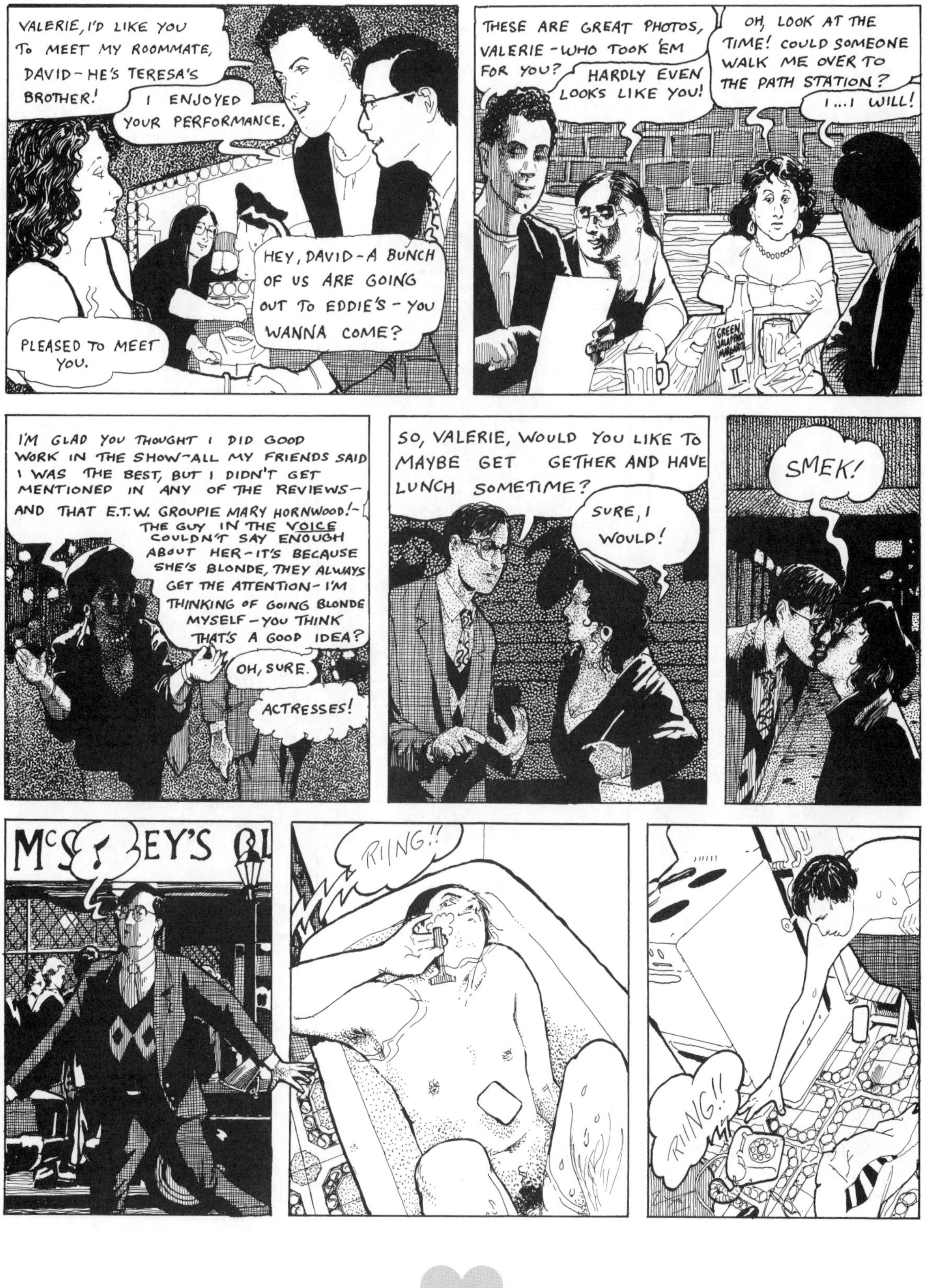
VALERIE, I'D LIKE YOU TO MEET MY ROOMMATE, DAVID - HE'S TERESA'S BROTHER!
I ENJOYED YOUR PERFORMANCE.
HEY, DAVID - A BUNCH OF US ARE GOING OUT TO EDDIE'S - YOU WANNA COME?
PLEASED TO MEET YOU.
THESE ARE GREAT PHOTOS, VALERIE - WHO TOOK 'EM FOR YOU?
HARDLY EVEN LOOKS LIKE YOU!
OH, LOOK AT THE TIME! COULD SOMEONE WALK ME OVER TO THE PATH STATION?
I...I WILL!
I'M GLAD YOU THOUGHT I DID GOOD WORK IN THE SHOW - ALL MY FRIENDS SAID I WAS THE BEST, BUT I DIDN'T GET MENTIONED IN ANY OF THE REVIEWS - AND THAT E.T.W. GROUPIE MARY HORNWOOD! - THE GUY IN THE VOICE COULDN'T SAY ENOUGH ABOUT HER - IT'S BECAUSE SHE'S BLONDE, THEY ALWAYS GET THE ATTENTION - I'M THINKING OF GOING BLONDE MYSELF - YOU THINK THAT'S A GOOD IDEA?
OH, SURE.
ACTRESSES!
SO, VALERIE, WOULD YOU LIKE TO MAYBE GET GETHER AND HAVE LUNCH SOMETIME?
SURE, I WOULD!
SMEK!
RIING!!
RIING!!

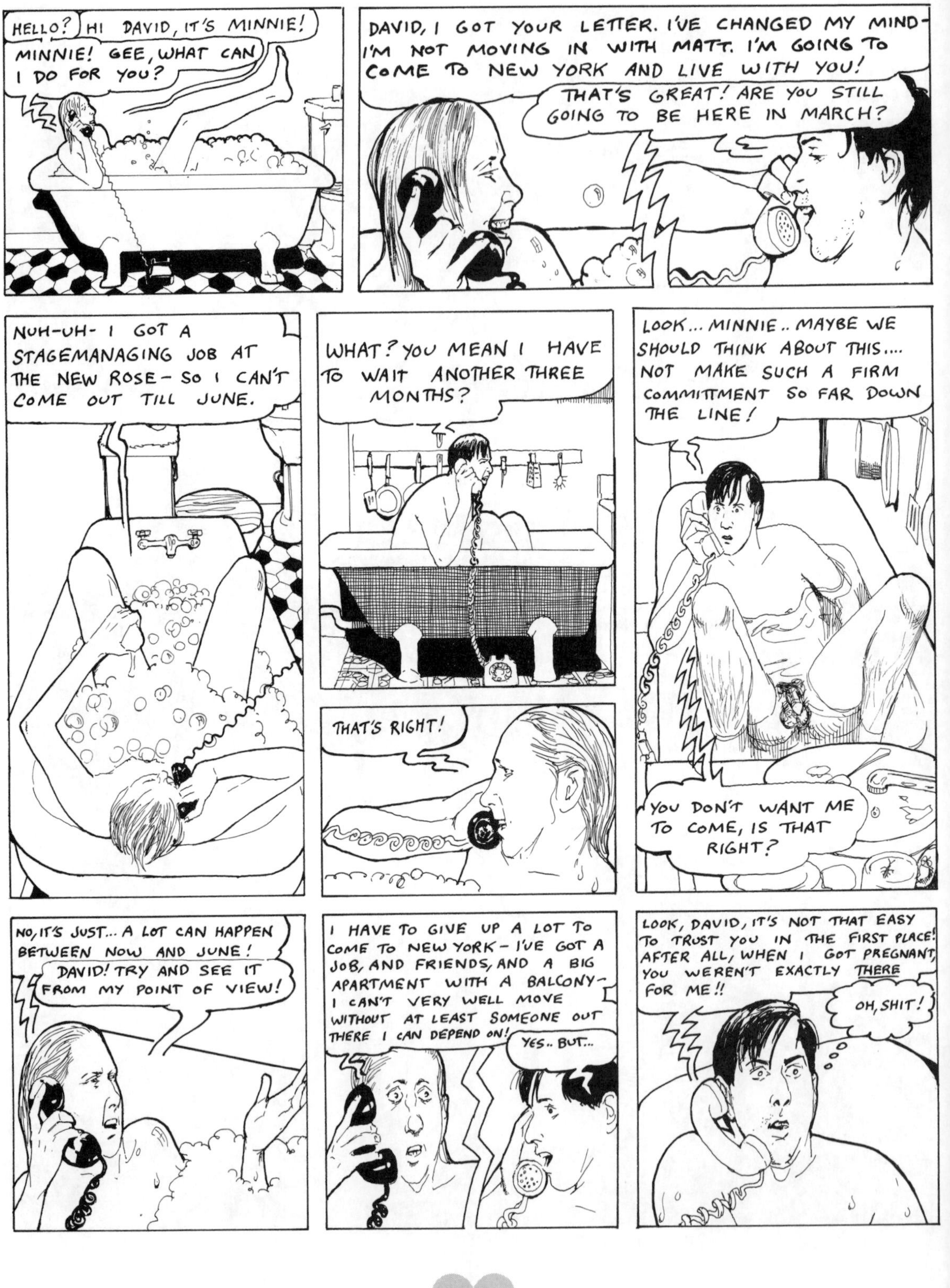
HELLO?
HI DAVID, IT'S MINNIE!
MINNIE! GEE, WHAT CAN I DO FOR YOU?
DAVID, I GOT YOUR LETTER. I'VE CHANGED MY MIND- I'M NOT MOVING IN WITH MATT. I'M GOING TO COME TO NEW YORK AND LIVE WITH YOU!
THAT'S GREAT! ARE YOU STILL GOING TO BE HERE IN MARCH?
NUH-UH- I GOT A STAGEMANAGING JOB AT THE NEW ROSE- SO I CAN'T COME OUT TILL JUNE.
WHAT? YOU MEAN I HAVE TO WAIT ANOTHER THREE MONTHS?
THAT'S RIGHT!
LOOK... MINNIE.. MAYBE WE SHOULD THINK ABOUT THIS.... NOT MAKE SUCH A FIRM COMMITTMENT SO FAR DOWN THE LINE!
YOU DON'T WANT ME TO COME, IS THAT RIGHT?
NO, IT'S JUST... A LOT CAN HAPPEN BETWEEN NOW AND JUNE!
DAVID! TRY AND SEE IT FROM MY POINT OF VIEW!
I HAVE TO GIVE UP A LOT TO COME TO NEW YORK - I'VE GOT A JOB, AND FRIENDS, AND A BIG APARTMENT WITH A BALCONY- I CAN'T VERY WELL MOVE WITHOUT AT LEAST SOMEONE OUT THERE I CAN DEPEND ON!
YES.. BUT...
LOOK, DAVID, IT'S NOT THAT EASY TO TRUST YOU IN THE FIRST PLACE! AFTER ALL, WHEN I GOT PREGNANT, YOU WEREN'T EXACTLY THERE FOR ME!!
OH, SHIT!

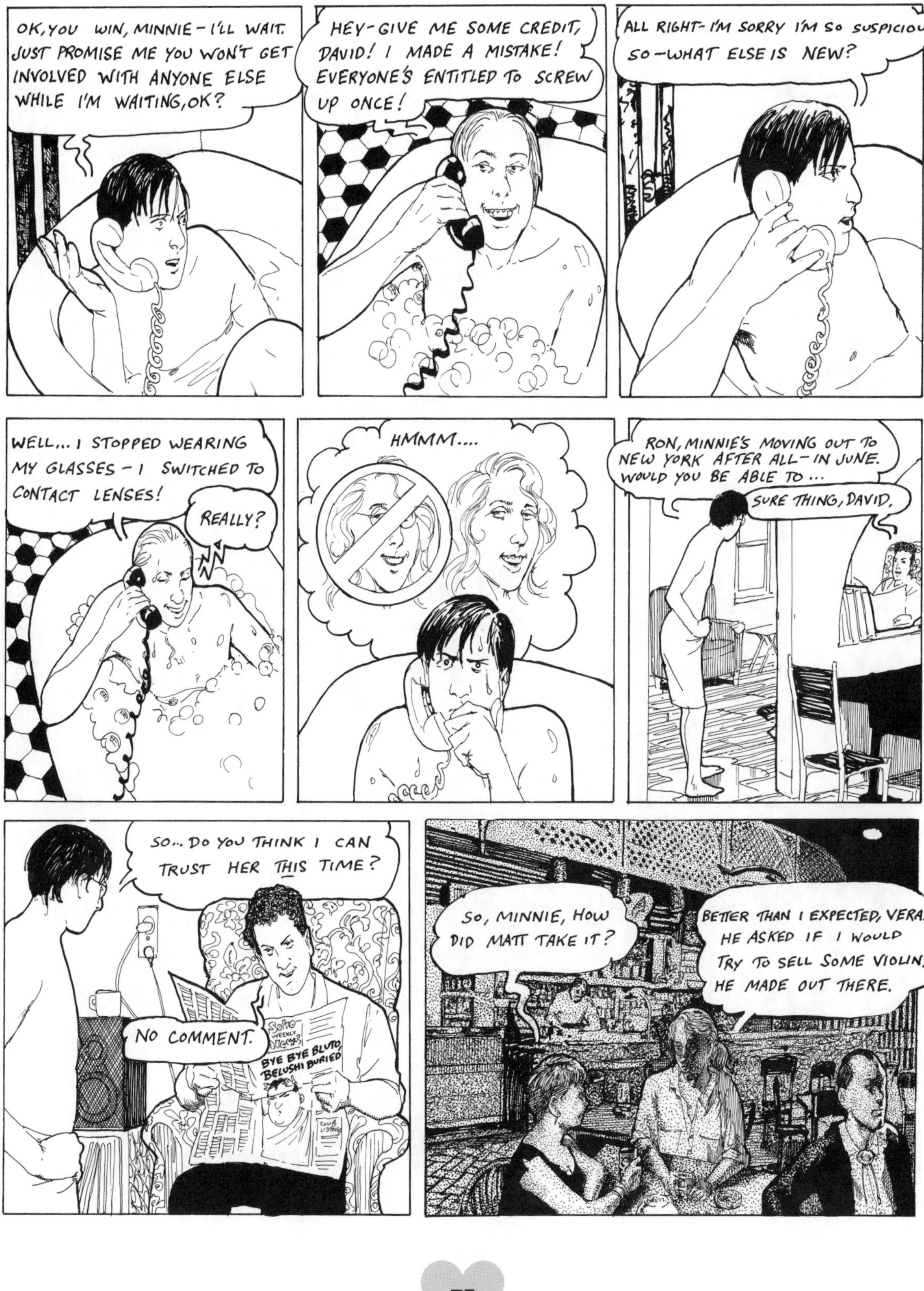
OK, YOU WIN, MINNIE - I'LL WAIT. JUST PROMISE ME YOU WON'T GET INVOLVED WITH ANYONE ELSE WHILE I'M WAITING, OK?
HEY- GIVE ME SOME CREDIT, DAVID! I MADE A MISTAKE! EVERYONE'S ENTITLED TO SCREW UP ONCE!
ALL RIGHT- I'M SORRY I'M SO SUSPICIOUS. SO—WHAT ELSE IS NEW?
WELL... I STOPPED WEARING MY GLASSES - I SWITCHED TO CONTACT LENSES!
REALLY?
HMMM....
RON, MINNIE'S MOVING OUT TO NEW YORK AFTER ALL- IN JUNE. WOULD YOU BE ABLE TO ...
SURE THING, DAVID.
SO... DO YOU THINK I CAN TRUST HER THIS TIME?
NO COMMENT.
SoHo WEEKLY NEWS
BYE BYE BLUTO, BELUSHI BURIED
CLUB LISTINGS
SO, MINNIE, HOW DID MATT TAKE IT?
BETTER THAN I EXPECTED, VERA. HE ASKED IF I WOULD TRY TO SELL SOME VIOLINS HE MADE OUT THERE.

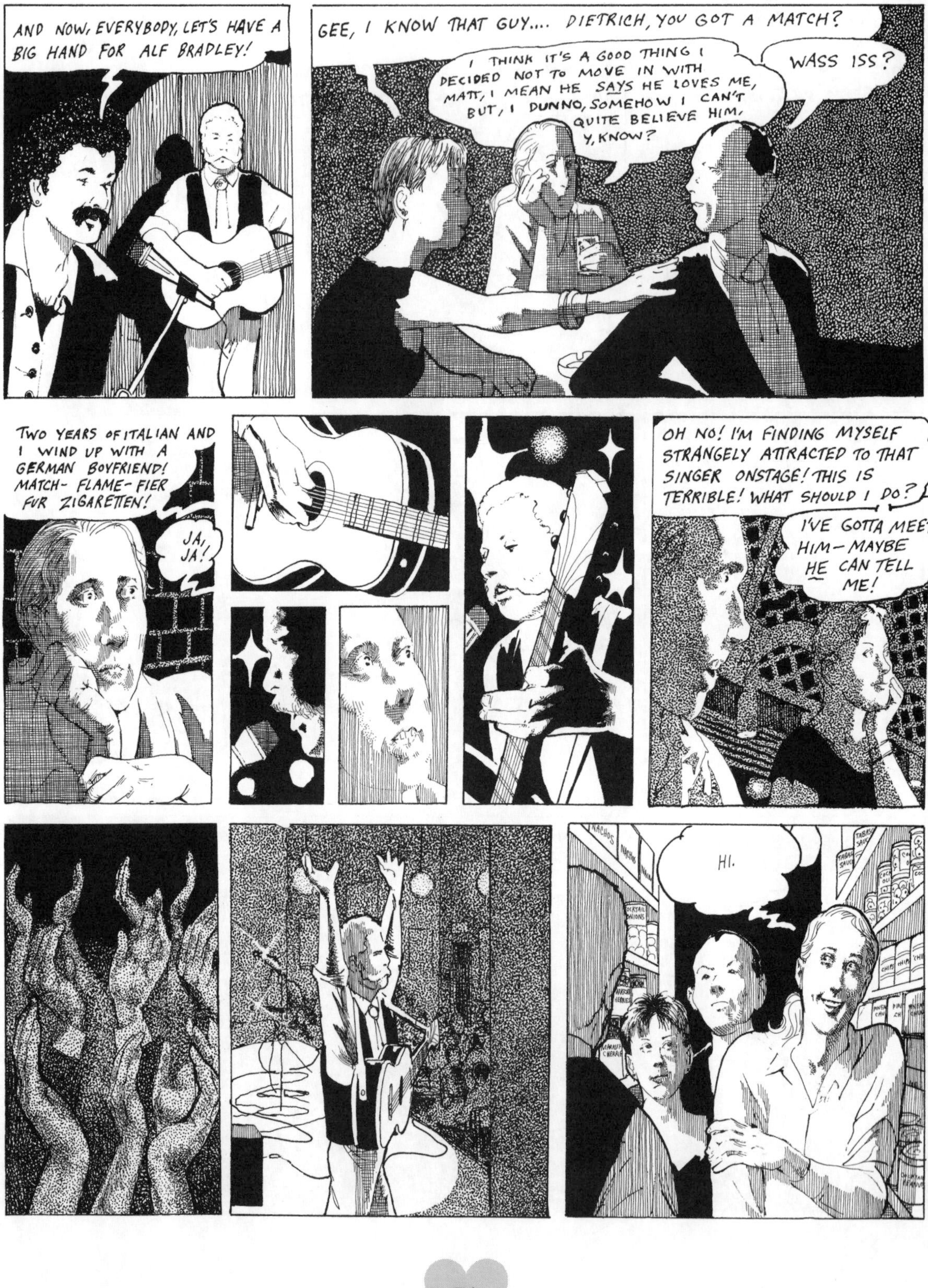
AND NOW, EVERYBODY, LET'S HAVE A BIG HAND FOR ALF BRADLEY!
GEE, I KNOW THAT GUY.... DIETRICH, YOU GOT A MATCH?
I THINK IT'S A GOOD THING I DECIDED NOT TO MOVE IN WITH MATT, I MEAN HE SAYS HE LOVES ME, BUT, I DUNNO, SOMEHOW I CAN'T QUITE BELIEVE HIM, Y, KNOW?
WASS ISS?
TWO YEARS OF ITALIAN AND I WIND UP WITH A GERMAN BOYFRIEND! MATCH- FLAME- FIER FUR ZIGARETTEN!
JA, JA!
OH NO! I'M FINDING MYSELF STRANGELY ATTRACTED TO THAT SINGER ONSTAGE! THIS IS TERRIBLE! WHAT SHOULD I DO?
I'VE GOTTA MEET HIM- MAYBE HE CAN TELL ME!
HI.

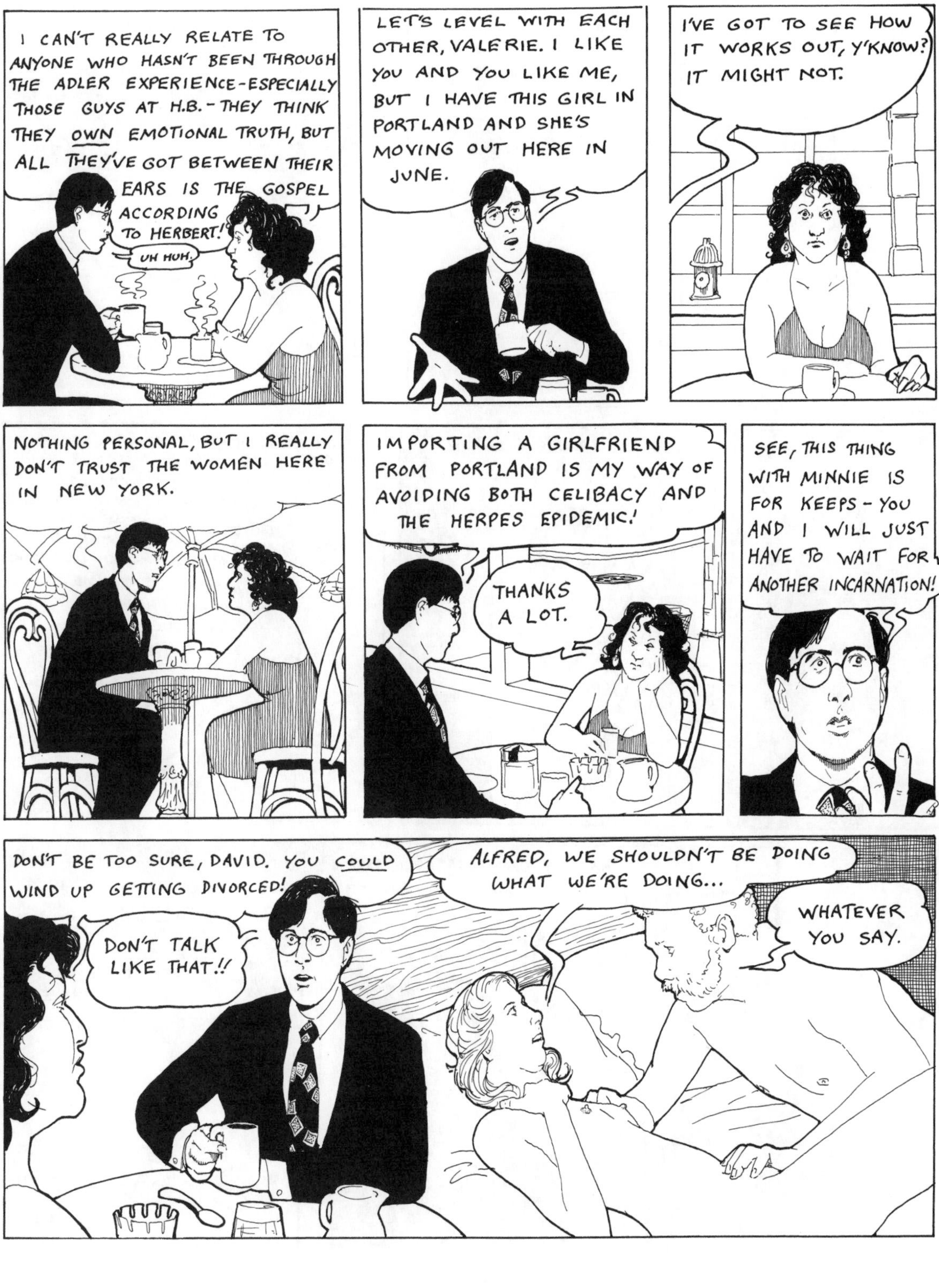
I CAN'T REALLY RELATE TO ANYONE WHO HASN'T BEEN THROUGH THE ADLER EXPERIENCE-ESPECIALLY THOSE GUYS AT H.B.-THEY THINK THEY OWN EMOTIONAL TRUTH, BUT ALL THEY'VE GOT BETWEEN THEIR EARS IS THE GOSPEL ACCORDING TO HERBERT!
UH HUH.
LET'S LEVEL WITH EACH OTHER, VALERIE. I LIKE YOU AND YOU LIKE ME, BUT I HAVE THIS GIRL IN PORTLAND AND SHE'S MOVING OUT HERE IN JUNE.
I'VE GOT TO SEE HOW IT WORKS OUT, Y'KNOW? IT MIGHT NOT.
NOTHING PERSONAL, BUT I REALLY DON'T TRUST THE WOMEN HERE IN NEW YORK.
IMPORTING A GIRLFRIEND FROM PORTLAND IS MY WAY OF AVOIDING BOTH CELIBACY AND THE HERPES EPIDEMIC!
THANKS A LOT.
SEE, THIS THING WITH MINNIE IS FOR KEEPS - YOU AND I WILL JUST HAVE TO WAIT FOR ANOTHER INCARNATION!
DON'T BE TOO SURE, DAVID. YOU COULD WIND UP GETTING DIVORCED!
DON'T TALK LIKE THAT!!
ALFRED, WE SHOULDN'T BE DOING WHAT WE'RE DOING...
WHATEVER YOU SAY.

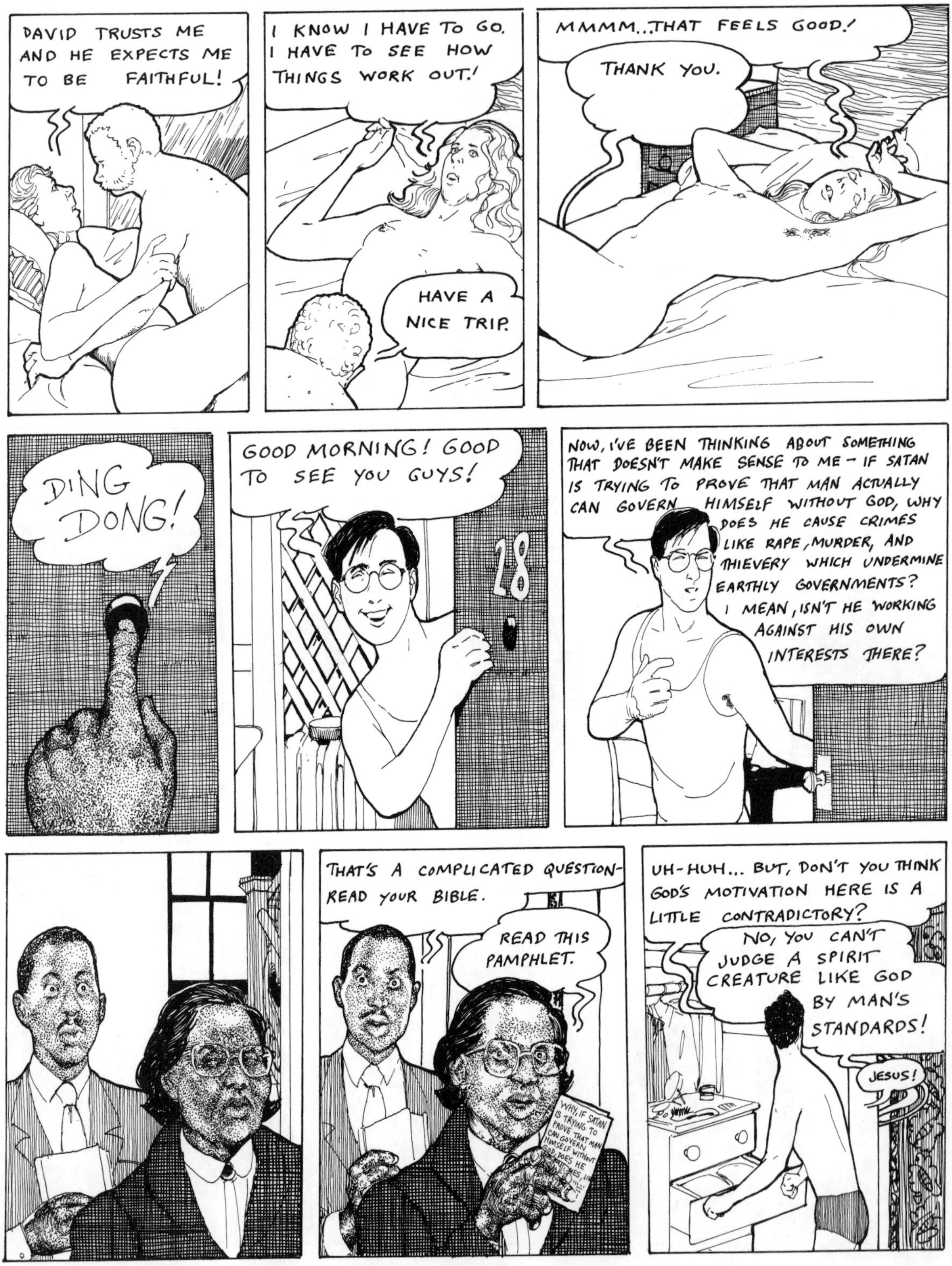
DAVID TRUSTS ME AND HE EXPECTS ME TO BE FAITHFUL!
I KNOW I HAVE TO GO. I HAVE TO SEE HOW THINGS WORK OUT!
HAVE A NICE TRIP.
MMMM...THAT FEELS GOOD!
THANK YOU.
DING DONG!
GOOD MORNING! GOOD TO SEE YOU GUYS!
28
NOW, I'VE BEEN THINKING ABOUT SOMETHING THAT DOESN'T MAKE SENSE TO ME - IF SATAN IS TRYING TO PROVE THAT MAN ACTUALLY CAN GOVERN HIMSELF WITHOUT GOD, WHY DOES HE CAUSE CRIMES LIKE RAPE, MURDER, AND THIEVERY WHICH UNDERMINE EARTHLY GOVERNMENTS? I MEAN, ISN'T HE WORKING AGAINST HIS OWN INTERESTS THERE?
THAT'S A COMPLICATED QUESTION- READ YOUR BIBLE.
READ THIS PAMPHLET.
UH-HUH... BUT, DON'T YOU THINK GOD'S MOTIVATION HERE IS A LITTLE CONTRADICTORY?
NO, YOU CAN'T JUDGE A SPIRIT CREATURE LIKE GOD BY MAN'S STANDARDS!
JESUS!

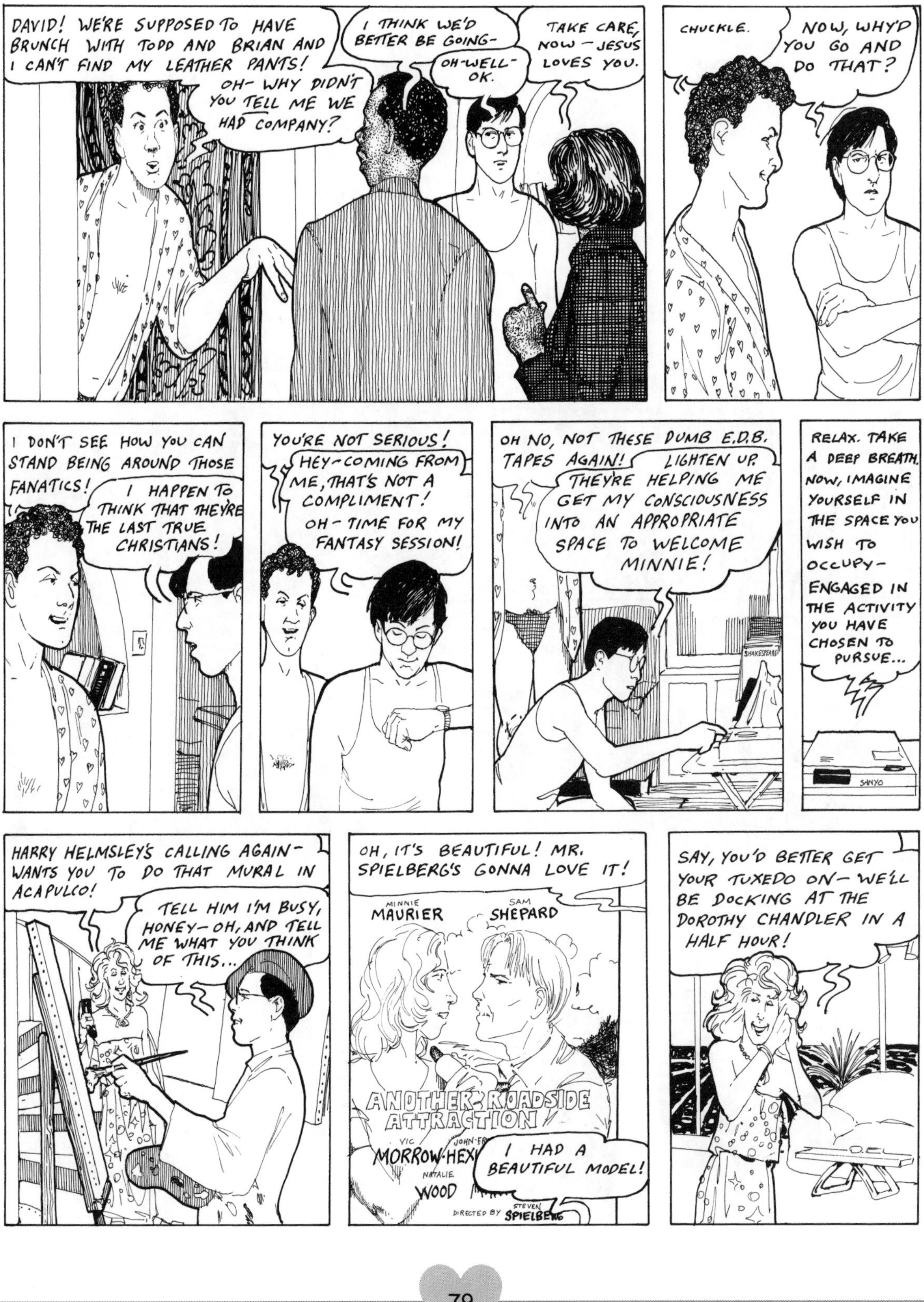
DAVID! WE'RE SUPPOSED TO HAVE BRUNCH WITH TODD AND BRIAN AND I CAN'T FIND MY LEATHER PANTS!
OH- WHY DIDN'T YOU TELL ME WE HAD COMPANY?
I THINK WE'D BETTER BE GOING-
OH-WELL- OK.
TAKE CARE, NOW - JESUS LOVES YOU.
CHUCKLE.
NOW, WHY'D YOU GO AND DO THAT?
I DON'T SEE HOW YOU CAN STAND BEING AROUND THOSE FANATICS!
I HAPPEN TO THINK THAT THEY'RE THE LAST TRUE CHRISTIANS!
YOU'RE NOT SERIOUS!
HEY- COMING FROM ME, THAT'S NOT A COMPLIMENT!
OH- TIME FOR MY FANTASY SESSION!
OH NO, NOT THESE DUMB E.D.B. TAPES AGAIN!
LIGHTEN UP. THEY'RE HELPING ME GET MY CONSCIOUSNESS INTO AN APPROPRIATE SPACE TO WELCOME MINNIE!
SHAKESPEARE
RELAX. TAKE A DEEP BREATH. NOW, IMAGINE YOURSELF IN THE SPACE YOU WISH TO OCCUPY- ENGAGED IN THE ACTIVITY YOU HAVE CHOSEN TO PURSUE...
SANYO
HARRY HELMSLEY'S CALLING AGAIN- WANTS YOU TO DO THAT MURAL IN ACAPULCO!
TELL HIM I'M BUSY, HONEY- OH, AND TELL ME WHAT YOU THINK OF THIS...
OH, IT'S BEAUTIFUL! MR. SPIELBERG'S GONNA LOVE IT!
MINNIE MAURIER
SAM SHEPARD
ANOTHER ROADSIDE ATTRACTION
VIC MORROW
NATALIE WOOD
I HAD A BEAUTIFUL MODEL!
DIRECTED BY STEVEN SPIELBERG
SAY, YOU'D BETTER GET YOUR TUXEDO ON- WE'LL BE DOCKING AT THE DOROTHY CHANDLER IN A HALF HOUR!

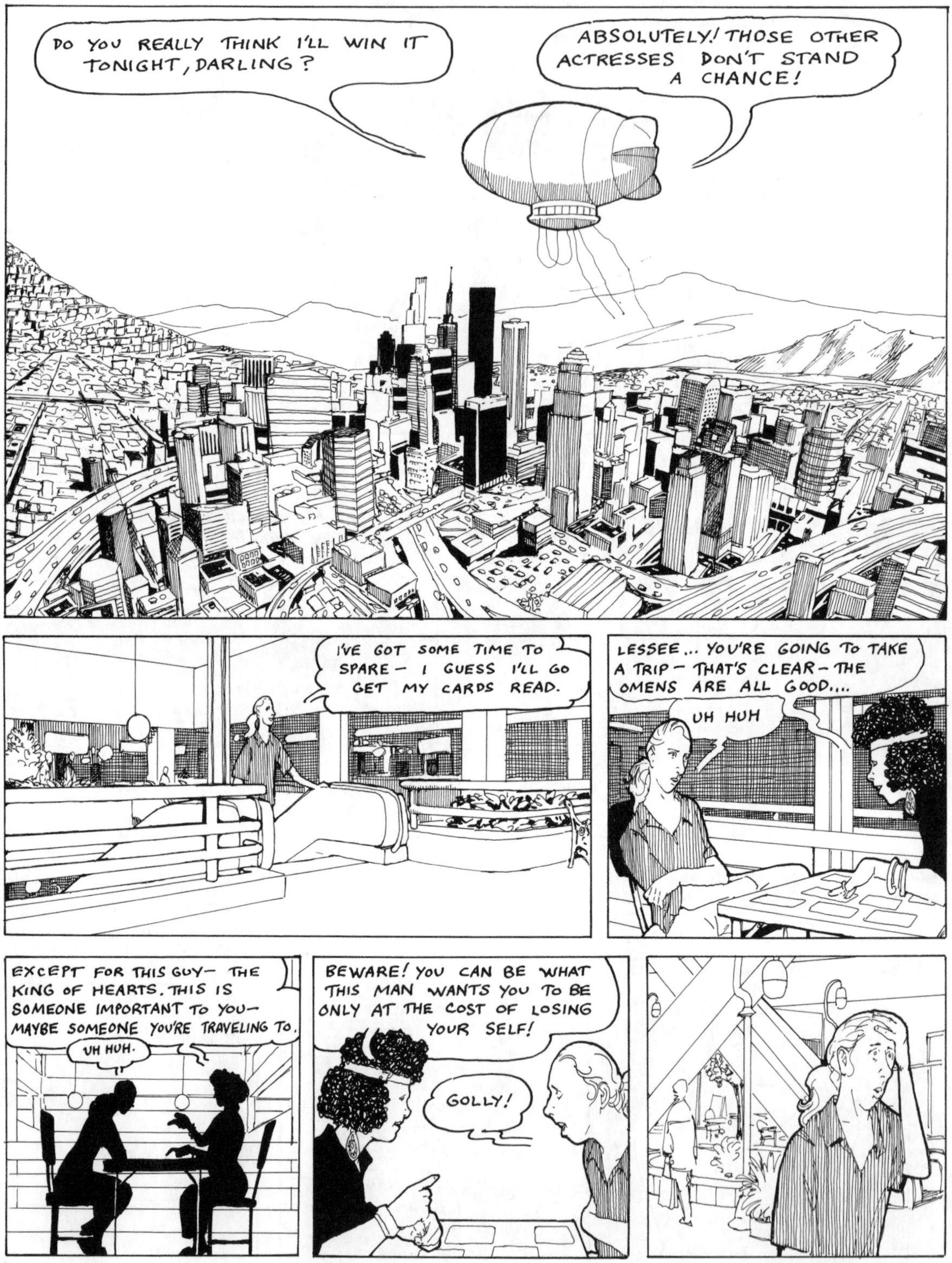
DO YOU REALLY THINK I'LL WIN IT TONIGHT, DARLING?
ABSOLUTELY! THOSE OTHER ACTRESSES DON'T STAND A CHANCE!
I'VE GOT SOME TIME TO SPARE — I GUESS I'LL GO GET MY CARDS READ.
LESSEE... YOU'RE GOING TO TAKE A TRIP — THAT'S CLEAR — THE OMENS ARE ALL GOOD....
UH HUH
EXCEPT FOR THIS GUY — THE KING OF HEARTS. THIS IS SOMEONE IMPORTANT TO YOU — MAYBE SOMEONE YOU'RE TRAVELING TO.
UH HUH.
BEWARE! YOU CAN BE WHAT THIS MAN WANTS YOU TO BE ONLY AT THE COST OF LOSING YOUR SELF!
GOLLY!

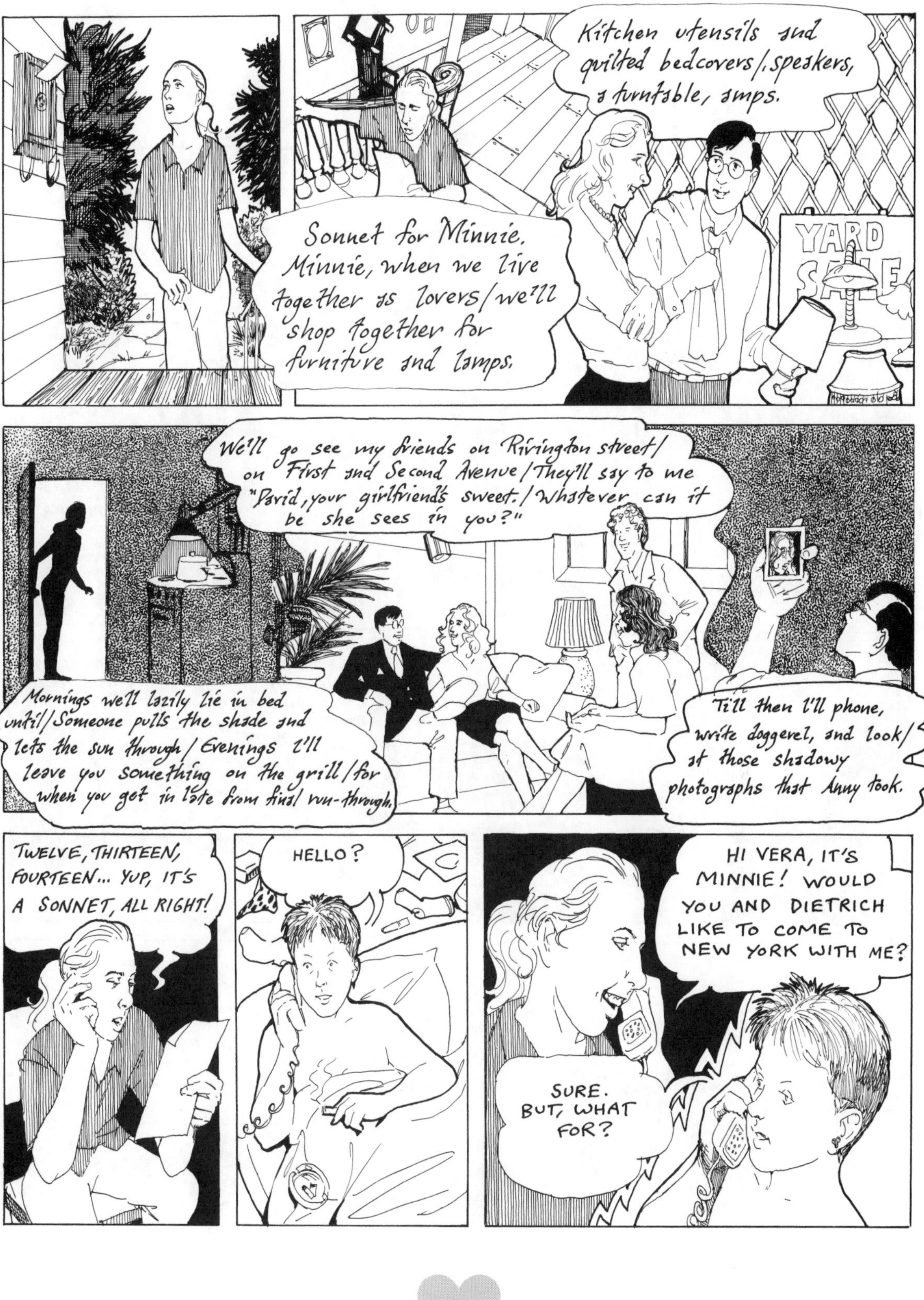
Kitchen utensils and quilted bedcovers/, speakers, a turntable, amps.
Sonnet for Minnie. Minnie, when we live together as lovers/ we'll shop together for furniture and lamps.
YARD SALE
We'll go see my friends on Rivington street/ on First and Second Avenue/ They'll say to me "David, your girlfriend's sweet./ Whatever can it be she sees in you?"
Mornings we'll lazily lie in bed until/ Someone pulls the shade and lets the sun through/ Evenings I'll leave you something on the grill/ for when you get in late from final run-through.
Till then I'll phone, write doggerel, and look/ at those shadowy photographs that Anny took.
TWELVE, THIRTEEN, FOURTEEN... YUP, IT'S A SONNET, ALL RIGHT!
HELLO?
HI VERA, IT'S MINNIE! WOULD YOU AND DIETRICH LIKE TO COME TO NEW YORK WITH ME?
SURE. BUT, WHAT FOR?

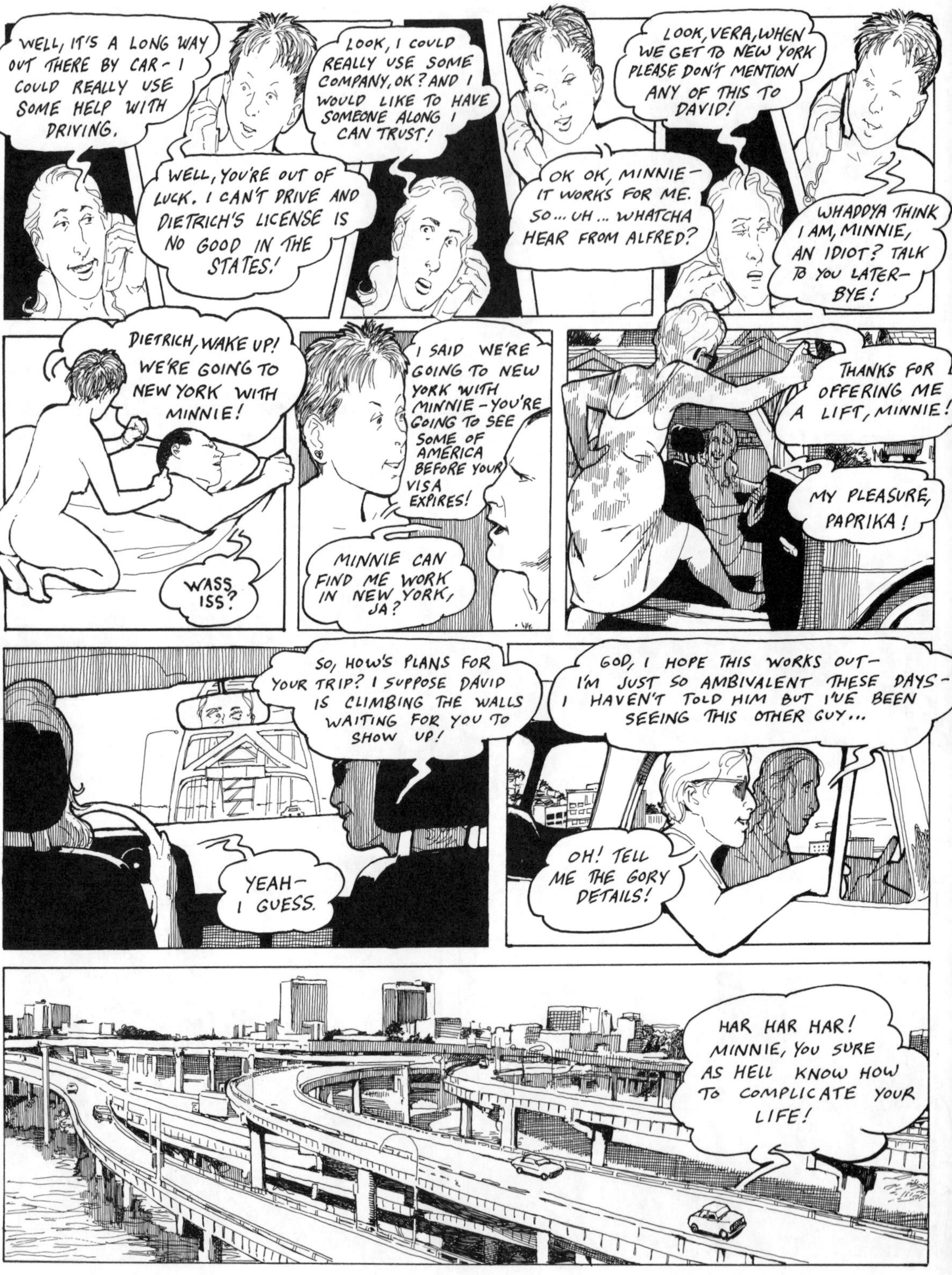
WELL, IT'S A LONG WAY OUT THERE BY CAR- I COULD REALLY USE SOME HELP WITH DRIVING.
WELL, YOU'RE OUT OF LUCK. I CAN'T DRIVE AND DIETRICH'S LICENSE IS NO GOOD IN THE STATES!
LOOK, I COULD REALLY USE SOME COMPANY, OK? AND I WOULD LIKE TO HAVE SOMEONE ALONG I CAN TRUST!
OK OK, MINNIE- IT WORKS FOR ME. SO... UH ... WHATCHA HEAR FROM ALFRED?
LOOK, VERA, WHEN WE GET TO NEW YORK PLEASE DON'T MENTION ANY OF THIS TO DAVID!
WHADDYA THINK I AM, MINNIE, AN IDIOT? TALK TO YOU LATER- BYE!
DIETRICH, WAKE UP! WE'RE GOING TO NEW YORK WITH MINNIE!
WASS ISS?
I SAID WE'RE GOING TO NEW YORK WITH MINNIE - YOU'RE GOING TO SEE SOME OF AMERICA BEFORE YOUR VISA EXPIRES!
MINNIE CAN FIND ME WORK IN NEW YORK, JA?
THANKS FOR OFFERING ME A LIFT, MINNIE!
MY PLEASURE, PAPRIKA!
SO, HOW'S PLANS FOR YOUR TRIP? I SUPPOSE DAVID IS CLIMBING THE WALLS WAITING FOR YOU TO SHOW UP!
YEAH- I GUESS.
GOD, I HOPE THIS WORKS OUT- I'M JUST SO AMBIVALENT THESE DAYS- I HAVEN'T TOLD HIM BUT I'VE BEEN SEEING THIS OTHER GUY...
OH! TELL ME THE GORY DETAILS!
HAR HAR HAR! MINNIE, YOU SURE AS HELL KNOW HOW TO COMPLICATE YOUR LIFE!

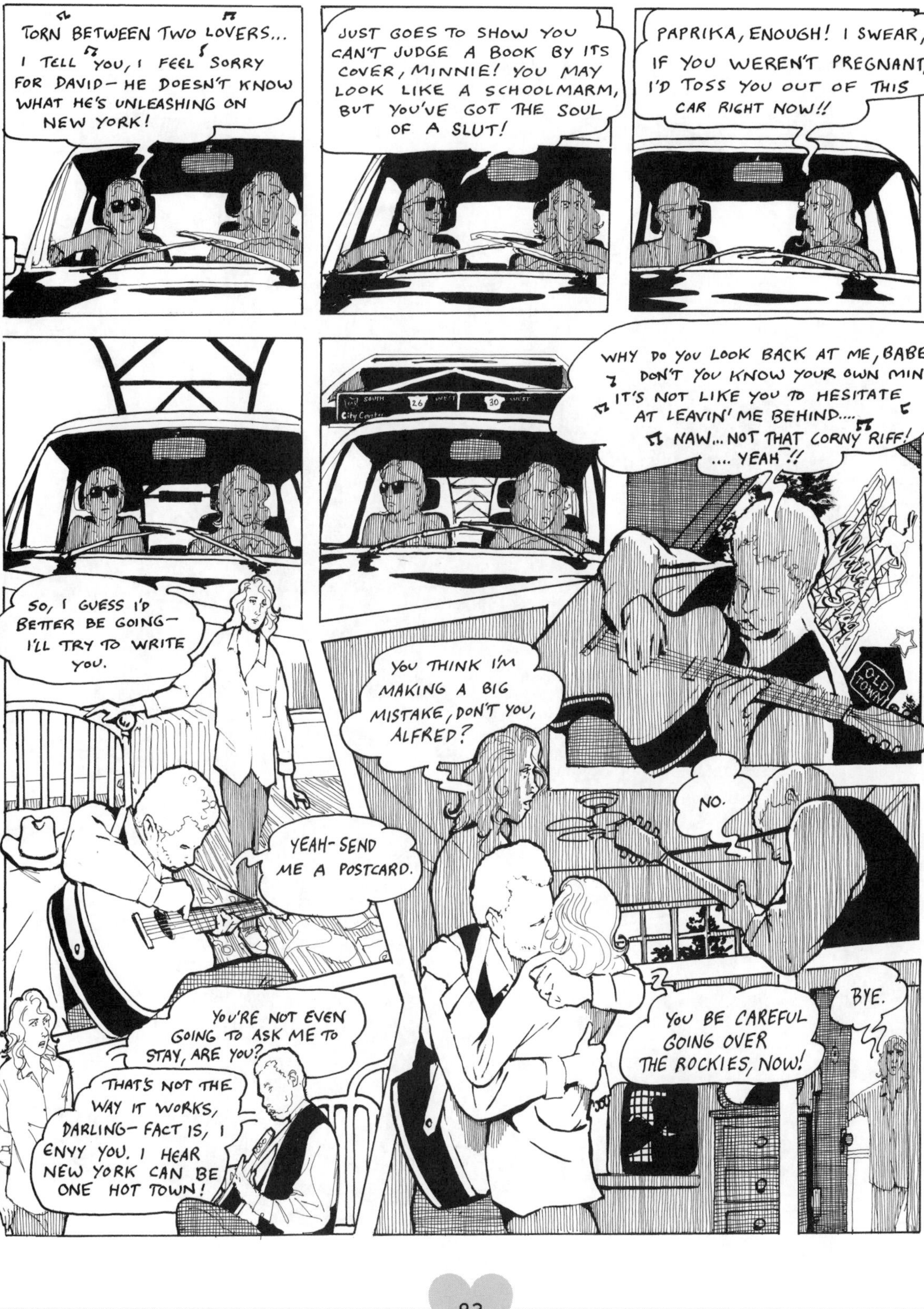
TORN BETWEEN TWO LOVERS...
I TELL YOU, I FEEL SORRY FOR DAVID– HE DOESN'T KNOW WHAT HE'S UNLEASHING ON NEW YORK!
JUST GOES TO SHOW YOU CAN'T JUDGE A BOOK BY ITS COVER, MINNIE! YOU MAY LOOK LIKE A SCHOOLMARM, BUT YOU'VE GOT THE SOUL OF A SLUT!
PAPRIKA, ENOUGH! I SWEAR, IF YOU WEREN'T PREGNANT, I'D TOSS YOU OUT OF THIS CAR RIGHT NOW!!
SOUTH 26 WEST 30 WEST
City Center
WHY DO YOU LOOK BACK AT ME, BABE? DON'T YOU KNOW YOUR OWN MIND? IT'S NOT LIKE YOU TO HESITATE AT LEAVIN' ME BEHIND....
NAW... NOT THAT CORNY RIFF! .... YEAH!!
OLD TOWN
SO, I GUESS I'D BETTER BE GOING– I'LL TRY TO WRITE YOU.
YEAH– SEND ME A POSTCARD.
YOU THINK I'M MAKING A BIG MISTAKE, DON'T YOU, ALFRED?
NO.
YOU'RE NOT EVEN GOING TO ASK ME TO STAY, ARE YOU?
THAT'S NOT THE WAY IT WORKS, DARLING– FACT IS, I ENVY YOU. I HEAR NEW YORK CAN BE ONE HOT TOWN!
YOU BE CAREFUL GOING OVER THE ROCKIES, NOW!
BYE.

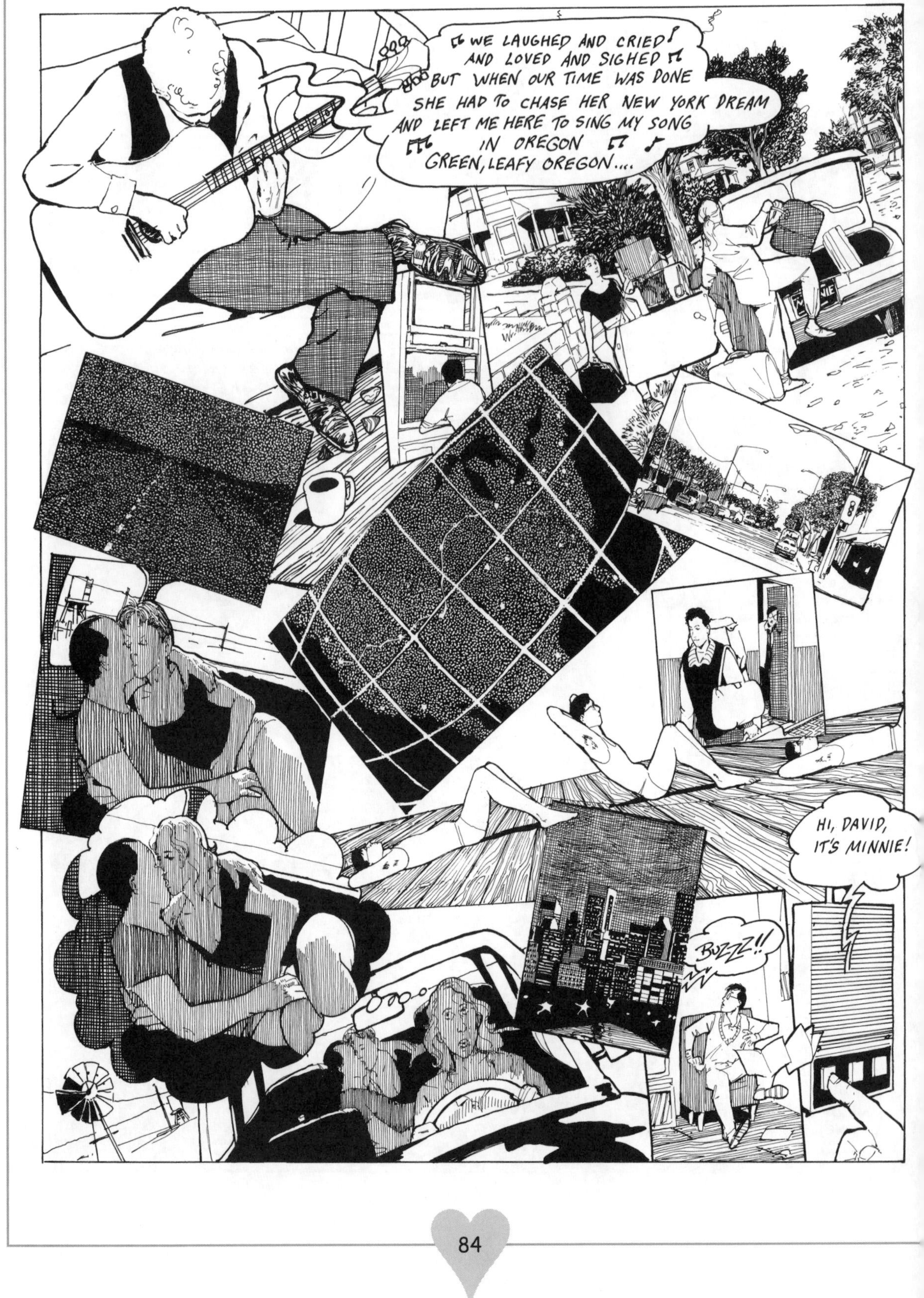
WE LAUGHED AND CRIED AND LOVED AND SIGHED BUT WHEN OUR TIME WAS DONE SHE HAD TO CHASE HER NEW YORK DREAM AND LEFT ME HERE TO SING MY SONG IN OREGON GREEN, LEAFY OREGON....
HI, DAVID, IT'S MINNIE!
BUZZZ!!

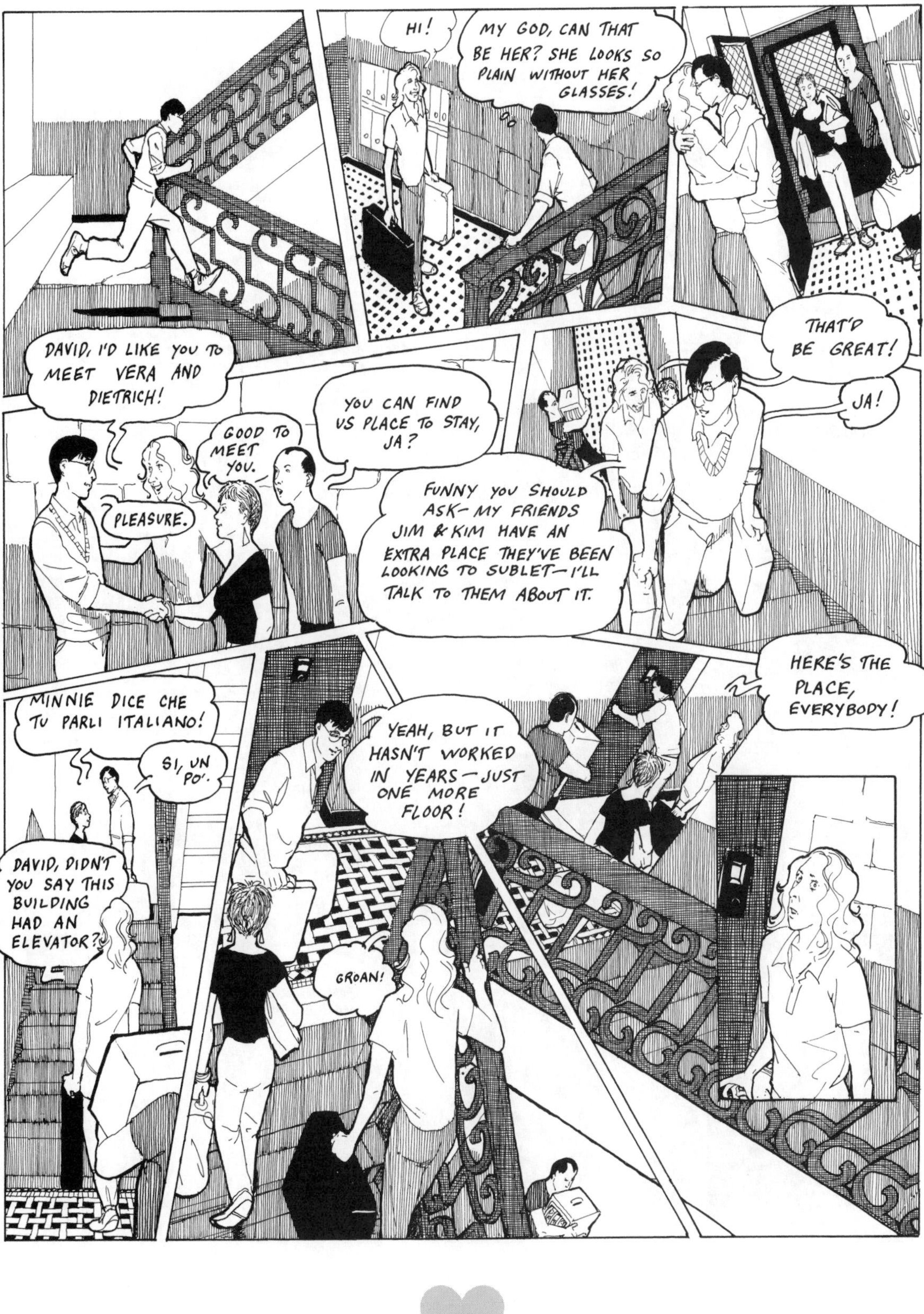
HI!
MY GOD, CAN THAT BE HER? SHE LOOKS SO PLAIN WITHOUT HER GLASSES!
DAVID, I'D LIKE YOU TO MEET VERA AND DIETRICH!
PLEASURE.
GOOD TO MEET YOU.
YOU CAN FIND US PLACE TO STAY, JA?
FUNNY YOU SHOULD ASK— MY FRIENDS JIM & KIM HAVE AN EXTRA PLACE THEY'VE BEEN LOOKING TO SUBLET— I'LL TALK TO THEM ABOUT IT.
THAT'D BE GREAT!
JA!
MINNIE DICE CHE TU PARLI ITALIANO!
SI, UN PO'.
DAVID, DIDN'T YOU SAY THIS BUILDING HAD AN ELEVATOR?
YEAH, BUT IT HASN'T WORKED IN YEARS— JUST ONE MORE FLOOR!
GROAN!
HERE'S THE PLACE, EVERYBODY!

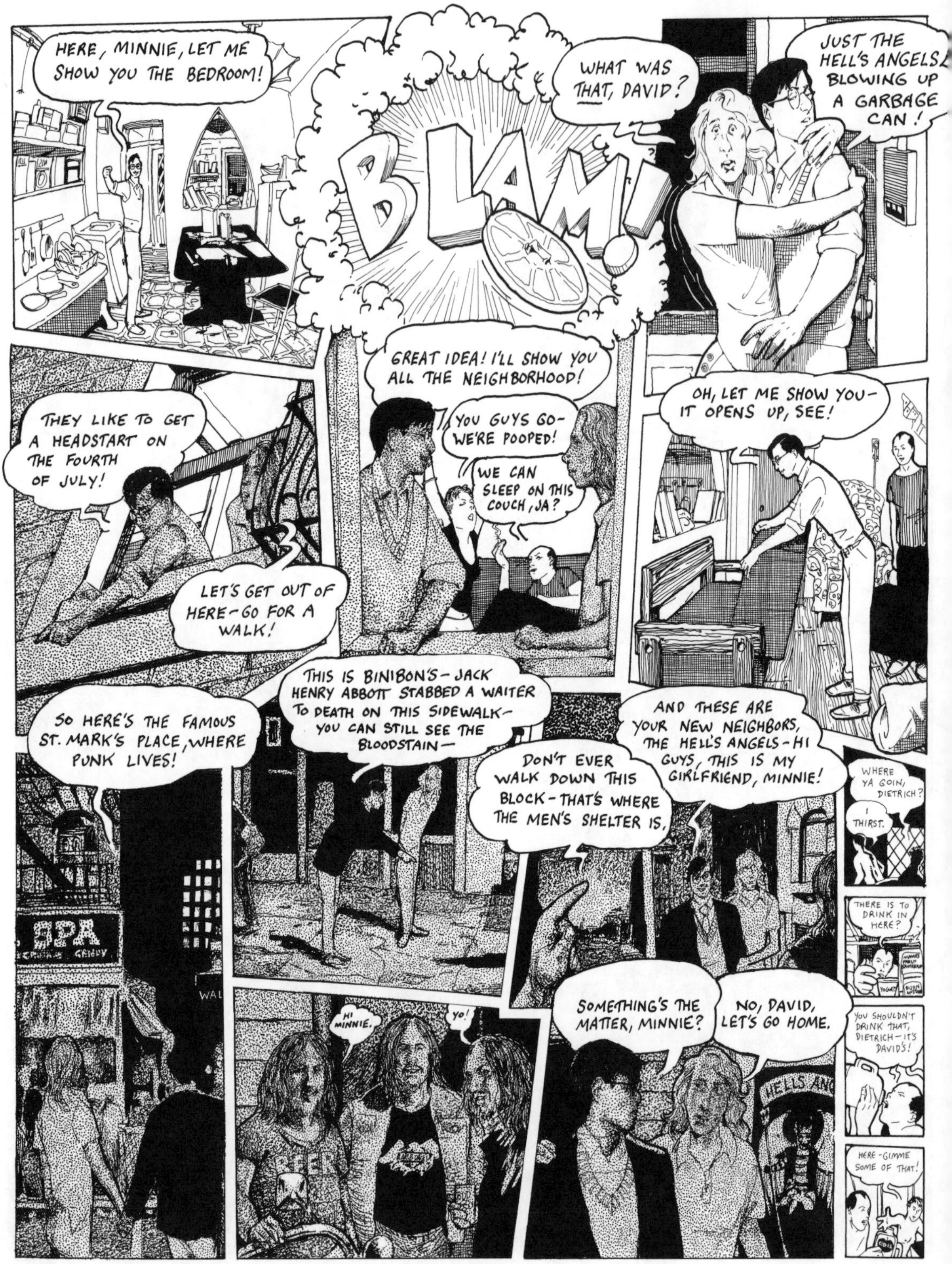
HERE, MINNIE, LET ME SHOW YOU THE BEDROOM!
BLAM!
WHAT WAS THAT, DAVID?
JUST THE HELL'S ANGELS BLOWING UP A GARBAGE CAN!
THEY LIKE TO GET A HEADSTART ON THE FOURTH OF JULY!
LET'S GET OUT OF HERE-GO FOR A WALK!
GREAT IDEA! I'LL SHOW YOU ALL THE NEIGHBORHOOD!
YOU GUYS GO-WE'RE POOPED!
WE CAN SLEEP ON THIS COUCH, JA?
OH, LET ME SHOW YOU-IT OPENS UP, SEE!
SO HERE'S THE FAMOUS ST. MARK'S PLACE, WHERE PUNK LIVES!
THIS IS BINIBON'S-JACK HENRY ABBOTT STABBED A WAITER TO DEATH ON THIS SIDEWALK-YOU CAN STILL SEE THE BLOODSTAIN-
DON'T EVER WALK DOWN THIS BLOCK-THAT'S WHERE THE MEN'S SHELTER IS.
AND THESE ARE YOUR NEW NEIGHBORS, THE HELL'S ANGELS-HI GUYS, THIS IS MY GIRLFRIEND, MINNIE!
WHERE YA GOIN, DIETRICH?
I THIRST.
THERE IS TO DRINK IN HERE?
YOGURT
HI MINNIE.
YO!
SOMETHING'S THE MATTER, MINNIE?
NO, DAVID, LET'S GO HOME.
YOU SHOULDN'T DRINK THAT, DIETRICH-IT'S DAVID'S!
HERE-GIMME SOME OF THAT!

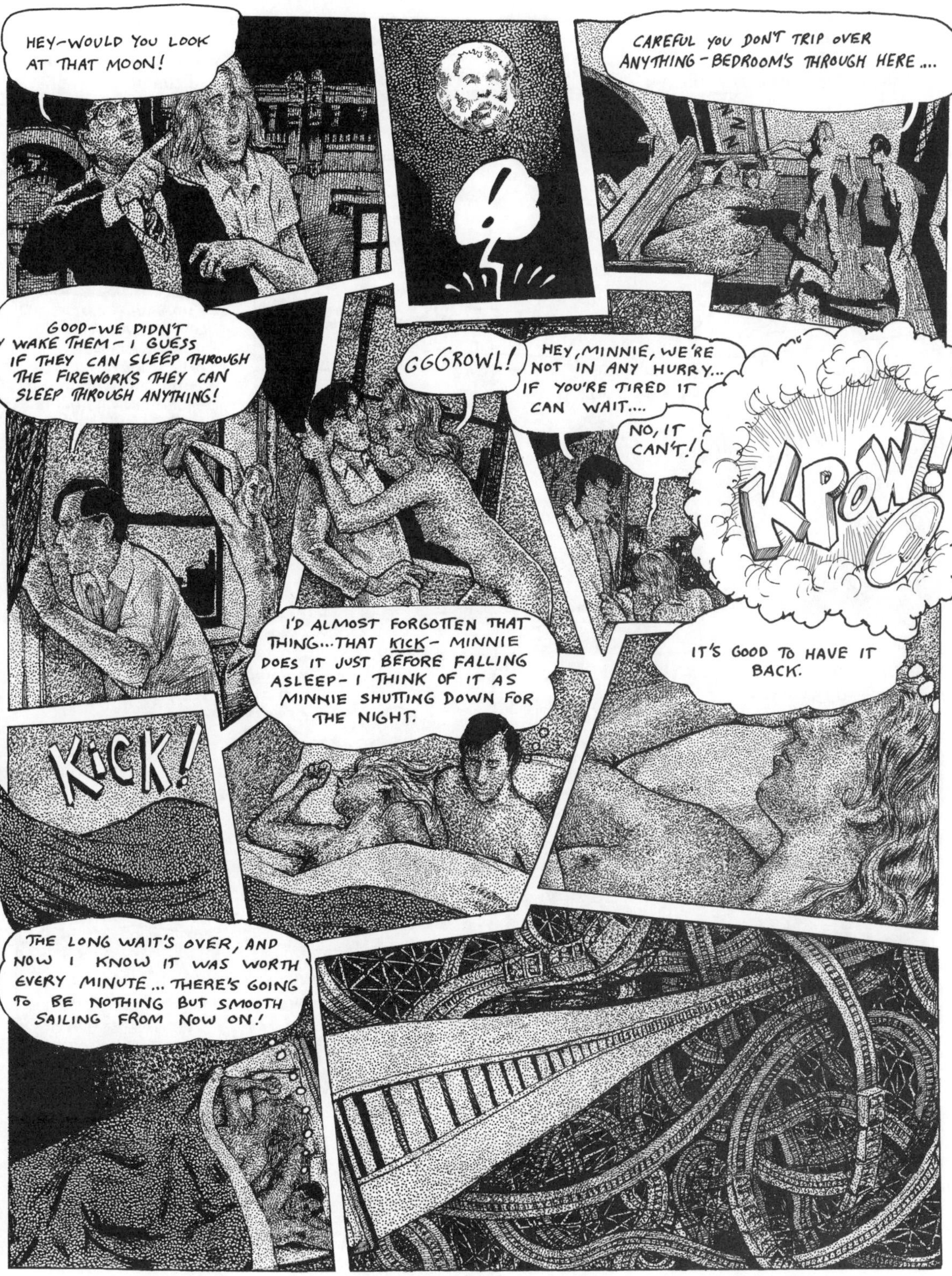

HEY-WOULD YOU LOOK AT THAT MOON!
!
CAREFUL YOU DON'T TRIP OVER ANYTHING-BEDROOM'S THROUGH HERE....
GOOD-WE DIDN'T WAKE THEM- I GUESS IF THEY CAN SLEEP THROUGH THE FIREWORKS THEY CAN SLEEP THROUGH ANYTHING!
GGGROWL!
HEY, MINNIE, WE'RE NOT IN ANY HURRY... IF YOU'RE TIRED IT CAN WAIT....
NO, IT CAN'T!
KPOW!
I'D ALMOST FORGOTTEN THAT THING...THAT KICK- MINNIE DOES IT JUST BEFORE FALLING ASLEEP- I THINK OF IT AS MINNIE SHUTTING DOWN FOR THE NIGHT.
KICK!
IT'S GOOD TO HAVE IT BACK.
THE LONG WAIT'S OVER, AND NOW I KNOW IT WAS WORTH EVERY MINUTE... THERE'S GOING TO BE NOTHING BUT SMOOTH SAILING FROM NOW ON!

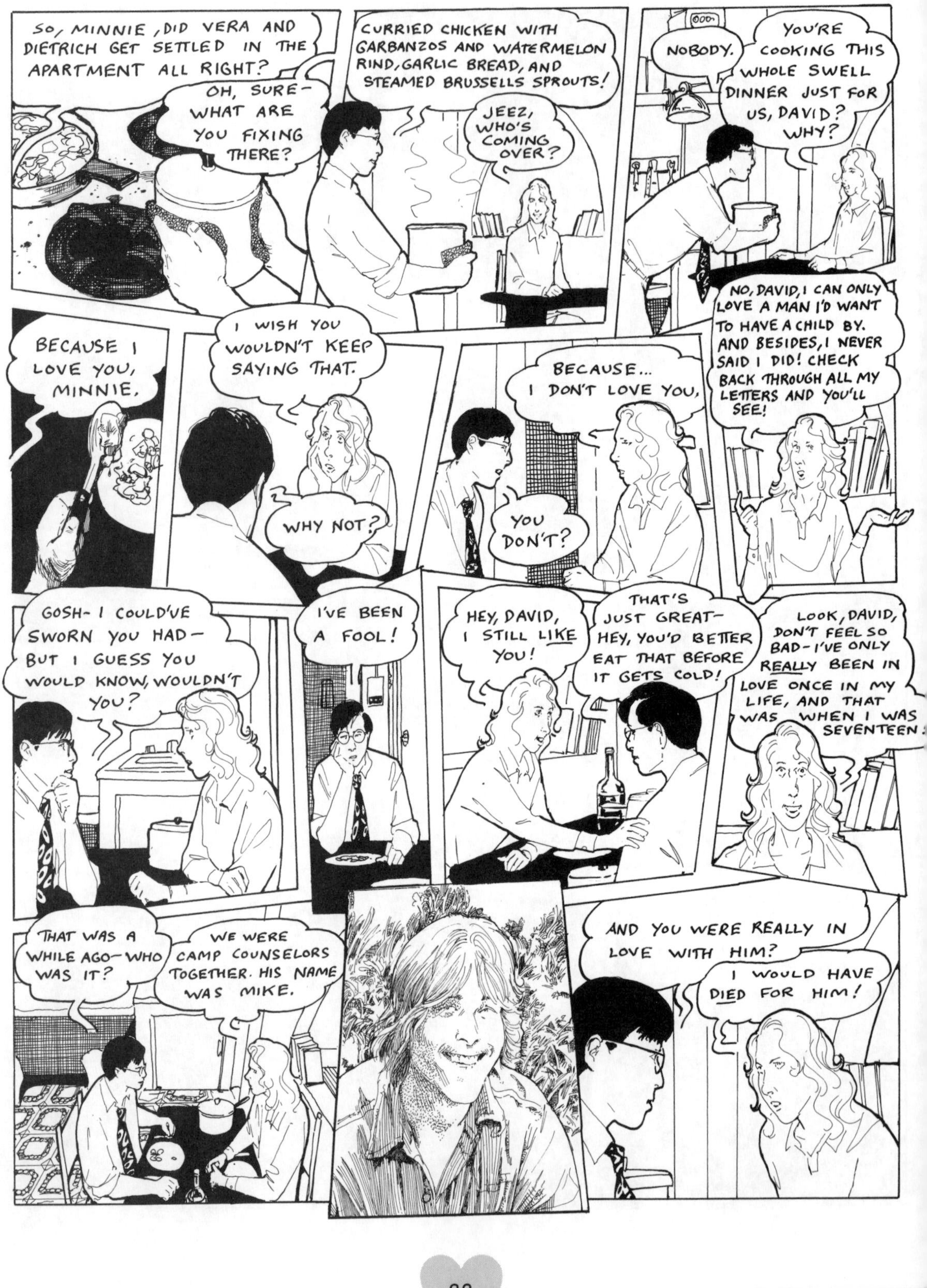
SO, MINNIE, DID VERA AND DIETRICH GET SETTLED IN THE APARTMENT ALL RIGHT?
OH, SURE- WHAT ARE YOU FIXING THERE?
CURRIED CHICKEN WITH GARBANZOS AND WATERMELON RIND, GARLIC BREAD, AND STEAMED BRUSSELLS SPROUTS!
JEEZ, WHO'S COMING OVER?
NOBODY.
YOU'RE COOKING THIS WHOLE SWELL DINNER JUST FOR US, DAVID? WHY?
BECAUSE I LOVE YOU, MINNIE.
I WISH YOU WOULDN'T KEEP SAYING THAT.
WHY NOT?
BECAUSE... I DON'T LOVE YOU.
YOU DON'T?
NO, DAVID, I CAN ONLY LOVE A MAN I'D WANT TO HAVE A CHILD BY. AND BESIDES, I NEVER SAID I DID! CHECK BACK THROUGH ALL MY LETTERS AND YOU'LL SEE!
GOSH- I COULD'VE SWORN YOU HAD- BUT I GUESS YOU WOULD KNOW, WOULDN'T YOU?
I'VE BEEN A FOOL!
HEY, DAVID, I STILL LIKE YOU!
THAT'S JUST GREAT- HEY, YOU'D BETTER EAT THAT BEFORE IT GETS COLD!
LOOK, DAVID, DON'T FEEL SO BAD- I'VE ONLY REALLY BEEN IN LOVE ONCE IN MY LIFE, AND THAT WAS WHEN I WAS SEVENTEEN.
THAT WAS A WHILE AGO- WHO WAS IT?
WE WERE CAMP COUNSELORS TOGETHER. HIS NAME WAS MIKE.
AND YOU WERE REALLY IN LOVE WITH HIM?
I WOULD HAVE DIED FOR HIM!

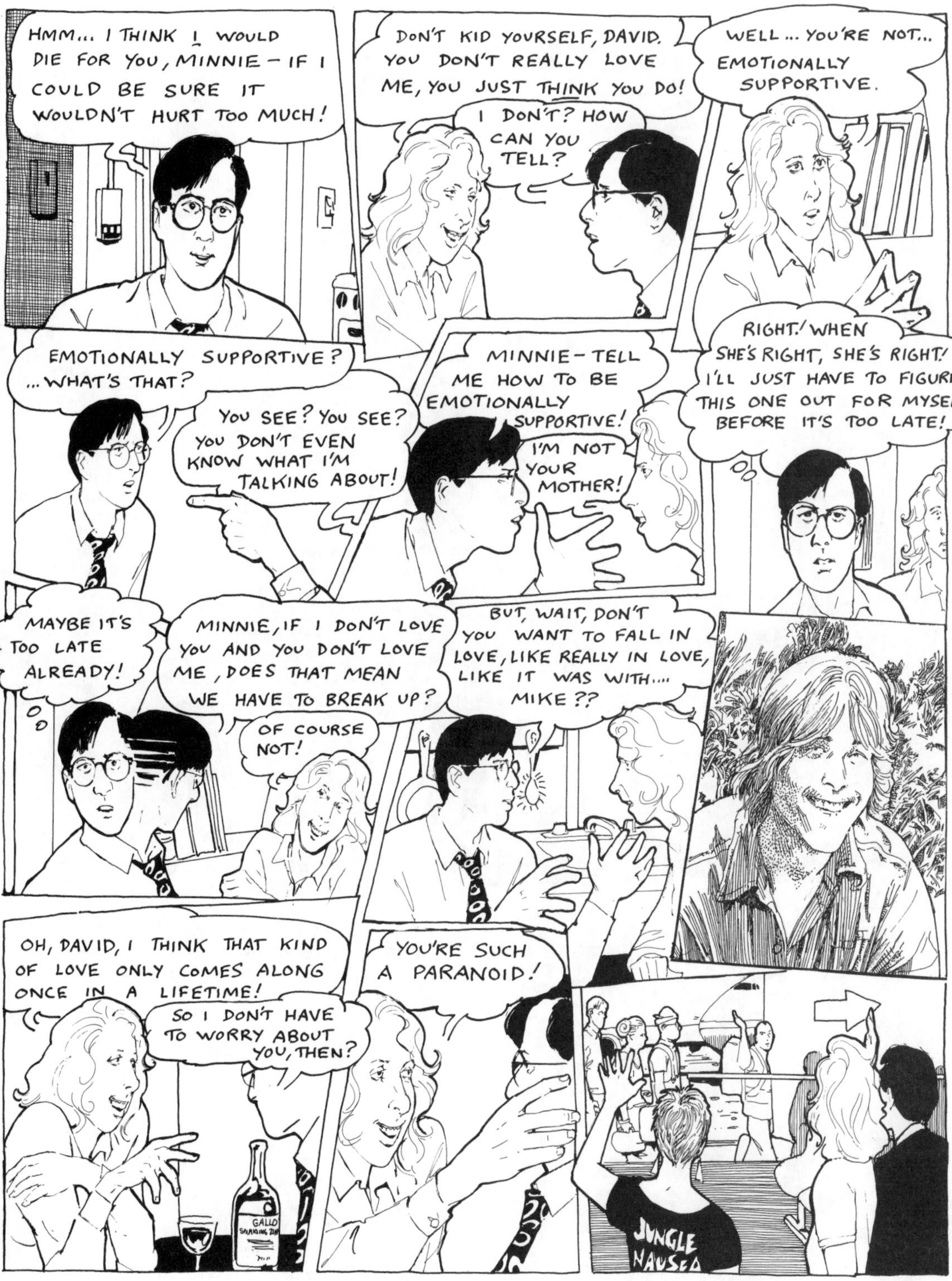

HMM... I THINK I WOULD DIE FOR YOU, MINNIE - IF I COULD BE SURE IT WOULDN'T HURT TOO MUCH!
DON'T KID YOURSELF, DAVID. YOU DON'T REALLY LOVE ME, YOU JUST THINK YOU DO!
I DON'T? HOW CAN YOU TELL?
WELL... YOU'RE NOT... EMOTIONALLY SUPPORTIVE.
EMOTIONALLY SUPPORTIVE? ...WHAT'S THAT?
YOU SEE? YOU SEE? YOU DON'T EVEN KNOW WHAT I'M TALKING ABOUT!
MINNIE - TELL ME HOW TO BE EMOTIONALLY SUPPORTIVE!
I'M NOT YOUR MOTHER!
RIGHT! WHEN SHE'S RIGHT, SHE'S RIGHT! I'LL JUST HAVE TO FIGURE THIS ONE OUT FOR MYSELF BEFORE IT'S TOO LATE!
MAYBE IT'S TOO LATE ALREADY!
MINNIE, IF I DON'T LOVE YOU AND YOU DON'T LOVE ME, DOES THAT MEAN WE HAVE TO BREAK UP?
OF COURSE NOT!
BUT, WAIT, DON'T YOU WANT TO FALL IN LOVE, LIKE REALLY IN LOVE, LIKE IT WAS WITH.... MIKE??
OH, DAVID, I THINK THAT KIND OF LOVE ONLY COMES ALONG ONCE IN A LIFETIME!
SO I DON'T HAVE TO WORRY ABOUT YOU, THEN?
YOU'RE SUCH A PARANOID!
GALLO
JUNGLE NAUSEA

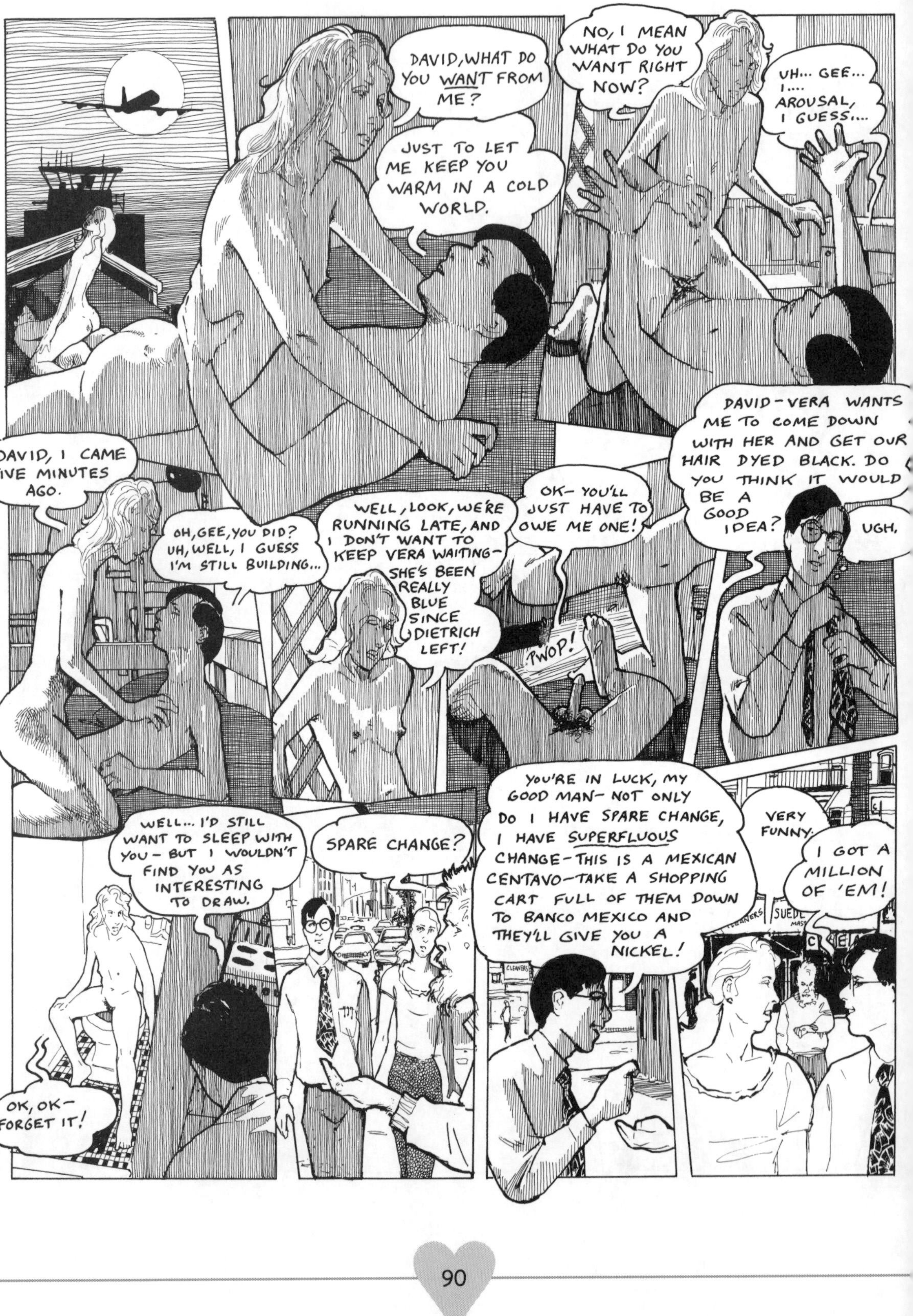
DAVID, WHAT DO YOU WANT FROM ME?
JUST TO LET ME KEEP YOU WARM IN A COLD WORLD.
NO, I MEAN WHAT DO YOU WANT RIGHT NOW?
UH... GEE... I.... AROUSAL, I GUESS....
DAVID, I CAME FIVE MINUTES AGO.
OH, GEE, YOU DID? UH, WELL, I GUESS I'M STILL BUILDING...
WELL, LOOK, WE'RE RUNNING LATE, AND I DON'T WANT TO KEEP VERA WAITING- SHE'S BEEN REALLY BLUE SINCE DIETRICH LEFT!
OK- YOU'LL JUST HAVE TO OWE ME ONE!
PWOP!
DAVID-VERA WANTS ME TO COME DOWN WITH HER AND GET OUR HAIR DYED BLACK. DO YOU THINK IT WOULD BE A GOOD IDEA?
UGH.
WELL... I'D STILL WANT TO SLEEP WITH YOU - BUT I WOULDN'T FIND YOU AS INTERESTING TO DRAW.
OK, OK- FORGET IT!
SPARE CHANGE?
YOU'RE IN LUCK, MY GOOD MAN- NOT ONLY DO I HAVE SPARE CHANGE, I HAVE SUPERFLUOUS CHANGE- THIS IS A MEXICAN CENTAVO- TAKE A SHOPPING CART FULL OF THEM DOWN TO BANCO MEXICO AND THEY'LL GIVE YOU A NICKEL!
VERY FUNNY.
I GOT A MILLION OF 'EM!

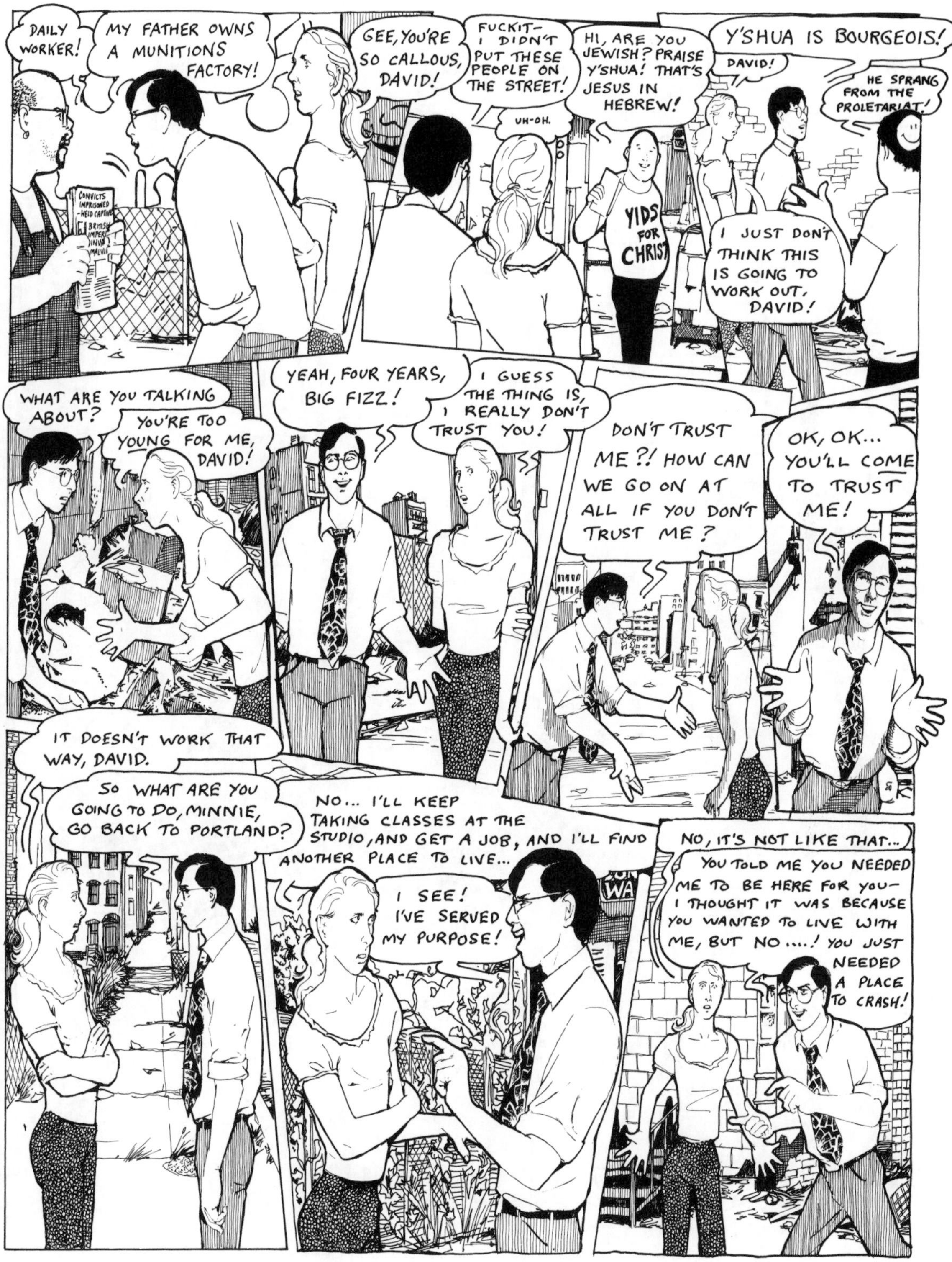
DAILY WORKER!
MY FATHER OWNS A MUNITIONS FACTORY!
CONVICTS IMPRISONED - HELD CAPTIVE
GEE, YOU'RE SO CALLOUS, DAVID!
FUCKIT- I DIDN'T PUT THESE PEOPLE ON THE STREET!
UH-OH.
HI, ARE YOU JEWISH? PRAISE Y'SHUA! THAT'S JESUS IN HEBREW!
YIDS FOR CHRIST
Y'SHUA IS BOURGEOIS!
DAVID!
HE SPRANG FROM THE PROLETARIAT!
I JUST DON'T THINK THIS IS GOING TO WORK OUT, DAVID!
WHAT ARE YOU TALKING ABOUT?
YOU'RE TOO YOUNG FOR ME, DAVID!
YEAH, FOUR YEARS, BIG FIZZ!
I GUESS THE THING IS, I REALLY DON'T TRUST YOU!
DON'T TRUST ME?! HOW CAN WE GO ON AT ALL IF YOU DON'T TRUST ME?
OK, OK... YOU'LL COME TO TRUST ME!
IT DOESN'T WORK THAT WAY, DAVID.
SO WHAT ARE YOU GOING TO DO, MINNIE, GO BACK TO PORTLAND?
NO... I'LL KEEP TAKING CLASSES AT THE STUDIO, AND GET A JOB, AND I'LL FIND ANOTHER PLACE TO LIVE...
I SEE! I'VE SERVED MY PURPOSE!
NO, IT'S NOT LIKE THAT...
YOU TOLD ME YOU NEEDED ME TO BE HERE FOR YOU- I THOUGHT IT WAS BECAUSE YOU WANTED TO LIVE WITH ME, BUT NO....! YOU JUST NEEDED A PLACE TO CRASH!

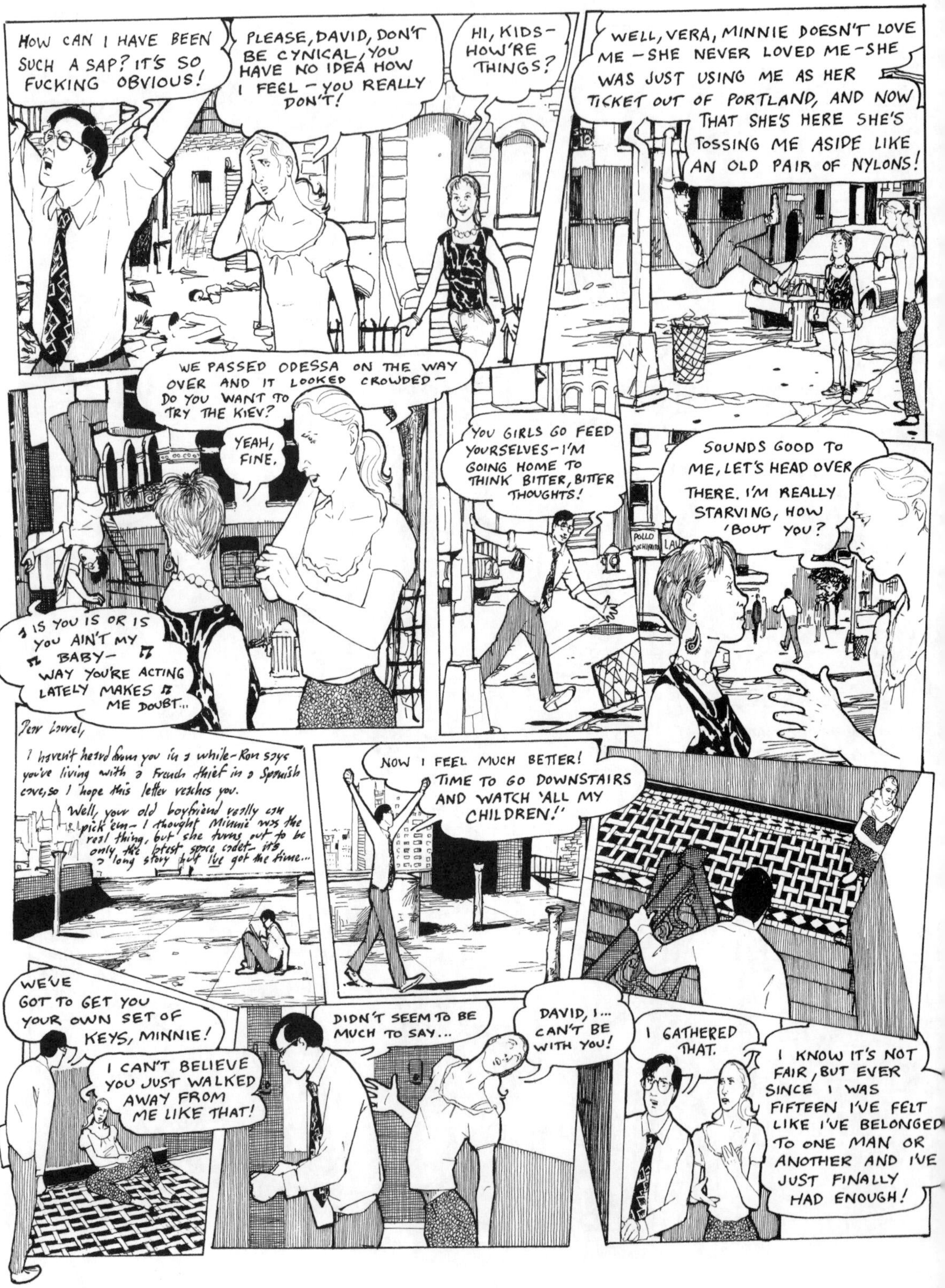

HOW CAN I HAVE BEEN SUCH A SAP? IT'S SO FUCKING OBVIOUS!
PLEASE, DAVID, DON'T BE CYNICAL, YOU HAVE NO IDEA HOW I FEEL - YOU REALLY DON'T!
HI, KIDS - HOW'RE THINGS?
WELL, VERA, MINNIE DOESN'T LOVE ME - SHE NEVER LOVED ME - SHE WAS JUST USING ME AS HER TICKET OUT OF PORTLAND, AND NOW THAT SHE'S HERE SHE'S TOSSING ME ASIDE LIKE AN OLD PAIR OF NYLONS!
WE PASSED ODESSA ON THE WAY OVER AND IT LOOKED CROWDED - DO YOU WANT TO TRY THE KIEV?
YEAH, FINE.
♪ IS YOU IS OR IS YOU AIN'T MY BABY - ♫ WAY YOU'RE ACTING LATELY MAKES ♫ ME DOUBT...
YOU GIRLS GO FEED YOURSELVES - I'M GOING HOME TO THINK BITTER, BITTER THOUGHTS!
SOUNDS GOOD TO ME, LET'S HEAD OVER THERE. I'M REALLY STARVING, HOW 'BOUT YOU?
POLLO
Dear Laurel,
I haven't heard from you in a while - Ron says you're living with a French thief in a Spanish cave, so I hope this letter reaches you.
Well, your old boyfriend really can pick 'em - I thought Minnie was the real thing, but she turns out to be only the latest space cadet - it's a long story but I've got the time...
NOW I FEEL MUCH BETTER! TIME TO GO DOWNSTAIRS AND WATCH 'ALL MY CHILDREN.'
WE'VE GOT TO GET YOU YOUR OWN SET OF KEYS, MINNIE!
I CAN'T BELIEVE YOU JUST WALKED AWAY FROM ME LIKE THAT!
DIDN'T SEEM TO BE MUCH TO SAY...
DAVID, I... CAN'T BE WITH YOU!
I GATHERED THAT.
I KNOW IT'S NOT FAIR, BUT EVER SINCE I WAS FIFTEEN I'VE FELT LIKE I'VE BELONGED TO ONE MAN OR ANOTHER AND I'VE JUST FINALLY HAD ENOUGH!

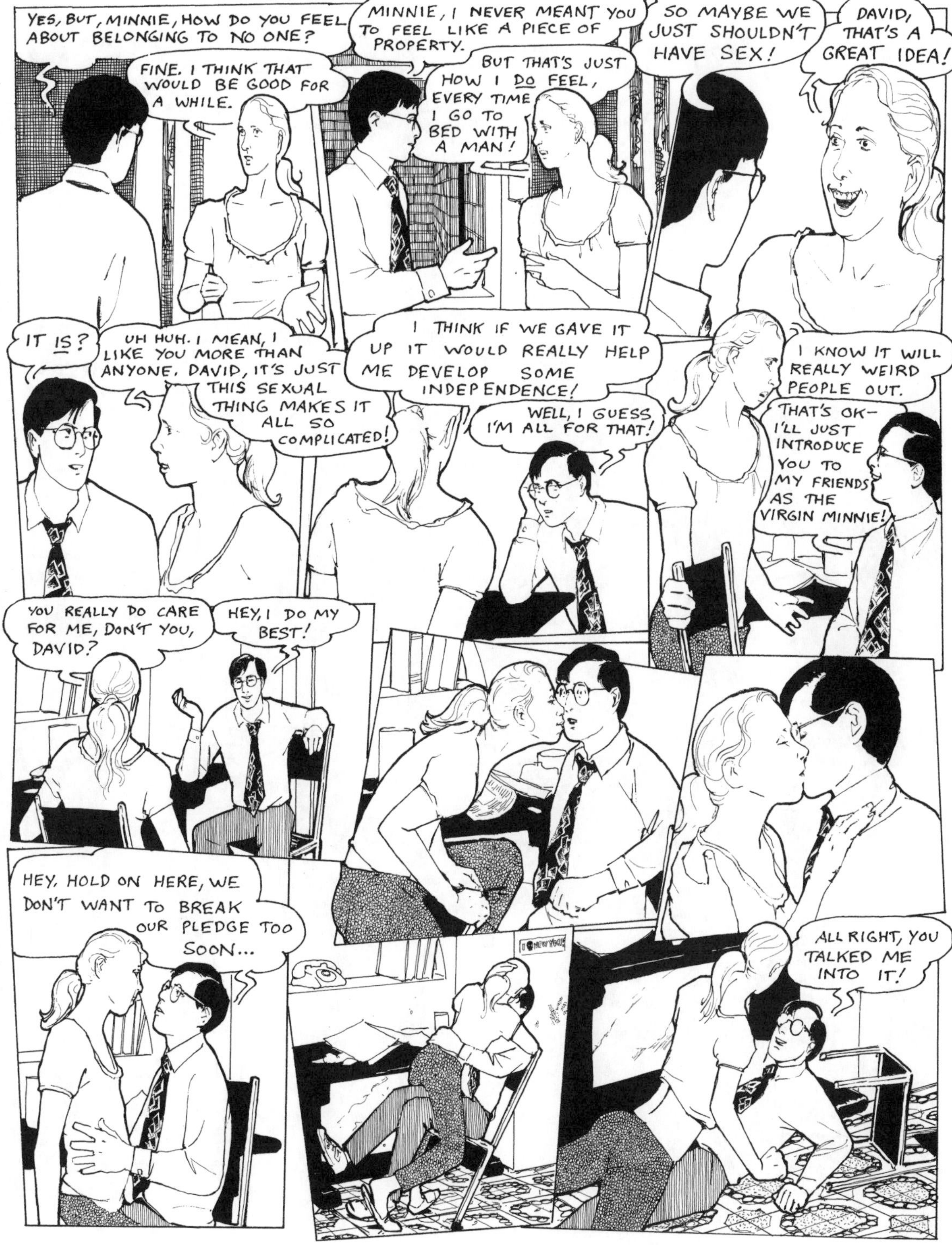
YES, BUT, MINNIE, HOW DO YOU FEEL ABOUT BELONGING TO NO ONE?
FINE. I THINK THAT WOULD BE GOOD FOR A WHILE.
MINNIE, I NEVER MEANT YOU TO FEEL LIKE A PIECE OF PROPERTY.
BUT THAT'S JUST HOW I DO FEEL, EVERY TIME I GO TO BED WITH A MAN!
SO MAYBE WE JUST SHOULDN'T HAVE SEX!
DAVID, THAT'S A GREAT IDEA!
IT IS?
UH HUH. I MEAN, I LIKE YOU MORE THAN ANYONE, DAVID, IT'S JUST THIS SEXUAL THING MAKES IT ALL SO COMPLICATED!
I THINK IF WE GAVE IT UP IT WOULD REALLY HELP ME DEVELOP SOME INDEPENDENCE!
WELL, I GUESS I'M ALL FOR THAT!
I KNOW IT WILL REALLY WEIRD PEOPLE OUT.
THAT'S OK— I'LL JUST INTRODUCE YOU TO MY FRIENDS AS THE VIRGIN MINNIE!
YOU REALLY DO CARE FOR ME, DON'T YOU, DAVID?
HEY, I DO MY BEST!
HEY, HOLD ON HERE, WE DON'T WANT TO BREAK OUR PLEDGE TOO SOON...
ALL RIGHT, YOU TALKED ME INTO IT!

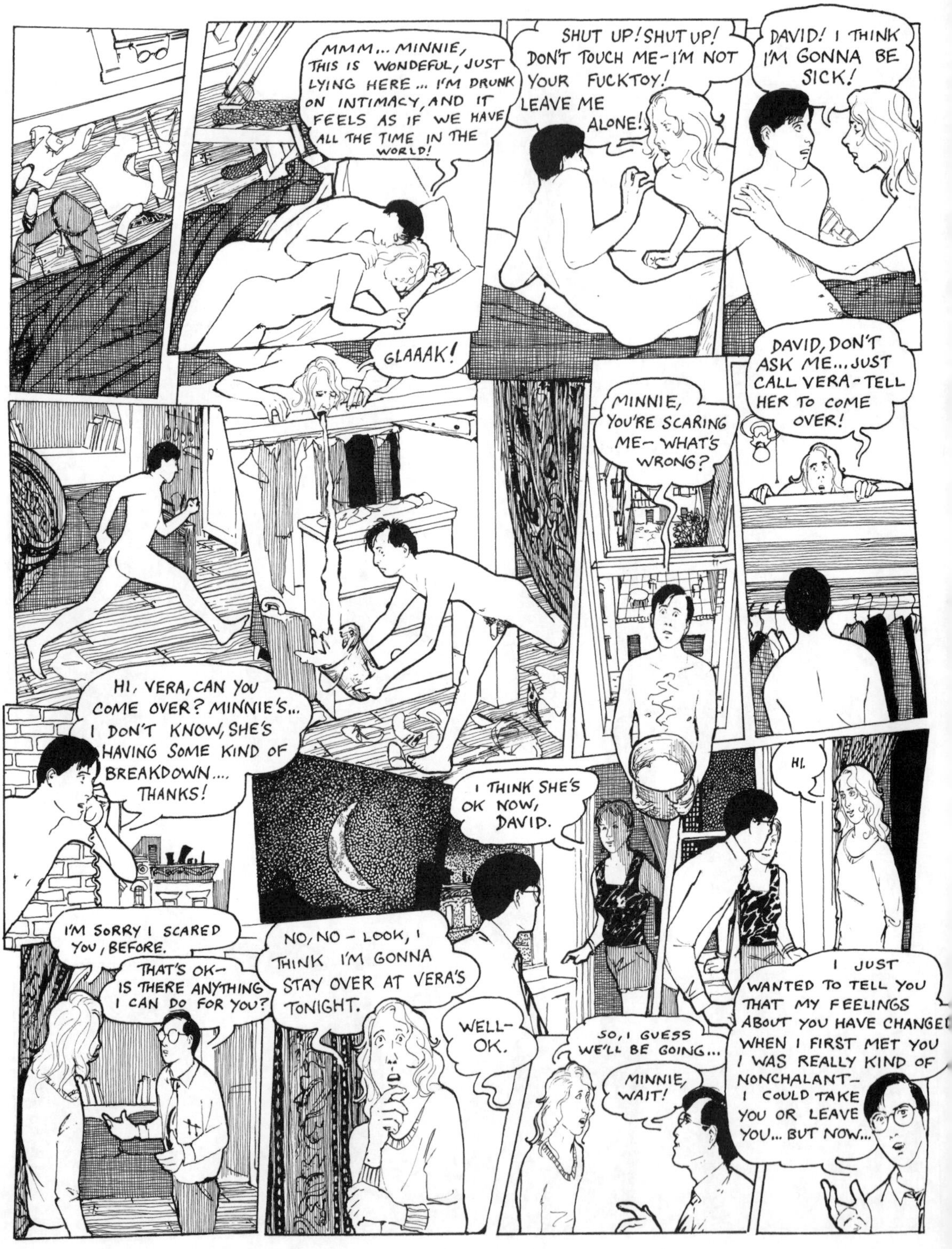
MMM... MINNIE, THIS IS WONDEFUL, JUST LYING HERE... I'M DRUNK ON INTIMACY, AND IT FEELS AS IF WE HAVE ALL THE TIME IN THE WORLD!
SHUT UP! SHUT UP! DON'T TOUCH ME- I'M NOT YOUR FUCKTOY! LEAVE ME ALONE!
DAVID! I THINK I'M GONNA BE SICK!
GLAAAK!
MINNIE, YOU'RE SCARING ME- WHAT'S WRONG?
DAVID, DON'T ASK ME... JUST CALL VERA- TELL HER TO COME OVER!
HI, VERA, CAN YOU COME OVER? MINNIE'S... I DON'T KNOW, SHE'S HAVING SOME KIND OF BREAKDOWN.... THANKS!
I THINK SHE'S OK NOW, DAVID.
HI.
I'M SORRY I SCARED YOU, BEFORE.
THAT'S OK- IS THERE ANYTHING I CAN DO FOR YOU?
NO, NO - LOOK, I THINK I'M GONNA STAY OVER AT VERA'S TONIGHT.
WELL- OK.
SO, I GUESS WE'LL BE GOING...
MINNIE, WAIT!
I JUST WANTED TO TELL YOU THAT MY FEELINGS ABOUT YOU HAVE CHANGED WHEN I FIRST MET YOU I WAS REALLY KIND OF NONCHALANT- I COULD TAKE YOU OR LEAVE YOU... BUT NOW...

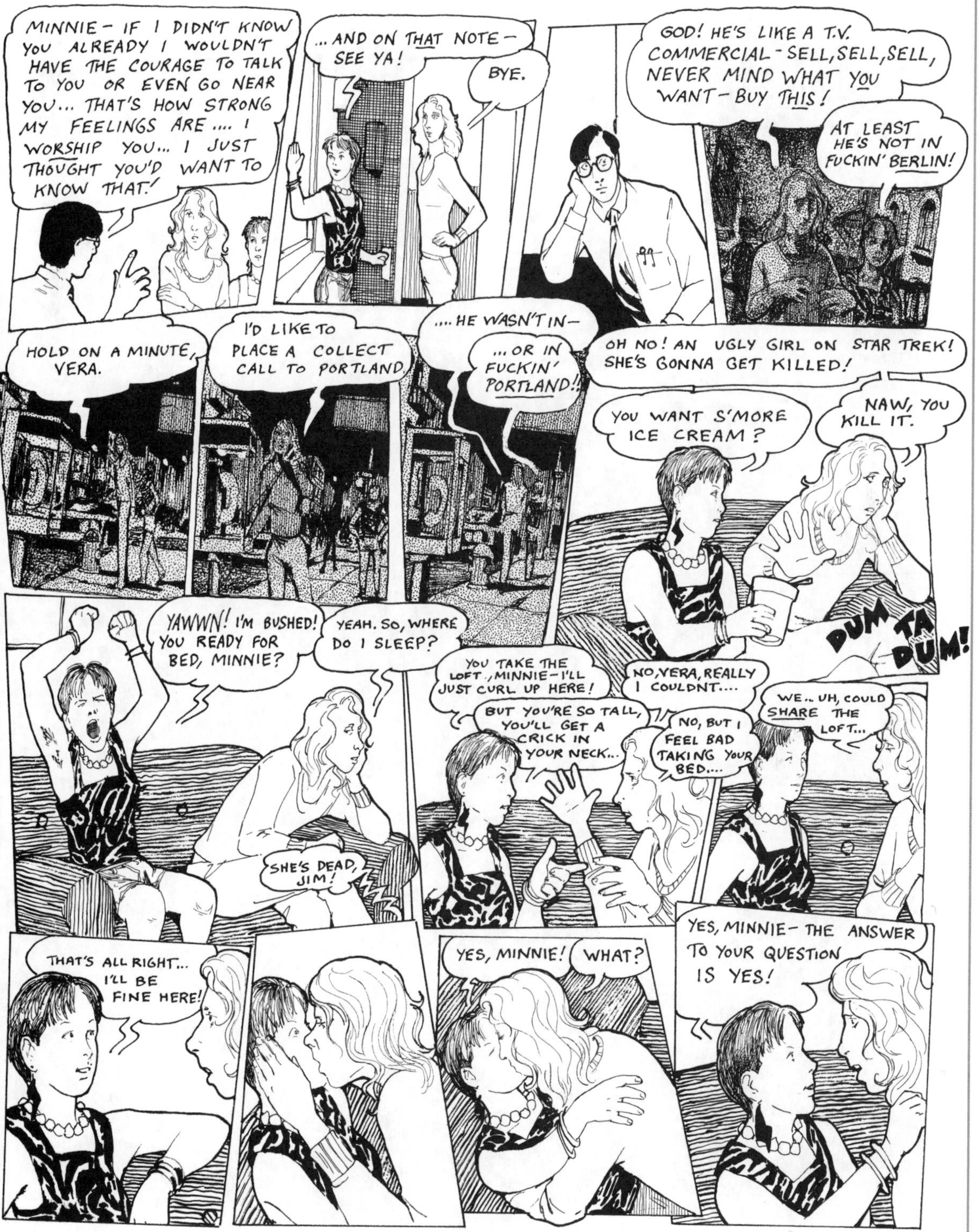
MINNIE- IF I DIDN'T KNOW YOU ALREADY I WOULDN'T HAVE THE COURAGE TO TALK TO YOU OR EVEN GO NEAR YOU... THAT'S HOW STRONG MY FEELINGS ARE .... I WORSHIP YOU... I JUST THOUGHT YOU'D WANT TO KNOW THAT!
...AND ON THAT NOTE- SEE YA!
BYE.
GOD! HE'S LIKE A T.V. COMMERCIAL- SELL, SELL, SELL, NEVER MIND WHAT YOU WANT- BUY THIS!
AT LEAST HE'S NOT IN FUCKIN' BERLIN!
HOLD ON A MINUTE, VERA.
I'D LIKE TO PLACE A COLLECT CALL TO PORTLAND
.... HE WASN'T IN-
...OR IN FUCKIN' PORTLAND!!
OH NO! AN UGLY GIRL ON STAR TREK! SHE'S GONNA GET KILLED!
YOU WANT S'MORE ICE CREAM?
NAW, YOU KILL IT.
DUM TA DUM!
YAWWN! I'M BUSHED! YOU READY FOR BED, MINNIE?
YEAH. SO, WHERE DO I SLEEP?
SHE'S DEAD, JIM!
YOU TAKE THE LOFT, MINNIE- I'LL JUST CURL UP HERE!
NO, VERA, REALLY I COULDNT....
BUT YOU'RE SO TALL, YOU'LL GET A CRICK IN YOUR NECK...
NO, BUT I FEEL BAD TAKING YOUR BED....
WE.. UH, COULD SHARE THE LOFT...
THAT'S ALL RIGHT... I'LL BE FINE HERE!
YES, MINNIE!
WHAT?
YES, MINNIE- THE ANSWER TO YOUR QUESTION IS YES!

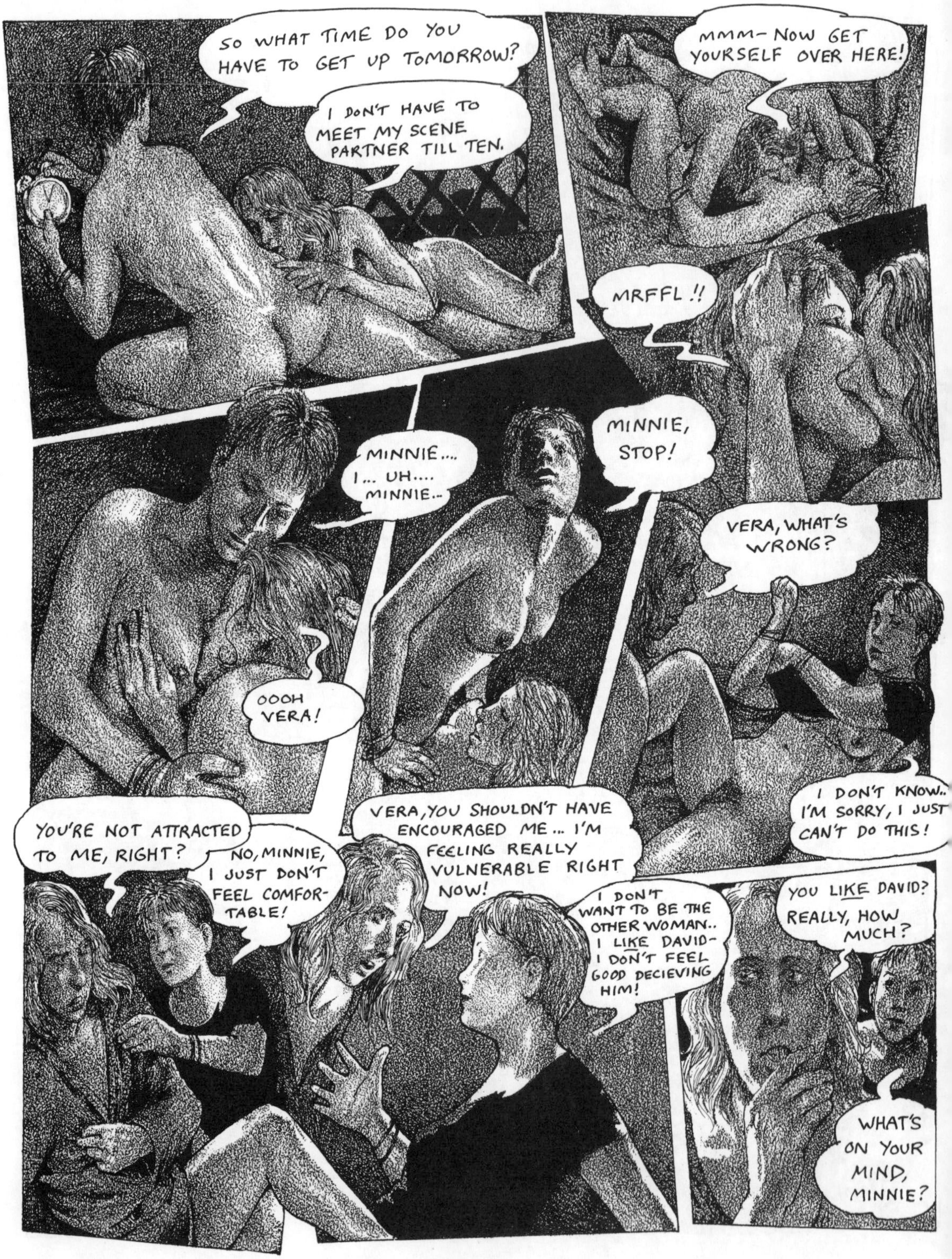
SO WHAT TIME DO YOU HAVE TO GET UP TOMORROW?
I DON'T HAVE TO MEET MY SCENE PARTNER TILL TEN.
MMM- NOW GET YOURSELF OVER HERE!
MRFFL !!
MINNIE.... I... UH.... MINNIE...
OOOH VERA!
MINNIE, STOP!
VERA, WHAT'S WRONG?
I DON'T KNOW.. I'M SORRY, I JUST CAN'T DO THIS!
YOU'RE NOT ATTRACTED TO ME, RIGHT?
NO, MINNIE, I JUST DON'T FEEL COMFORTABLE!
VERA, YOU SHOULDN'T HAVE ENCOURAGED ME... I'M FEELING REALLY VULNERABLE RIGHT NOW!
I DON'T WANT TO BE THE OTHER WOMAN.. I LIKE DAVID- I DON'T FEEL GOOD DECIEVING HIM!
YOU LIKE DAVID? REALLY, HOW MUCH?
WHAT'S ON YOUR MIND, MINNIE?

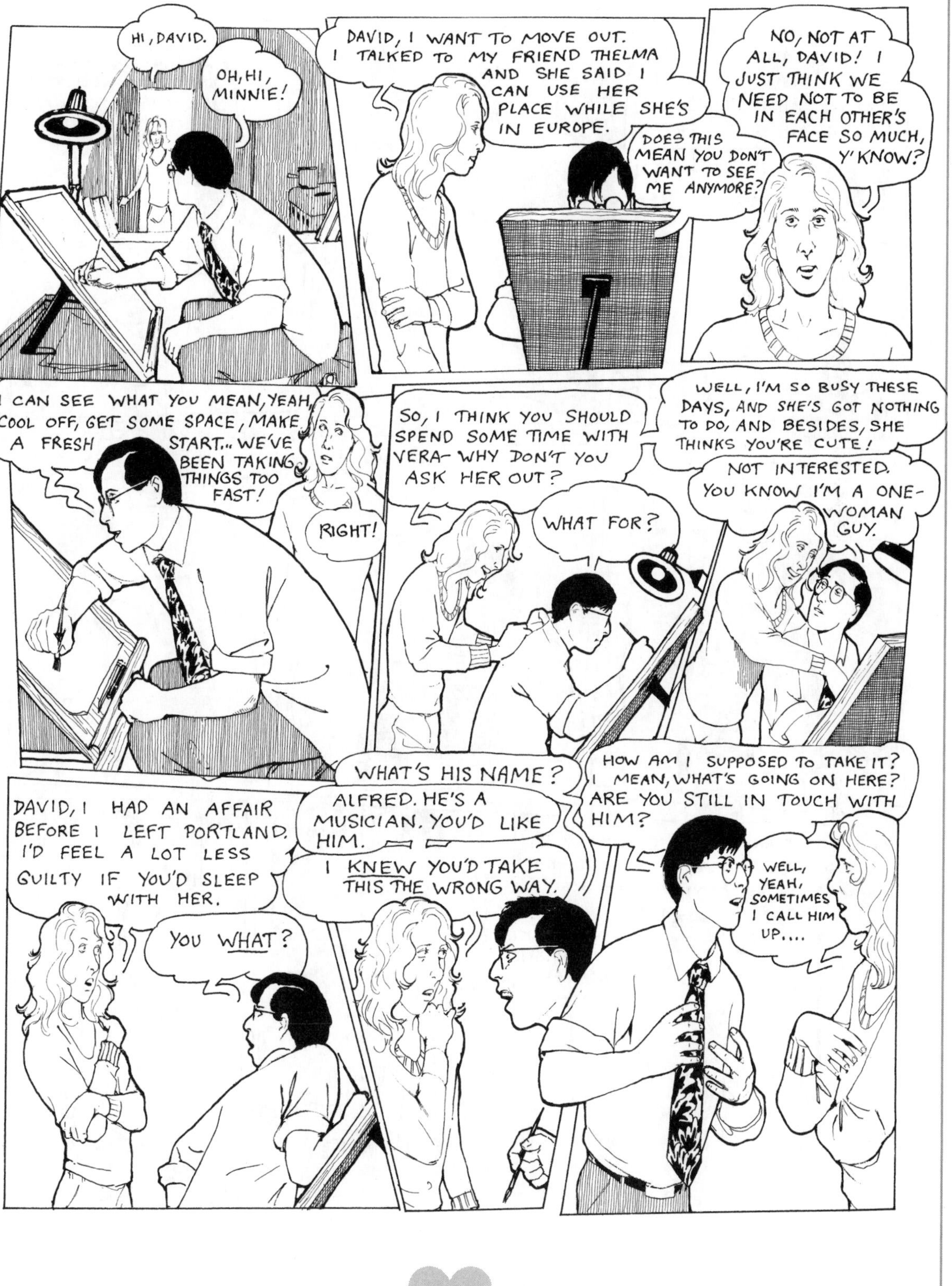
HI, DAVID.
OH, HI, MINNIE!
DAVID, I WANT TO MOVE OUT. I TALKED TO MY FRIEND THELMA AND SHE SAID I CAN USE HER PLACE WHILE SHE'S IN EUROPE.
DOES THIS MEAN YOU DON'T WANT TO SEE ME ANYMORE?
NO, NOT AT ALL, DAVID! I JUST THINK WE NEED NOT TO BE IN EACH OTHER'S FACE SO MUCH, Y'KNOW?
I CAN SEE WHAT YOU MEAN, YEAH, COOL OFF, GET SOME SPACE, MAKE A FRESH START.. WE'VE BEEN TAKING THINGS TOO FAST!
RIGHT!
SO, I THINK YOU SHOULD SPEND SOME TIME WITH VERA- WHY DON'T YOU ASK HER OUT?
WHAT FOR?
WELL, I'M SO BUSY THESE DAYS, AND SHE'S GOT NOTHING TO DO, AND BESIDES, SHE THINKS YOU'RE CUTE!
NOT INTERESTED. YOU KNOW I'M A ONE-WOMAN GUY.
DAVID, I HAD AN AFFAIR BEFORE I LEFT PORTLAND. I'D FEEL A LOT LESS GUILTY IF YOU'D SLEEP WITH HER.
YOU WHAT?
WHAT'S HIS NAME?
ALFRED. HE'S A MUSICIAN. YOU'D LIKE HIM.
I KNEW YOU'D TAKE THIS THE WRONG WAY.
HOW AM I SUPPOSED TO TAKE IT? I MEAN, WHAT'S GOING ON HERE? ARE YOU STILL IN TOUCH WITH HIM?
WELL, YEAH, SOMETIMES I CALL HIM UP....

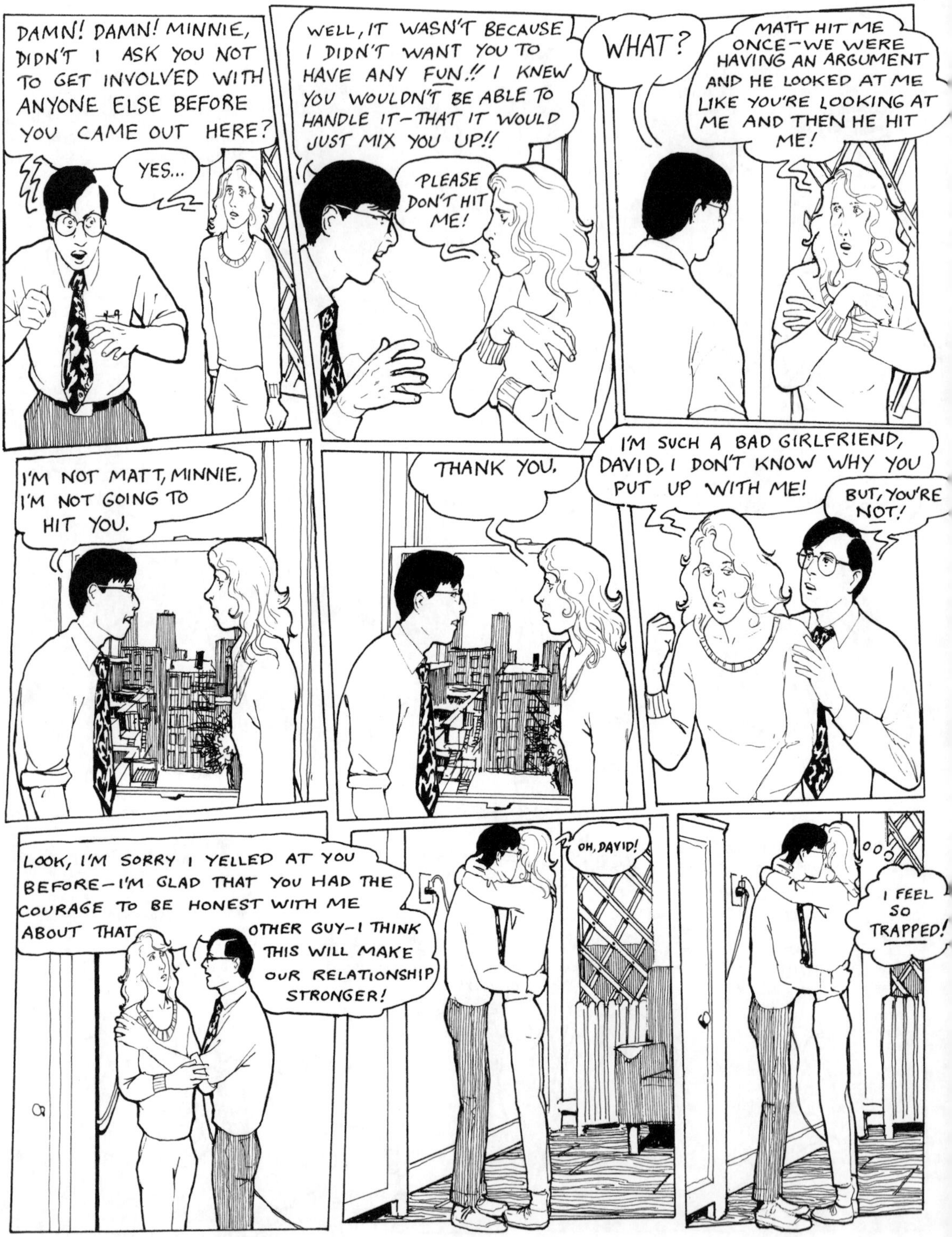
DAMN! DAMN! MINNIE, DIDN'T I ASK YOU NOT TO GET INVOLVED WITH ANYONE ELSE BEFORE YOU CAME OUT HERE?
YES...
WELL, IT WASN'T BECAUSE I DIDN'T WANT YOU TO HAVE ANY FUN!! I KNEW YOU WOULDN'T BE ABLE TO HANDLE IT—THAT IT WOULD JUST MIX YOU UP!!
PLEASE DON'T HIT ME!
WHAT?
MATT HIT ME ONCE—WE WERE HAVING AN ARGUMENT AND HE LOOKED AT ME LIKE YOU'RE LOOKING AT ME AND THEN HE HIT ME!
I'M NOT MATT, MINNIE. I'M NOT GOING TO HIT YOU.
THANK YOU.
I'M SUCH A BAD GIRLFRIEND, DAVID, I DON'T KNOW WHY YOU PUT UP WITH ME!
BUT, YOU'RE NOT!
LOOK, I'M SORRY I YELLED AT YOU BEFORE—I'M GLAD THAT YOU HAD THE COURAGE TO BE HONEST WITH ME ABOUT THAT OTHER GUY—I THINK THIS WILL MAKE OUR RELATIONSHIP STRONGER!
OH, DAVID!
I FEEL SO TRAPPED!

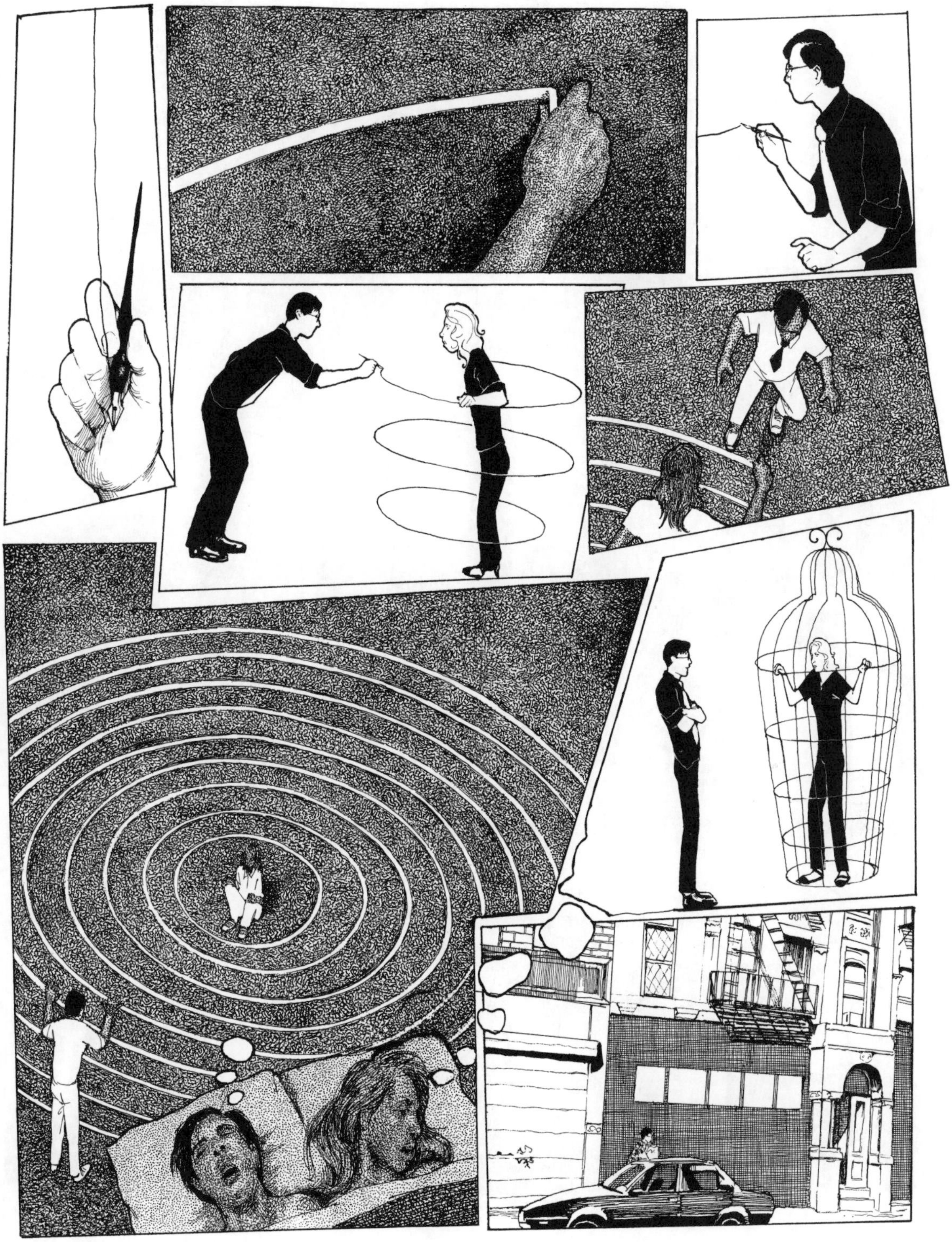

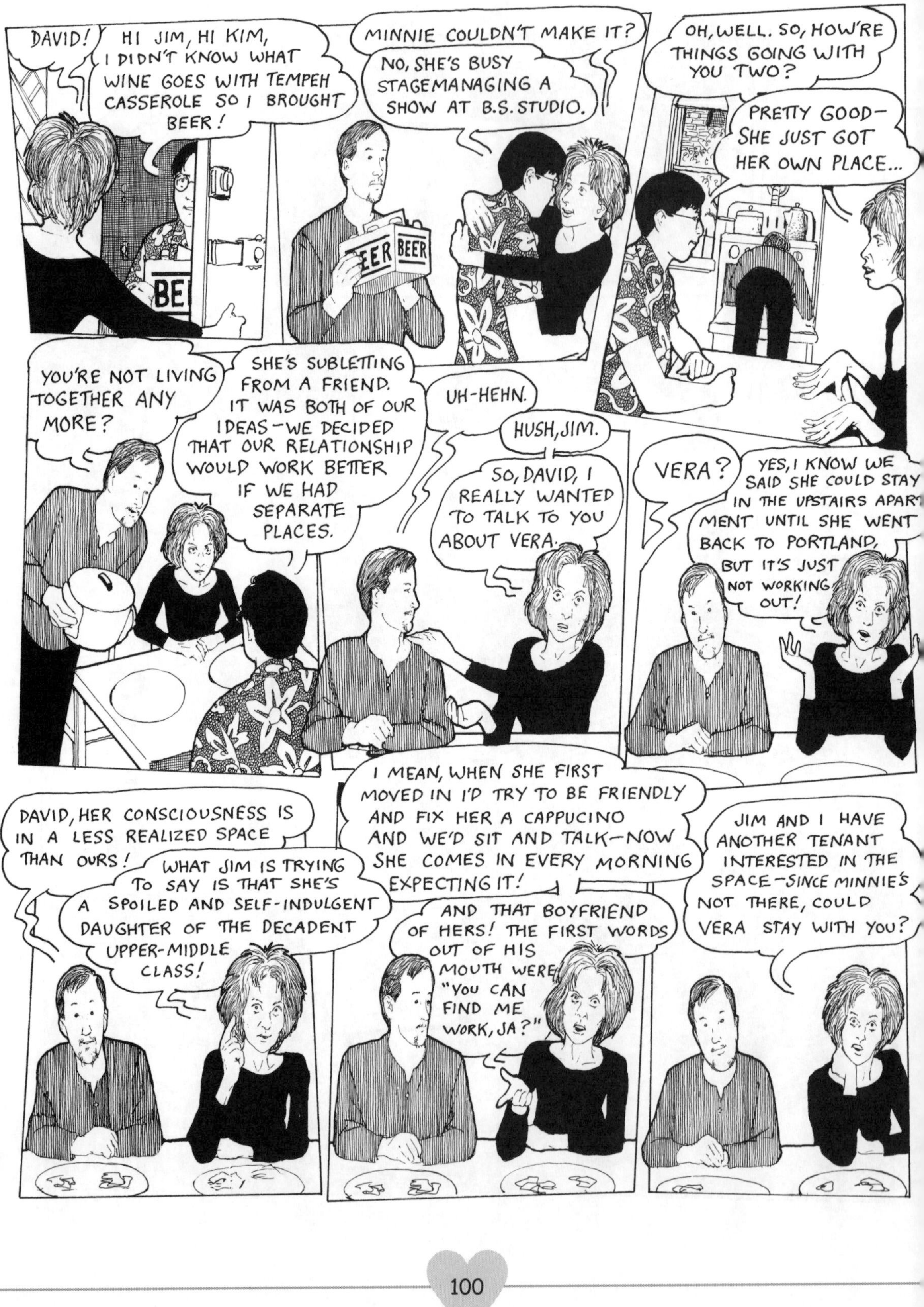
DAVID!
HI JIM, HI KIM, I DIDN'T KNOW WHAT WINE GOES WITH TEMPEH CASSEROLE SO I BROUGHT BEER!
BEER
BEER
BEER
MINNIE COULDN'T MAKE IT?
NO, SHE'S BUSY STAGEMANAGING A SHOW AT B.S. STUDIO.
OH, WELL. SO, HOW'RE THINGS GOING WITH YOU TWO?
PRETTY GOOD—SHE JUST GOT HER OWN PLACE...
YOU'RE NOT LIVING TOGETHER ANY MORE?
SHE'S SUBLETTING FROM A FRIEND. IT WAS BOTH OF OUR IDEAS—WE DECIDED THAT OUR RELATIONSHIP WOULD WORK BETTER IF WE HAD SEPARATE PLACES.
UH-HEHN.
HUSH, JIM.
SO, DAVID, I REALLY WANTED TO TALK TO YOU ABOUT VERA.
VERA?
YES, I KNOW WE SAID SHE COULD STAY IN THE UPSTAIRS APARTMENT UNTIL SHE WENT BACK TO PORTLAND, BUT IT'S JUST NOT WORKING OUT!
DAVID, HER CONSCIOUSNESS IS IN A LESS REALIZED SPACE THAN OURS!
WHAT JIM IS TRYING TO SAY IS THAT SHE'S A SPOILED AND SELF-INDULGENT DAUGHTER OF THE DECADENT UPPER-MIDDLE CLASS!
I MEAN, WHEN SHE FIRST MOVED IN I'D TRY TO BE FRIENDLY AND FIX HER A CAPPUCINO AND WE'D SIT AND TALK—NOW SHE COMES IN EVERY MORNING EXPECTING IT!
AND THAT BOYFRIEND OF HERS! THE FIRST WORDS OUT OF HIS MOUTH WERE "YOU CAN FIND ME WORK, JA?"
JIM AND I HAVE ANOTHER TENANT INTERESTED IN THE SPACE—SINCE MINNIE'S NOT THERE, COULD VERA STAY WITH YOU?

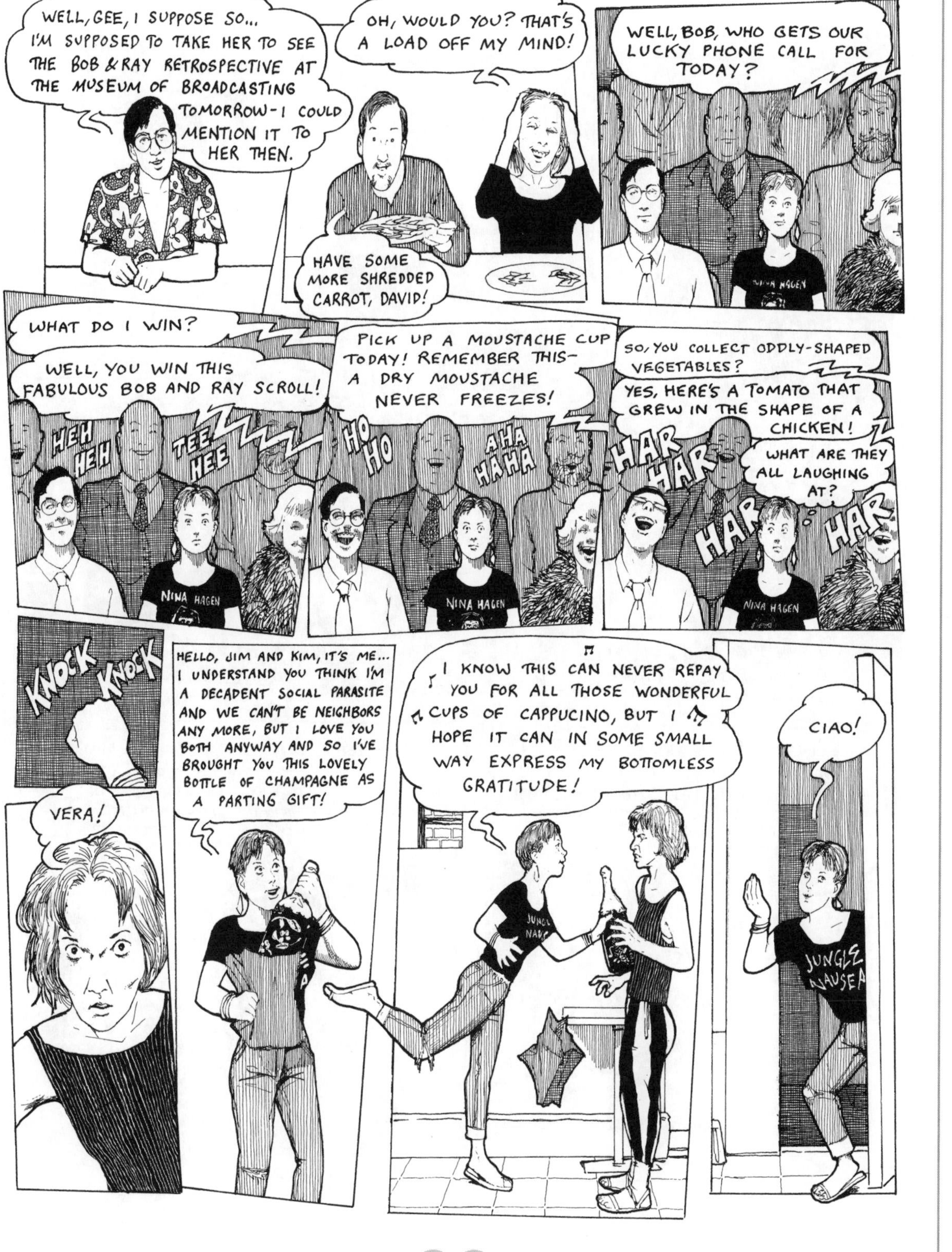
WELL, GEE, I SUPPOSE SO... I'M SUPPOSED TO TAKE HER TO SEE THE BOB & RAY RETROSPECTIVE AT THE MUSEUM OF BROADCASTING TOMORROW - I COULD MENTION IT TO HER THEN.
OH, WOULD YOU? THAT'S A LOAD OFF MY MIND!
HAVE SOME MORE SHREDDED CARROT, DAVID!
WELL, BOB, WHO GETS OUR LUCKY PHONE CALL FOR TODAY?
WHAT DO I WIN?
WELL, YOU WIN THIS FABULOUS BOB AND RAY SCROLL!
HEH HEH
TEE HEE
NINA HAGEN
PICK UP A MOUSTACHE CUP TODAY! REMEMBER THIS - A DRY MOUSTACHE NEVER FREEZES!
HO HO
AHA HAHA
NINA HAGEN
SO, YOU COLLECT ODDLY-SHAPED VEGETABLES?
YES, HERE'S A TOMATO THAT GREW IN THE SHAPE OF A CHICKEN!
HAR HAR
WHAT ARE THEY ALL LAUGHING AT?
HAR HAR
NINA HAGEN
KNOCK KNOCK
VERA!
HELLO, JIM AND KIM, IT'S ME... I UNDERSTAND YOU THINK I'M A DECADENT SOCIAL PARASITE AND WE CAN'T BE NEIGHBORS ANY MORE, BUT I LOVE YOU BOTH ANYWAY AND SO I'VE BROUGHT YOU THIS LOVELY BOTTLE OF CHAMPAGNE AS A PARTING GIFT!
I KNOW THIS CAN NEVER REPAY YOU FOR ALL THOSE WONDERFUL CUPS OF CAPPUCINO, BUT I HOPE IT CAN IN SOME SMALL WAY EXPRESS MY BOTTOMLESS GRATITUDE!
CIAO!
JUNGLE NAUSEA

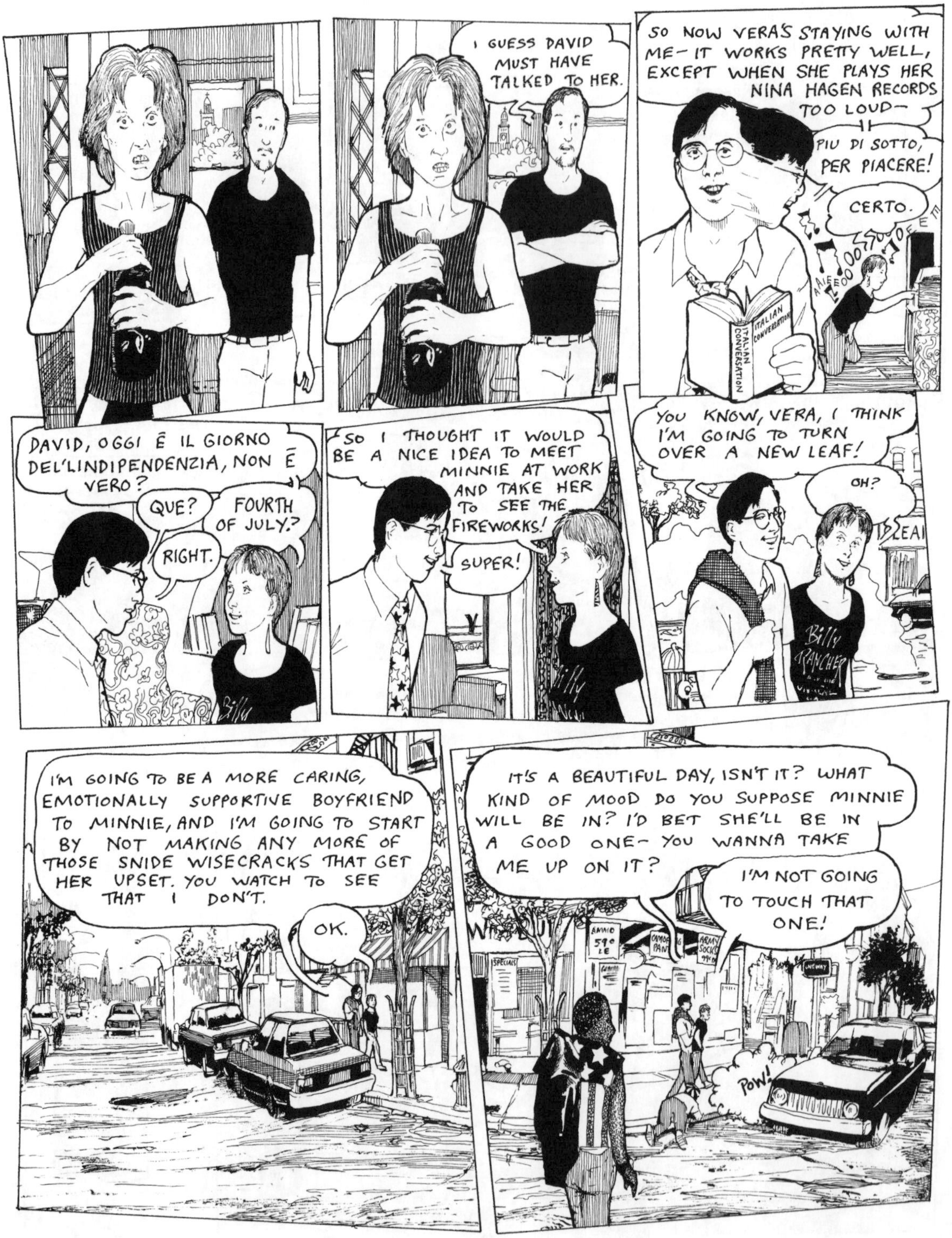
I GUESS DAVID MUST HAVE TALKED TO HER.
SO NOW VERA'S STAYING WITH ME— IT WORKS PRETTY WELL, EXCEPT WHEN SHE PLAYS HER NINA HAGEN RECORDS TOO LOUD—
PIU DI SOTTO, PER PIACERE!
CERTO.
ITALIAN CONVERSATION
DAVID, OGGI Ē IL GIORNO DEL'LINDIPENDENZIA, NON Ē VERO?
QUE?
FOURTH OF JULY?
RIGHT.
SO I THOUGHT IT WOULD BE A NICE IDEA TO MEET MINNIE AT WORK AND TAKE HER TO SEE THE FIREWORKS!
SUPER!
YOU KNOW, VERA, I THINK I'M GOING TO TURN OVER A NEW LEAF!
OH?
Billy Rancher
I'M GOING TO BE A MORE CARING, EMOTIONALLY SUPPORTIVE BOYFRIEND TO MINNIE, AND I'M GOING TO START BY NOT MAKING ANY MORE OF THOSE SNIDE WISECRACKS THAT GET HER UPSET. YOU WATCH TO SEE THAT I DON'T.
OK.
IT'S A BEAUTIFUL DAY, ISN'T IT? WHAT KIND OF MOOD DO YOU SUPPOSE MINNIE WILL BE IN? I'D BET SHE'LL BE IN A GOOD ONE— YOU WANNA TAKE ME UP ON IT?
I'M NOT GOING TO TOUCH THAT ONE!
POW!

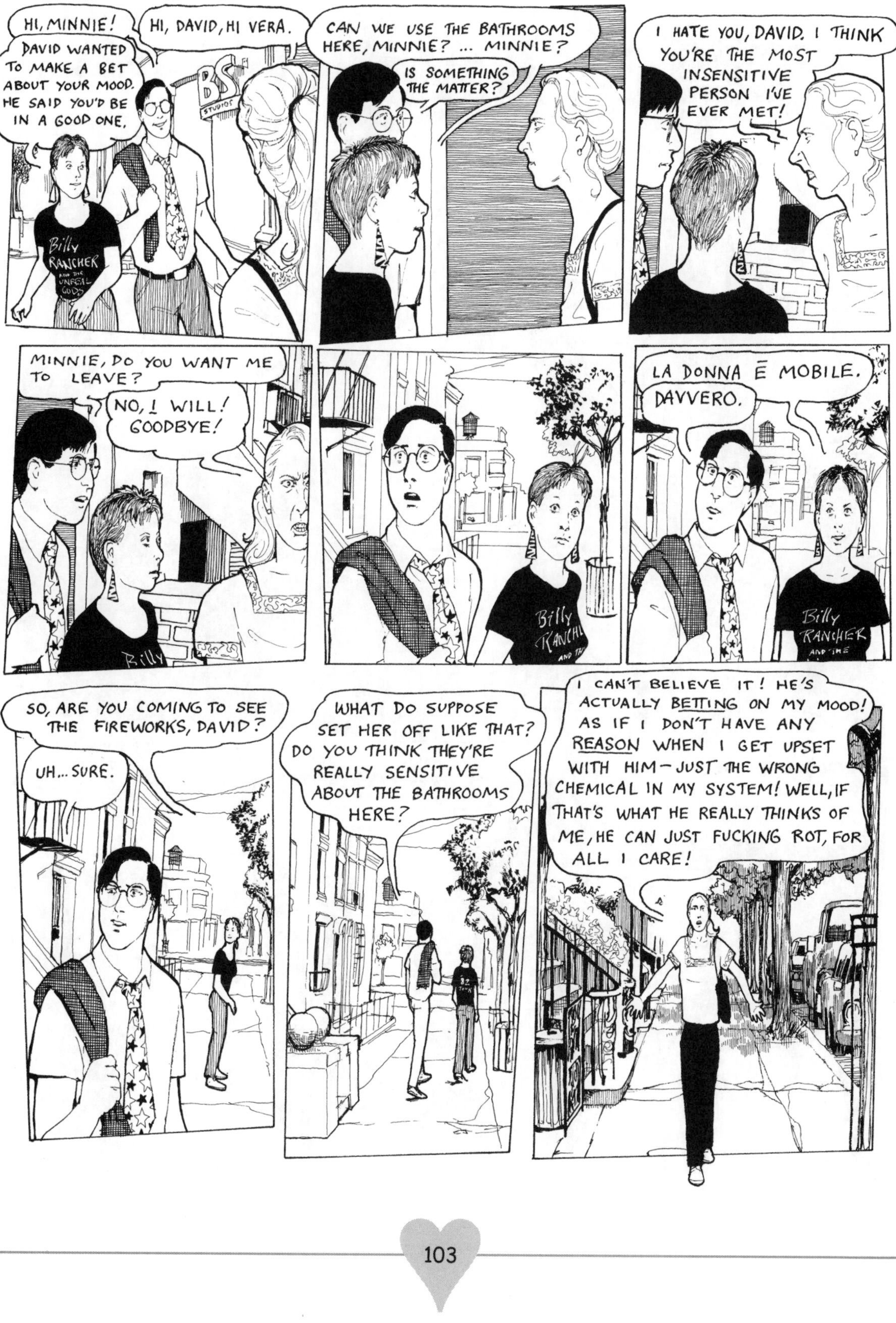
HI, MINNIE!
DAVID WANTED TO MAKE A BET ABOUT YOUR MOOD. HE SAID YOU'D BE IN A GOOD ONE.
HI, DAVID, HI VERA.
BS STUDIOS
Billy RANCHER AND THE UNREAL GODS
CAN WE USE THE BATHROOMS HERE, MINNIE? ... MINNIE?
IS SOMETHING THE MATTER?
I HATE YOU, DAVID. I THINK YOU'RE THE MOST INSENSITIVE PERSON I'VE EVER MET!
MINNIE, DO YOU WANT ME TO LEAVE?
NO, I WILL! GOODBYE!
LA DONNA È MOBILE.
DAVVERO.
SO, ARE YOU COMING TO SEE THE FIREWORKS, DAVID?
UH... SURE.
WHAT DO SUPPOSE SET HER OFF LIKE THAT? DO YOU THINK THEY'RE REALLY SENSITIVE ABOUT THE BATHROOMS HERE?
I CAN'T BELIEVE IT! HE'S ACTUALLY BETTING ON MY MOOD! AS IF I DON'T HAVE ANY REASON WHEN I GET UPSET WITH HIM—JUST THE WRONG CHEMICAL IN MY SYSTEM! WELL, IF THAT'S WHAT HE REALLY THINKS OF ME, HE CAN JUST FUCKING ROT, FOR ALL I CARE!

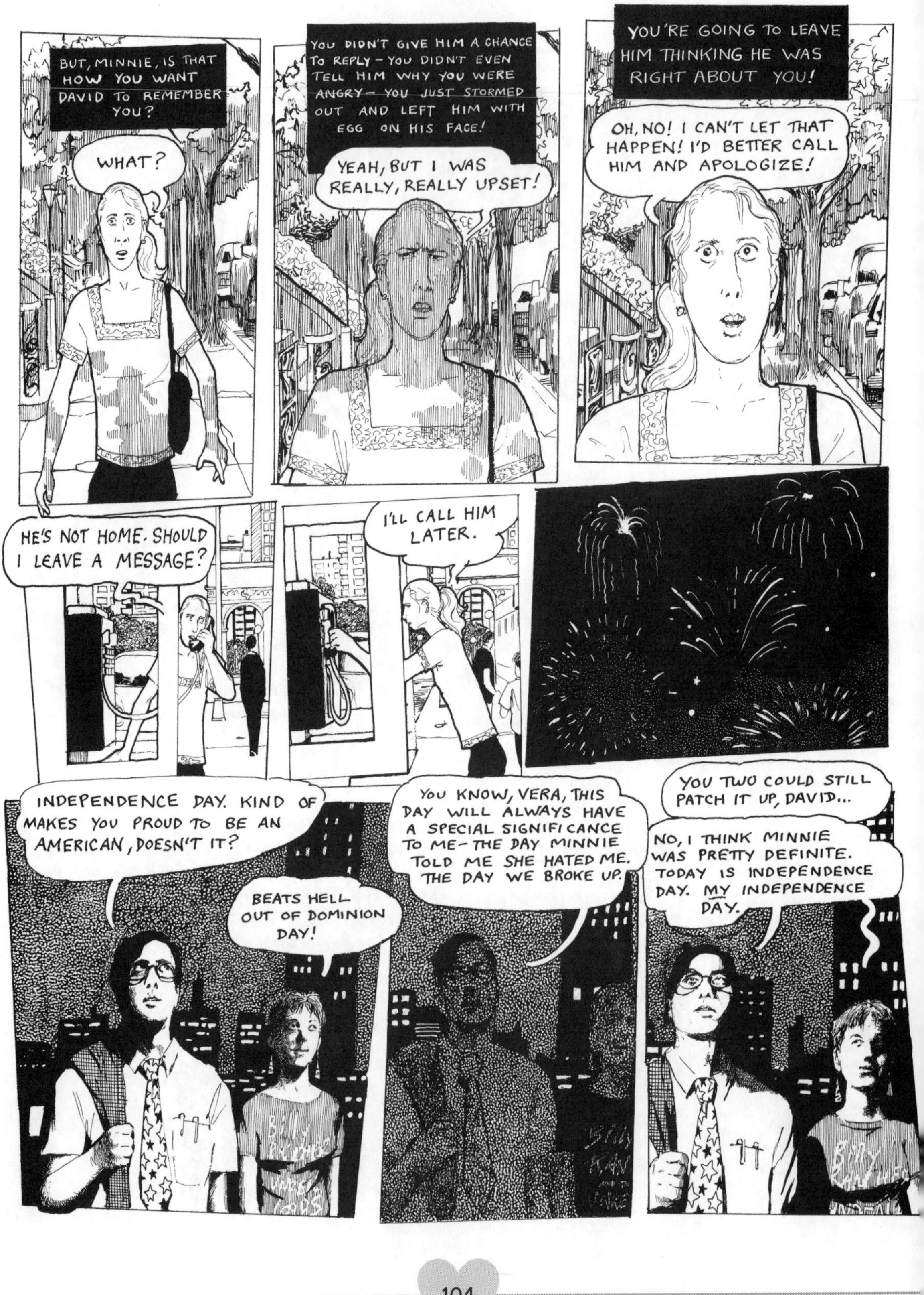

BUT, MINNIE, IS THAT HOW YOU WANT DAVID TO REMEMBER YOU?
WHAT?
YOU DIDN'T GIVE HIM A CHANCE TO REPLY - YOU DIDN'T EVEN TELL HIM WHY YOU WERE ANGRY - YOU JUST STORMED OUT AND LEFT HIM WITH EGG ON HIS FACE!
YEAH, BUT I WAS REALLY, REALLY UPSET!
YOU'RE GOING TO LEAVE HIM THINKING HE WAS RIGHT ABOUT YOU!
OH, NO! I CAN'T LET THAT HAPPEN! I'D BETTER CALL HIM AND APOLOGIZE!
HE'S NOT HOME. SHOULD I LEAVE A MESSAGE?
I'LL CALL HIM LATER.
INDEPENDENCE DAY. KIND OF MAKES YOU PROUD TO BE AN AMERICAN, DOESN'T IT?
BEATS HELL OUT OF DOMINION DAY!
YOU KNOW, VERA, THIS DAY WILL ALWAYS HAVE A SPECIAL SIGNIFICANCE TO ME - THE DAY MINNIE TOLD ME SHE HATED ME. THE DAY WE BROKE UP.
YOU TWO COULD STILL PATCH IT UP, DAVID...
NO, I THINK MINNIE WAS PRETTY DEFINITE. TODAY IS INDEPENDENCE DAY. MY INDEPENDENCE DAY.

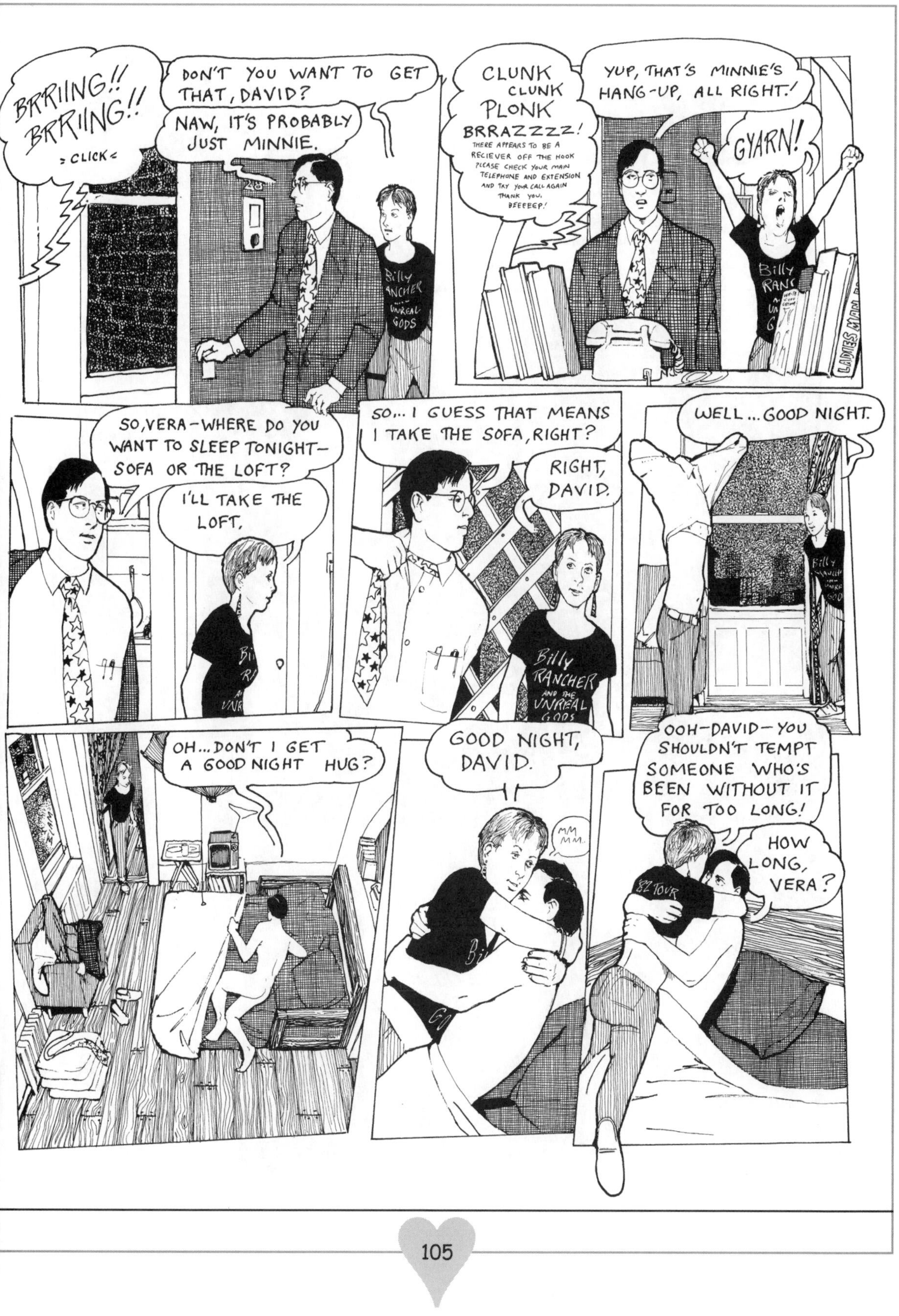
BRRIING!! BRRIING!!
> CLICK <
DON'T YOU WANT TO GET THAT, DAVID?
NAW, IT'S PROBABLY JUST MINNIE.
CLUNK CLUNK PLONK BRRAZZZZ!
THERE APPEARS TO BE A RECIEVER OFF THE HOOK PLEASE CHECK YOUR MAIN TELEPHONE AND EXTENSION AND TRY YOUR CALL AGAIN THANK YOU. BEEEEEP!
YUP, THAT'S MINNIE'S HANG-UP, ALL RIGHT!
GYARN!
LADIES MAN
SO, VERA—WHERE DO YOU WANT TO SLEEP TONIGHT—SOFA OR THE LOFT?
I'LL TAKE THE LOFT.
SO... I GUESS THAT MEANS I TAKE THE SOFA, RIGHT?
RIGHT, DAVID.
Billy RANCHER AND THE UNREAL GODS
WELL ... GOOD NIGHT.
OH... DON'T I GET A GOOD NIGHT HUG?
GOOD NIGHT, DAVID.
MM MM.
OOH—DAVID—YOU SHOULDN'T TEMPT SOMEONE WHO'S BEEN WITHOUT IT FOR TOO LONG!
'82 TOUR
HOW LONG, VERA?

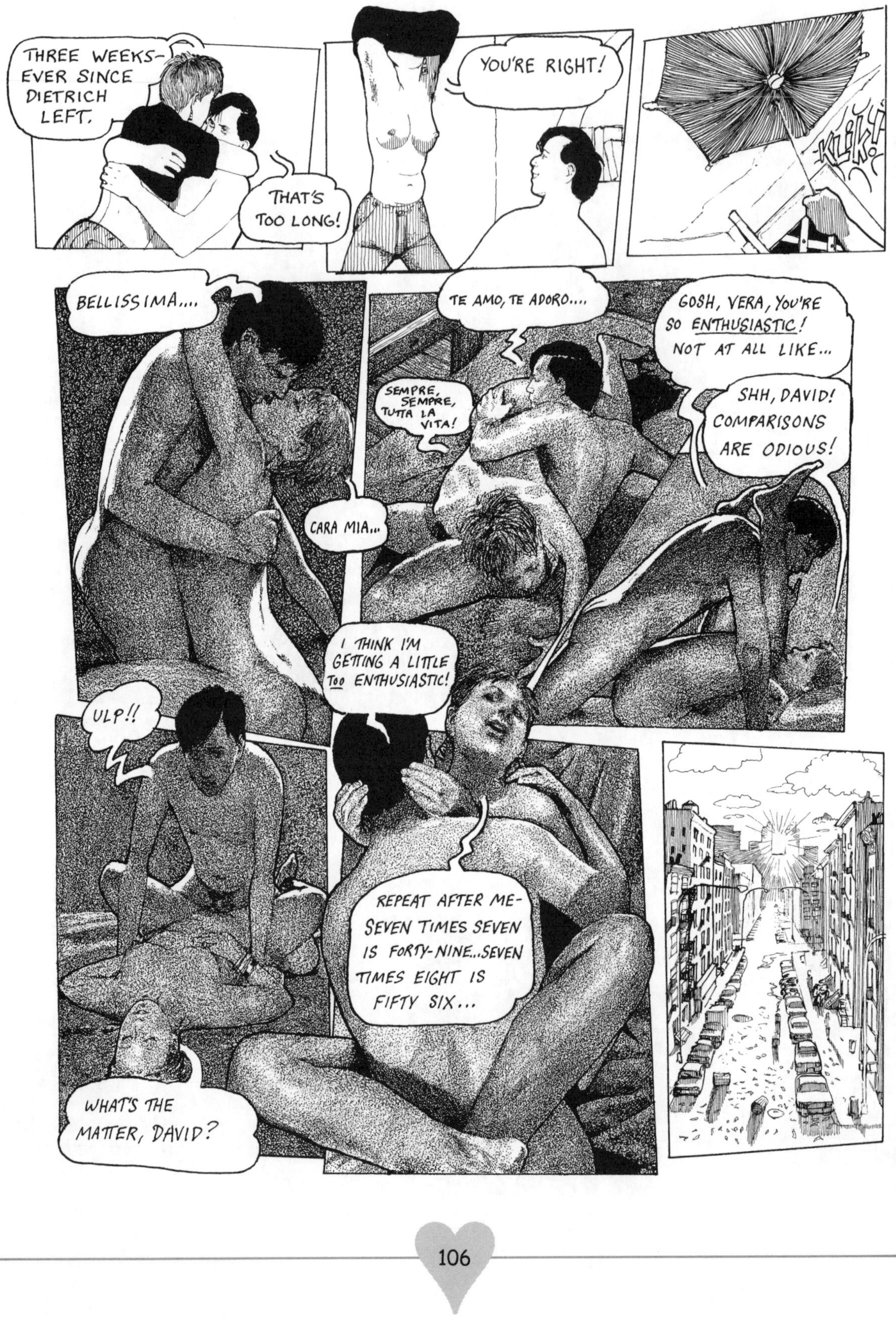
THREE WEEKS- EVER SINCE DIETRICH LEFT.
THAT'S TOO LONG!
YOU'RE RIGHT!
KLIK!
BELLISSIMA....
TE AMO, TE ADORO....
SEMPRE, SEMPRE, TUTTA LA VITA!
CARA MIA...
GOSH, VERA, YOU'RE SO ENTHUSIASTIC! NOT AT ALL LIKE...
SHH, DAVID! COMPARISONS ARE ODIOUS!
ULP!!
I THINK I'M GETTING A LITTLE TOO ENTHUSIASTIC!
REPEAT AFTER ME- SEVEN TIMES SEVEN IS FORTY-NINE...SEVEN TIMES EIGHT IS FIFTY SIX...
WHAT'S THE MATTER, DAVID?

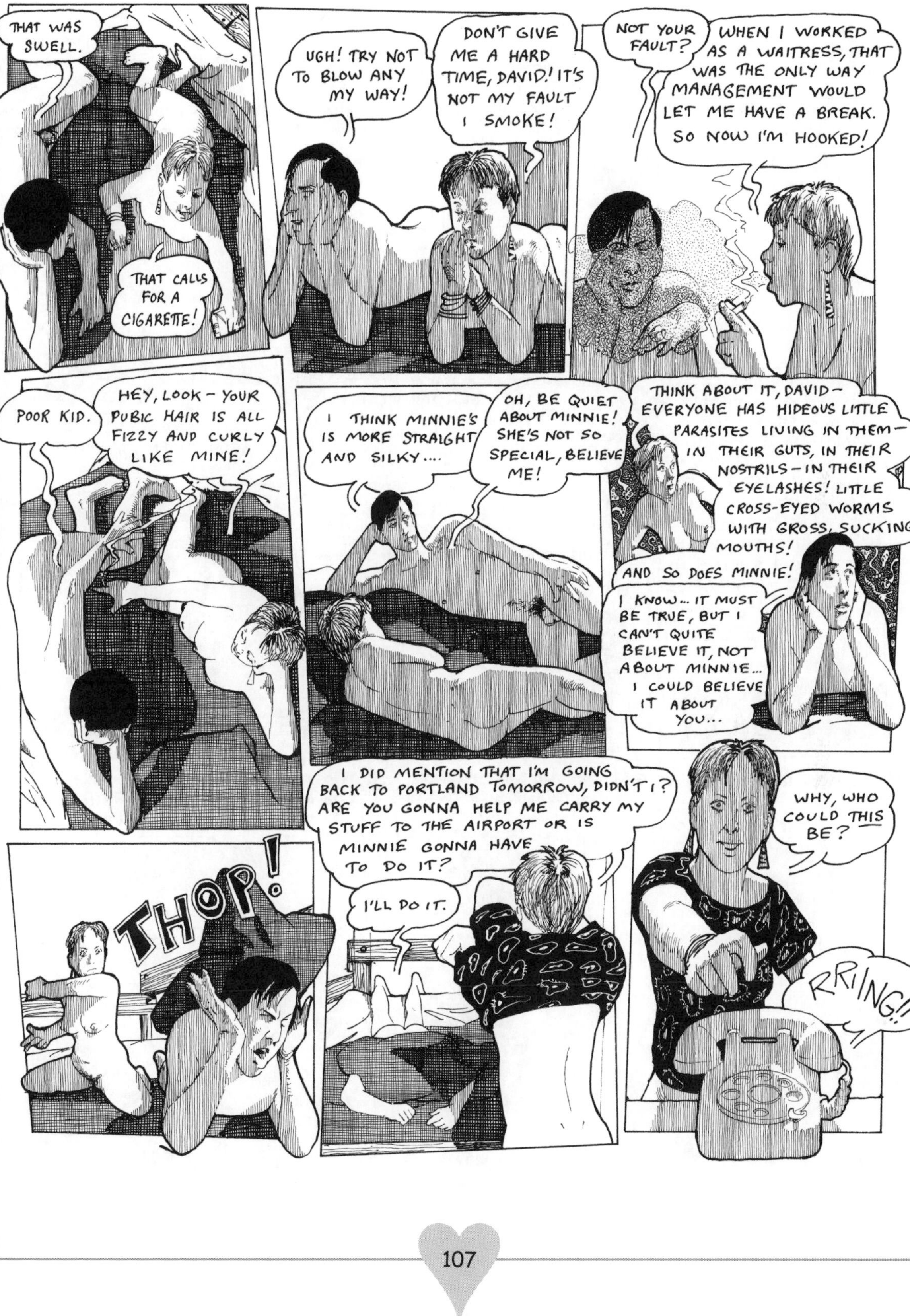
THAT WAS SWELL.
THAT CALLS FOR A CIGARETTE!
UGH! TRY NOT TO BLOW ANY MY WAY!
DON'T GIVE ME A HARD TIME, DAVID! IT'S NOT MY FAULT I SMOKE!
NOT YOUR FAULT?
WHEN I WORKED AS A WAITRESS, THAT WAS THE ONLY WAY MANAGEMENT WOULD LET ME HAVE A BREAK. SO NOW I'M HOOKED!
POOR KID.
HEY, LOOK - YOUR PUBIC HAIR IS ALL FIZZY AND CURLY LIKE MINE!
I THINK MINNIE'S IS MORE STRAIGHT AND SILKY....
OH, BE QUIET ABOUT MINNIE! SHE'S NOT SO SPECIAL, BELIEVE ME!
THINK ABOUT IT, DAVID - EVERYONE HAS HIDEOUS LITTLE PARASITES LIVING IN THEM - IN THEIR GUTS, IN THEIR NOSTRILS - IN THEIR EYELASHES! LITTLE CROSS-EYED WORMS WITH GROSS, SUCKING MOUTHS!
AND SO DOES MINNIE!
I KNOW... IT MUST BE TRUE, BUT I CAN'T QUITE BELIEVE IT, NOT ABOUT MINNIE... I COULD BELIEVE IT ABOUT YOU...
THOP!
I DID MENTION THAT I'M GOING BACK TO PORTLAND TOMORROW, DIDN'T I? ARE YOU GONNA HELP ME CARRY MY STUFF TO THE AIRPORT OR IS MINNIE GONNA HAVE TO DO IT?
I'LL DO IT.
WHY, WHO COULD THIS BE?
RRIING!!

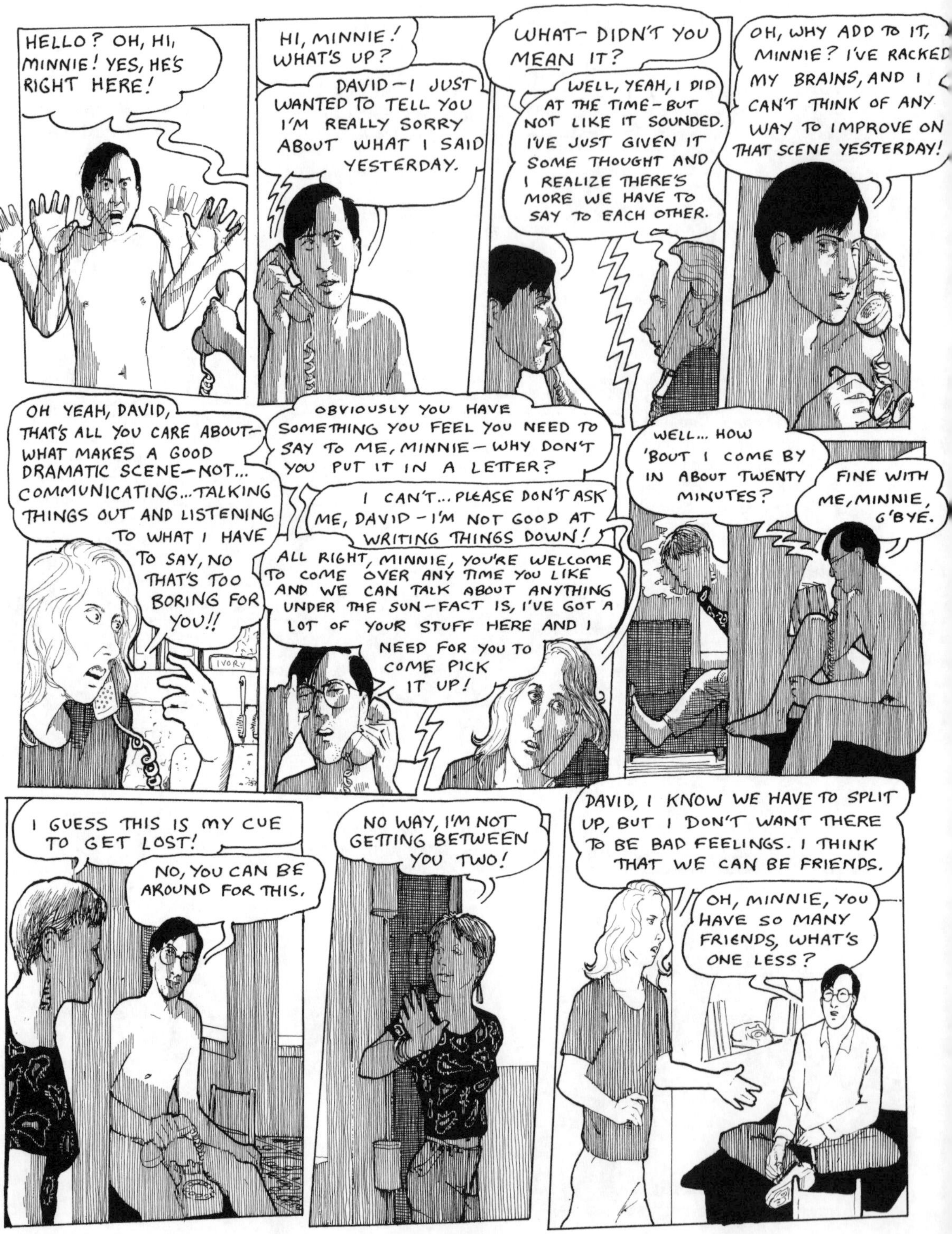
HELLO? OH, HI, MINNIE! YES, HE'S RIGHT HERE!
HI, MINNIE! WHAT'S UP?
DAVID—I JUST WANTED TO TELL YOU I'M REALLY SORRY ABOUT WHAT I SAID YESTERDAY.
WHAT- DIDN'T YOU MEAN IT?
WELL, YEAH, I DID AT THE TIME—BUT NOT LIKE IT SOUNDED. I'VE JUST GIVEN IT SOME THOUGHT AND I REALIZE THERE'S MORE WE HAVE TO SAY TO EACH OTHER.
OH, WHY ADD TO IT, MINNIE? I'VE RACKED MY BRAINS, AND I CAN'T THINK OF ANY WAY TO IMPROVE ON THAT SCENE YESTERDAY!
OH YEAH, DAVID, THAT'S ALL YOU CARE ABOUT—WHAT MAKES A GOOD DRAMATIC SCENE—NOT... COMMUNICATING...TALKING THINGS OUT AND LISTENING TO WHAT I HAVE TO SAY, NO THAT'S TOO BORING FOR YOU!!
IVORY
OBVIOUSLY YOU HAVE SOMETHING YOU FEEL YOU NEED TO SAY TO ME, MINNIE—WHY DON'T YOU PUT IT IN A LETTER?
I CAN'T...PLEASE DON'T ASK ME, DAVID—I'M NOT GOOD AT WRITING THINGS DOWN!
ALL RIGHT, MINNIE, YOU'RE WELCOME TO COME OVER ANY TIME YOU LIKE AND WE CAN TALK ABOUT ANYTHING UNDER THE SUN—FACT IS, I'VE GOT A LOT OF YOUR STUFF HERE AND I NEED FOR YOU TO COME PICK IT UP!
WELL... HOW 'BOUT I COME BY IN ABOUT TWENTY MINUTES?
FINE WITH ME, MINNIE, G'BYE.
I GUESS THIS IS MY CUE TO GET LOST!
NO, YOU CAN BE AROUND FOR THIS.
NO WAY, I'M NOT GETTING BETWEEN YOU TWO!
DAVID, I KNOW WE HAVE TO SPLIT UP, BUT I DON'T WANT THERE TO BE BAD FEELINGS. I THINK THAT WE CAN BE FRIENDS.
OH, MINNIE, YOU HAVE SO MANY FRIENDS, WHAT'S ONE LESS?

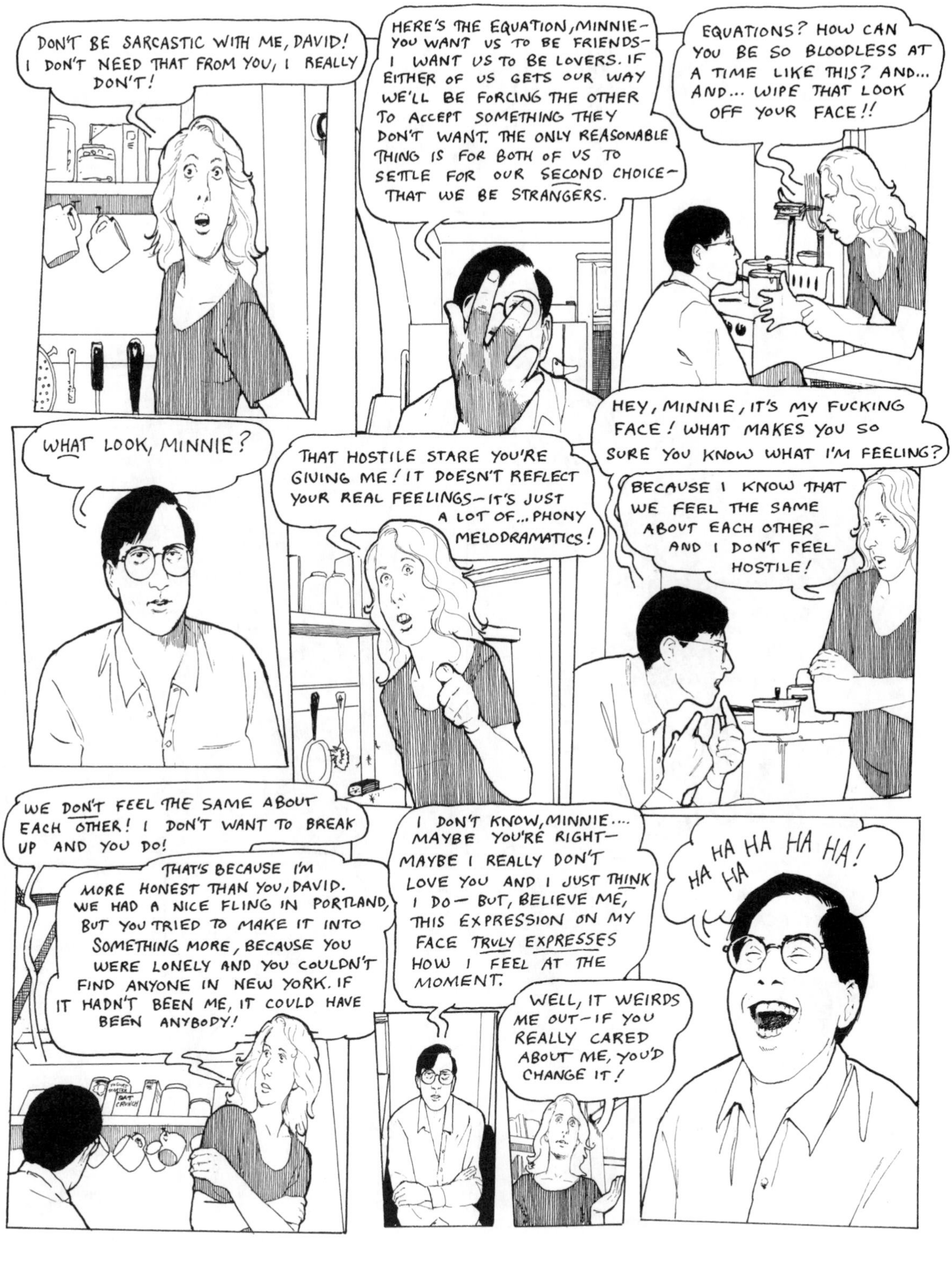
DON'T BE SARCASTIC WITH ME, DAVID! I DON'T NEED THAT FROM YOU, I REALLY DON'T!
HERE'S THE EQUATION, MINNIE- YOU WANT US TO BE FRIENDS- I WANT US TO BE LOVERS. IF EITHER OF US GETS OUR WAY WE'LL BE FORCING THE OTHER TO ACCEPT SOMETHING THEY DON'T WANT. THE ONLY REASONABLE THING IS FOR BOTH OF US TO SETTLE FOR OUR SECOND CHOICE- THAT WE BE STRANGERS.
EQUATIONS? HOW CAN YOU BE SO BLOODLESS AT A TIME LIKE THIS? AND... AND... WIPE THAT LOOK OFF YOUR FACE!!
WHAT LOOK, MINNIE?
THAT HOSTILE STARE YOU'RE GIVING ME! IT DOESN'T REFLECT YOUR REAL FEELINGS- IT'S JUST A LOT OF... PHONY MELODRAMATICS!
HEY, MINNIE, IT'S MY FUCKING FACE! WHAT MAKES YOU SO SURE YOU KNOW WHAT I'M FEELING?
BECAUSE I KNOW THAT WE FEEL THE SAME ABOUT EACH OTHER- AND I DON'T FEEL HOSTILE!
WE DON'T FEEL THE SAME ABOUT EACH OTHER! I DON'T WANT TO BREAK UP AND YOU DO!
THAT'S BECAUSE I'M MORE HONEST THAN YOU, DAVID. WE HAD A NICE FLING IN PORTLAND, BUT YOU TRIED TO MAKE IT INTO SOMETHING MORE, BECAUSE YOU WERE LONELY AND YOU COULDN'T FIND ANYONE IN NEW YORK. IF IT HADN'T BEEN ME, IT COULD HAVE BEEN ANYBODY!
I DON'T KNOW, MINNIE.... MAYBE YOU'RE RIGHT- MAYBE I REALLY DON'T LOVE YOU AND I JUST THINK I DO- BUT, BELIEVE ME, THIS EXPRESSION ON MY FACE TRULY EXPRESSES HOW I FEEL AT THE MOMENT.
WELL, IT WEIRDS ME OUT- IF YOU REALLY CARED ABOUT ME, YOU'D CHANGE IT!
HA HA HA HA HA HA HA!

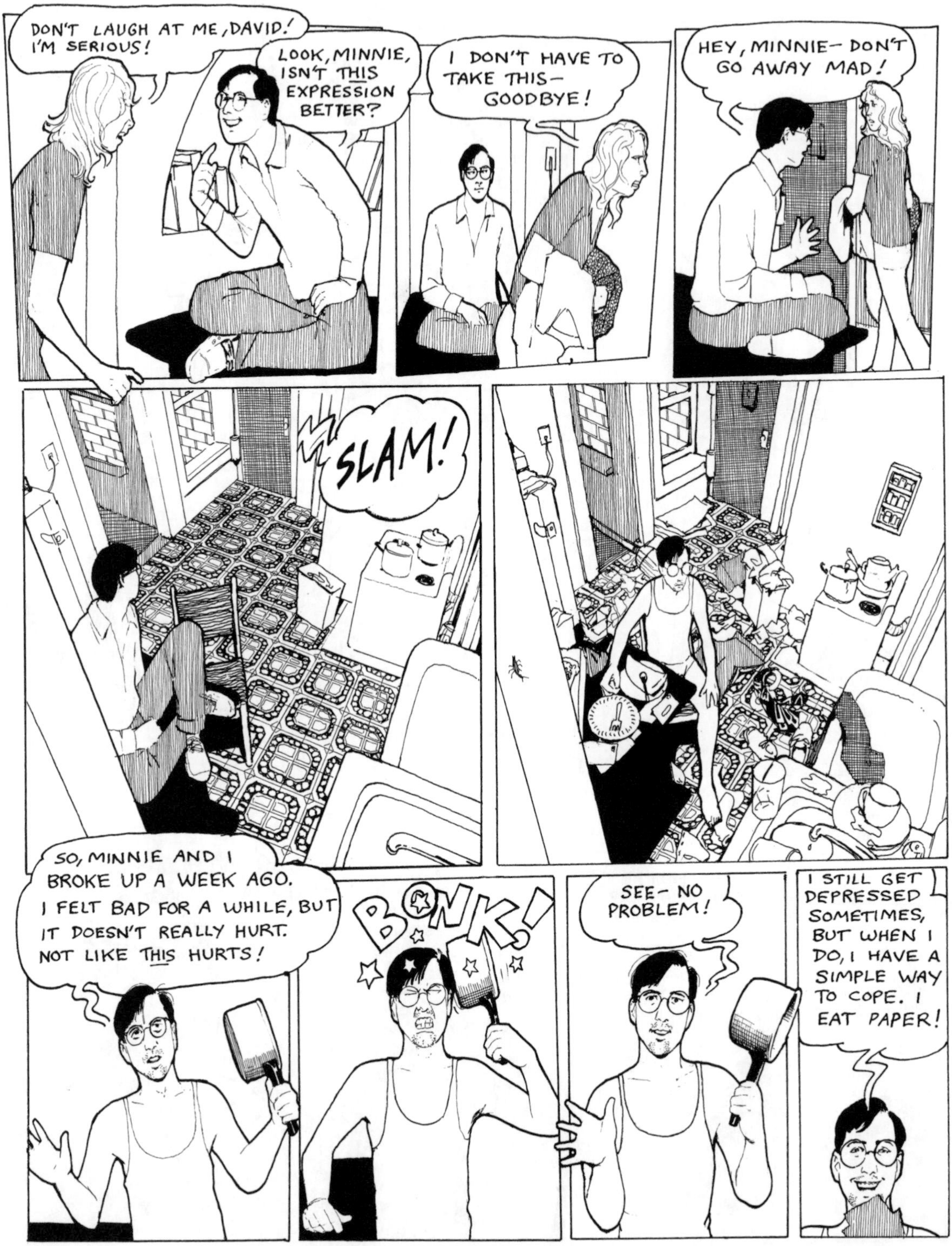
DON'T LAUGH AT ME, DAVID! I'M SERIOUS!
LOOK, MINNIE, ISN'T THIS EXPRESSION BETTER?
I DON'T HAVE TO TAKE THIS— GOODBYE!
HEY, MINNIE— DON'T GO AWAY MAD!
SLAM!
SO, MINNIE AND I BROKE UP A WEEK AGO. I FELT BAD FOR A WHILE, BUT IT DOESN'T REALLY HURT. NOT LIKE THIS HURTS!
BONK!
SEE— NO PROBLEM!
I STILL GET DEPRESSED SOMETIMES, BUT WHEN I DO, I HAVE A SIMPLE WAY TO COPE. I EAT PAPER!

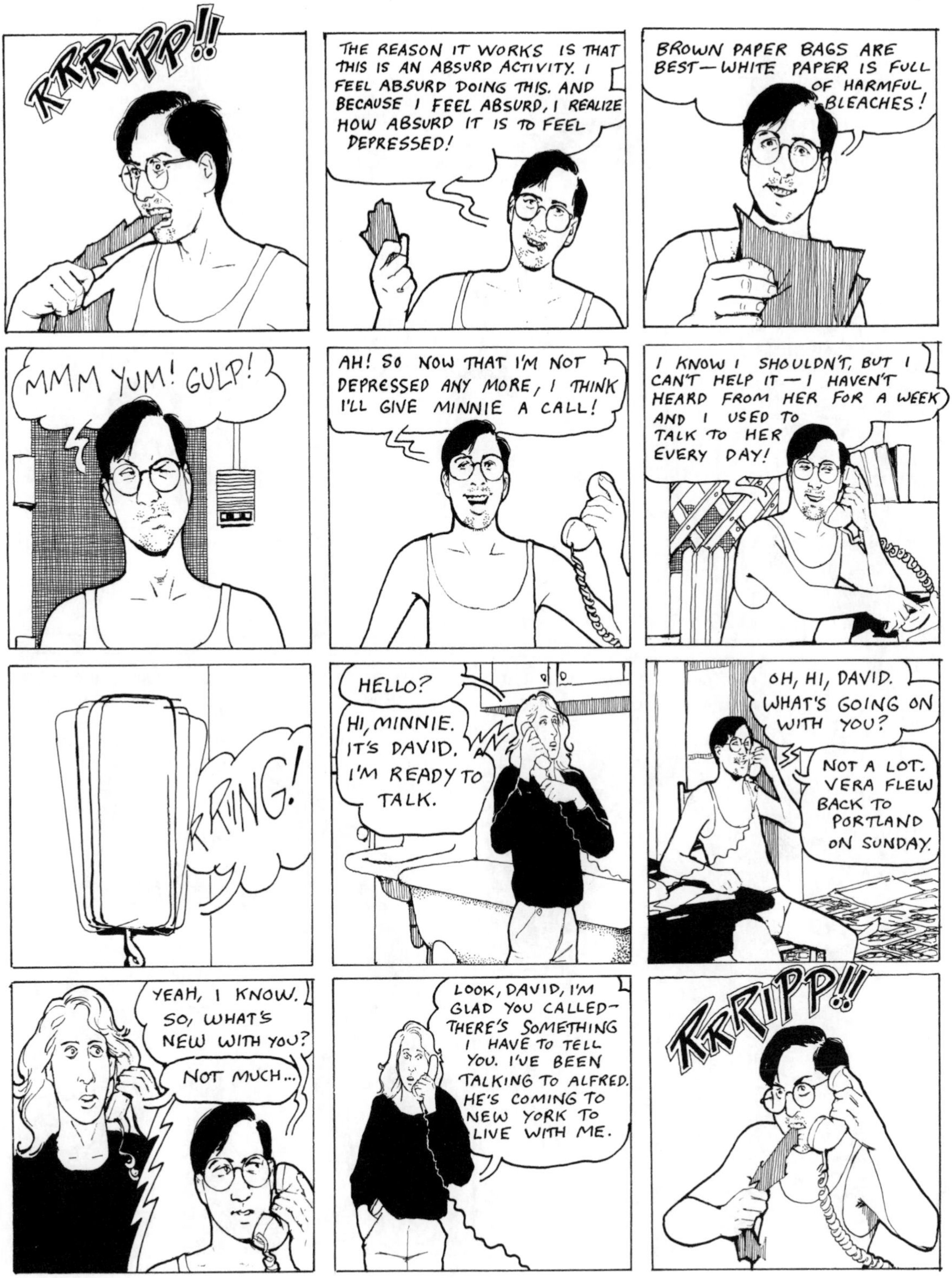
RRRIPP!!
THE REASON IT WORKS IS THAT THIS IS AN ABSURD ACTIVITY. I FEEL ABSURD DOING THIS. AND BECAUSE I FEEL ABSURD, I REALIZE HOW ABSURD IT IS TO FEEL DEPRESSED!
BROWN PAPER BAGS ARE BEST—WHITE PAPER IS FULL OF HARMFUL BLEACHES!
MMM YUM! GULP!
AH! SO NOW THAT I'M NOT DEPRESSED ANY MORE, I THINK I'LL GIVE MINNIE A CALL!
I KNOW I SHOULDN'T, BUT I CAN'T HELP IT—I HAVEN'T HEARD FROM HER FOR A WEEK AND I USED TO TALK TO HER EVERY DAY!
KRING!
HELLO?
HI, MINNIE. IT'S DAVID. I'M READY TO TALK.
OH, HI, DAVID. WHAT'S GOING ON WITH YOU?
NOT A LOT. VERA FLEW BACK TO PORTLAND ON SUNDAY.
YEAH, I KNOW. SO, WHAT'S NEW WITH YOU?
NOT MUCH...
LOOK, DAVID, I'M GLAD YOU CALLED—THERE'S SOMETHING I HAVE TO TELL YOU. I'VE BEEN TALKING TO ALFRED. HE'S COMING TO NEW YORK TO LIVE WITH ME.
RRRIPP!!

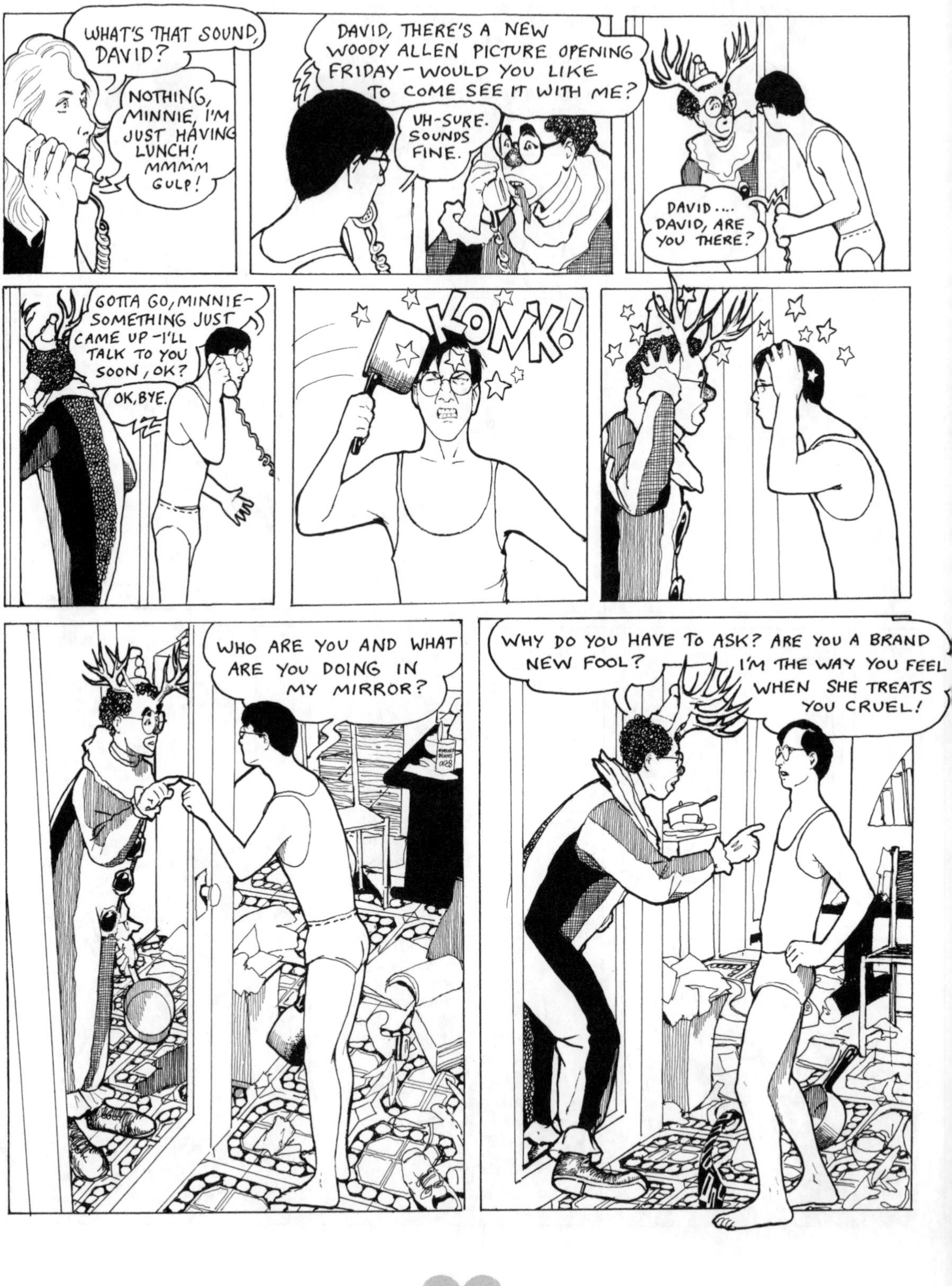
WHAT'S THAT SOUND, DAVID?
NOTHING, MINNIE, I'M JUST HAVING LUNCH! MMMM GULP!
DAVID, THERE'S A NEW WOODY ALLEN PICTURE OPENING FRIDAY - WOULD YOU LIKE TO COME SEE IT WITH ME?
UH-SURE. SOUNDS FINE.
DAVID.... DAVID, ARE YOU THERE?
GOTTA GO, MINNIE - SOMETHING JUST CAME UP - I'LL TALK TO YOU SOON, OK?
OK, BYE.
KONK!
WHO ARE YOU AND WHAT ARE YOU DOING IN MY MIRROR?
WHY DO YOU HAVE TO ASK? ARE YOU A BRAND NEW FOOL?
I'M THE WAY YOU FEEL WHEN SHE TREATS YOU CRUEL!

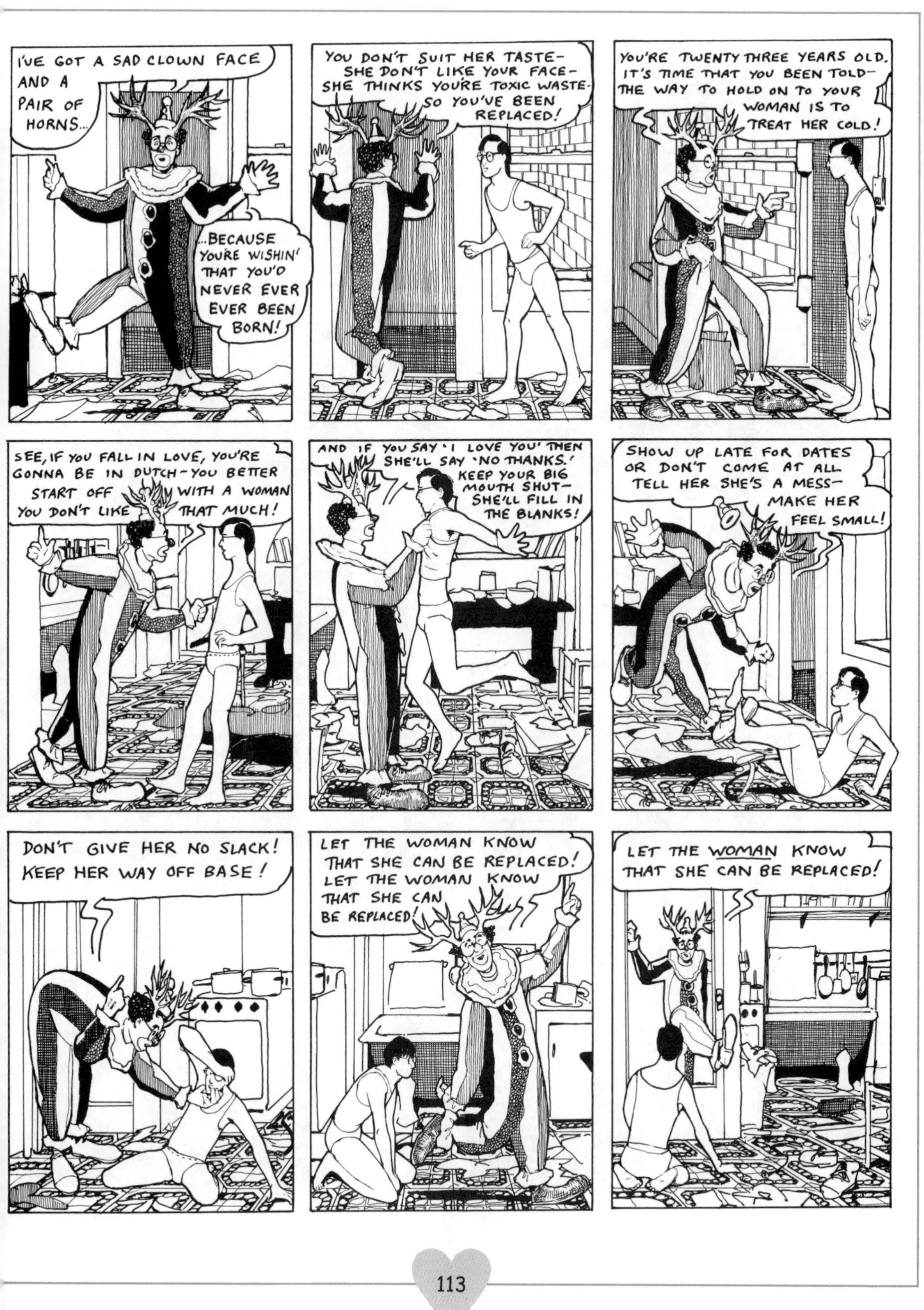
I'VE GOT A SAD CLOWN FACE AND A PAIR OF HORNS...
...BECAUSE YOU'RE WISHIN' THAT YOU'D NEVER EVER EVER BEEN BORN!
YOU DON'T SUIT HER TASTE- SHE DON'T LIKE YOUR FACE- SHE THINKS YOU'RE TOXIC WASTE- SO YOU'VE BEEN REPLACED!
YOU'RE TWENTY THREE YEARS OLD. IT'S TIME THAT YOU BEEN TOLD- THE WAY TO HOLD ON TO YOUR WOMAN IS TO TREAT HER COLD!
SEE, IF YOU FALL IN LOVE, YOU'RE GONNA BE IN DUTCH- YOU BETTER START OFF WITH A WOMAN YOU DON'T LIKE THAT MUCH!
AND IF YOU SAY 'I LOVE YOU' THEN SHE'LL SAY 'NO THANKS.' KEEP YOUR BIG MOUTH SHUT- SHE'LL FILL IN THE BLANKS!
SHOW UP LATE FOR DATES OR DON'T COME AT ALL TELL HER SHE'S A MESS- MAKE HER FEEL SMALL!
DON'T GIVE HER NO SLACK! KEEP HER WAY OFF BASE!
LET THE WOMAN KNOW THAT SHE CAN BE REPLACED! LET THE WOMAN KNOW THAT SHE CAN BE REPLACED!
LET THE WOMAN KNOW THAT SHE CAN BE REPLACED!

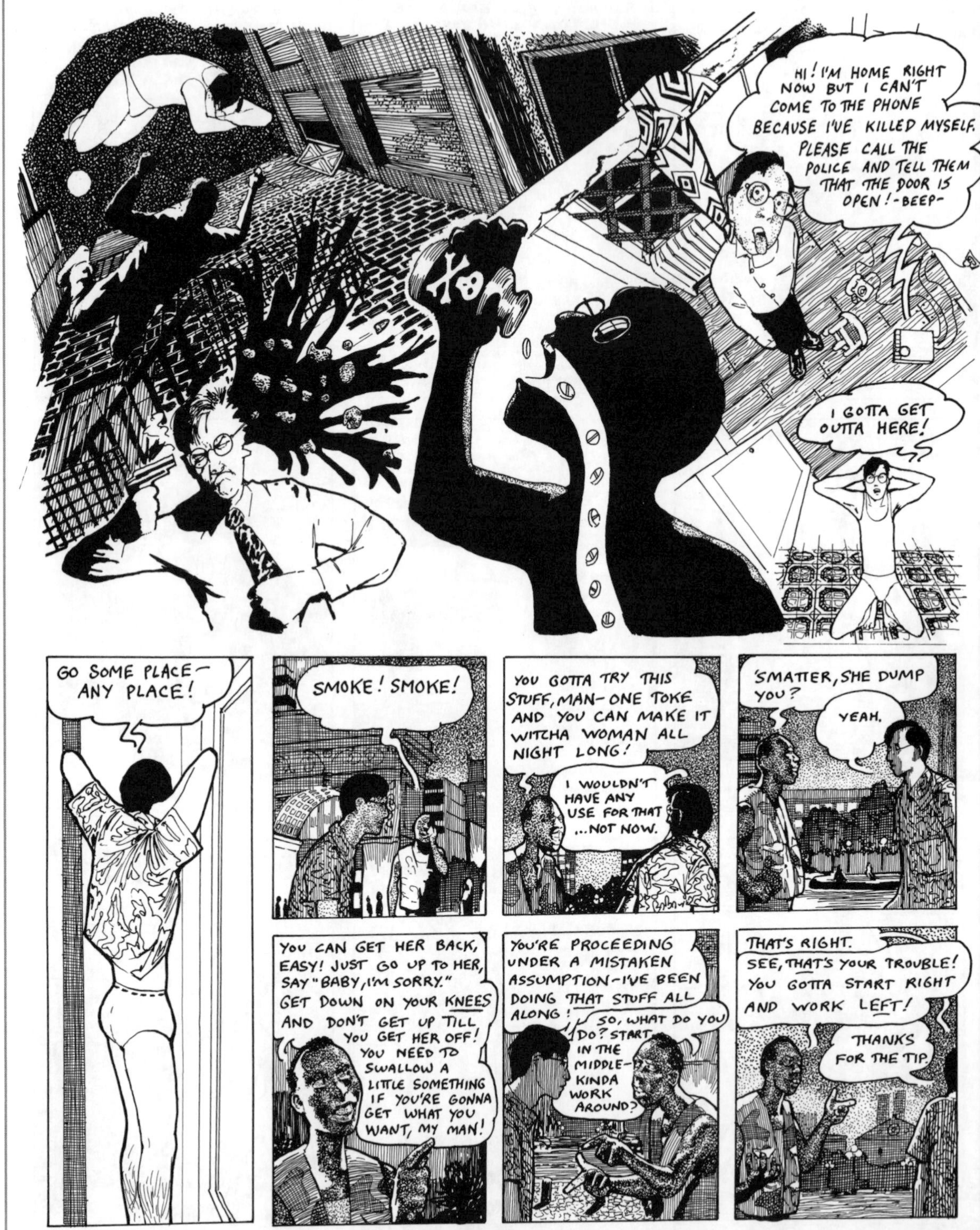

HI! I'M HOME RIGHT NOW BUT I CAN'T COME TO THE PHONE BECAUSE I'VE KILLED MYSELF. PLEASE CALL THE POLICE AND TELL THEM THAT THE DOOR IS OPEN! -BEEP-
I GOTTA GET OUTTA HERE!
GO SOME PLACE- ANY PLACE!
SMOKE! SMOKE!
YOU GOTTA TRY THIS STUFF, MAN- ONE TOKE AND YOU CAN MAKE IT WITCHA WOMAN ALL NIGHT LONG!
I WOULDN'T HAVE ANY USE FOR THAT ...NOT NOW.
'SMATTER, SHE DUMP YOU?
YEAH.
YOU CAN GET HER BACK, EASY! JUST GO UP TO HER, SAY "BABY, I'M SORRY." GET DOWN ON YOUR KNEES AND DON'T GET UP TILL YOU GET HER OFF! YOU NEED TO SWALLOW A LITTLE SOMETHING IF YOU'RE GONNA GET WHAT YOU WANT, MY MAN!
YOU'RE PROCEEDING UNDER A MISTAKEN ASSUMPTION- I'VE BEEN DOING THAT STUFF ALL ALONG!
SO, WHAT DO YOU DO? START IN THE MIDDLE- KINDA WORK AROUND?
THAT'S RIGHT.
SEE, THAT'S YOUR TROUBLE! YOU GOTTA START RIGHT AND WORK LEFT!
THANKS FOR THE TIP.

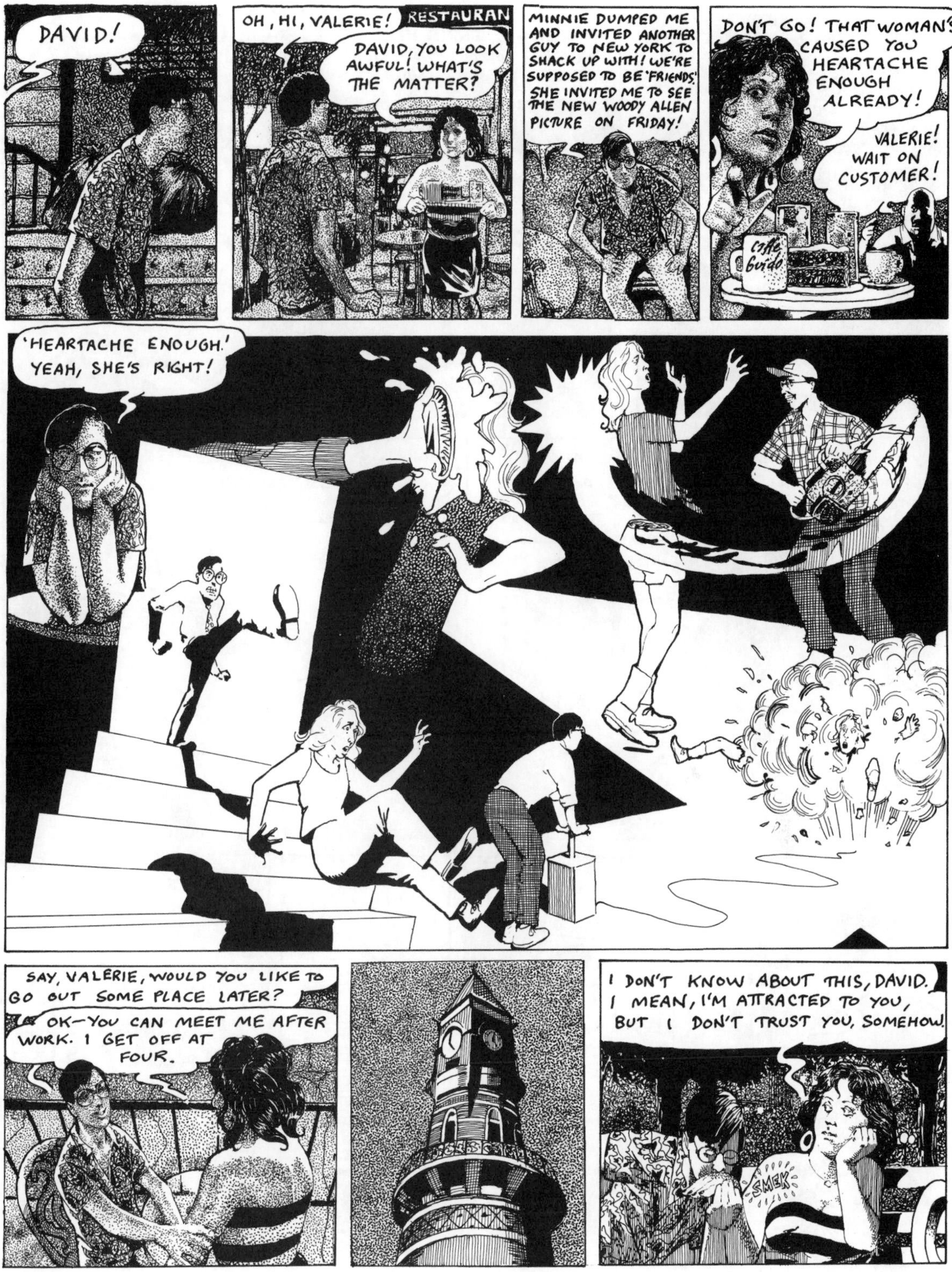
DAVID!
OH, HI, VALERIE!
RESTAURAN
DAVID, YOU LOOK AWFUL! WHAT'S THE MATTER?
MINNIE DUMPED ME AND INVITED ANOTHER GUY TO NEW YORK TO SHACK UP WITH! WE'RE SUPPOSED TO BE 'FRIENDS.' SHE INVITED ME TO SEE THE NEW WOODY ALLEN PICTURE ON FRIDAY!
DON'T GO! THAT WOMAN'S CAUSED YOU HEARTACHE ENOUGH ALREADY!
VALERIE! WAIT ON CUSTOMER!
Caffe Guido
'HEARTACHE ENOUGH.' YEAH, SHE'S RIGHT!
SAY, VALERIE, WOULD YOU LIKE TO GO OUT SOME PLACE LATER?
OK—YOU CAN MEET ME AFTER WORK. I GET OFF AT FOUR.
I DON'T KNOW ABOUT THIS, DAVID. I MEAN, I'M ATTRACTED TO YOU, BUT I DON'T TRUST YOU, SOMEHOW.
SMEK

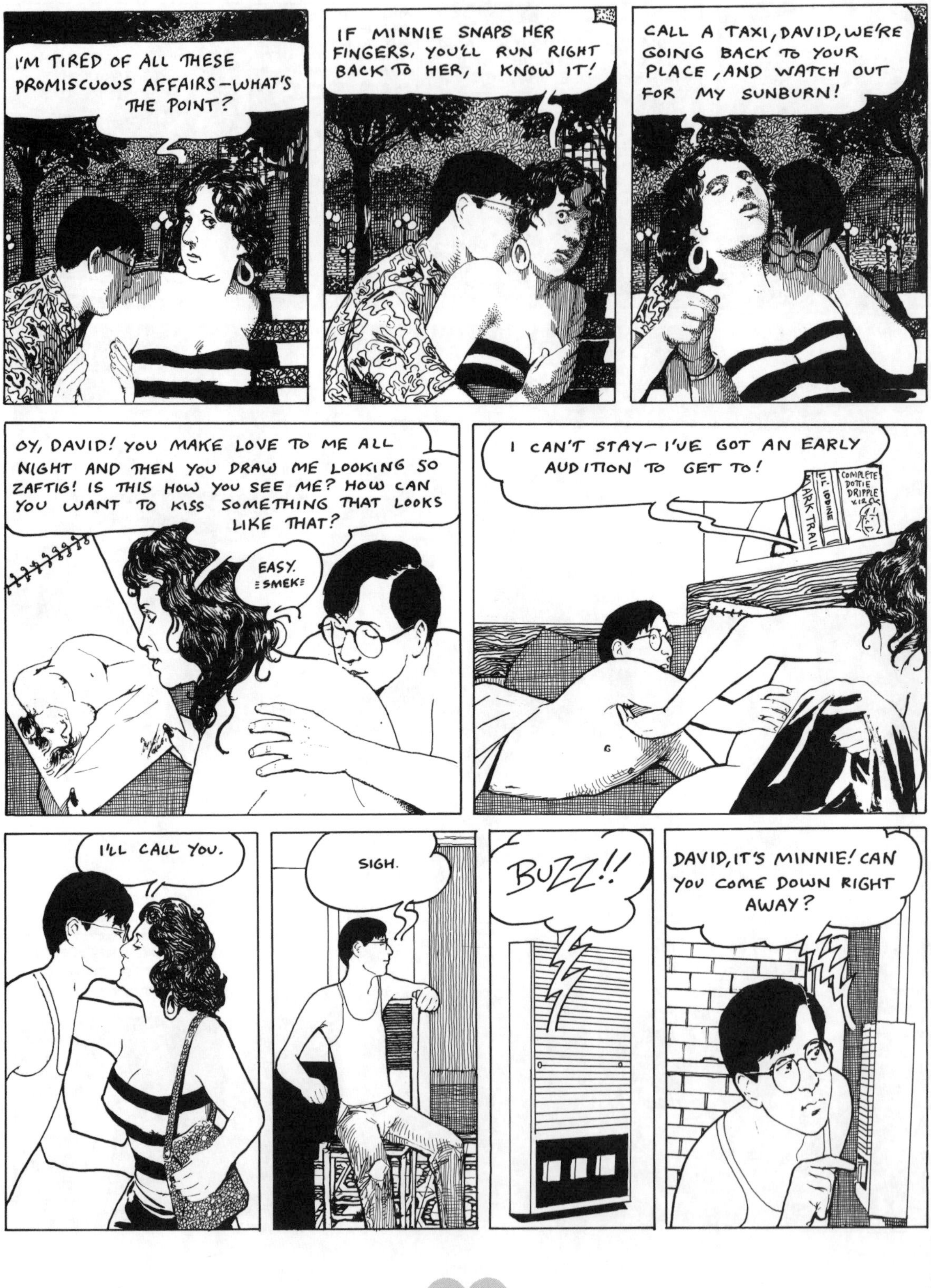
I'M TIRED OF ALL THESE PROMISCUOUS AFFAIRS—WHAT'S THE POINT?
IF MINNIE SNAPS HER FINGERS, YOU'LL RUN RIGHT BACK TO HER, I KNOW IT!
CALL A TAXI, DAVID, WE'RE GOING BACK TO YOUR PLACE, AND WATCH OUT FOR MY SUNBURN!
OY, DAVID! YOU MAKE LOVE TO ME ALL NIGHT AND THEN YOU DRAW ME LOOKING SO ZAFTIG! IS THIS HOW YOU SEE ME? HOW CAN YOU WANT TO KISS SOMETHING THAT LOOKS LIKE THAT?
EASY. =SMEK=
I CAN'T STAY—I'VE GOT AN EARLY AUDITION TO GET TO!
ARK TRAIL
LI'L IODINE
COMPLETE DOTTIE DRIPPLE
I'LL CALL YOU.
SIGH.
BUZZ!!
DAVID, IT'S MINNIE! CAN YOU COME DOWN RIGHT AWAY?

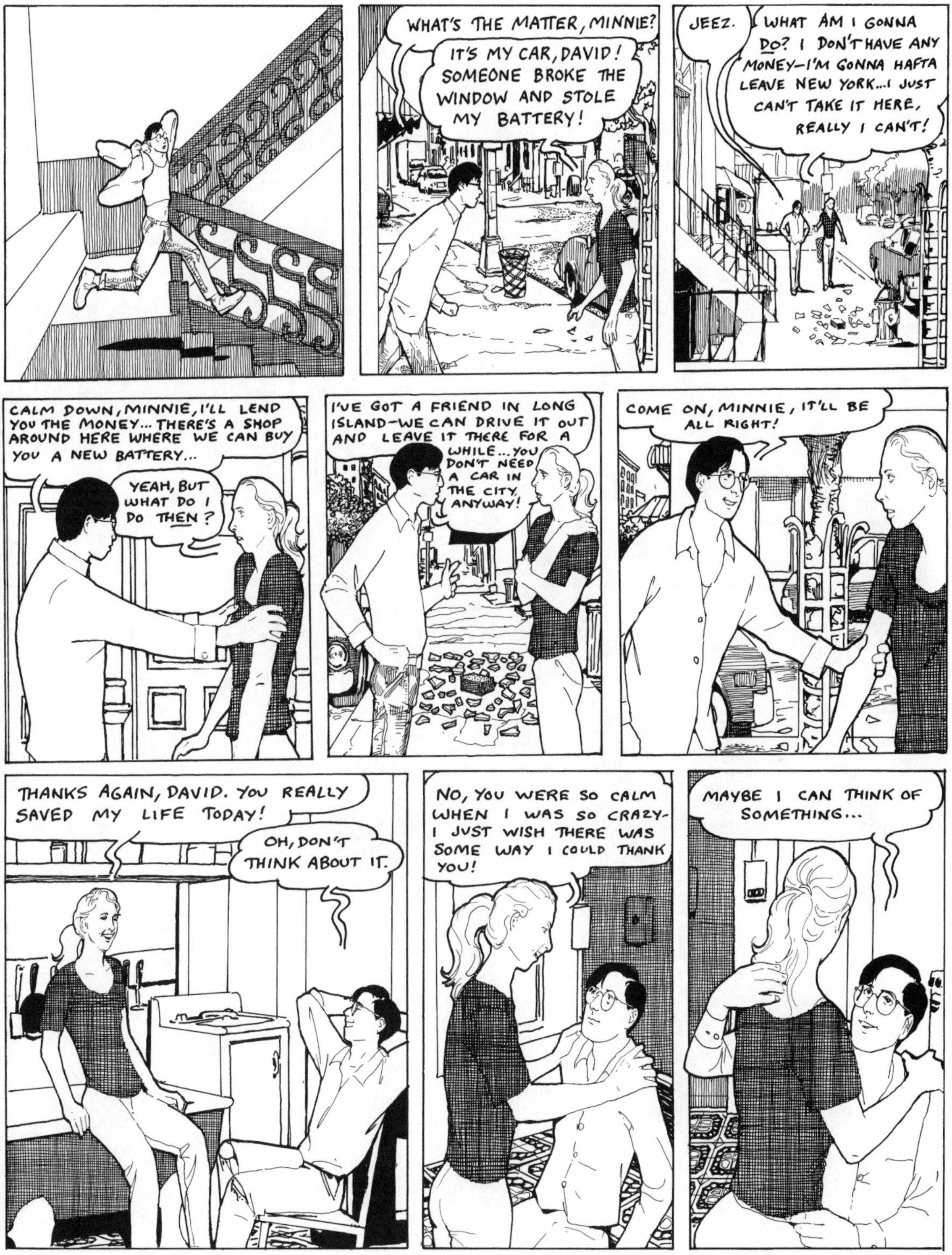

WHAT'S THE MATTER, MINNIE?
IT'S MY CAR, DAVID! SOMEONE BROKE THE WINDOW AND STOLE MY BATTERY!
JEEZ.
WHAT AM I GONNA DO? I DON'T HAVE ANY MONEY—I'M GONNA HAFTA LEAVE NEW YORK...I JUST CAN'T TAKE IT HERE, REALLY I CAN'T!
CALM DOWN, MINNIE, I'LL LEND YOU THE MONEY... THERE'S A SHOP AROUND HERE WHERE WE CAN BUY YOU A NEW BATTERY...
YEAH, BUT WHAT DO I DO THEN?
I'VE GOT A FRIEND IN LONG ISLAND—WE CAN DRIVE IT OUT AND LEAVE IT THERE FOR A WHILE... YOU DON'T NEED A CAR IN THE CITY, ANYWAY!
COME ON, MINNIE, IT'LL BE ALL RIGHT!
THANKS AGAIN, DAVID. YOU REALLY SAVED MY LIFE TODAY!
OH, DON'T THINK ABOUT IT.
NO, YOU WERE SO CALM WHEN I WAS SO CRAZY—I JUST WISH THERE WAS SOME WAY I COULD THANK YOU!
MAYBE I CAN THINK OF SOMETHING...

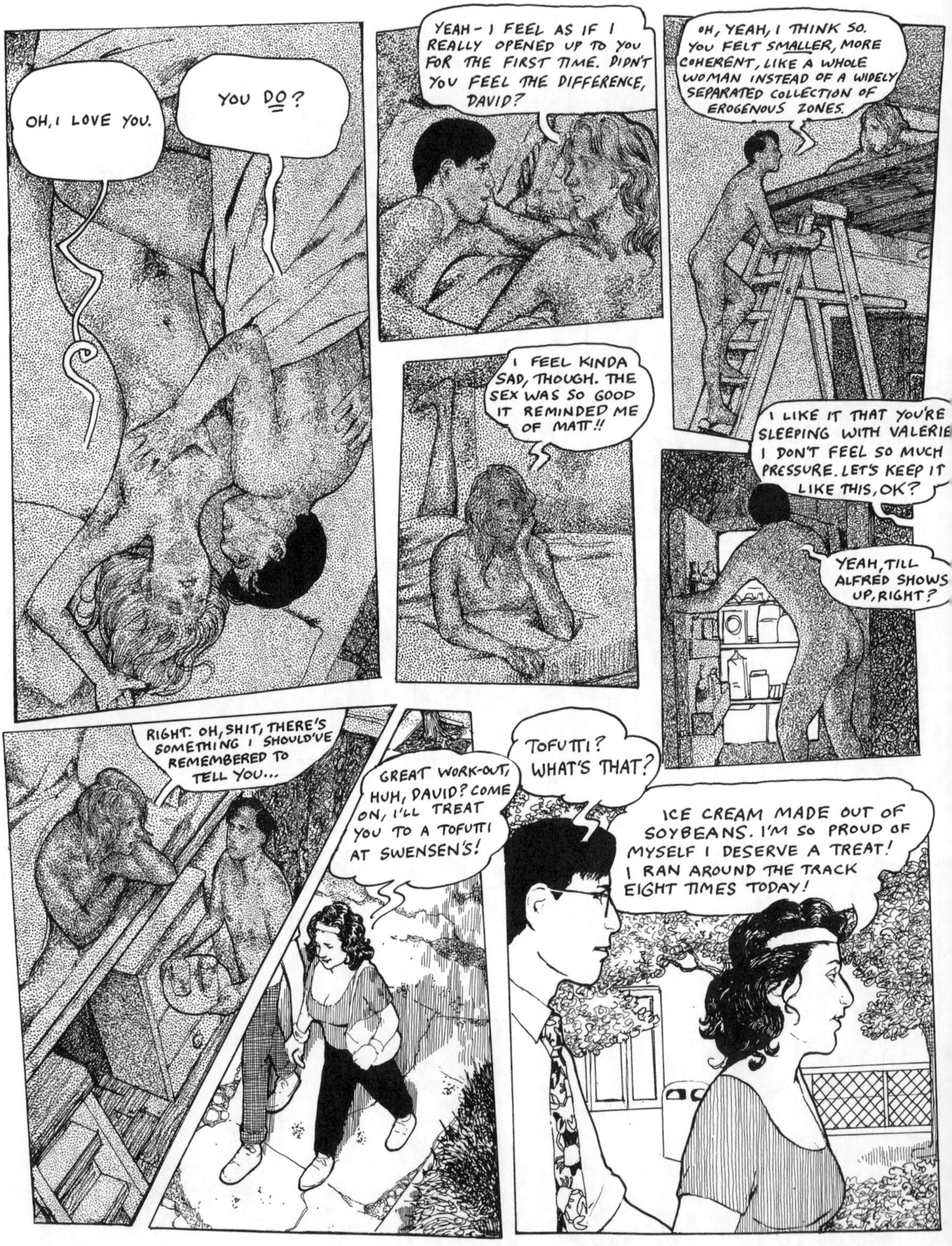
OH, I LOVE YOU.
YOU DO?
YEAH - I FEEL AS IF I REALLY OPENED UP TO YOU FOR THE FIRST TIME. DIDN'T YOU FEEL THE DIFFERENCE, DAVID?
OH, YEAH, I THINK SO. YOU FELT SMALLER, MORE COHERENT, LIKE A WHOLE WOMAN INSTEAD OF A WIDELY SEPARATED COLLECTION OF EROGENOUS ZONES.
I FEEL KINDA SAD, THOUGH. THE SEX WAS SO GOOD IT REMINDED ME OF MATT!!
I LIKE IT THAT YOU'RE SLEEPING WITH VALERIE. I DON'T FEEL SO MUCH PRESSURE. LET'S KEEP IT LIKE THIS, OK?
YEAH, TILL ALFRED SHOWS UP, RIGHT?
RIGHT. OH, SHIT, THERE'S SOMETHING I SHOULD'VE REMEMBERED TO TELL YOU...
GREAT WORK-OUT, HUH, DAVID? COME ON, I'LL TREAT YOU TO A TOFUTTI AT SWENSEN'S!
TOFUTTI? WHAT'S THAT?
ICE CREAM MADE OUT OF SOYBEANS. I'M SO PROUD OF MYSELF I DESERVE A TREAT! I RAN AROUND THE TRACK EIGHT TIMES TODAY!

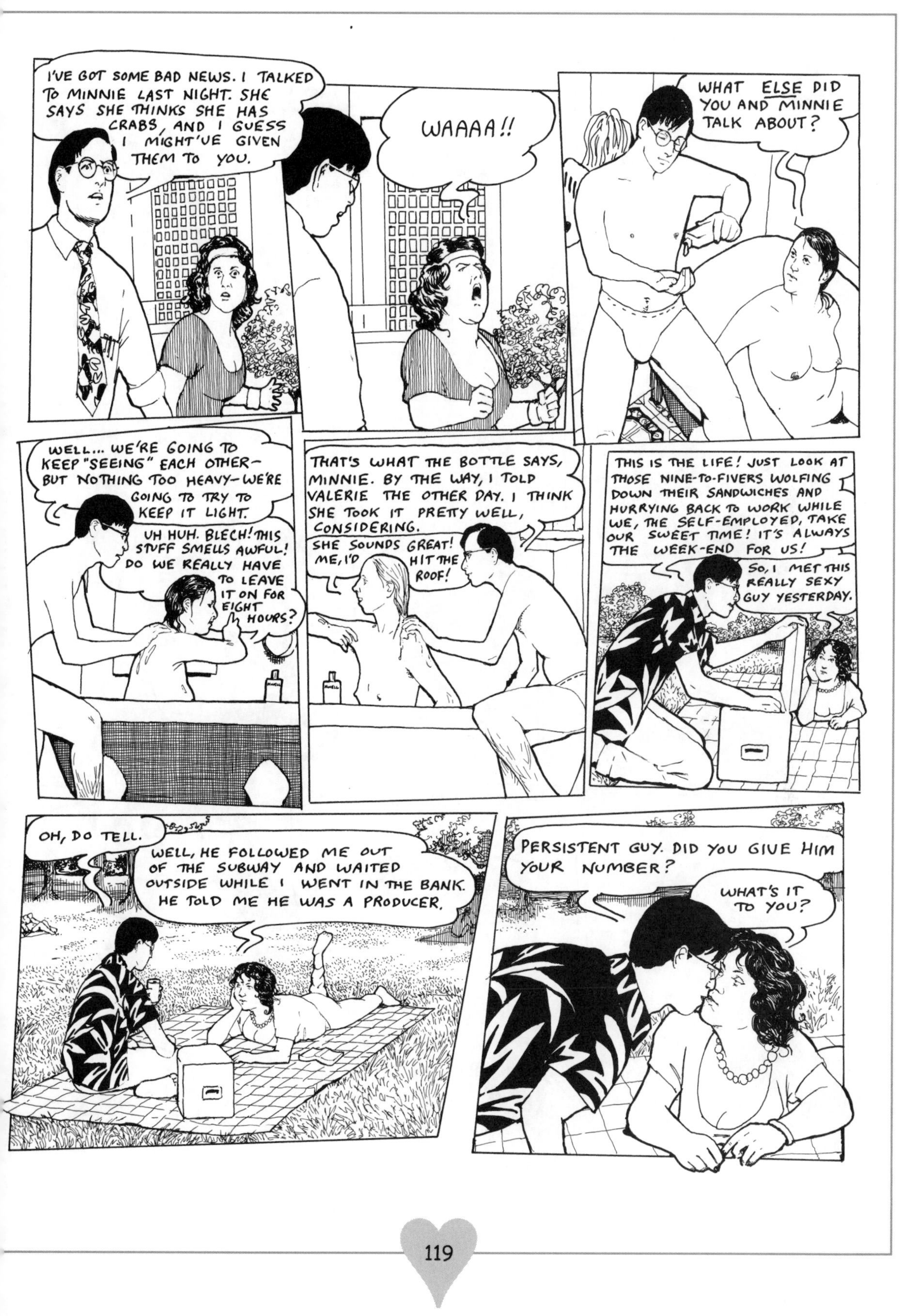
I'VE GOT SOME BAD NEWS. I TALKED TO MINNIE LAST NIGHT. SHE SAYS SHE THINKS SHE HAS CRABS, AND I GUESS I MIGHT'VE GIVEN THEM TO YOU.
WAAAA!!
WHAT ELSE DID YOU AND MINNIE TALK ABOUT?
WELL... WE'RE GOING TO KEEP "SEEING" EACH OTHER- BUT NOTHING TOO HEAVY- WE'RE GOING TO TRY TO KEEP IT LIGHT.
UH HUH. BLECH! THIS STUFF SMELLS AWFUL! DO WE REALLY HAVE TO LEAVE IT ON FOR EIGHT HOURS?
THAT'S WHAT THE BOTTLE SAYS, MINNIE. BY THE WAY, I TOLD VALERIE THE OTHER DAY. I THINK SHE TOOK IT PRETTY WELL, CONSIDERING.
SHE SOUNDS GREAT! ME, I'D HIT THE ROOF!
THIS IS THE LIFE! JUST LOOK AT THOSE NINE-TO-FIVERS WOLFING DOWN THEIR SANDWICHES AND HURRYING BACK TO WORK WHILE WE, THE SELF-EMPLOYED, TAKE OUR SWEET TIME! IT'S ALWAYS THE WEEK-END FOR US!
SO, I MET THIS REALLY SEXY GUY YESTERDAY.
OH, DO TELL.
WELL, HE FOLLOWED ME OUT OF THE SUBWAY AND WAITED OUTSIDE WHILE I WENT IN THE BANK. HE TOLD ME HE WAS A PRODUCER.
PERSISTENT GUY. DID YOU GIVE HIM YOUR NUMBER?
WHAT'S IT TO YOU?

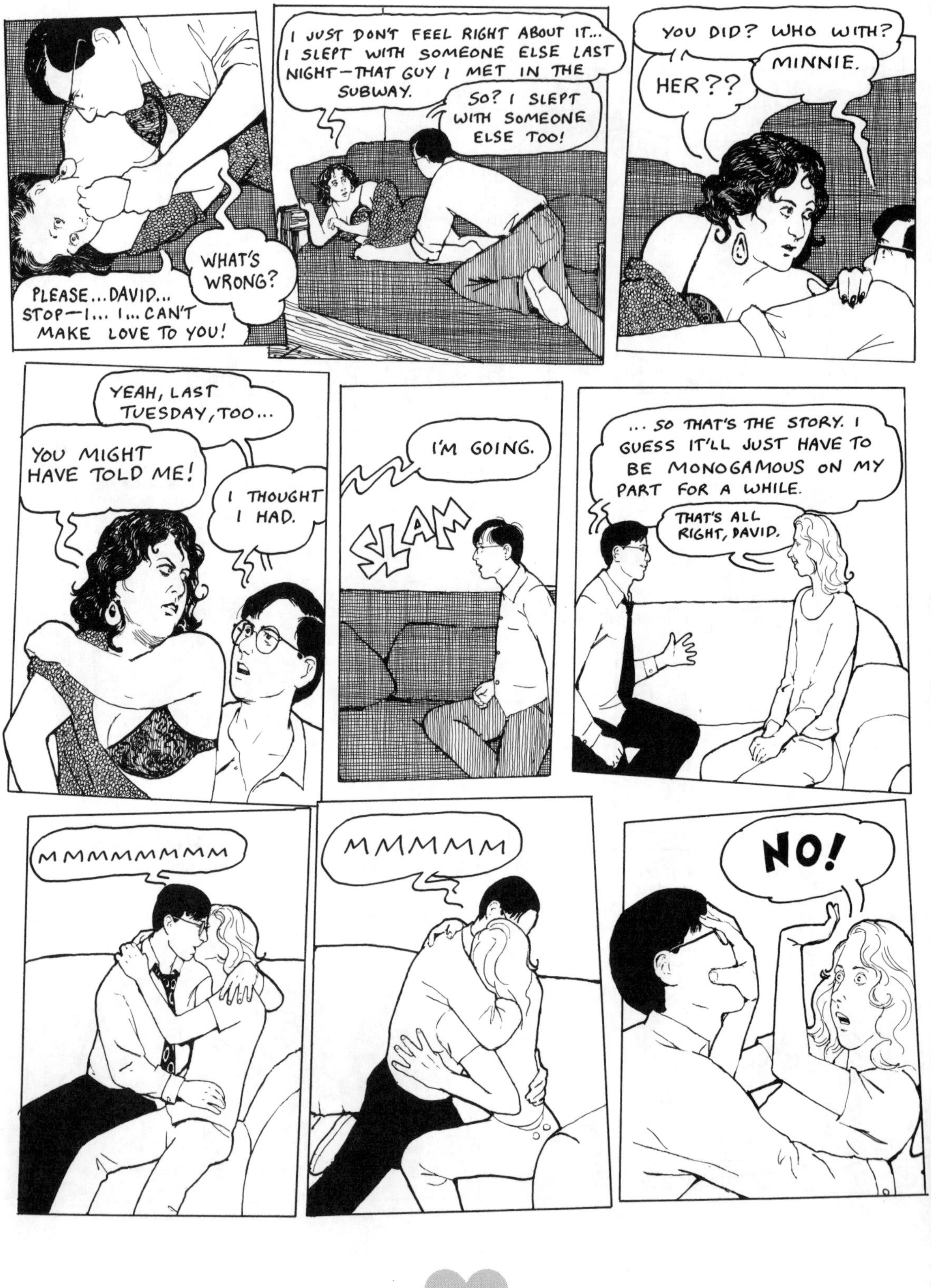
WHAT'S WRONG?
PLEASE... DAVID... STOP—I... I... CAN'T MAKE LOVE TO YOU!
I JUST DON'T FEEL RIGHT ABOUT IT... I SLEPT WITH SOMEONE ELSE LAST NIGHT—THAT GUY I MET IN THE SUBWAY.
SO? I SLEPT WITH SOMEONE ELSE TOO!
YOU DID? WHO WITH?
MINNIE.
HER??
YEAH, LAST TUESDAY, TOO...
YOU MIGHT HAVE TOLD ME!
I THOUGHT I HAD.
I'M GOING.
SLAM
... SO THAT'S THE STORY. I GUESS IT'LL JUST HAVE TO BE MONOGAMOUS ON MY PART FOR A WHILE.
THAT'S ALL RIGHT, DAVID.
MMMMMMMM
MMMMM
NO!

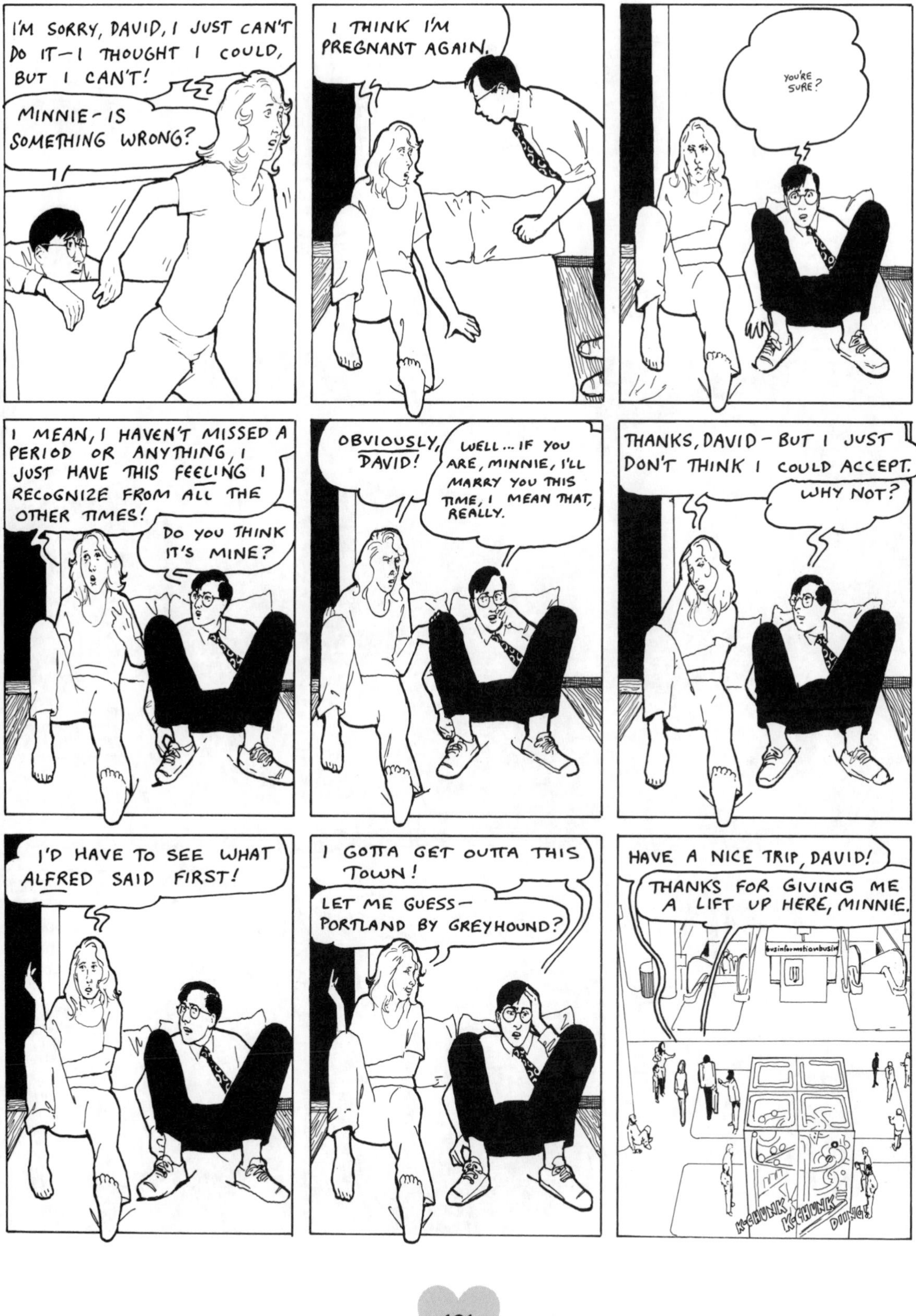
I'M SORRY, DAVID, I JUST CAN'T DO IT—I THOUGHT I COULD, BUT I CAN'T!
MINNIE-IS SOMETHING WRONG?
I THINK I'M PREGNANT AGAIN.
YOU'RE SURE?
I MEAN, I HAVEN'T MISSED A PERIOD OR ANYTHING, I JUST HAVE THIS FEELING I RECOGNIZE FROM ALL THE OTHER TIMES!
DO YOU THINK IT'S MINE?
OBVIOUSLY, DAVID!
WELL... IF YOU ARE, MINNIE, I'LL MARRY YOU THIS TIME, I MEAN THAT, REALLY.
THANKS, DAVID - BUT I JUST DON'T THINK I COULD ACCEPT.
WHY NOT?
I'D HAVE TO SEE WHAT ALFRED SAID FIRST!
I GOTTA GET OUTTA THIS TOWN!
LET ME GUESS-PORTLAND BY GREYHOUND?
HAVE A NICE TRIP, DAVID!
THANKS FOR GIVING ME A LIFT UP HERE, MINNIE.
businformationbusin
K-CHUNK
K-CHUNK
DING!

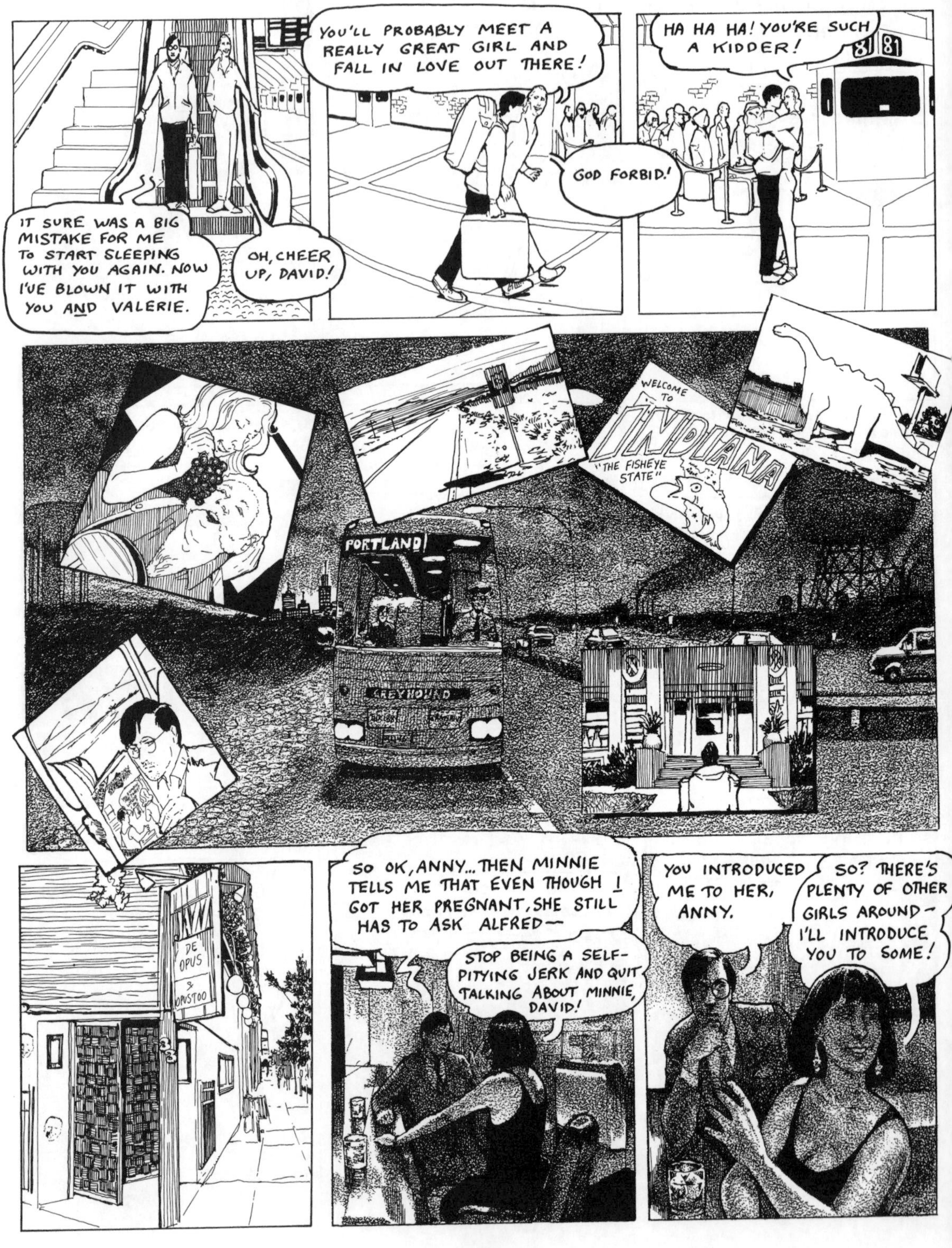
IT SURE WAS A BIG MISTAKE FOR ME TO START SLEEPING WITH YOU AGAIN. NOW I'VE BLOWN IT WITH YOU AND VALERIE.
OH, CHEER UP, DAVID!
YOU'LL PROBABLY MEET A REALLY GREAT GIRL AND FALL IN LOVE OUT THERE!
GOD FORBID!
HA HA HA! YOU'RE SUCH A KIDDER!
81
81
WELCOME TO INDIANA
"THE FISHEYE STATE"
PORTLAND
GREYHOUND
DE OPUS
OPUSTOO
SO OK, ANNY... THEN MINNIE TELLS ME THAT EVEN THOUGH I GOT HER PREGNANT, SHE STILL HAS TO ASK ALFRED—
STOP BEING A SELF-PITYING JERK AND QUIT TALKING ABOUT MINNIE, DAVID!
YOU INTRODUCED ME TO HER, ANNY.
SO? THERE'S PLENTY OF OTHER GIRLS AROUND— I'LL INTRODUCE YOU TO SOME!

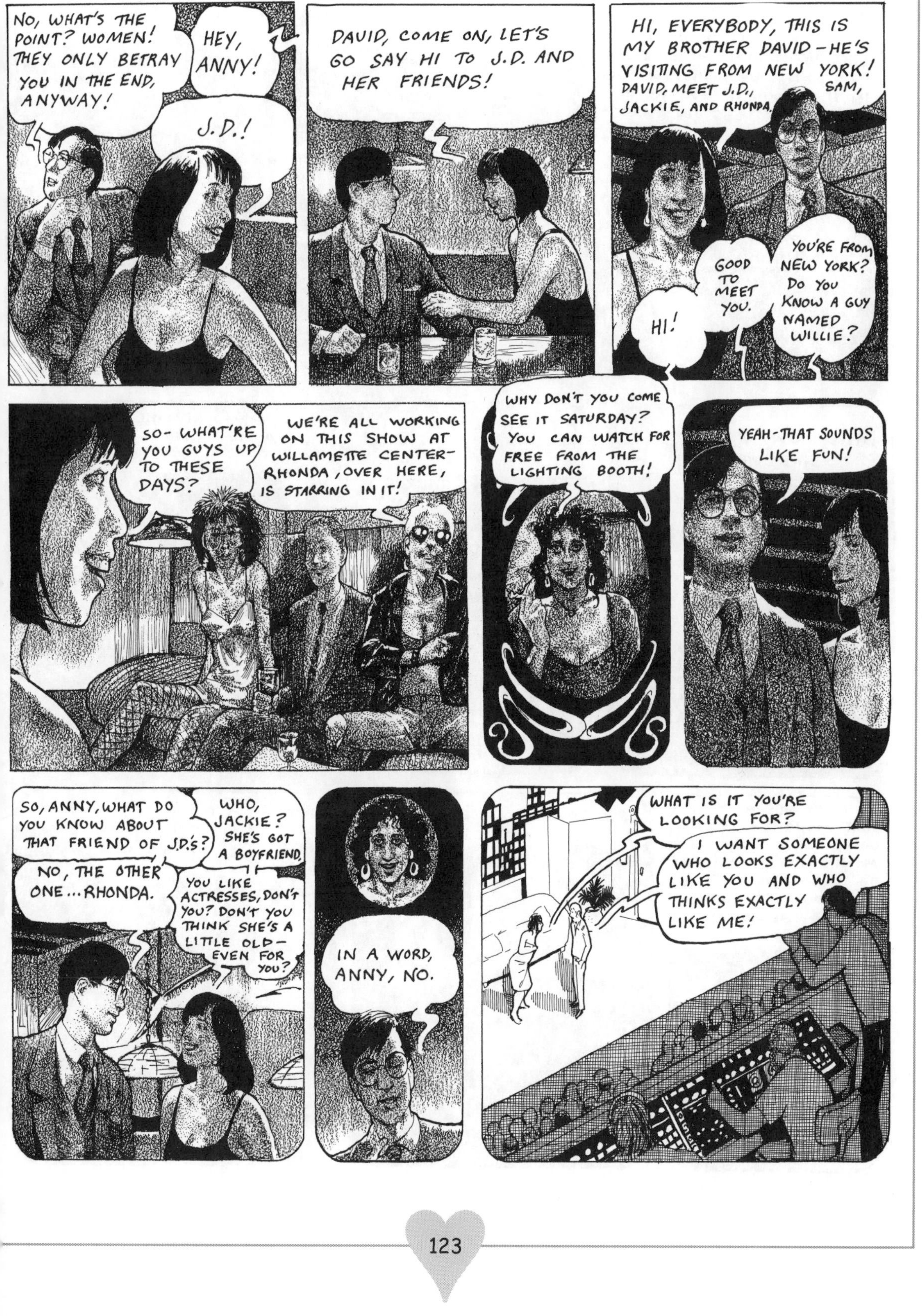

NO, WHAT'S THE POINT? WOMEN! THEY ONLY BETRAY YOU IN THE END, ANYWAY!
HEY, ANNY!
J.D.!
DAVID, COME ON, LET'S GO SAY HI TO J.D. AND HER FRIENDS!
HI, EVERYBODY, THIS IS MY BROTHER DAVID - HE'S VISITING FROM NEW YORK! DAVID, MEET J.D., SAM, JACKIE, AND RHONDA.
HI!
GOOD TO MEET YOU.
YOU'RE FROM NEW YORK? DO YOU KNOW A GUY NAMED WILLIE?
SO- WHAT'RE YOU GUYS UP TO THESE DAYS?
WE'RE ALL WORKING ON THIS SHOW AT WILLAMETTE CENTER- RHONDA, OVER HERE, IS STARRING IN IT!
WHY DON'T YOU COME SEE IT SATURDAY? YOU CAN WATCH FOR FREE FROM THE LIGHTING BOOTH!
YEAH-THAT SOUNDS LIKE FUN!
SO, ANNY, WHAT DO YOU KNOW ABOUT THAT FRIEND OF J.D.'S?
WHO, JACKIE? SHE'S GOT A BOYFRIEND.
NO, THE OTHER ONE... RHONDA.
YOU LIKE ACTRESSES, DON'T YOU? DON'T YOU THINK SHE'S A LITTLE OLD- EVEN FOR YOU?
IN A WORD, ANNY, NO.
WHAT IS IT YOU'RE LOOKING FOR?
I WANT SOMEONE WHO LOOKS EXACTLY LIKE YOU AND WHO THINKS EXACTLY LIKE ME!

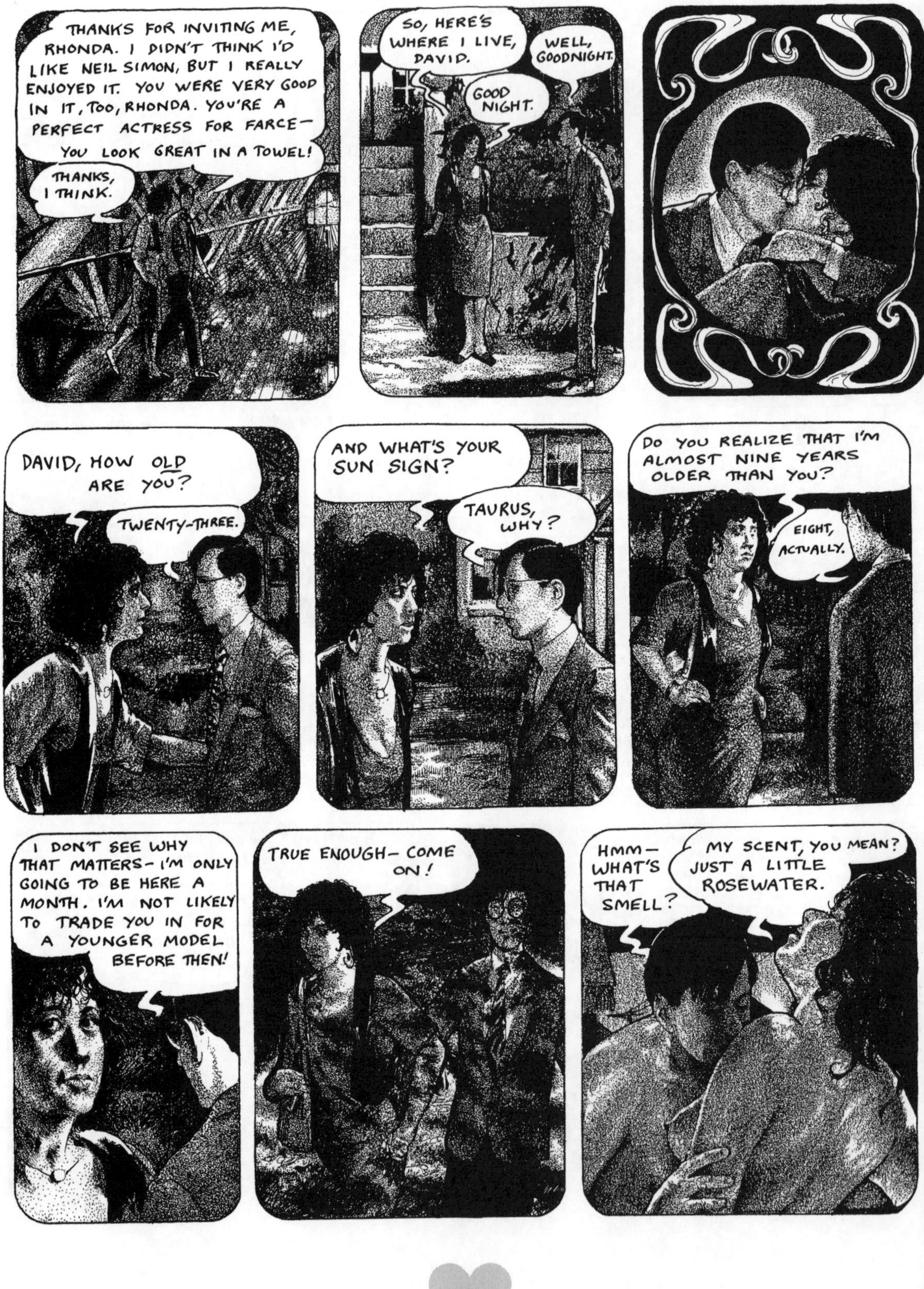
THANKS FOR INVITING ME, RHONDA. I DIDN'T THINK I'D LIKE NEIL SIMON, BUT I REALLY ENJOYED IT. YOU WERE VERY GOOD IN IT, TOO, RHONDA. YOU'RE A PERFECT ACTRESS FOR FARCE— YOU LOOK GREAT IN A TOWEL!
THANKS, I THINK.
SO, HERE'S WHERE I LIVE, DAVID.
GOOD NIGHT.
WELL, GOODNIGHT.
DAVID, HOW OLD ARE YOU?
TWENTY-THREE.
AND WHAT'S YOUR SUN SIGN?
TAURUS, WHY?
DO YOU REALIZE THAT I'M ALMOST NINE YEARS OLDER THAN YOU?
EIGHT, ACTUALLY.
I DON'T SEE WHY THAT MATTERS– I'M ONLY GOING TO BE HERE A MONTH. I'M NOT LIKELY TO TRADE YOU IN FOR A YOUNGER MODEL BEFORE THEN!
TRUE ENOUGH– COME ON!
HMM– WHAT'S THAT SMELL?
MY SCENT, YOU MEAN? JUST A LITTLE ROSEWATER.

IT REMINDS ME OF SOMETHING—
I CAN'T QUITE THINK WHAT...

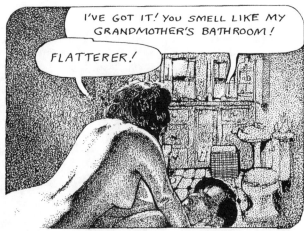

I'VE GOT IT! YOU SMELL LIKE MY GRANDMOTHER'S BATHROOM!

FLATTERER!

IT'S WONDERFUL SPENDING TIME WITH YOU, DAVID—YOU'RE SO LAID-BACK!

WELL, OK, JUST SO I'M NOT MELLOW!

SEE, BEFORE I WAS WITH YOU, I WAS WITH THIS GUY WHO WAS SO CONTROLLING HE WOULDN'T LET ME OUT OF HIS SIGHT—EVER!

REALLY? WHAT IF YOU HAD TO GO TO THE LADIES' ROOM?

THAT'S THE DIFFERENCE BETWEEN PORTLAND AND NEW YORK—IN NEW YORK ROBERT WOULD BE AN ARTIST. HERE HE'S JUST PSYCHOTIC.

WE WOUND UP NOT GOING OUTSIDE MUCH.

REMINDS ME OF THESE TWO CONCEPTUAL ARTISTS WHO HAD THEMSELVES ROPED TOGETHER FOR A YEAR.

HI DAVID!

PAPRIKA!

PAPRIKA, THIS IS RHONDA.

AND WHO'S THIS LITTLE GUY?

HIS NAME'S ANDAMO. SO, DAVID—WHAT BRINGS YOU BACK HERE?

OH, JUST KIND OF A VACATION FROM EVERYTHING IN NEW YORK....

SO, HOW'S MINNIE?

UHM... SHE'S MOVED IN WITH ANOTHER GUY.

COOCHIE COO!

125

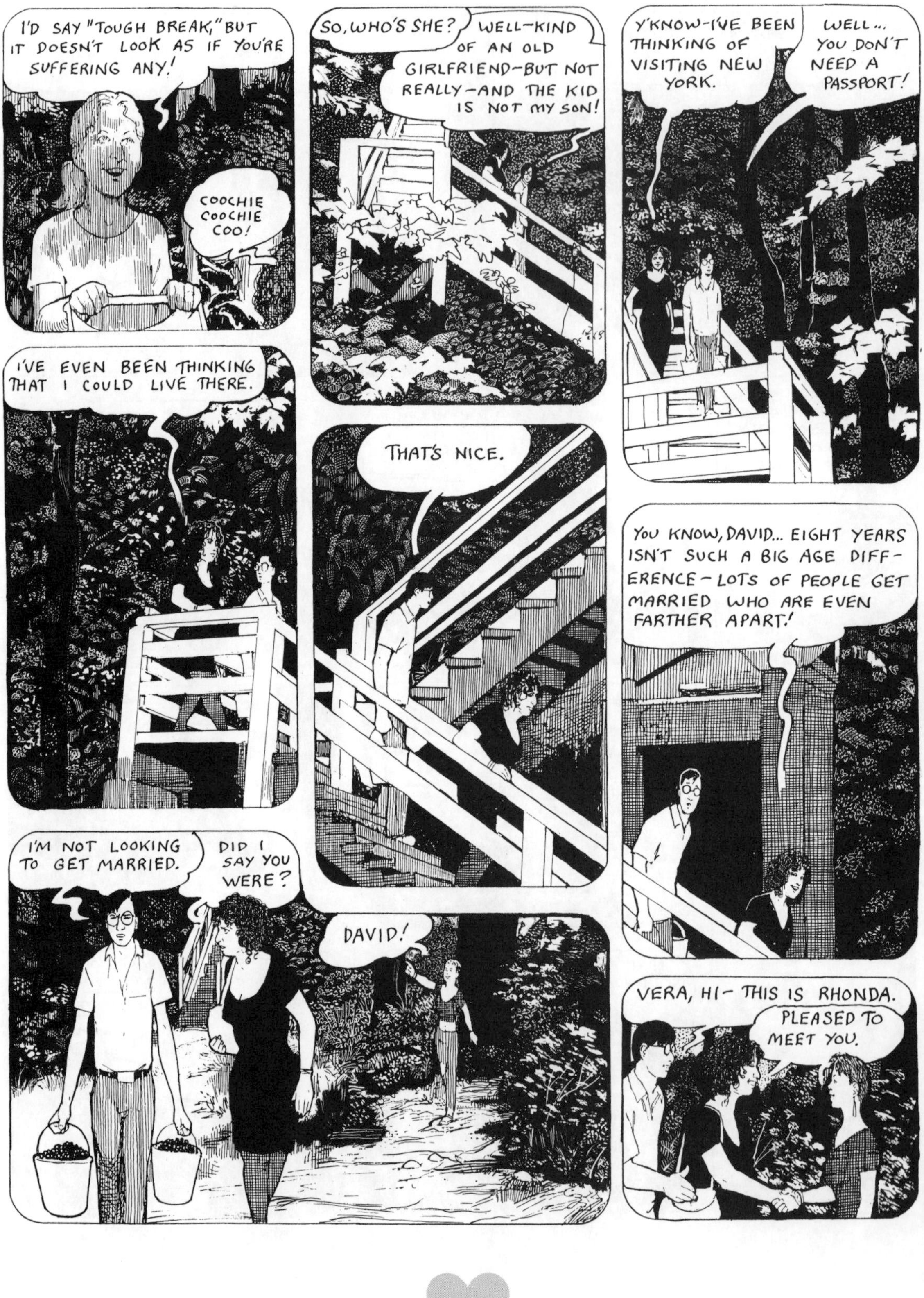
I'D SAY "TOUGH BREAK," BUT IT DOESN'T LOOK AS IF YOU'RE SUFFERING ANY!
COOCHIE COOCHIE COO!
SO, WHO'S SHE?
WELL—KIND OF AN OLD GIRLFRIEND—BUT NOT REALLY—AND THE KID IS NOT MY SON!
Y'KNOW—I'VE BEEN THINKING OF VISITING NEW YORK.
WELL... YOU DON'T NEED A PASSPORT!
I'VE EVEN BEEN THINKING THAT I COULD LIVE THERE.
THAT'S NICE.
YOU KNOW, DAVID... EIGHT YEARS ISN'T SUCH A BIG AGE DIFF-ERENCE—LOTS OF PEOPLE GET MARRIED WHO ARE EVEN FARTHER APART!
I'M NOT LOOKING TO GET MARRIED.
DID I SAY YOU WERE?
DAVID!
VERA, HI—THIS IS RHONDA.
PLEASED TO MEET YOU.

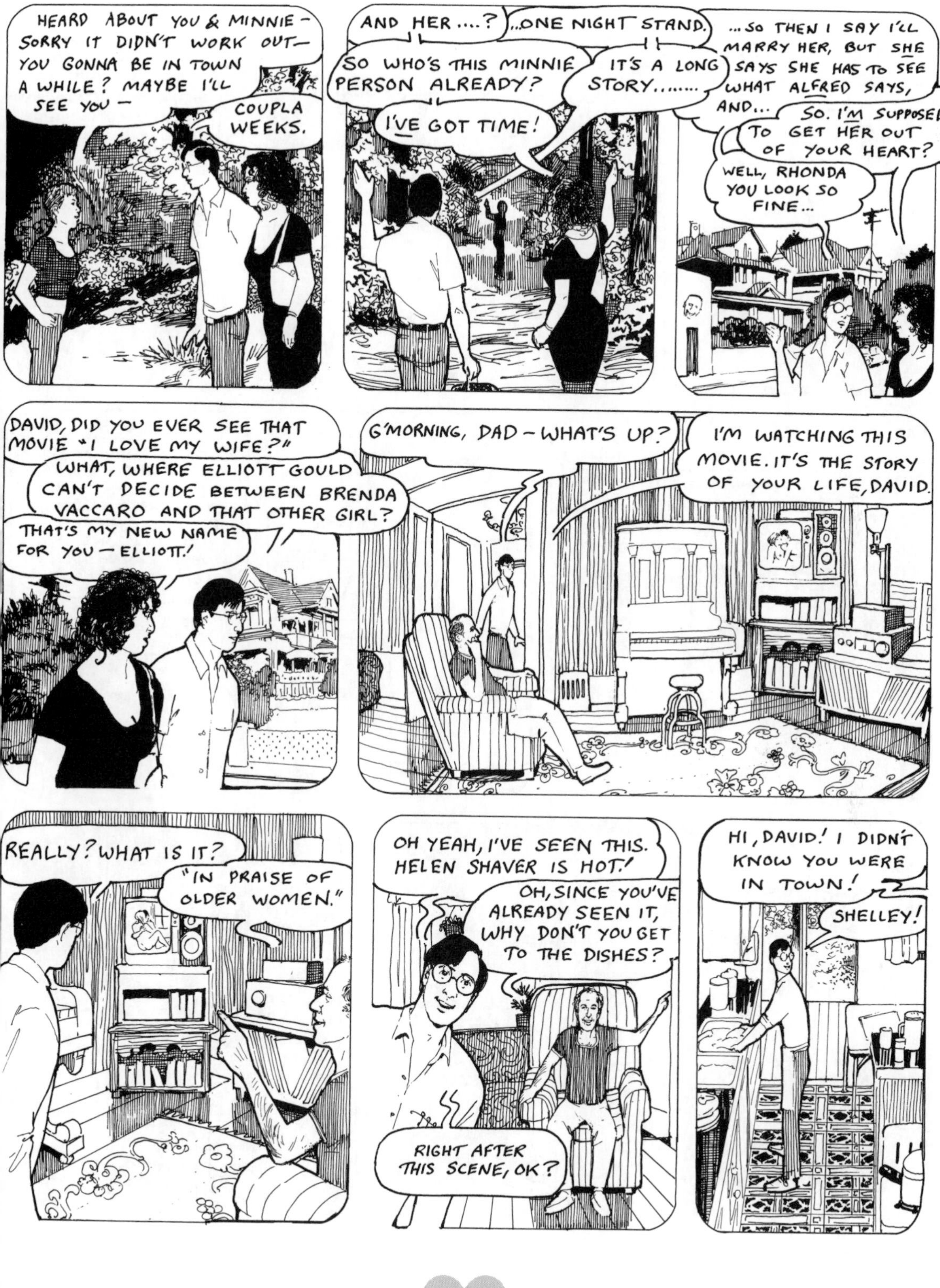
HEARD ABOUT YOU & MINNIE - SORRY IT DIDN'T WORK OUT- YOU GONNA BE IN TOWN A WHILE? MAYBE I'LL SEE YOU -
COUPLA WEEKS.
AND HER....?
...ONE NIGHT STAND.
SO WHO'S THIS MINNIE PERSON ALREADY?
IT'S A LONG STORY.......
I'VE GOT TIME!
...SO THEN I SAY I'LL MARRY HER, BUT SHE SAYS SHE HAS TO SEE WHAT ALFRED SAYS, AND...
SO. I'M SUPPOSED TO GET HER OUT OF YOUR HEART?
WELL, RHONDA YOU LOOK SO FINE...
DAVID, DID YOU EVER SEE THAT MOVIE "I LOVE MY WIFE?"
WHAT, WHERE ELLIOTT GOULD CAN'T DECIDE BETWEEN BRENDA VACCARO AND THAT OTHER GIRL?
THAT'S MY NEW NAME FOR YOU - ELLIOTT!
G'MORNING, DAD - WHAT'S UP?
I'M WATCHING THIS MOVIE. IT'S THE STORY OF YOUR LIFE, DAVID.
REALLY? WHAT IS IT?
"IN PRAISE OF OLDER WOMEN."
OH YEAH, I'VE SEEN THIS. HELEN SHAVER IS HOT!
OH, SINCE YOU'VE ALREADY SEEN IT, WHY DON'T YOU GET TO THE DISHES?
RIGHT AFTER THIS SCENE, OK?
HI, DAVID! I DIDN'T KNOW YOU WERE IN TOWN!
SHELLEY!

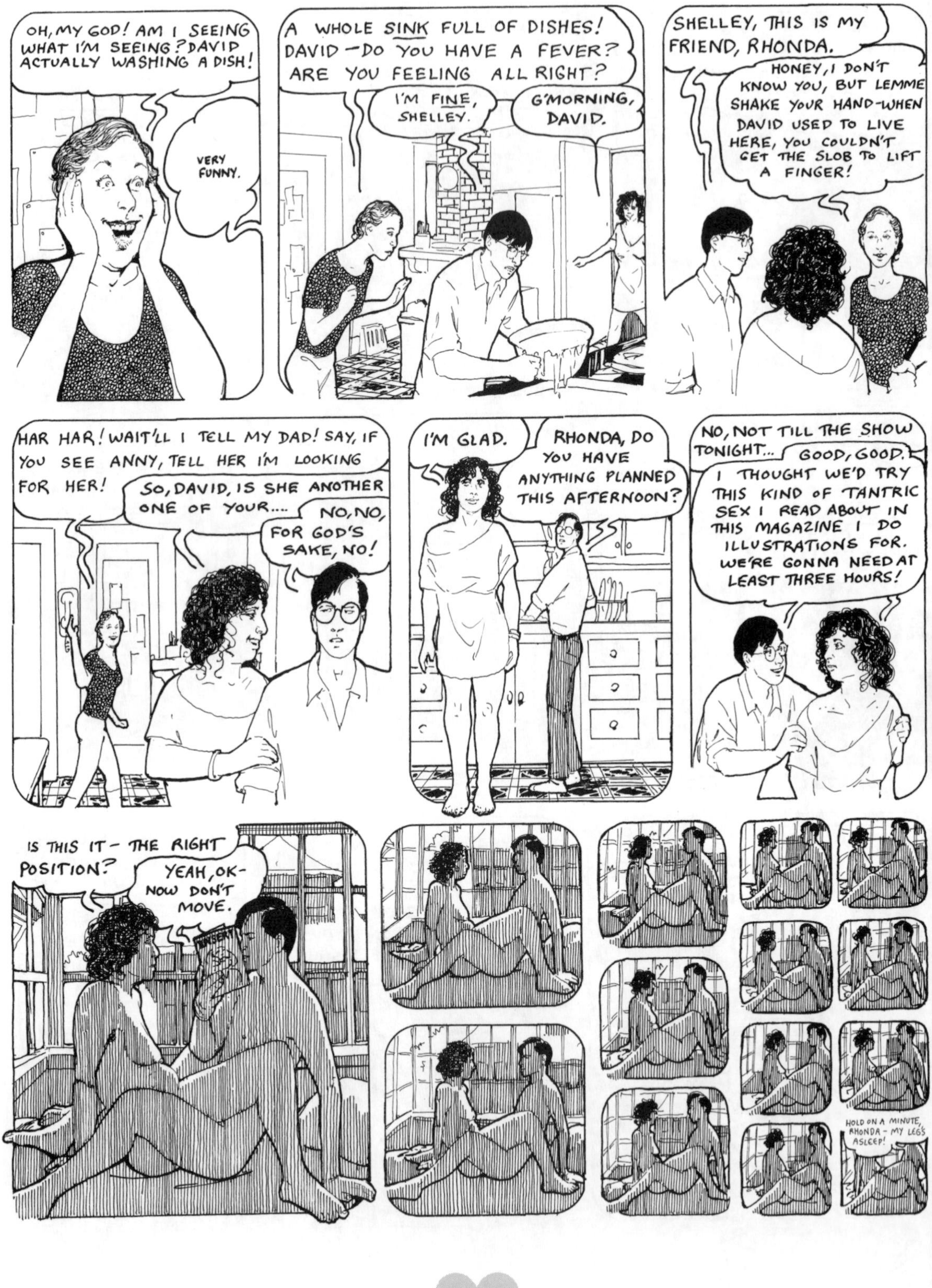
OH, MY GOD! AM I SEEING WHAT I'M SEEING? DAVID ACTUALLY WASHING A DISH!
VERY FUNNY.
A WHOLE SINK FULL OF DISHES! DAVID—DO YOU HAVE A FEVER? ARE YOU FEELING ALL RIGHT?
I'M FINE, SHELLEY.
G'MORNING, DAVID.
SHELLEY, THIS IS MY FRIEND, RHONDA.
HONEY, I DON'T KNOW YOU, BUT LEMME SHAKE YOUR HAND—WHEN DAVID USED TO LIVE HERE, YOU COULDN'T GET THE SLOB TO LIFT A FINGER!
HAR HAR! WAIT'LL I TELL MY DAD! SAY, IF YOU SEE ANNY, TELL HER I'M LOOKING FOR HER!
SO, DAVID, IS SHE ANOTHER ONE OF YOUR....
NO, NO, FOR GOD'S SAKE, NO!
I'M GLAD.
RHONDA, DO YOU HAVE ANYTHING PLANNED THIS AFTERNOON?
NO, NOT TILL THE SHOW TONIGHT...
GOOD, GOOD. I THOUGHT WE'D TRY THIS KIND OF TANTRIC SEX I READ ABOUT IN THIS MAGAZINE I DO ILLUSTRATIONS FOR. WE'RE GONNA NEED AT LEAST THREE HOURS!
IS THIS IT—THE RIGHT POSITION?
YEAH, OK—NOW DON'T MOVE.
HOLD ON A MINUTE, RHONDA—MY LEG'S ASLEEP!

IS YOUR BACK ANY BETTER TODAY, RHONDA?
IT'S STILL A LITTLE STIFF.
STEPPING STONE
RHONDA, I'VE BEEN THINKING— I CAN'T PROMISE TO WAIT FOR YOU IF YOU PLAN TO MOVE TO NEW YORK. SEE, I JUST WENT THROUGH THE SAME THING WITH MINNIE!
DAVID, I'M NOT MINNIE!
I KNOW THAT, BUT YOU DON'T UNDERSTAND WHAT I'VE BEEN THROUGH— YOU DON'T KNOW WHAT SHE'S LIKE— YOU'VE NEVER MET HER!
SURE I HAVE!
YOU HAVE?
J.D.'S A GOOD FRIEND OF HERS— I DIDN'T KNOW WHO YOU WERE TALKING ABOUT, BUT J.D REMINDED ME. ISN'T THAT HER PHOTO ON THE WALL?
EGAD! IT IS— HOW DO SUPPOSE IT GOT THERE?
ISN'T THAT WHY YOU PICKED THIS BOOTH?
NO, HONESTLY, RHONDA, I HAD NO IDEA...
RELAX, DAVID, I BELIEVE YOU. SAY, I HAVE A FRIEND WHO CAN GET ME SOME ACID. WOULD YOU LIKE TO TAKE IT WITH ME?
WELL— I...UH...SORTA PROMISED MINNIE I'D DO IT FIRST WITH HER— ON THE BEACH.
GREAT!
YOU'VE BEEN TELLING ME FOR WEEKS HOW ROTTEN SHE TREATED YOU— I DON'T THINK YOU OWE HER ANYTHING!
YEAH, I S'POZE NOT— BUT... YOU'RE SURE IT'S SAFE?
OH, DON'T BE SUCH A BABY! I'VE BEEN TAKING IT FOR FIFTEEN YEARS AND I'M FINE!
WELL... ALL RIGHT.
YOU WON'T BE SORRY!
SERVES YOU RIGHT!

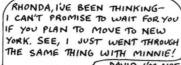

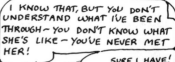

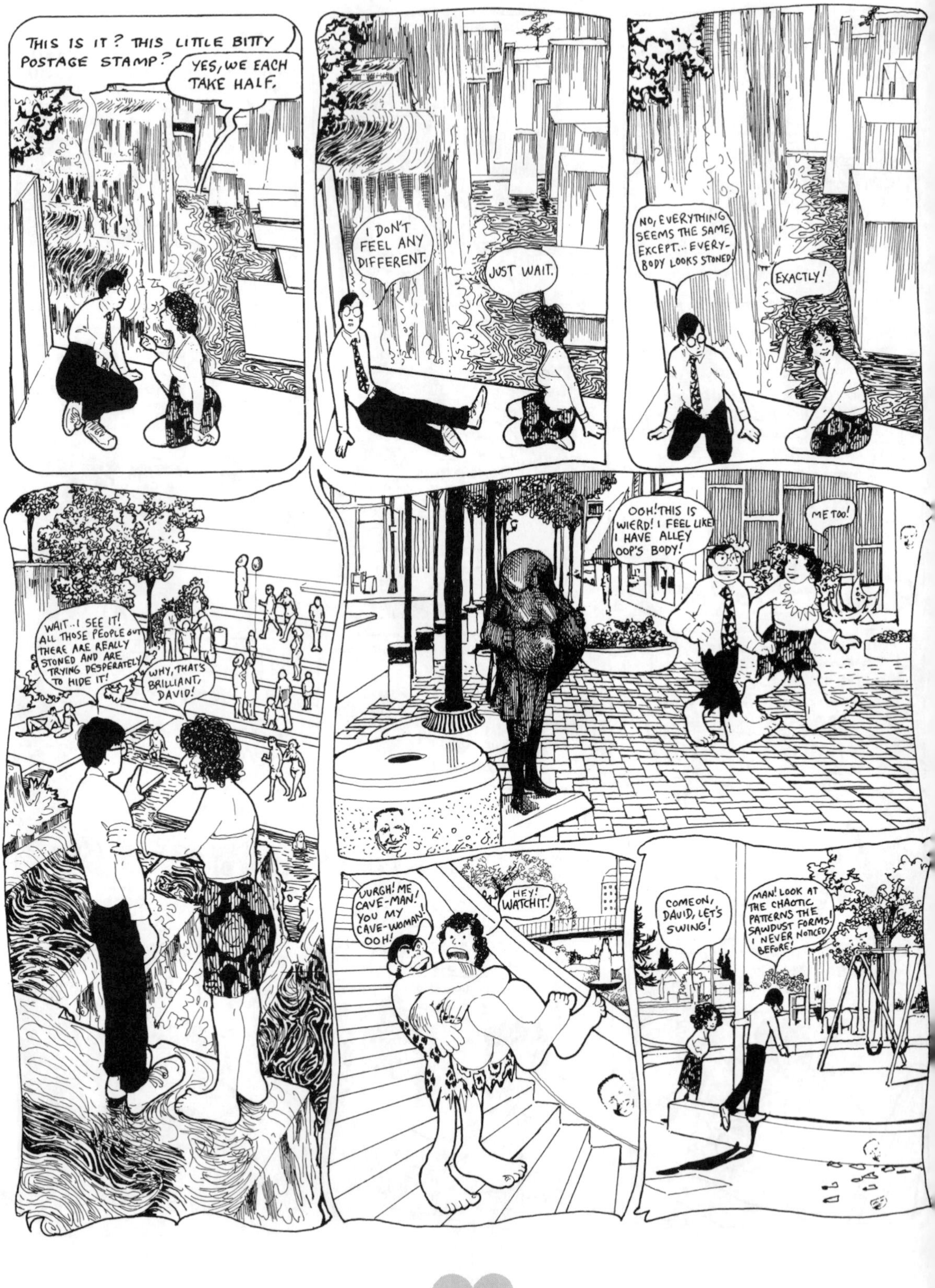
THIS IS IT? THIS LITTLE BITTY POSTAGE STAMP?
YES, WE EACH TAKE HALF.
I DON'T FEEL ANY DIFFERENT.
JUST WAIT.
NO, EVERYTHING SEEMS THE SAME, EXCEPT... EVERY-BODY LOOKS STONED!
EXACTLY!
WAIT..I SEE IT! ALL THOSE PEOPLE OUT THERE ARE REALLY STONED AND ARE TRYING DESPERATELY TO HIDE IT!
WHY, THAT'S BRILLIANT, DAVID!
OOH! THIS IS WIERD! I FEEL LIKE I HAVE ALLEY OOP'S BODY!
ME TOO!
UURGH! ME CAVE-MAN! YOU MY CAVE-WOMAN! OOH!
HEY! WATCHIT!
COMEON, DAVID, LET'S SWING!
MAN! LOOK AT THE CHAOTIC PATTERNS THE SAWDUST FORMS! I NEVER NOTICED BEFORE!

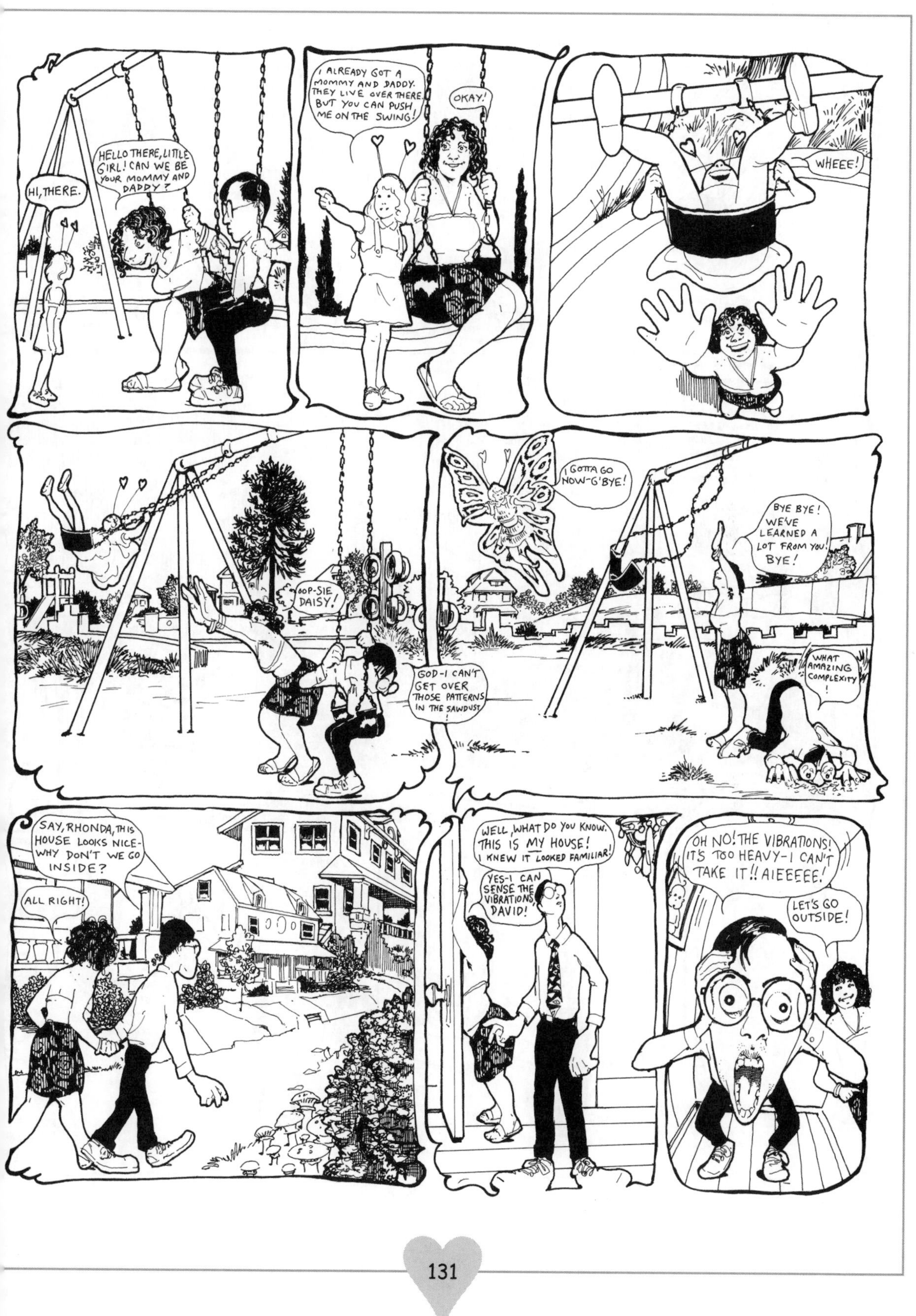
HI, THERE.
HELLO THERE, LITTLE GIRL! CAN WE BE YOUR MOMMY AND DADDY?
I ALREADY GOT A MOMMY AND DADDY. THEY LIVE OVER THERE. BUT YOU CAN PUSH ME ON THE SWING!
OKAY!
WHEEE!
OOP-SIE DAISY!
GOD-I CAN'T GET OVER THOSE PATTERNS IN THE SAWDUST!
I GOTTA GO NOW-G'BYE!
BYE BYE! WE'VE LEARNED A LOT FROM YOU! BYE!
WHAT AMAZING COMPLEXITY!
SAY, RHONDA, THIS HOUSE LOOKS NICE-WHY DON'T WE GO INSIDE?
ALL RIGHT!
WELL, WHAT DO YOU KNOW. THIS IS MY HOUSE! I KNEW IT LOOKED FAMILIAR!
YES-I CAN SENSE THE VIBRATIONS, DAVID!
OH NO! THE VIBRATIONS! IT'S TOO HEAVY-I CAN'T TAKE IT!! AIEEEEE!
LET'S GO OUTSIDE!

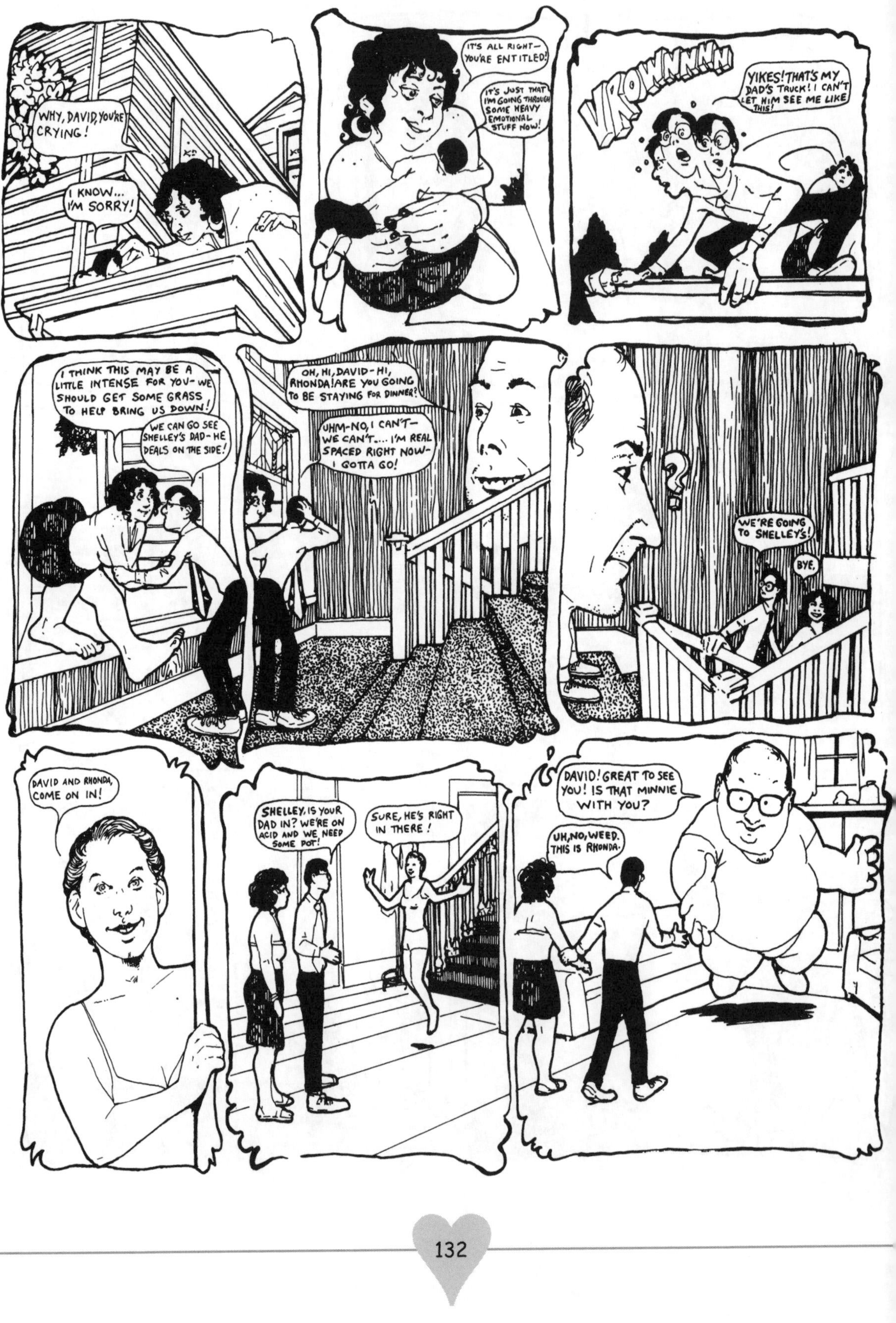
WHY, DAVID, YOU'RE CRYING!
I KNOW... I'M SORRY!
IT'S ALL RIGHT— YOU'RE ENTITLED!
IT'S JUST THAT I'M GOING THROUGH SOME HEAVY EMOTIONAL STUFF NOW!
VROWNNNN
YIKES! THAT'S MY DAD'S TRUCK! I CAN'T LET HIM SEE ME LIKE THIS!
I THINK THIS MAY BE A LITTLE INTENSE FOR YOU- WE SHOULD GET SOME GRASS TO HELP BRING US DOWN!
WE CAN GO SEE SHELLEY'S DAD- HE DEALS ON THE SIDE!
OH, HI, DAVID- HI, RHONDA! ARE YOU GOING TO BE STAYING FOR DINNER?
UHM-NO, I CAN'T- WE CAN'T.... I'M REAL SPACED RIGHT NOW- I GOTTA GO!
?
WE'RE GOING TO SHELLEY'S!
BYE.
DAVID AND RHONDA, COME ON IN!
SHELLEY, IS YOUR DAD IN? WE'RE ON ACID AND WE NEED SOME POT!
SURE, HE'S RIGHT IN THERE!
¡
DAVID! GREAT TO SEE YOU! IS THAT MINNIE WITH YOU?
UH, NO, WEED. THIS IS RHONDA.

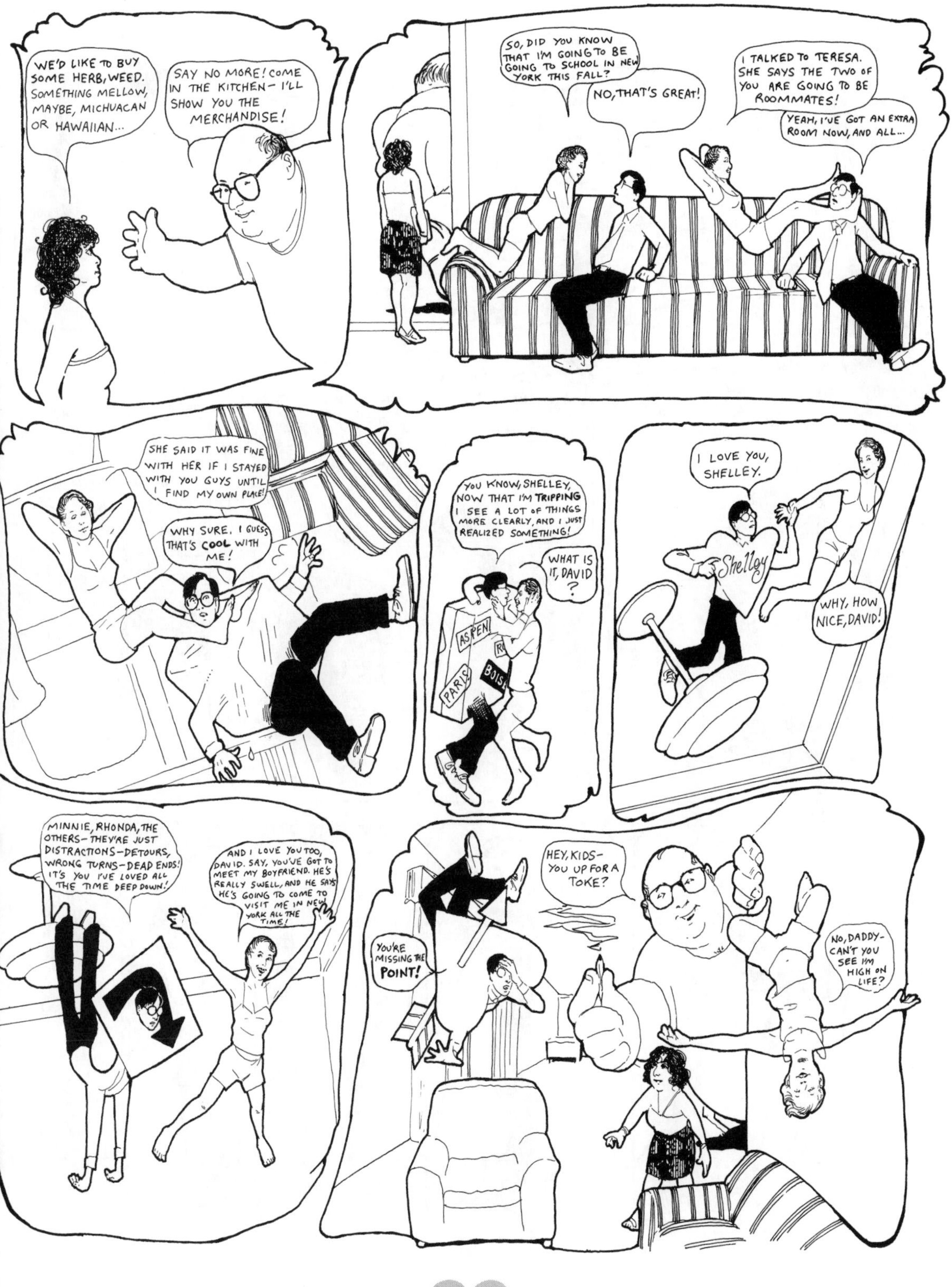
WE'D LIKE TO BUY SOME HERB, WEED. SOMETHING MELLOW, MAYBE, MICHUACAN OR HAWAIIAN...
SAY NO MORE! COME IN THE KITCHEN— I'LL SHOW YOU THE MERCHANDISE!
SO, DID YOU KNOW THAT I'M GOING TO BE GOING TO SCHOOL IN NEW YORK THIS FALL?
NO, THAT'S GREAT!
I TALKED TO TERESA. SHE SAYS THE TWO OF YOU ARE GOING TO BE ROOMMATES!
YEAH, I'VE GOT AN EXTRA ROOM NOW, AND ALL...
SHE SAID IT WAS FINE WITH HER IF I STAYED WITH YOU GUYS UNTIL I FIND MY OWN PLACE!
WHY SURE, I GUESS THAT'S **COOL** WITH ME!
YOU KNOW, SHELLEY, NOW THAT I'M **TRIPPING** I SEE A LOT OF THINGS MORE CLEARLY, AND I JUST REALIZED SOMETHING!
WHAT IS IT, DAVID ?
ASPEN
PARIS
BOISE
I LOVE YOU, SHELLEY.
Shelley
WHY, HOW NICE, DAVID!
MINNIE, RHONDA, THE OTHERS— THEY'RE JUST DISTRACTIONS—DETOURS, WRONG TURNS—DEAD ENDS! IT'S YOU I'VE LOVED ALL THE TIME DEEP DOWN!
AND I LOVE YOU TOO, DAVID. SAY, YOU'VE GOT TO MEET MY BOYFRIEND. HE'S REALLY SWELL, AND HE SAYS HE'S GOING TO COME TO VISIT ME IN NEW YORK ALL THE TIME!
HEY, KIDS— YOU UP FOR A TOKE?
YOU'RE MISSING THE **POINT!**
NO, DADDY— CAN'T YOU SEE I'M HIGH ON LIFE?

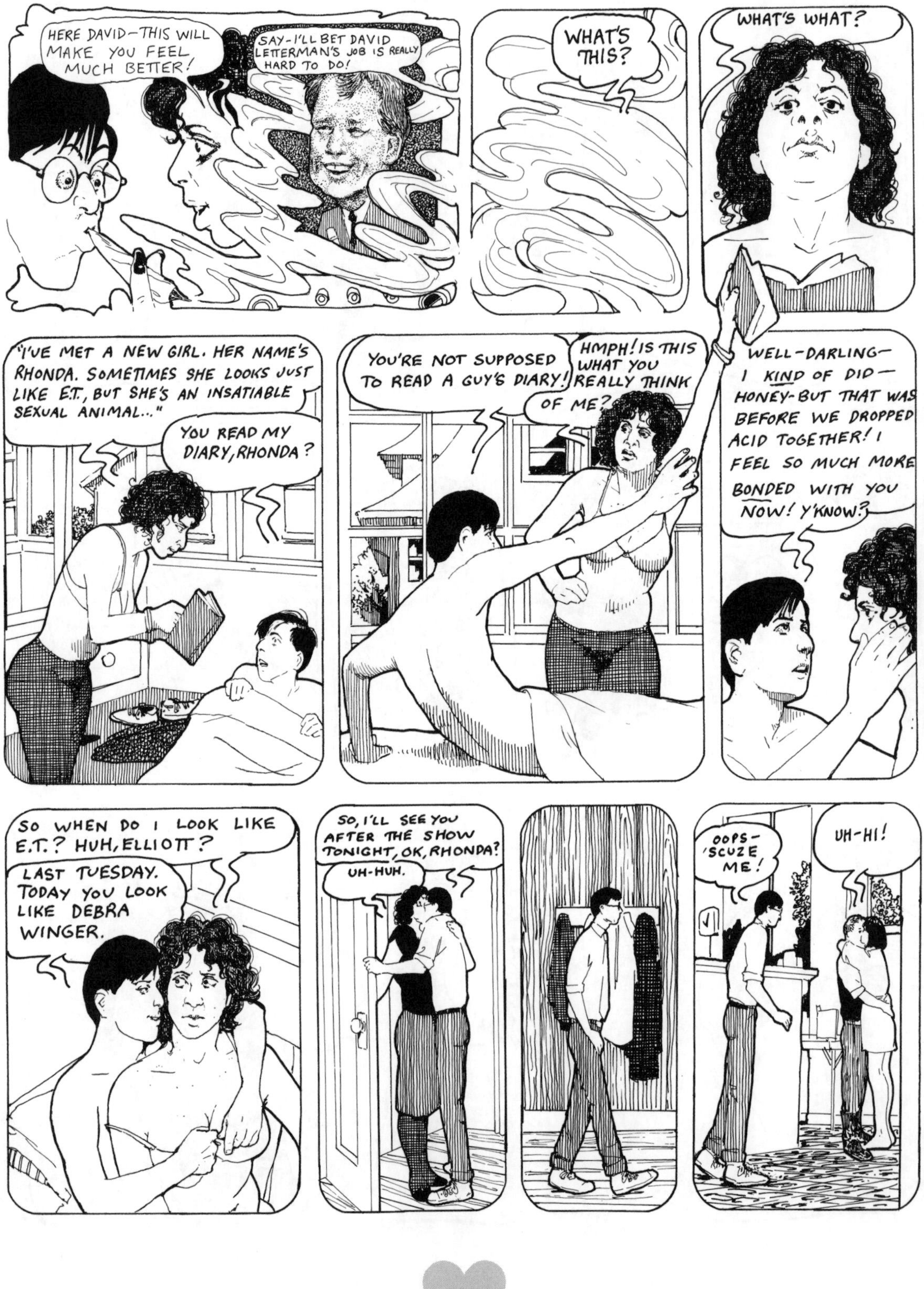
HERE DAVID—THIS WILL MAKE YOU FEEL MUCH BETTER!
SAY-I'LL BET DAVID LETTERMAN'S JOB IS REALLY HARD TO DO!
WHAT'S THIS?
WHAT'S WHAT?
"I'VE MET A NEW GIRL. HER NAME'S RHONDA. SOMETIMES SHE LOOKS JUST LIKE E.T., BUT SHE'S AN INSATIABLE SEXUAL ANIMAL..."
YOU READ MY DIARY, RHONDA?
YOU'RE NOT SUPPOSED TO READ A GUY'S DIARY!
HMPH! IS THIS WHAT YOU REALLY THINK OF ME?
WELL-DARLING-I KIND OF DID-HONEY-BUT THAT WAS BEFORE WE DROPPED ACID TOGETHER! I FEEL SO MUCH MORE BONDED WITH YOU NOW! Y'KNOW?
SO WHEN DO I LOOK LIKE E.T.? HUH, ELLIOTT?
LAST TUESDAY. TODAY YOU LOOK LIKE DEBRA WINGER.
SO, I'LL SEE YOU AFTER THE SHOW TONIGHT, OK, RHONDA?
UH-HUH.
OOPS-'SCUZE ME!
UH-HI!

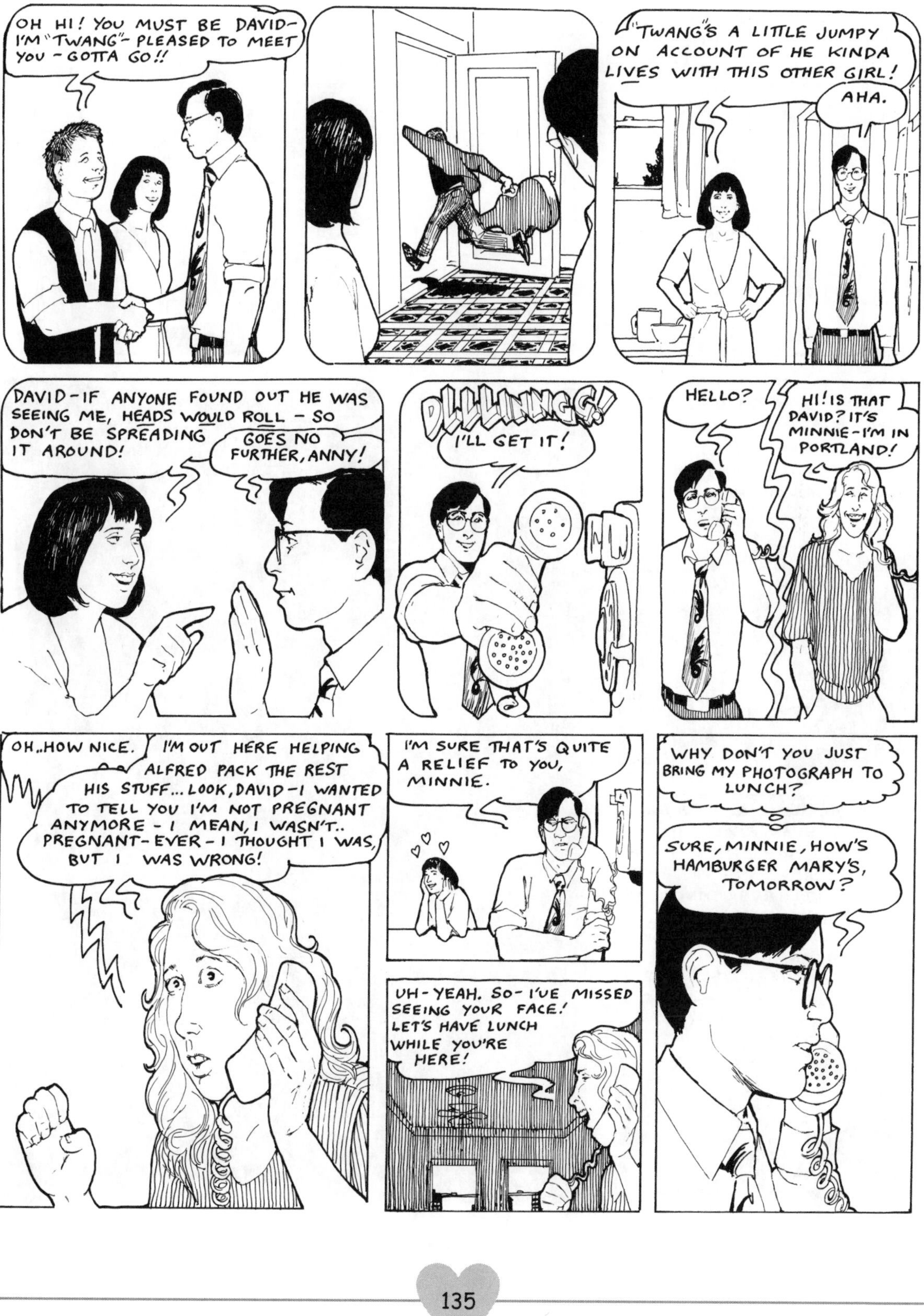
OH HI! YOU MUST BE DAVID- I'M "TWANG"- PLEASED TO MEET YOU - GOTTA GO!!
"TWANG"S A LITTLE JUMPY ON ACCOUNT OF HE KINDA LIVES WITH THIS OTHER GIRL!
AHA.
DAVID- IF ANYONE FOUND OUT HE WAS SEEING ME, HEADS WOULD ROLL - SO DON'T BE SPREADING IT AROUND!
GOES NO FURTHER, ANNY!
DLLLINNGG!
I'LL GET IT!
HELLO?
HI! IS THAT DAVID? IT'S MINNIE- I'M IN PORTLAND!
OH..HOW NICE.
I'M OUT HERE HELPING ALFRED PACK THE REST HIS STUFF... LOOK, DAVID- I WANTED TO TELL YOU I'M NOT PREGNANT ANYMORE - I MEAN, I WASN'T.. PREGNANT- EVER - I THOUGHT I WAS, BUT I WAS WRONG!
I'M SURE THAT'S QUITE A RELIEF TO YOU, MINNIE.
UH- YEAH. SO- I'VE MISSED SEEING YOUR FACE! LET'S HAVE LUNCH WHILE YOU'RE HERE!
WHY DON'T YOU JUST BRING MY PHOTOGRAPH TO LUNCH?
SURE, MINNIE, HOW'S HAMBURGER MARY'S, TOMORROW?

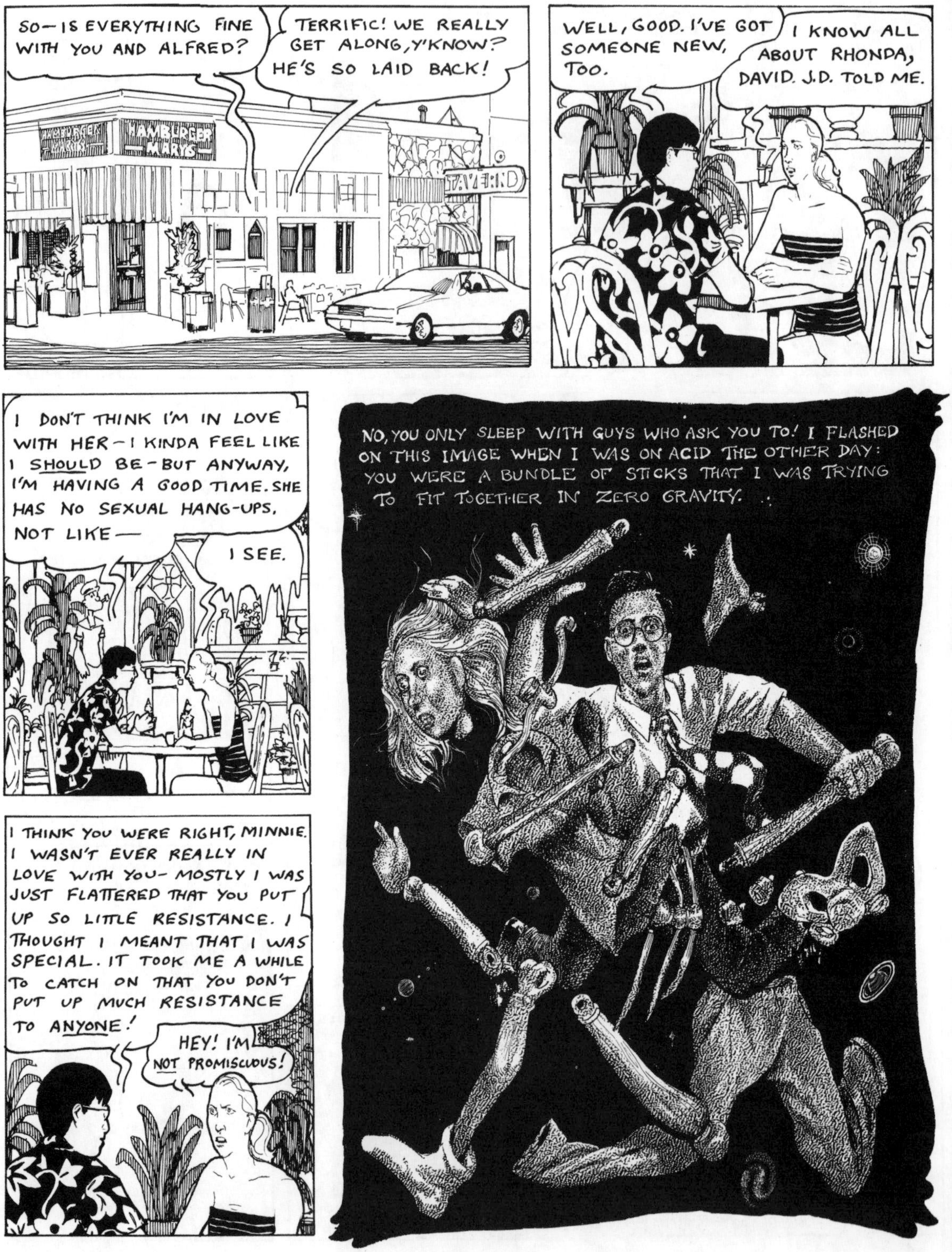
SO—IS EVERYTHING FINE WITH YOU AND ALFRED?
TERRIFIC! WE REALLY GET ALONG, Y'KNOW? HE'S SO LAID BACK!
HAMBURGER MARY'S
TAVERN
WELL, GOOD. I'VE GOT SOMEONE NEW, TOO.
I KNOW ALL ABOUT RHONDA, DAVID. J.D. TOLD ME.
I DON'T THINK I'M IN LOVE WITH HER—I KINDA FEEL LIKE I SHOULD BE—BUT ANYWAY, I'M HAVING A GOOD TIME. SHE HAS NO SEXUAL HANG-UPS, NOT LIKE—
I SEE.
I THINK YOU WERE RIGHT, MINNIE. I WASN'T EVER REALLY IN LOVE WITH YOU—MOSTLY I WAS JUST FLATTERED THAT YOU PUT UP SO LITTLE RESISTANCE. I THOUGHT I MEANT THAT I WAS SPECIAL. IT TOOK ME A WHILE TO CATCH ON THAT YOU DON'T PUT UP MUCH RESISTANCE TO ANYONE!
HEY! I'M NOT PROMISCUOUS!
NO, YOU ONLY SLEEP WITH GUYS WHO ASK YOU TO! I FLASHED ON THIS IMAGE WHEN I WAS ON ACID THE OTHER DAY: YOU WERE A BUNDLE OF STICKS THAT I WAS TRYING TO FIT TOGETHER IN ZERO GRAVITY.

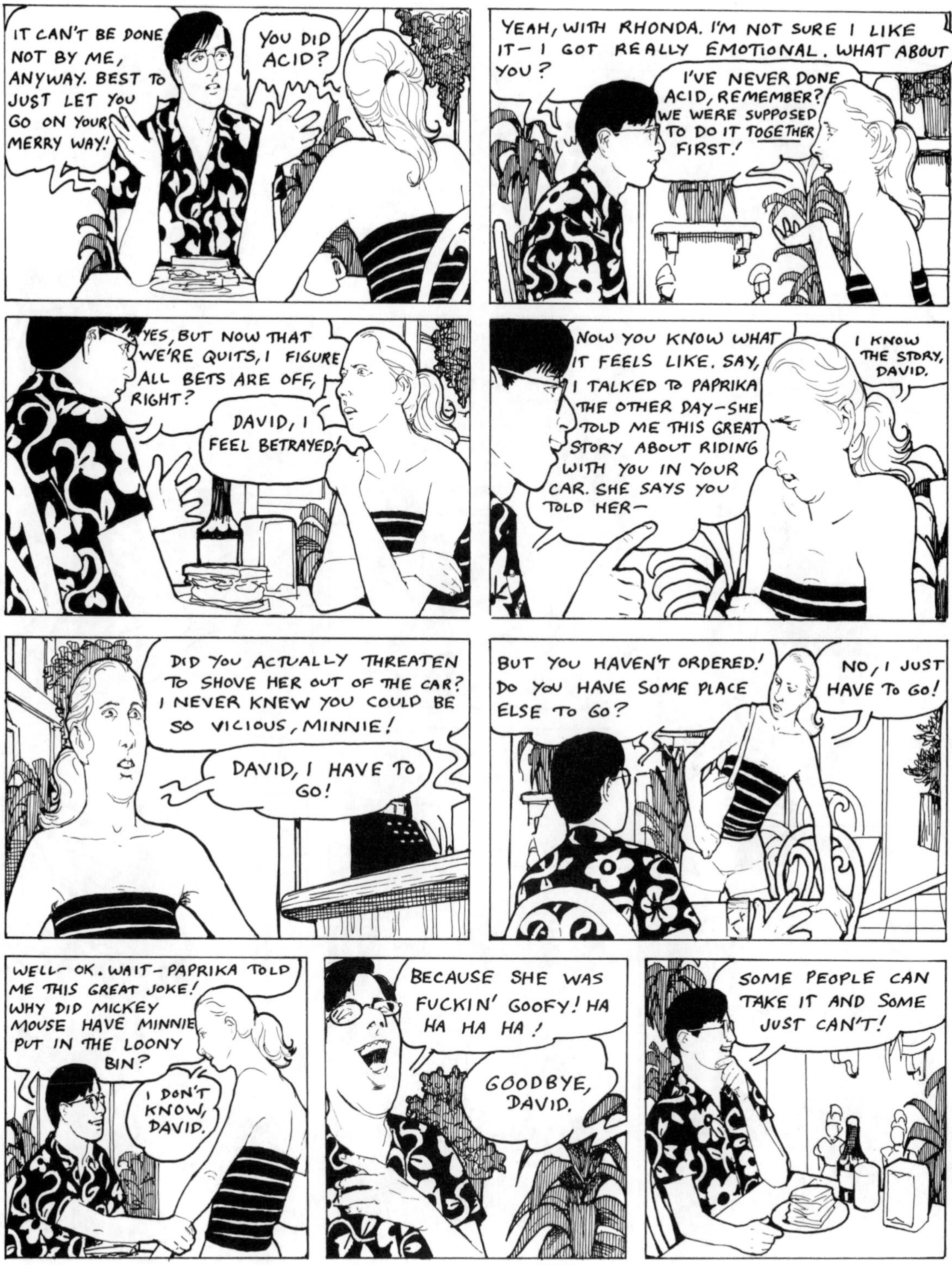

IT CAN'T BE DONE NOT BY ME, ANYWAY. BEST TO JUST LET YOU GO ON YOUR MERRY WAY!
YOU DID ACID?
YEAH, WITH RHONDA. I'M NOT SURE I LIKE IT— I GOT REALLY EMOTIONAL. WHAT ABOUT YOU?
I'VE NEVER DONE ACID, REMEMBER? WE WERE SUPPOSED TO DO IT TOGETHER FIRST!
YES, BUT NOW THAT WE'RE QUITS, I FIGURE ALL BETS ARE OFF, RIGHT?
DAVID, I FEEL BETRAYED!
NOW YOU KNOW WHAT IT FEELS LIKE. SAY, I TALKED TO PAPRIKA THE OTHER DAY—SHE TOLD ME THIS GREAT STORY ABOUT RIDING WITH YOU IN YOUR CAR. SHE SAYS YOU TOLD HER—
I KNOW THE STORY, DAVID.
DID YOU ACTUALLY THREATEN TO SHOVE HER OUT OF THE CAR? I NEVER KNEW YOU COULD BE SO VICIOUS, MINNIE!
DAVID, I HAVE TO GO!
BUT YOU HAVEN'T ORDERED! DO YOU HAVE SOME PLACE ELSE TO GO?
NO, I JUST HAVE TO GO!
WELL- OK. WAIT- PAPRIKA TOLD ME THIS GREAT JOKE! WHY DID MICKEY MOUSE HAVE MINNIE PUT IN THE LOONY BIN?
I DON'T KNOW, DAVID.
BECAUSE SHE WAS FUCKIN' GOOFY! HA HA HA HA!
GOODBYE, DAVID.
SOME PEOPLE CAN TAKE IT AND SOME JUST CAN'T!

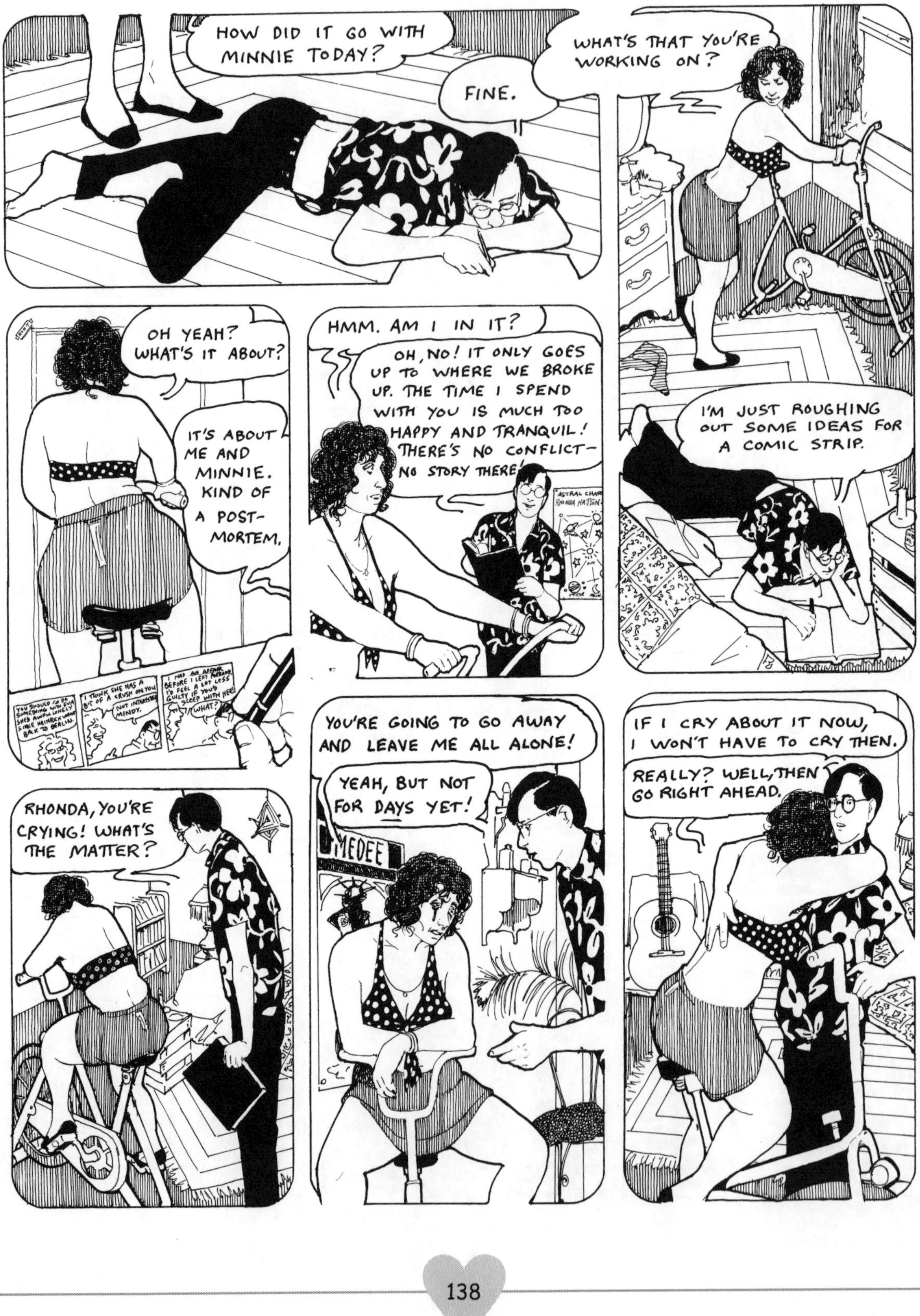

HOW DID IT GO WITH MINNIE TODAY?
FINE.
WHAT'S THAT YOU'RE WORKING ON?
I'M JUST ROUGHING OUT SOME IDEAS FOR A COMIC STRIP.
OH YEAH? WHAT'S IT ABOUT?
IT'S ABOUT ME AND MINNIE. KIND OF A POST-MORTEM.
YOU SHOULD GO DO SOMETHING WITH EVA SHE'S AWFUL LONELY SINCE HEINRICH WENT BACK TO BERLIN.
I THINK SHE HAS A BIT OF A CRUSH ON YOU.
NOT INTERESTED MINDY.
I HAD AN AFFAIR BEFORE I LEFT PORTLAND. I'D FEEL A LOT LESS GUILTY IF YOU'D SLEEP WITH HER!
WHAT?
HMM. AM I IN IT?
OH, NO! IT ONLY GOES UP TO WHERE WE BROKE UP. THE TIME I SPEND WITH YOU IS MUCH TOO HAPPY AND TRANQUIL! THERE'S NO CONFLICT— NO STORY THERE!
ASTRAL CHART
RHONDA HATTON
RHONDA, YOU'RE CRYING! WHAT'S THE MATTER?
YOU'RE GOING TO GO AWAY AND LEAVE ME ALL ALONE!
YEAH, BUT NOT FOR DAYS YET!
MEDEE
IF I CRY ABOUT IT NOW, I WON'T HAVE TO CRY THEN.
REALLY? WELL, THEN GO RIGHT AHEAD.

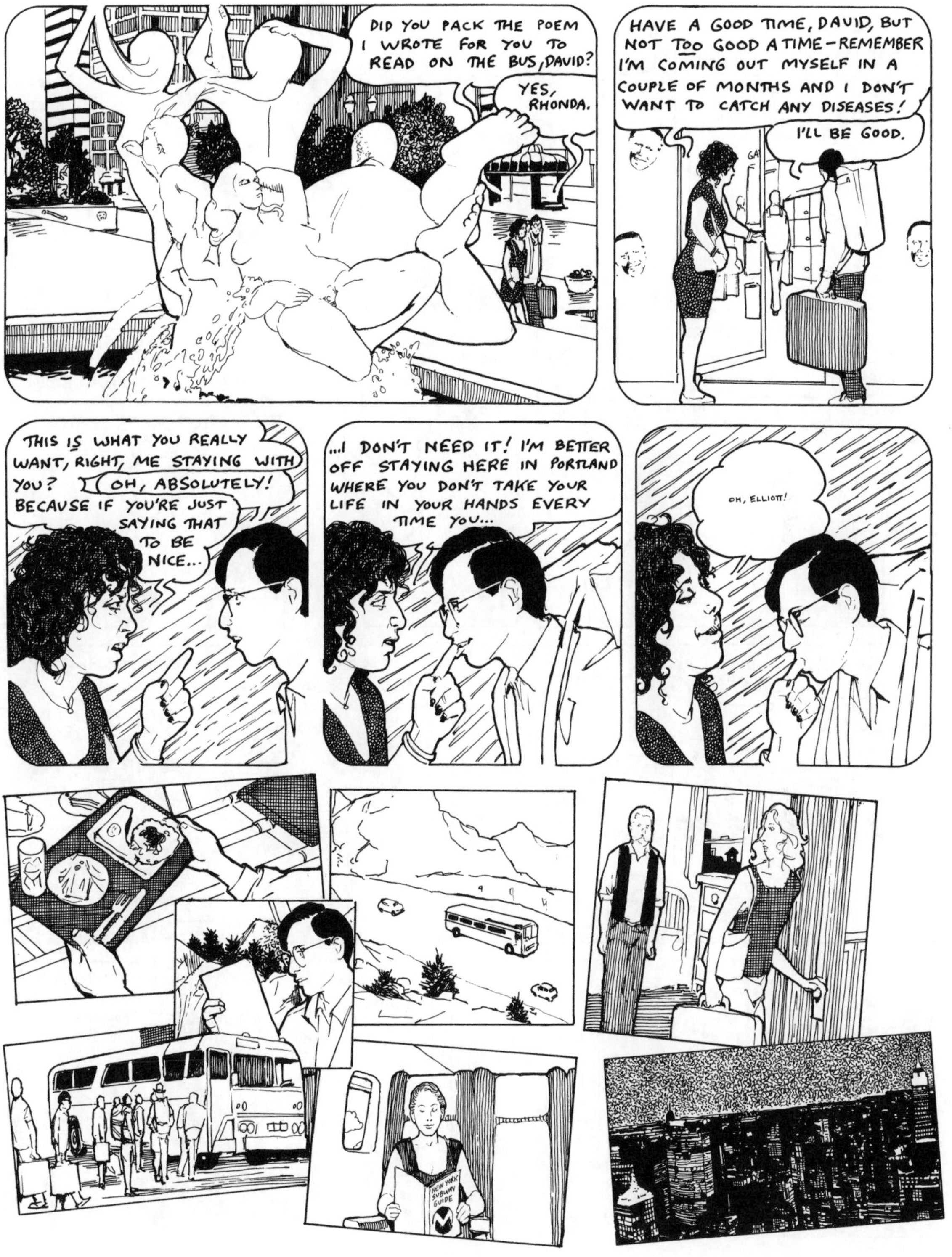
DID YOU PACK THE POEM I WROTE FOR YOU TO READ ON THE BUS, DAVID?
YES, RHONDA.
HAVE A GOOD TIME, DAVID, BUT NOT TOO GOOD A TIME—REMEMBER I'M COMING OUT MYSELF IN A COUPLE OF MONTHS AND I DON'T WANT TO CATCH ANY DISEASES!
I'LL BE GOOD.
THIS IS WHAT YOU REALLY WANT, RIGHT, ME STAYING WITH YOU?
OH, ABSOLUTELY!
BECAUSE IF YOU'RE JUST SAYING THAT TO BE NICE...
...I DON'T NEED IT! I'M BETTER OFF STAYING HERE IN PORTLAND WHERE YOU DON'T TAKE YOUR LIFE IN YOUR HANDS EVERY TIME YOU...
OH, ELLIOTT!
NEW YORK SUBWAY GUIDE

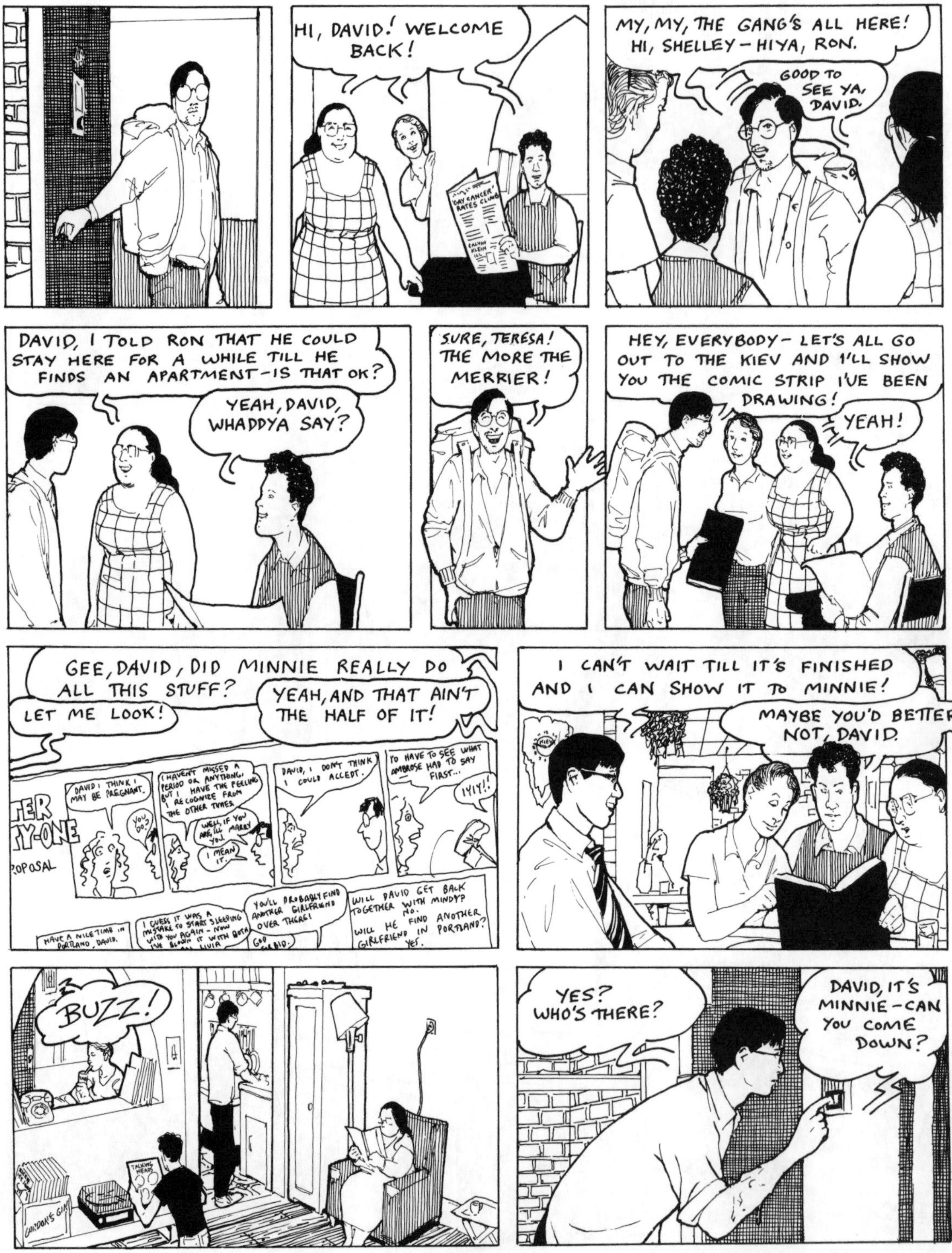
HI, DAVID! WELCOME BACK!
MY, MY, THE GANG'S ALL HERE! HI, SHELLEY - HIYA, RON.
GOOD TO SEE YA, DAVID.
DAVID, I TOLD RON THAT HE COULD STAY HERE FOR A WHILE TILL HE FINDS AN APARTMENT - IS THAT OK?
YEAH, DAVID, WHADDYA SAY?
SURE, TERESA! THE MORE THE MERRIER!
HEY, EVERYBODY - LET'S ALL GO OUT TO THE KIEV AND I'LL SHOW YOU THE COMIC STRIP I'VE BEEN DRAWING!
YEAH!
GEE, DAVID, DID MINNIE REALLY DO ALL THIS STUFF?
LET ME LOOK!
YEAH, AND THAT AIN'T THE HALF OF IT!
I CAN'T WAIT TILL IT'S FINISHED AND I CAN SHOW IT TO MINNIE!
MAYBE YOU'D BETTER NOT, DAVID.
BUZZ!
YES? WHO'S THERE?
DAVID, IT'S MINNIE - CAN YOU COME DOWN?

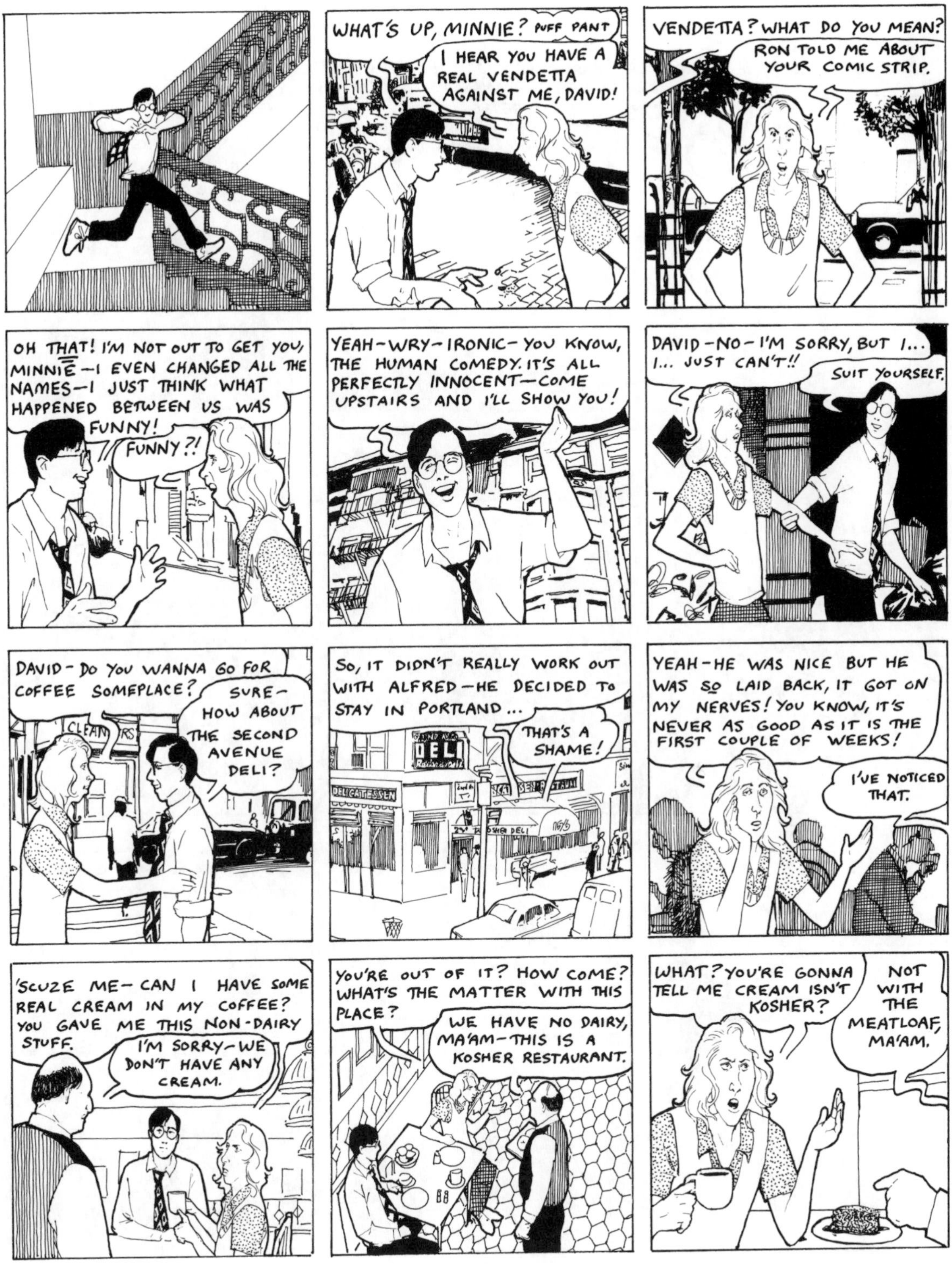
WHAT'S UP, MINNIE? PUFF PANT
I HEAR YOU HAVE A REAL VENDETTA AGAINST ME, DAVID!
VENDETTA? WHAT DO YOU MEAN?
RON TOLD ME ABOUT YOUR COMIC STRIP.
OH THAT! I'M NOT OUT TO GET YOU, MINNIE—I EVEN CHANGED ALL THE NAMES—I JUST THINK WHAT HAPPENED BETWEEN US WAS FUNNY!
FUNNY?!
YEAH—WRY—IRONIC—YOU KNOW, THE HUMAN COMEDY. IT'S ALL PERFECTLY INNOCENT—COME UPSTAIRS AND I'LL SHOW YOU!
DAVID—NO—I'M SORRY, BUT I... I... JUST CAN'T!!
SUIT YOURSELF.
DAVID—DO YOU WANNA GO FOR COFFEE SOMEPLACE?
SURE—HOW ABOUT THE SECOND AVENUE DELI?
CLEANERS
SO, IT DIDN'T REALLY WORK OUT WITH ALFRED—HE DECIDED TO STAY IN PORTLAND...
THAT'S A SHAME!
DELI
DELICATESSEN
YEAH—HE WAS NICE BUT HE WAS SO LAID BACK, IT GOT ON MY NERVES! YOU KNOW, IT'S NEVER AS GOOD AS IT IS THE FIRST COUPLE OF WEEKS!
I'VE NOTICED THAT.
'SCUZE ME—CAN I HAVE SOME REAL CREAM IN MY COFFEE? YOU GAVE ME THIS NON-DAIRY STUFF.
I'M SORRY—WE DON'T HAVE ANY CREAM.
YOU'RE OUT OF IT? HOW COME? WHAT'S THE MATTER WITH THIS PLACE?
WE HAVE NO DAIRY, MA'AM—THIS IS A KOSHER RESTAURANT.
WHAT? YOU'RE GONNA TELL ME CREAM ISN'T KOSHER?
NOT WITH THE MEATLOAF, MA'AM.

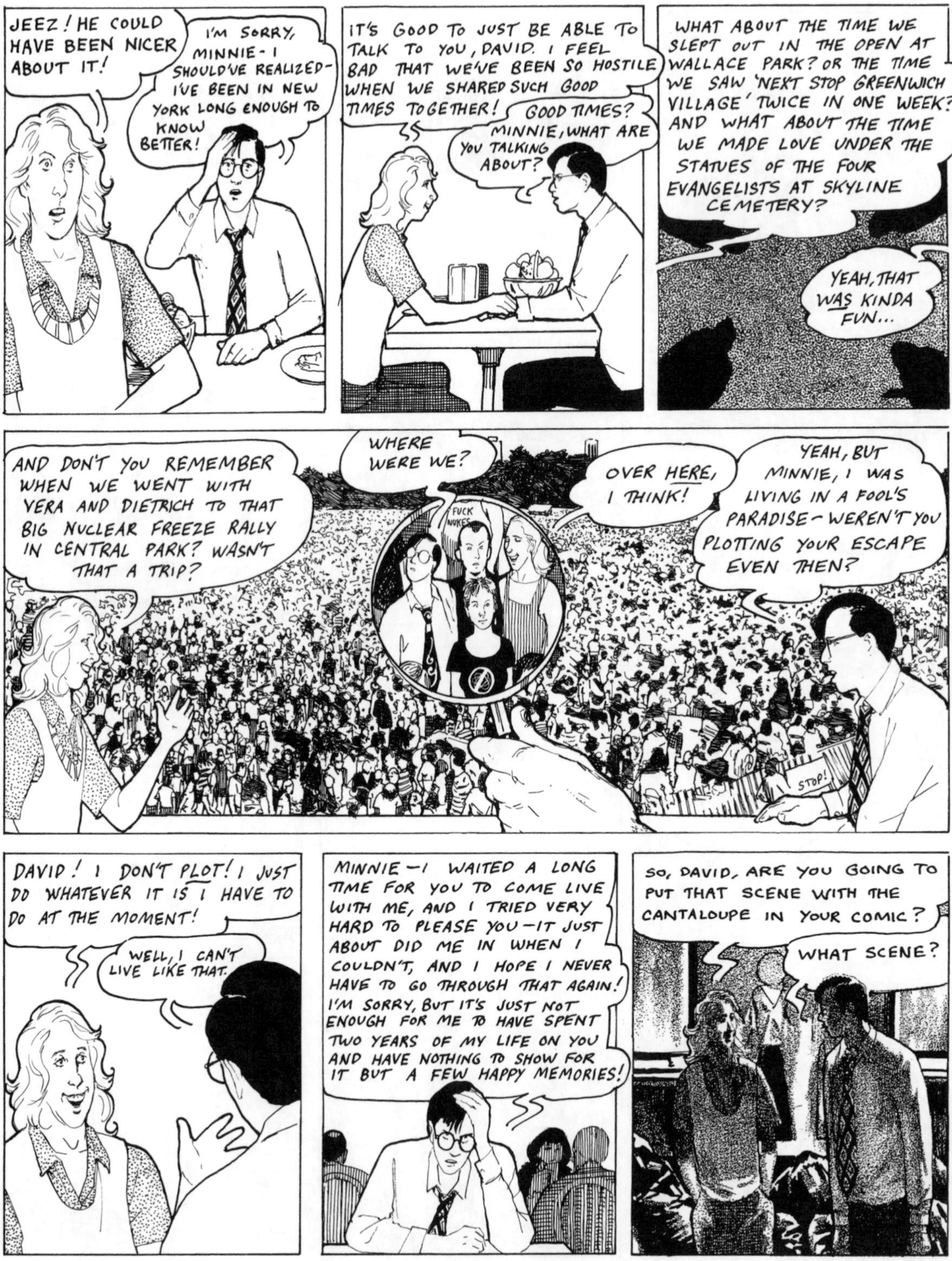
JEEZ! HE COULD HAVE BEEN NICER ABOUT IT!
I'M SORRY, MINNIE- I SHOULD'VE REALIZED- I'VE BEEN IN NEW YORK LONG ENOUGH TO KNOW BETTER!
IT'S GOOD TO JUST BE ABLE TO TALK TO YOU, DAVID. I FEEL BAD THAT WE'VE BEEN SO HOSTILE WHEN WE SHARED SUCH GOOD TIMES TOGETHER!
GOOD TIMES? MINNIE, WHAT ARE YOU TALKING ABOUT?
WHAT ABOUT THE TIME WE SLEPT OUT IN THE OPEN AT WALLACE PARK? OR THE TIME WE SAW 'NEXT STOP GREENWICH VILLAGE' TWICE IN ONE WEEK? AND WHAT ABOUT THE TIME WE MADE LOVE UNDER THE STATUES OF THE FOUR EVANGELISTS AT SKYLINE CEMETERY?
YEAH, THAT WAS KINDA FUN...
AND DON'T YOU REMEMBER WHEN WE WENT WITH VERA AND DIETRICH TO THAT BIG NUCLEAR FREEZE RALLY IN CENTRAL PARK? WASN'T THAT A TRIP?
WHERE WERE WE?
FUCK NUKES
OVER HERE, I THINK!
YEAH, BUT MINNIE, I WAS LIVING IN A FOOL'S PARADISE- WEREN'T YOU PLOTTING YOUR ESCAPE EVEN THEN?
STOP!
DAVID! I DON'T PLOT! I JUST DO WHATEVER IT IS I HAVE TO DO AT THE MOMENT!
WELL, I CAN'T LIVE LIKE THAT.
MINNIE —I WAITED A LONG TIME FOR YOU TO COME LIVE WITH ME, AND I TRIED VERY HARD TO PLEASE YOU —IT JUST ABOUT DID ME IN WHEN I COULDN'T, AND I HOPE I NEVER HAVE TO GO THROUGH THAT AGAIN! I'M SORRY, BUT IT'S JUST NOT ENOUGH FOR ME TO HAVE SPENT TWO YEARS OF MY LIFE ON YOU AND HAVE NOTHING TO SHOW FOR IT BUT A FEW HAPPY MEMORIES!
SO, DAVID, ARE YOU GOING TO PUT THAT SCENE WITH THE CANTALOUPE IN YOUR COMIC?
WHAT SCENE?

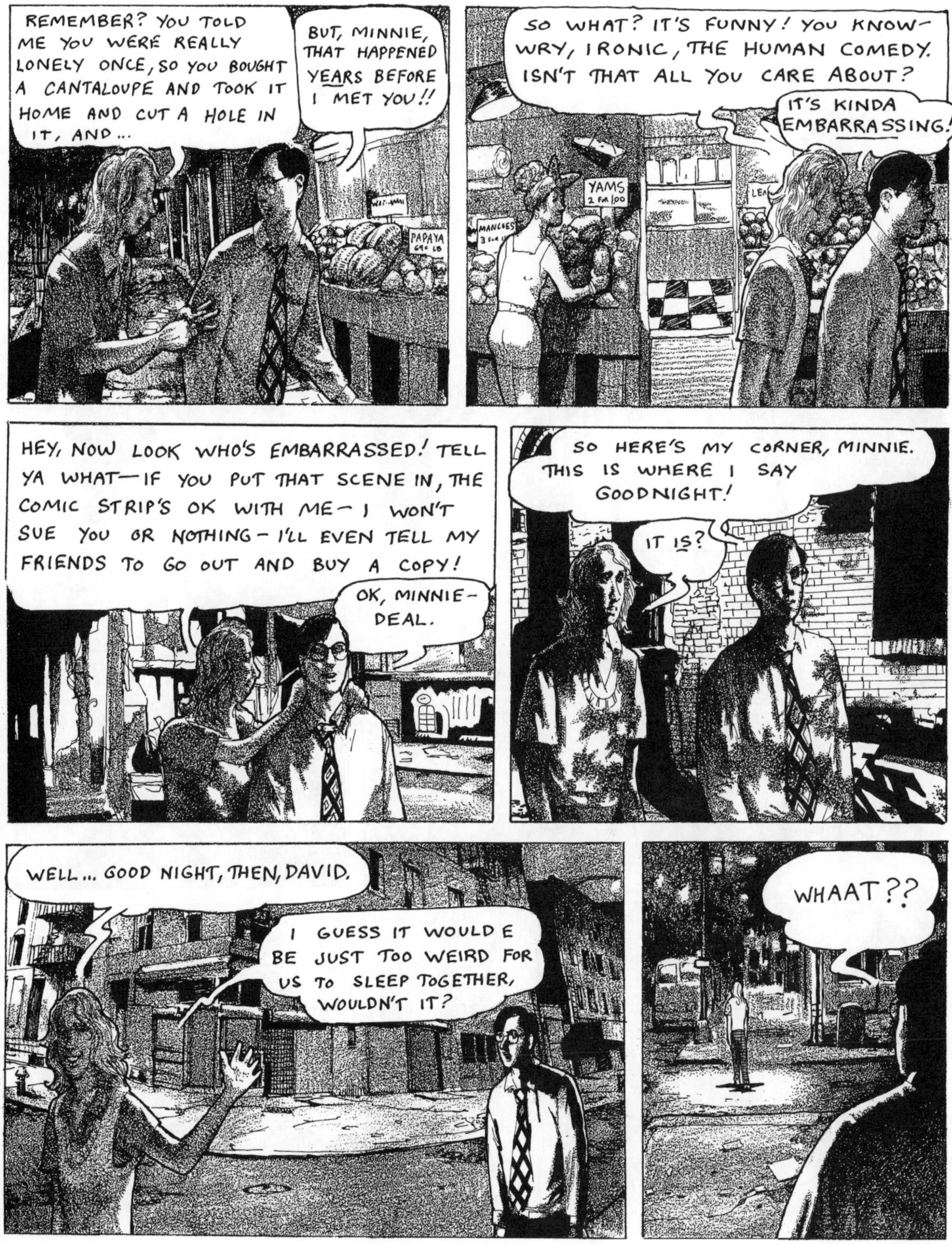
REMEMBER? YOU TOLD ME YOU WERE REALLY LONELY ONCE, SO YOU BOUGHT A CANTALOUPE AND TOOK IT HOME AND CUT A HOLE IN IT, AND...
BUT, MINNIE, THAT HAPPENED YEARS BEFORE I MET YOU!!
PAPAYA 69¢ LB
SO WHAT? IT'S FUNNY! YOU KNOW- WRY, IRONIC, THE HUMAN COMEDY. ISN'T THAT ALL YOU CARE ABOUT?
IT'S KINDA EMBARRASSING!
YAMS 2 FOR 100
HEY, NOW LOOK WHO'S EMBARRASSED! TELL YA WHAT—IF YOU PUT THAT SCENE IN, THE COMIC STRIP'S OK WITH ME- I WON'T SUE YOU OR NOTHING- I'LL EVEN TELL MY FRIENDS TO GO OUT AND BUY A COPY!
OK, MINNIE- DEAL.
SO HERE'S MY CORNER, MINNIE. THIS IS WHERE I SAY GOODNIGHT!
IT IS?
WELL... GOOD NIGHT, THEN, DAVID.
I GUESS IT WOULD E BE JUST TOO WEIRD FOR US TO SLEEP TOGETHER, WOULDN'T IT?
WHAAT??

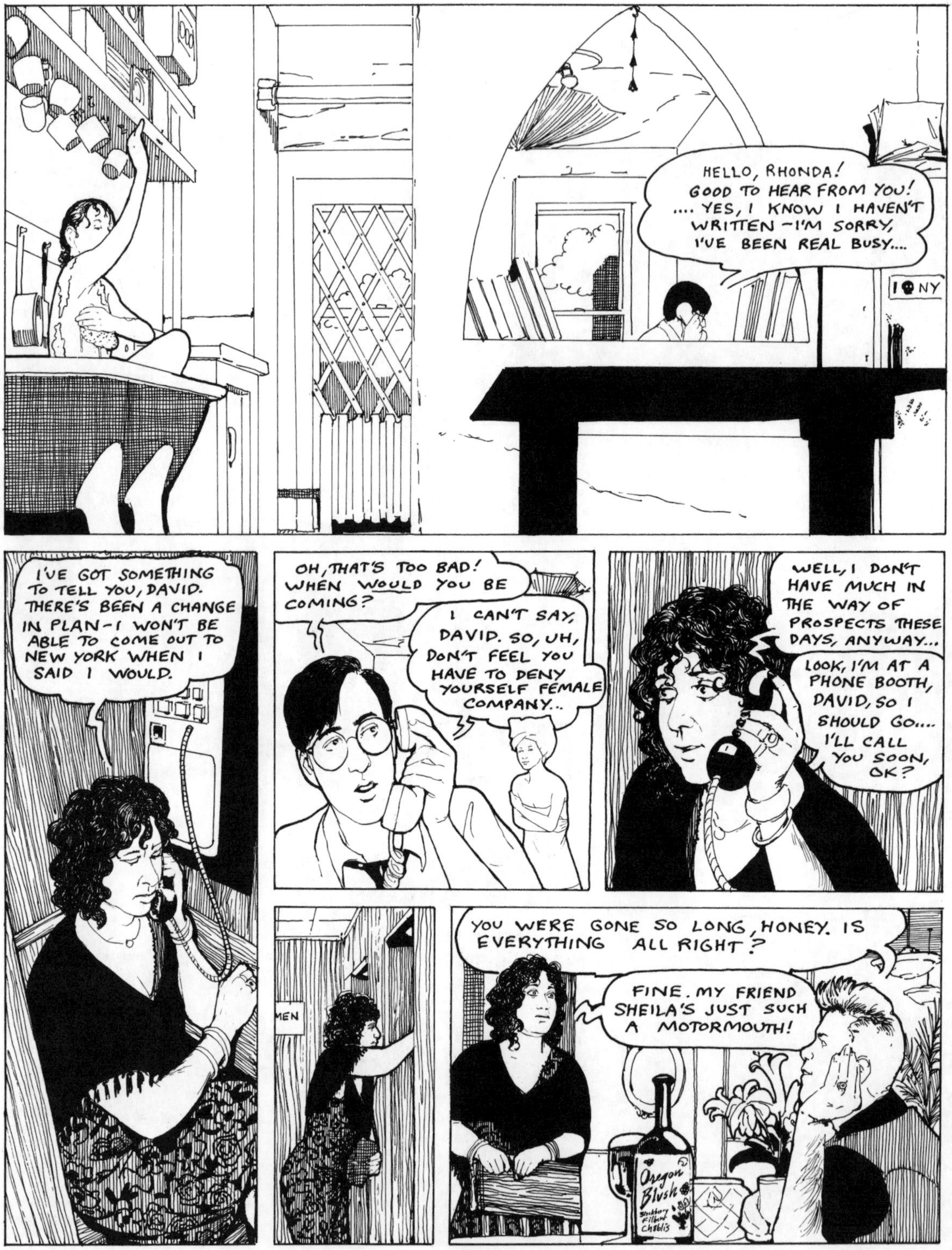

HELLO, RHONDA! GOOD TO HEAR FROM YOU! .... YES, I KNOW I HAVEN'T WRITTEN - I'M SORRY, I'VE BEEN REAL BUSY....
I'VE GOT SOMETHING TO TELL YOU, DAVID. THERE'S BEEN A CHANGE IN PLAN - I WON'T BE ABLE TO COME OUT TO NEW YORK WHEN I SAID I WOULD.
OH, THAT'S TOO BAD! WHEN WOULD YOU BE COMING?
I CAN'T SAY, DAVID. SO, UH, DON'T FEEL YOU HAVE TO DENY YOURSELF FEMALE COMPANY..
WELL, I DON'T HAVE MUCH IN THE WAY OF PROSPECTS THESE DAYS, ANYWAY...
LOOK, I'M AT A PHONE BOOTH, DAVID, SO I SHOULD GO.... I'LL CALL YOU SOON, OK?
MEN
YOU WERE GONE SO LONG, HONEY. IS EVERYTHING ALL RIGHT?
FINE. MY FRIEND SHEILA'S JUST SUCH A MOTORMOUTH!
Oregon Blush

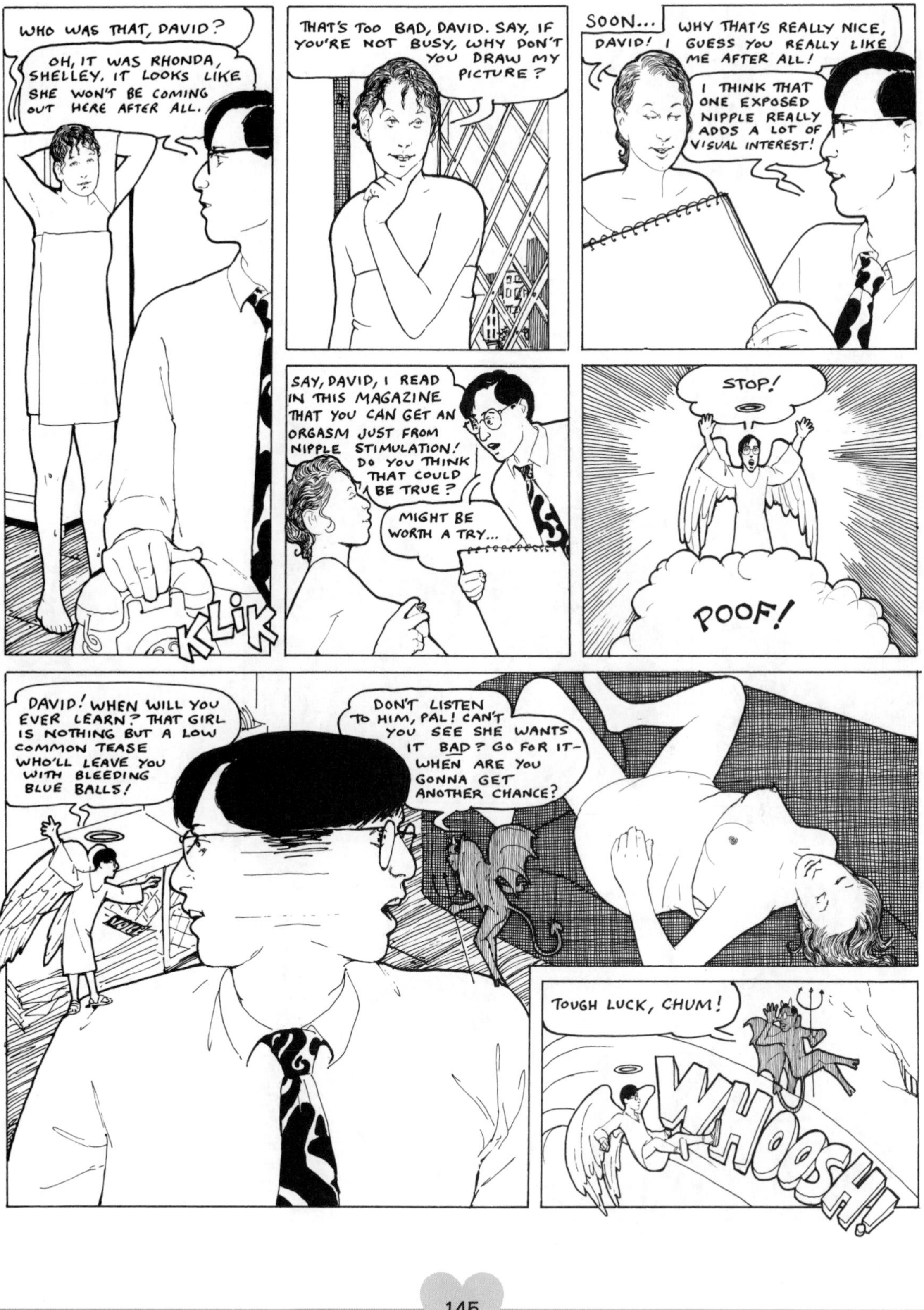
WHO WAS THAT, DAVID?
OH, IT WAS RHONDA, SHELLEY. IT LOOKS LIKE SHE WON'T BE COMING OUT HERE AFTER ALL.
KLIK
THAT'S TOO BAD, DAVID. SAY, IF YOU'RE NOT BUSY, WHY DON'T YOU DRAW MY PICTURE?
SOON...
WHY THAT'S REALLY NICE, DAVID! I GUESS YOU REALLY LIKE ME AFTER ALL!
I THINK THAT ONE EXPOSED NIPPLE REALLY ADDS A LOT OF VISUAL INTEREST!
SAY, DAVID, I READ IN THIS MAGAZINE THAT YOU CAN GET AN ORGASM JUST FROM NIPPLE STIMULATION!
DO YOU THINK THAT COULD BE TRUE?
MIGHT BE WORTH A TRY...
STOP!
POOF!
DAVID! WHEN WILL YOU EVER LEARN? THAT GIRL IS NOTHING BUT A LOW COMMON TEASE WHO'LL LEAVE YOU WITH BLEEDING BLUE BALLS!
DON'T LISTEN TO HIM, PAL! CAN'T YOU SEE SHE WANTS IT BAD? GO FOR IT- WHEN ARE YOU GONNA GET ANOTHER CHANCE?
TOUGH LUCK, CHUM!
WHOOSH!

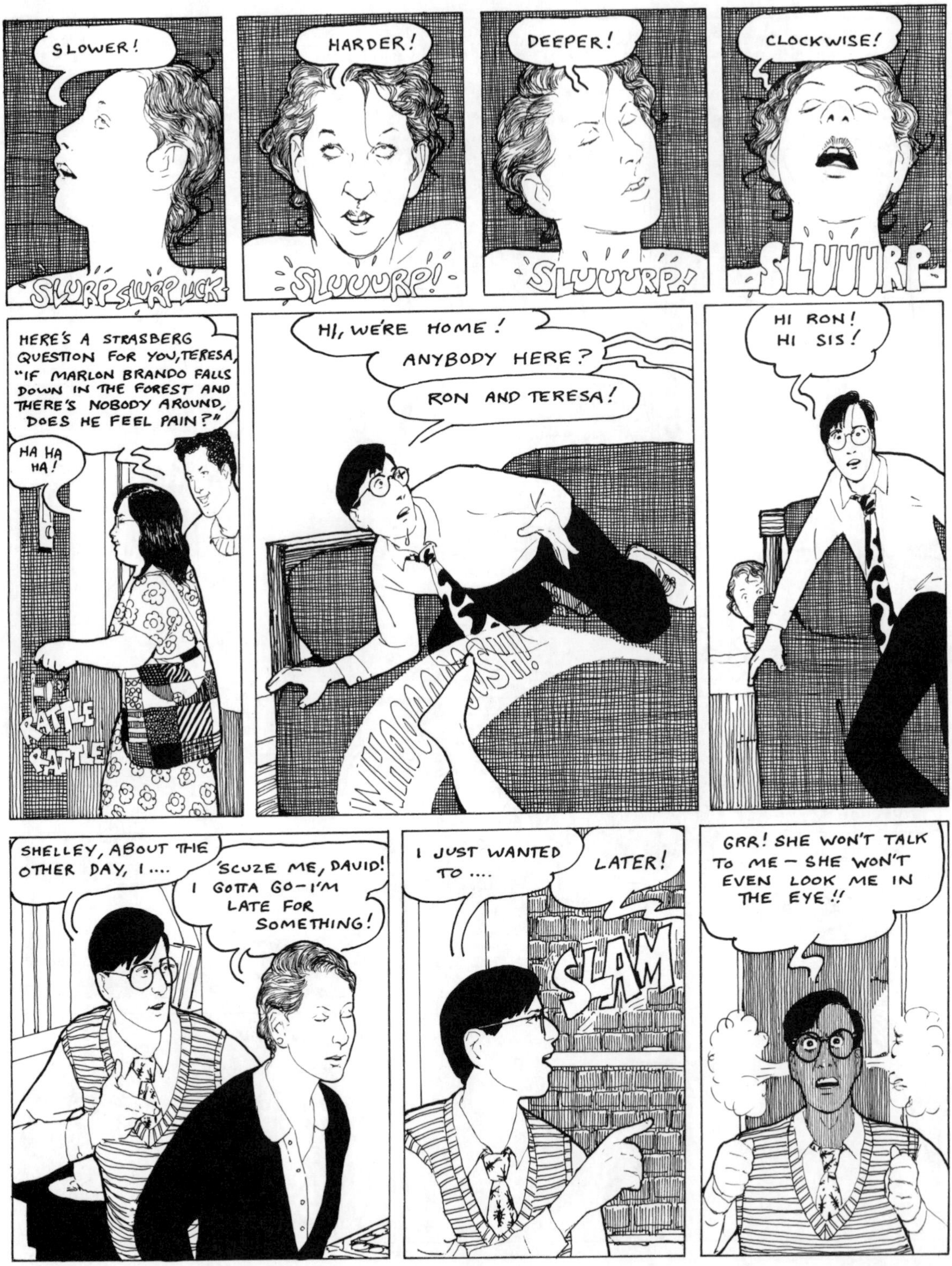
SLOWER!
SLURP SLURP LICK
HARDER!
SLUUURP!
DEEPER!
SLUUURP!
CLOCKWISE!
SLUUURP
HERE'S A STRASBERG QUESTION FOR YOU, TERESA, "IF MARLON BRANDO FALLS DOWN IN THE FOREST AND THERE'S NOBODY AROUND, DOES HE FEEL PAIN?"
HA HA HA!
RATTLE RATTLE
HI, WE'RE HOME!
ANYBODY HERE?
RON AND TERESA!
WHOOOOOSH!
HI RON! HI SIS!
SHELLEY, ABOUT THE OTHER DAY, I....
'SCUZE ME, DAVID! I GOTTA GO-I'M LATE FOR SOMETHING!
I JUST WANTED TO....
LATER!
SLAM
GRR! SHE WON'T TALK TO ME - SHE WON'T EVEN LOOK ME IN THE EYE!!

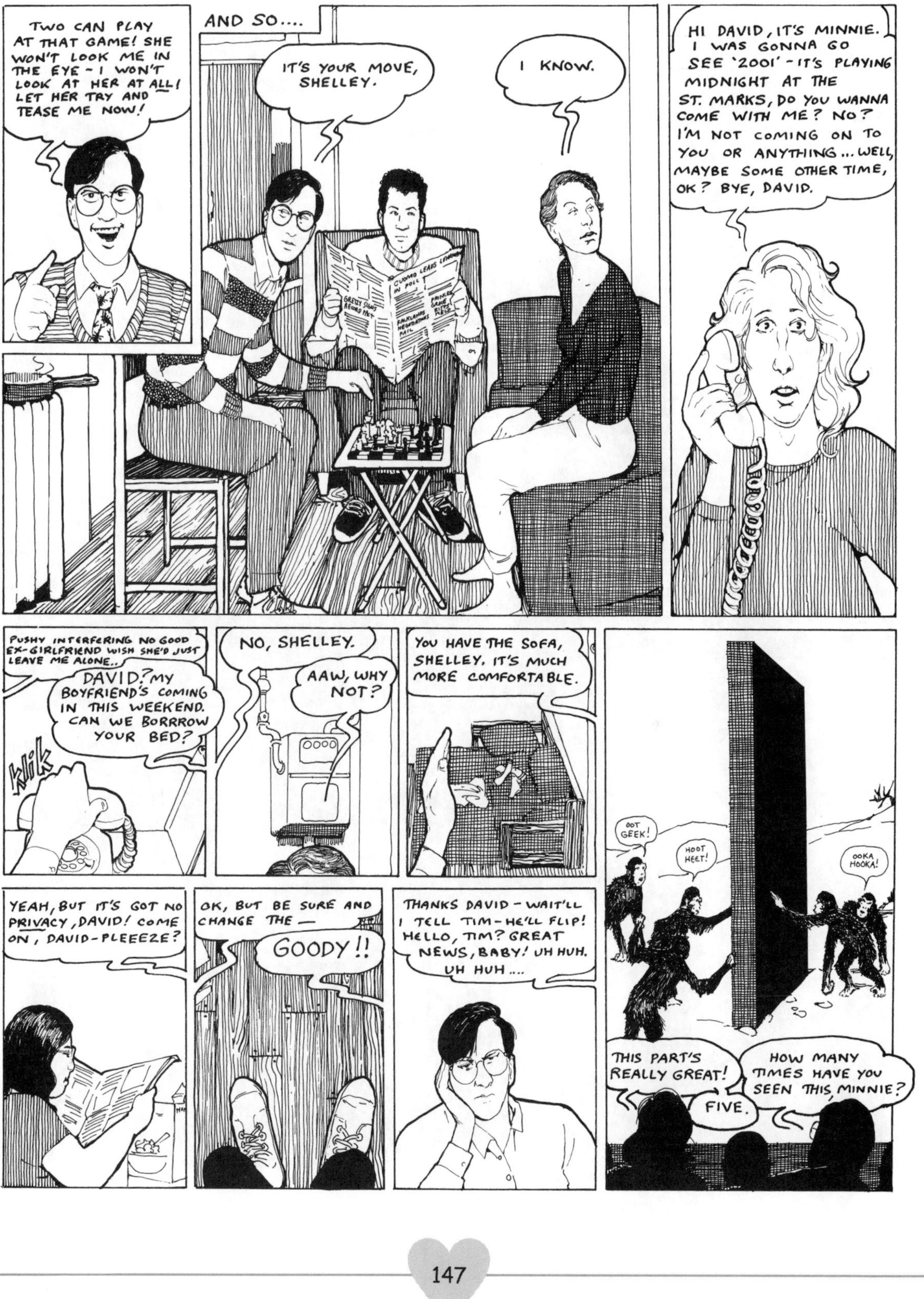

TWO CAN PLAY AT THAT GAME! SHE WON'T LOOK ME IN THE EYE - I WON'T LOOK AT HER AT ALL! LET HER TRY AND TEASE ME NOW!
AND SO....
IT'S YOUR MOVE, SHELLEY.
I KNOW.
HI DAVID, IT'S MINNIE. I WAS GONNA GO SEE '2001' - IT'S PLAYING MIDNIGHT AT THE ST. MARKS, DO YOU WANNA COME WITH ME? NO? I'M NOT COMING ON TO YOU OR ANYTHING... WELL, MAYBE SOME OTHER TIME, OK? BYE, DAVID.
PUSHY INTERFERING NO GOOD EX-GIRLFRIEND WISH SHE'D JUST LEAVE ME ALONE..
DAVID? MY BOYFRIEND'S COMING IN THIS WEEKEND. CAN WE BORRROW YOUR BED?
klik
NO, SHELLEY.
AAW, WHY NOT?
YOU HAVE THE SOFA, SHELLEY. IT'S MUCH MORE COMFORTABLE.
OOT GEEK!
HOOT HEET!
OOKA HOOKA!
YEAH, BUT IT'S GOT NO PRIVACY, DAVID! COME ON, DAVID-PLEEEZE?
OK, BUT BE SURE AND CHANGE THE —
GOODY!!
THANKS DAVID - WAIT'LL I TELL TIM - HE'LL FLIP! HELLO, TIM? GREAT NEWS, BABY! UH HUH. UH HUH....
THIS PART'S REALLY GREAT!
HOW MANY TIMES HAVE YOU SEEN THIS, MINNIE?
FIVE.

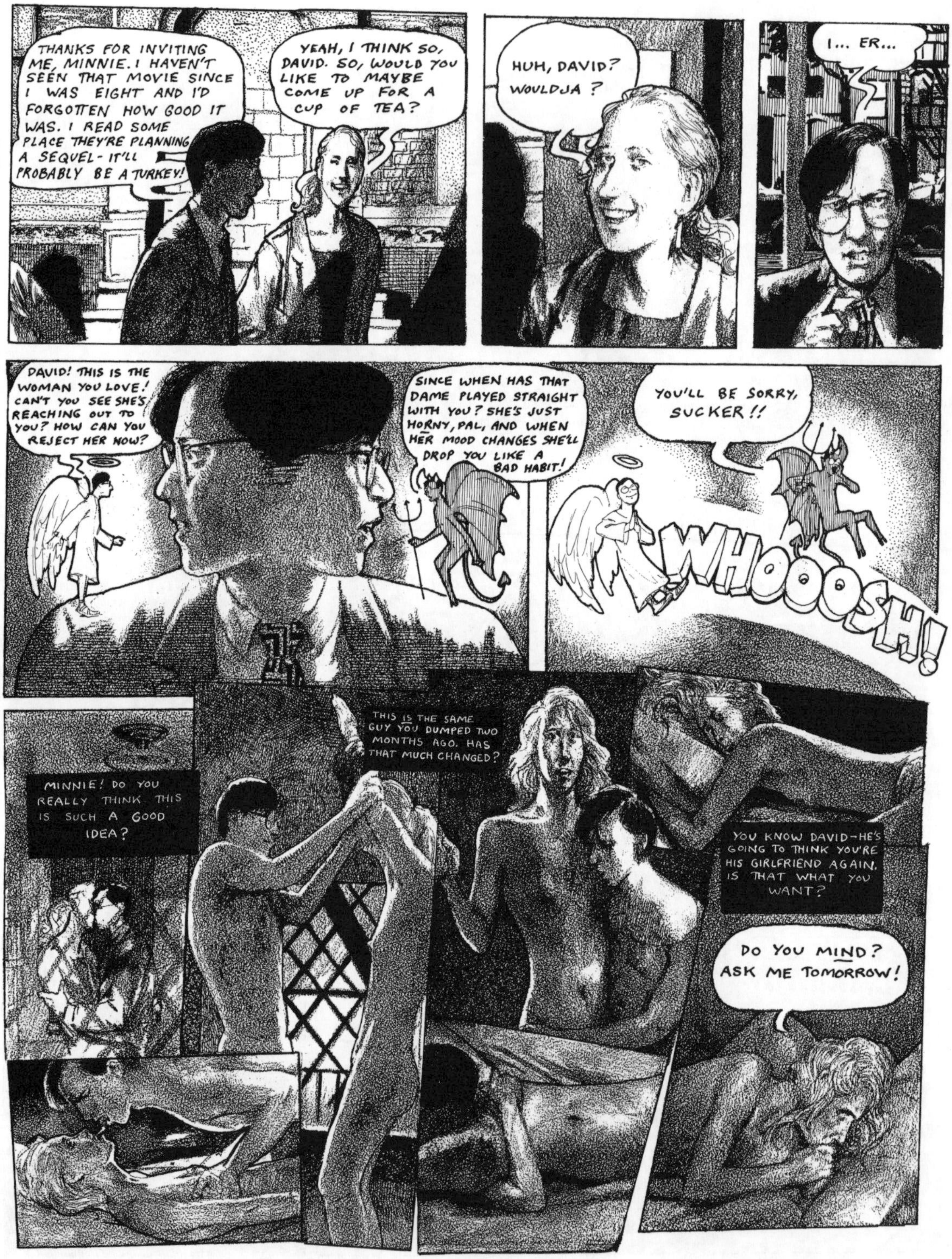
THANKS FOR INVITING ME, MINNIE. I HAVEN'T SEEN THAT MOVIE SINCE I WAS EIGHT AND I'D FORGOTTEN HOW GOOD IT WAS. I READ SOME PLACE THEY'RE PLANNING A SEQUEL- IT'LL PROBABLY BE A TURKEY!
YEAH, I THINK SO, DAVID. SO, WOULD YOU LIKE TO MAYBE COME UP FOR A CUP OF TEA?
HUH, DAVID? WOULDJA?
I... ER...
DAVID! THIS IS THE WOMAN YOU LOVE! CAN'T YOU SEE SHE'S REACHING OUT TO YOU? HOW CAN YOU REJECT HER NOW?
SINCE WHEN HAS THAT DAME PLAYED STRAIGHT WITH YOU? SHE'S JUST HORNY, PAL, AND WHEN HER MOOD CHANGES SHE'LL DROP YOU LIKE A BAD HABIT!
YOU'LL BE SORRY, SUCKER!!
WHOOOOSH!
MINNIE! DO YOU REALLY THINK THIS IS SUCH A GOOD IDEA?
THIS IS THE SAME GUY YOU DUMPED TWO MONTHS AGO. HAS THAT MUCH CHANGED?
YOU KNOW DAVID-HE'S GOING TO THINK YOU'RE HIS GIRLFRIEND AGAIN. IS THAT WHAT YOU WANT?
DO YOU MIND? ASK ME TOMORROW!

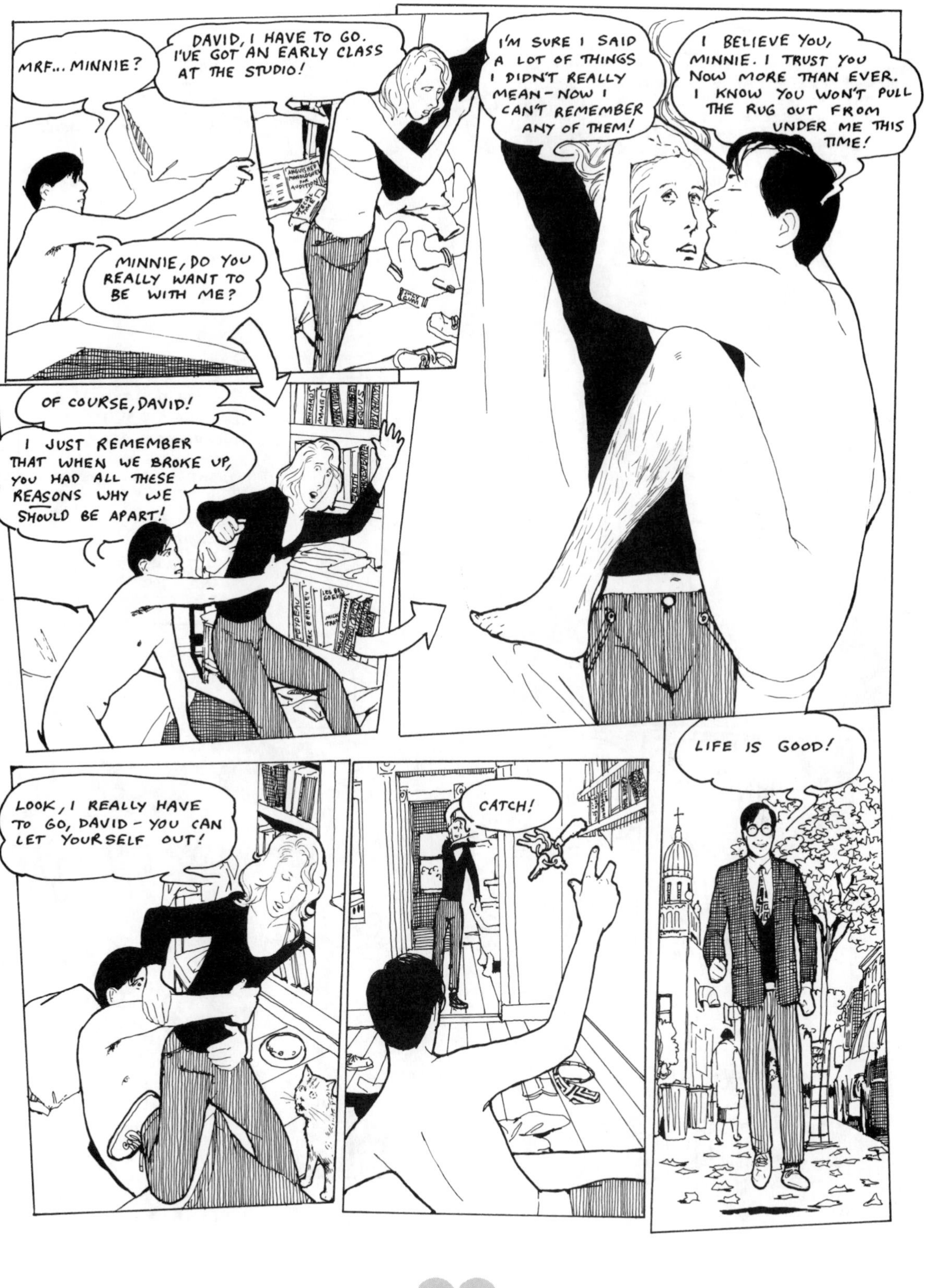
MRF... MINNIE?
DAVID, I HAVE TO GO. I'VE GOT AN EARLY CLASS AT THE STUDIO!
MINNIE, DO YOU REALLY WANT TO BE WITH ME?
OF COURSE, DAVID!
I JUST REMEMBER THAT WHEN WE BROKE UP, YOU HAD ALL THESE REASONS WHY WE SHOULD BE APART!
I'M SURE I SAID A LOT OF THINGS I DIDN'T REALLY MEAN - NOW I CAN'T REMEMBER ANY OF THEM!
I BELIEVE YOU, MINNIE. I TRUST YOU NOW MORE THAN EVER. I KNOW YOU WON'T PULL THE RUG OUT FROM UNDER ME THIS TIME!
LOOK, I REALLY HAVE TO GO, DAVID - YOU CAN LET YOURSELF OUT!
CATCH!
LIFE IS GOOD!

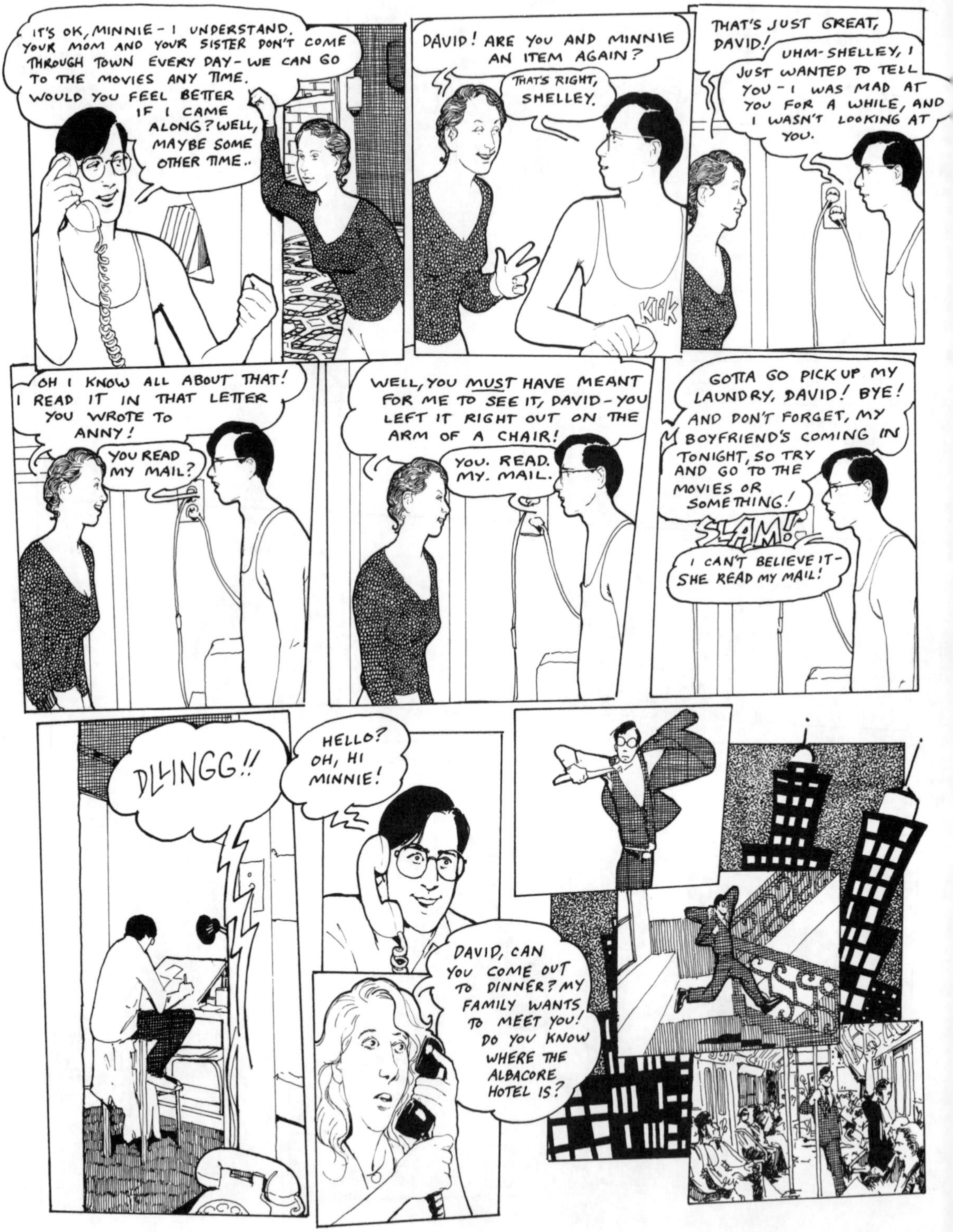
IT'S OK, MINNIE - I UNDERSTAND. YOUR MOM AND YOUR SISTER DON'T COME THROUGH TOWN EVERY DAY - WE CAN GO TO THE MOVIES ANY TIME. WOULD YOU FEEL BETTER IF I CAME ALONG? WELL, MAYBE SOME OTHER TIME..
DAVID! ARE YOU AND MINNIE AN ITEM AGAIN?
THAT'S RIGHT, SHELLEY.
KLIK
THAT'S JUST GREAT, DAVID!
UHM-SHELLEY, I JUST WANTED TO TELL YOU - I WAS MAD AT YOU FOR A WHILE, AND I WASN'T LOOKING AT YOU.
OH I KNOW ALL ABOUT THAT! I READ IT IN THAT LETTER YOU WROTE TO ANNY!
YOU READ MY MAIL?
WELL, YOU MUST HAVE MEANT FOR ME TO SEE IT, DAVID - YOU LEFT IT RIGHT OUT ON THE ARM OF A CHAIR!
YOU. READ. MY. MAIL.
GOTTA GO PICK UP MY LAUNDRY, DAVID! BYE! AND DON'T FORGET, MY BOYFRIEND'S COMING IN TONIGHT, SO TRY AND GO TO THE MOVIES OR SOMETHING!
SLAM!
I CAN'T BELIEVE IT - SHE READ MY MAIL!
DLLINGG!!
HELLO? OH, HI MINNIE!
DAVID, CAN YOU COME OUT TO DINNER? MY FAMILY WANTS TO MEET YOU! DO YOU KNOW WHERE THE ALBACORE HOTEL IS?

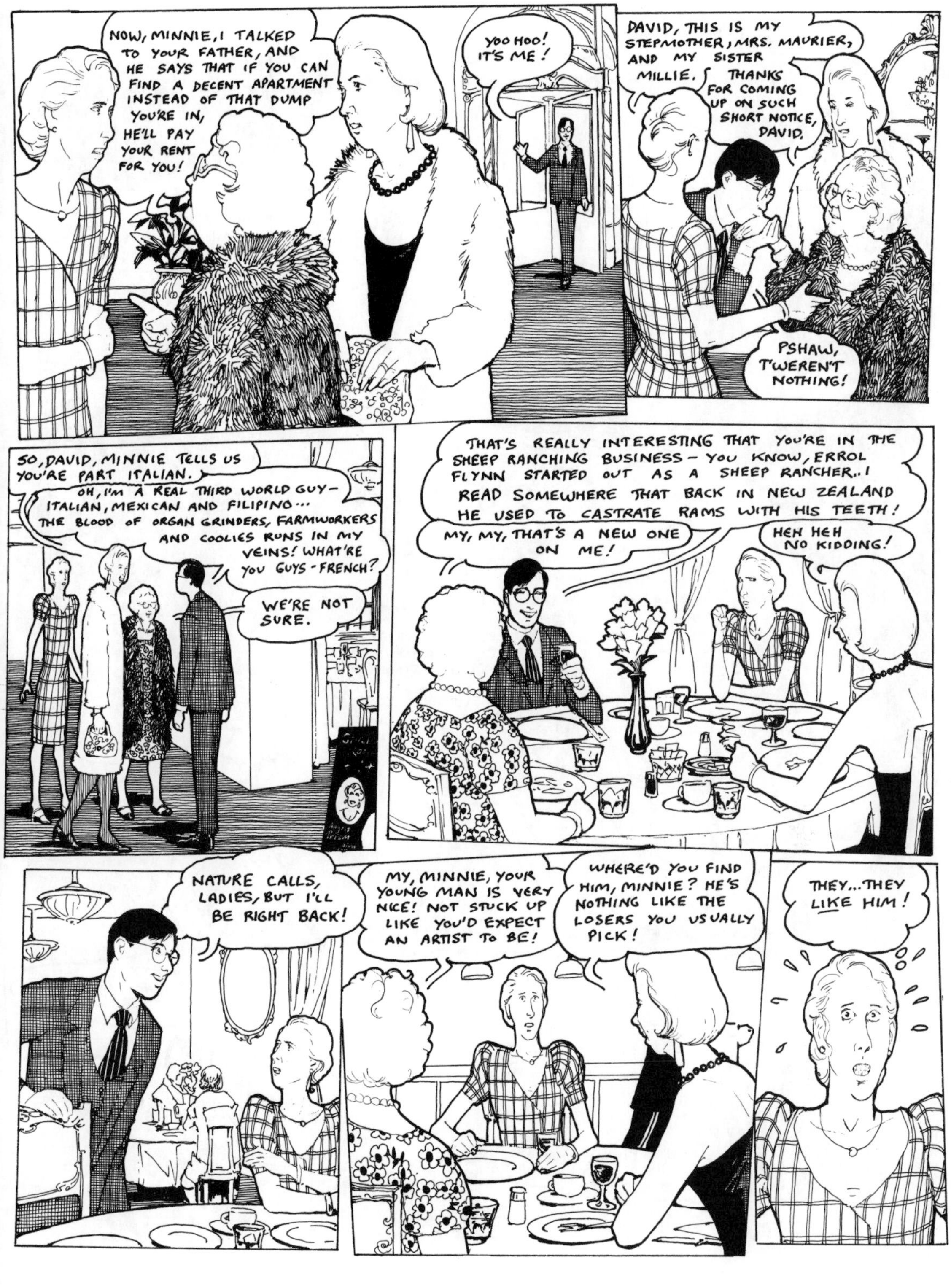
NOW, MINNIE, I TALKED TO YOUR FATHER, AND HE SAYS THAT IF YOU CAN FIND A DECENT APARTMENT INSTEAD OF THAT DUMP YOU'RE IN, HE'LL PAY YOUR RENT FOR YOU!
YOO HOO! IT'S ME!
DAVID, THIS IS MY STEPMOTHER, MRS. MAURIER, AND MY SISTER MILLIE.
THANKS FOR COMING UP ON SUCH SHORT NOTICE, DAVID.
PSHAW, T'WEREN'T NOTHING!
SO, DAVID, MINNIE TELLS US YOU'RE PART ITALIAN.
OH, I'M A REAL THIRD WORLD GUY- ITALIAN, MEXICAN AND FILIPINO... THE BLOOD OF ORGAN GRINDERS, FARMWORKERS AND COOLIES RUNS IN MY VEINS! WHAT'RE YOU GUYS - FRENCH?
WE'RE NOT SURE.
THAT'S REALLY INTERESTING THAT YOU'RE IN THE SHEEP RANCHING BUSINESS - YOU KNOW, ERROL FLYNN STARTED OUT AS A SHEEP RANCHER.. I READ SOMEWHERE THAT BACK IN NEW ZEALAND HE USED TO CASTRATE RAMS WITH HIS TEETH!
MY, MY, THAT'S A NEW ONE ON ME!
HEH HEH NO KIDDING!
NATURE CALLS, LADIES, BUT I'LL BE RIGHT BACK!
MY, MINNIE, YOUR YOUNG MAN IS VERY NICE! NOT STUCK UP LIKE YOU'D EXPECT AN ARTIST TO BE!
WHERE'D YOU FIND HIM, MINNIE? HE'S NOTHING LIKE THE LOSERS YOU USUALLY PICK!
THEY... THEY LIKE HIM!

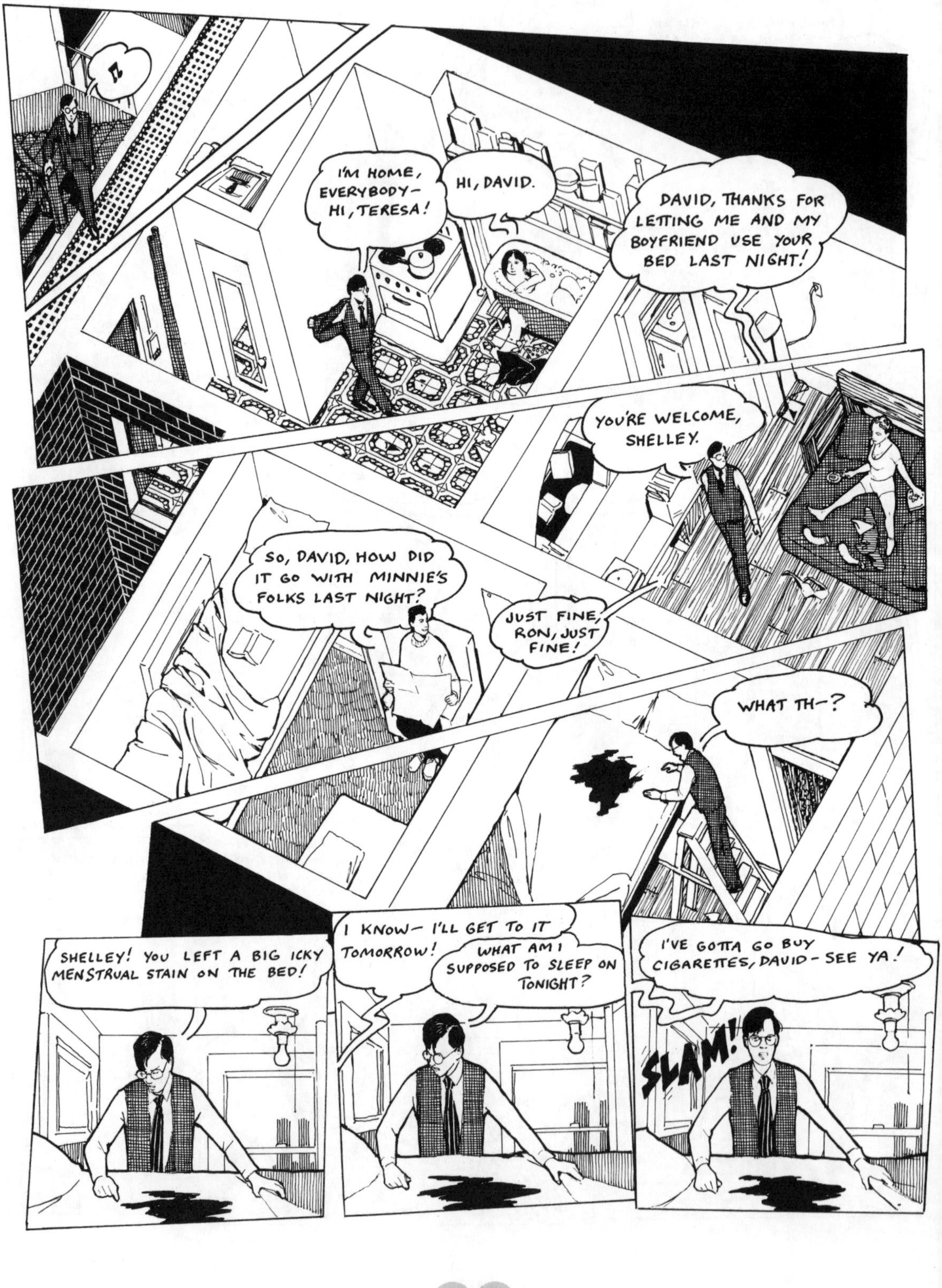
I'M HOME, EVERYBODY- HI, TERESA!
HI, DAVID.
DAVID, THANKS FOR LETTING ME AND MY BOYFRIEND USE YOUR BED LAST NIGHT!
YOU'RE WELCOME, SHELLEY.
SO, DAVID, HOW DID IT GO WITH MINNIE'S FOLKS LAST NIGHT?
JUST FINE, RON, JUST FINE!
WHAT TH-?
SHELLEY! YOU LEFT A BIG ICKY MENSTRUAL STAIN ON THE BED!
I KNOW- I'LL GET TO IT TOMORROW!
WHAT AM I SUPPOSED TO SLEEP ON TONIGHT?
I'VE GOTTA GO BUY CIGARETTES, DAVID- SEE YA!
SLAM!

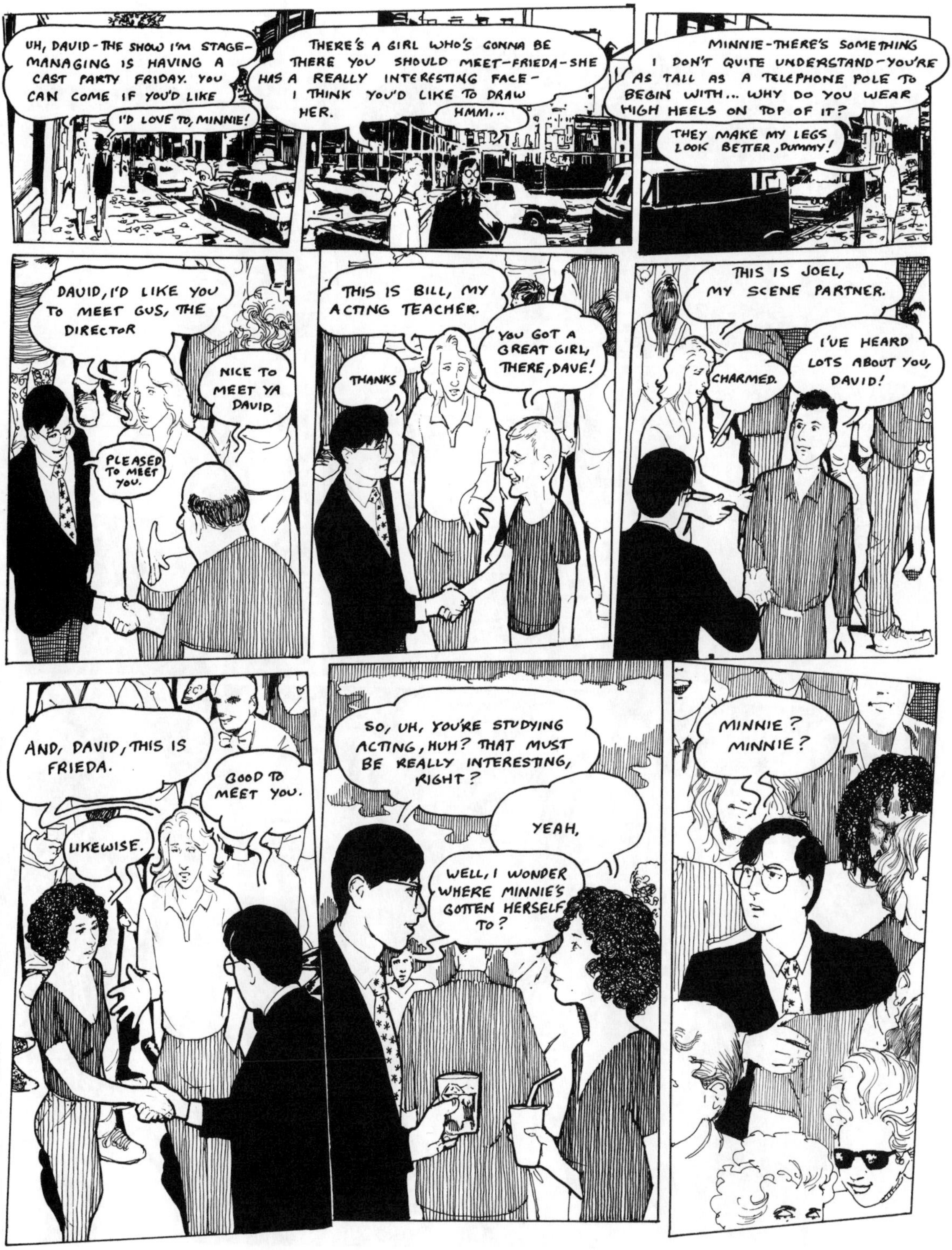
UH, DAVID-THE SHOW I'M STAGE-MANAGING IS HAVING A CAST PARTY FRIDAY. YOU CAN COME IF YOU'D LIKE
I'D LOVE TO, MINNIE!
THERE'S A GIRL WHO'S GONNA BE THERE YOU SHOULD MEET-FRIEDA-SHE HAS A REALLY INTERESTING FACE-I THINK YOU'D LIKE TO DRAW HER.
HMM..
MINNIE-THERE'S SOMETHING I DON'T QUITE UNDERSTAND-YOU'RE AS TALL AS A TELEPHONE POLE TO BEGIN WITH... WHY DO YOU WEAR HIGH HEELS ON TOP OF IT?
THEY MAKE MY LEGS LOOK BETTER, DUMMY!
DAVID, I'D LIKE YOU TO MEET GUS, THE DIRECTOR
NICE TO MEET YA DAVID.
PLEASED TO MEET YOU.
THIS IS BILL, MY ACTING TEACHER.
YOU GOT A GREAT GIRL, THERE, DAVE!
THANKS
THIS IS JOEL, MY SCENE PARTNER.
I'VE HEARD LOTS ABOUT YOU, DAVID!
CHARMED.
AND, DAVID, THIS IS FRIEDA.
GOOD TO MEET YOU.
LIKEWISE.
SO, UH, YOU'RE STUDYING ACTING, HUH? THAT MUST BE REALLY INTERESTING, RIGHT?
YEAH,
WELL, I WONDER WHERE MINNIE'S GOTTEN HERSELF TO?
MINNIE? MINNIE?

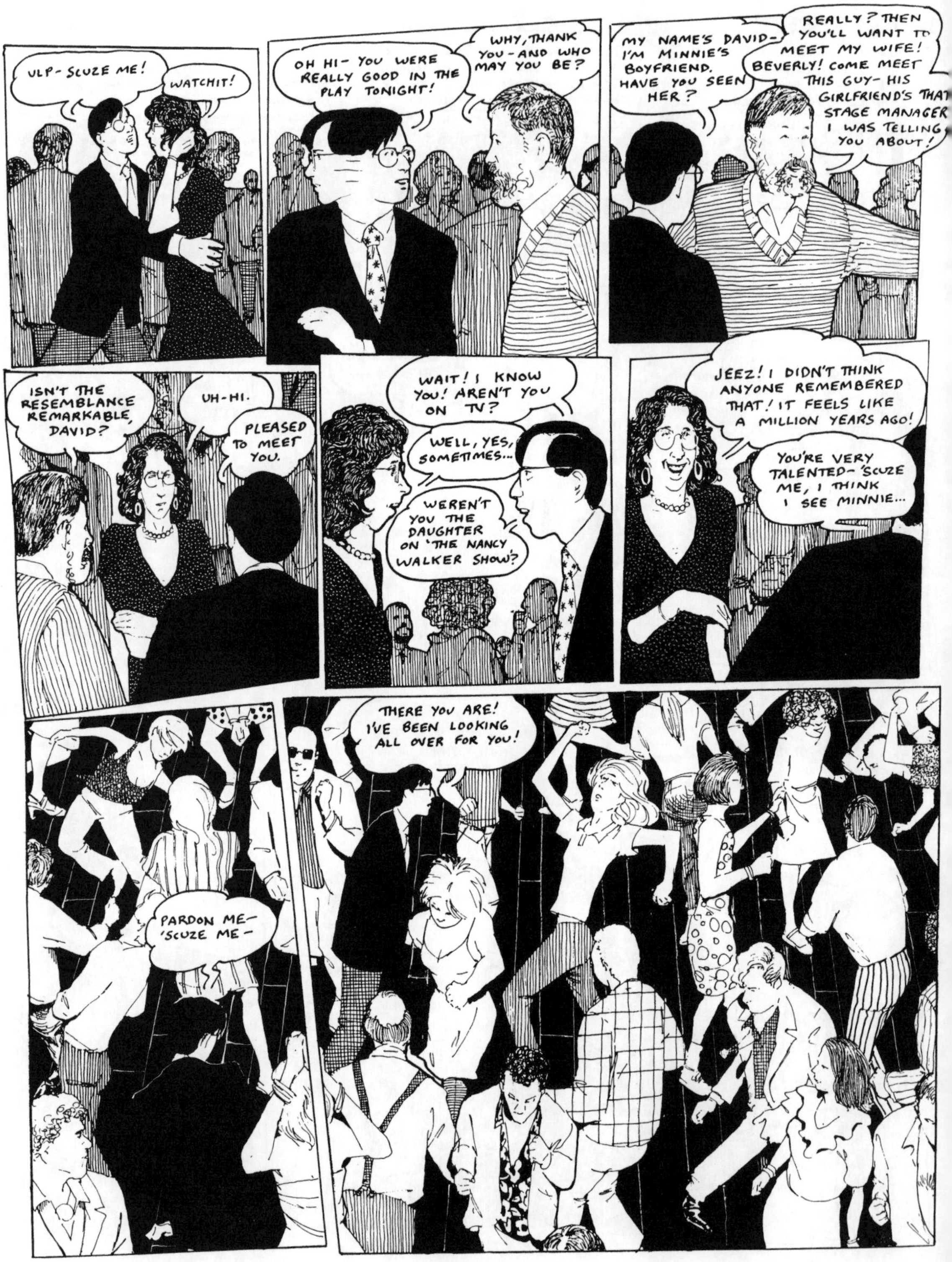
ULP-SCUZE ME!
WATCHIT!
OH HI- YOU WERE REALLY GOOD IN THE PLAY TONIGHT!
WHY, THANK YOU - AND WHO MAY YOU BE?
MY NAME'S DAVID- I'M MINNIE'S BOYFRIEND. HAVE YOU SEEN HER?
REALLY? THEN YOU'LL WANT TO MEET MY WIFE! BEVERLY! COME MEET THIS GUY- HIS GIRLFRIEND'S THAT STAGE MANAGER I WAS TELLING YOU ABOUT!
ISN'T THE RESEMBLANCE REMARKABLE, DAVID?
UH-HI.
PLEASED TO MEET YOU.
WAIT! I KNOW YOU! AREN'T YOU ON TV?
WELL, YES, SOMETIMES...
WEREN'T YOU THE DAUGHTER ON 'THE NANCY WALKER SHOW'?
JEEZ! I DIDN'T THINK ANYONE REMEMBERED THAT! IT FEELS LIKE A MILLION YEARS AGO!
YOU'RE VERY TALENTED- 'SCUZE ME, I THINK I SEE MINNIE...
PARDON ME- 'SCUZE ME-
THERE YOU ARE! I'VE BEEN LOOKING ALL OVER FOR YOU!

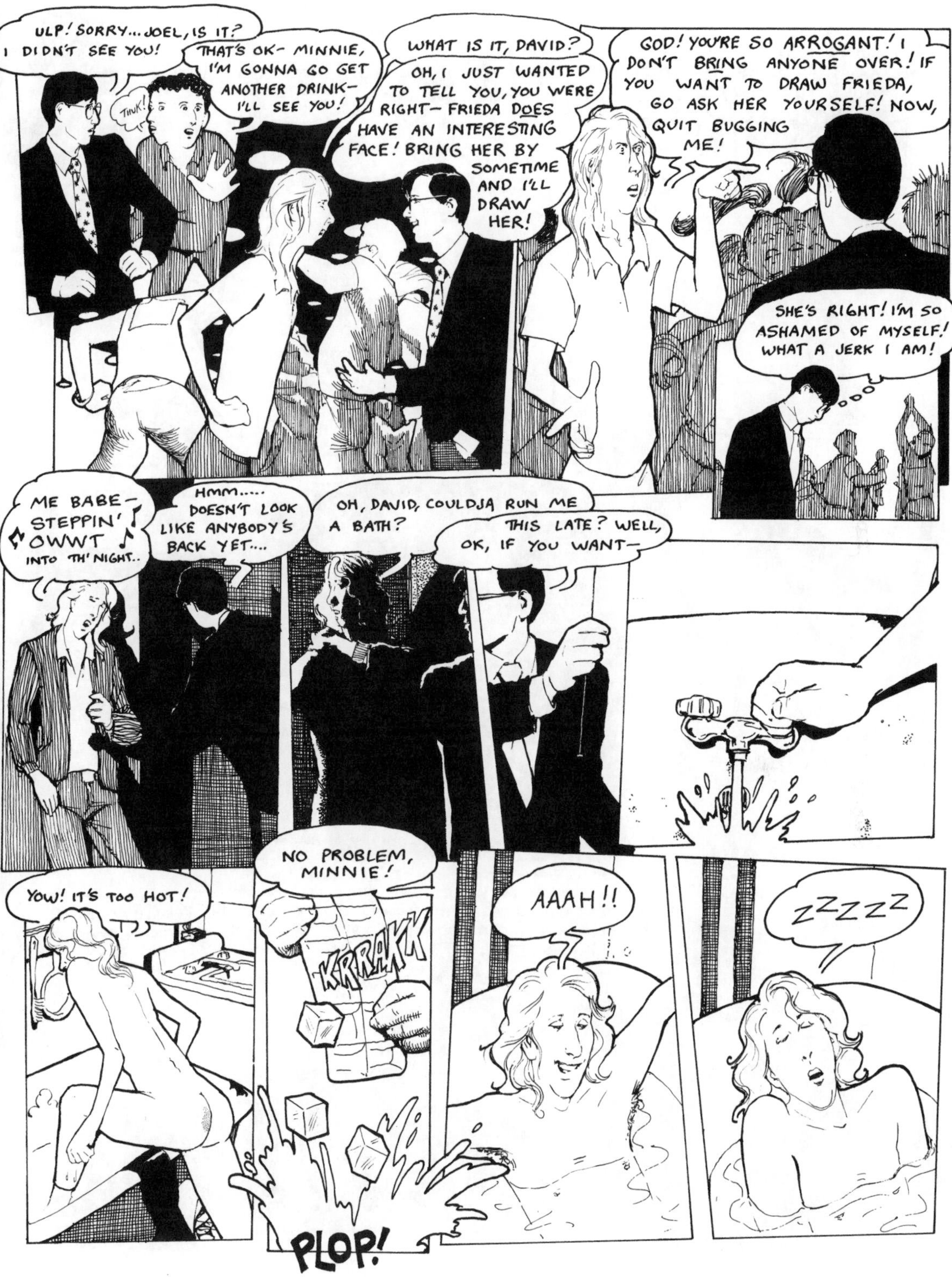
ULP! SORRY... JOEL, IS IT? I DIDN'T SEE YOU!
THUK!
THAT'S OK- MINNIE, I'M GONNA GO GET ANOTHER DRINK- I'LL SEE YOU!
WHAT IS IT, DAVID?
OH, I JUST WANTED TO TELL YOU, YOU WERE RIGHT- FRIEDA DOES HAVE AN INTERESTING FACE! BRING HER BY SOMETIME AND I'LL DRAW HER!
GOD! YOU'RE SO ARROGANT! I DON'T BRING ANYONE OVER! IF YOU WANT TO DRAW FRIEDA, GO ASK HER YOURSELF! NOW, QUIT BUGGING ME!
SHE'S RIGHT! I'M SO ASHAMED OF MYSELF! WHAT A JERK I AM!
ME BABE- STEPPIN' OWWT INTO TH' NIGHT..
HMM..... DOESN'T LOOK LIKE ANYBODY'S BACK YET....
OH, DAVID, COULDJA RUN ME A BATH?
THIS LATE? WELL, OK, IF YOU WANT-
YOW! IT'S TOO HOT!
NO PROBLEM, MINNIE!
KRRAKK
PLOP!
AAAH!!
ZZZZZ

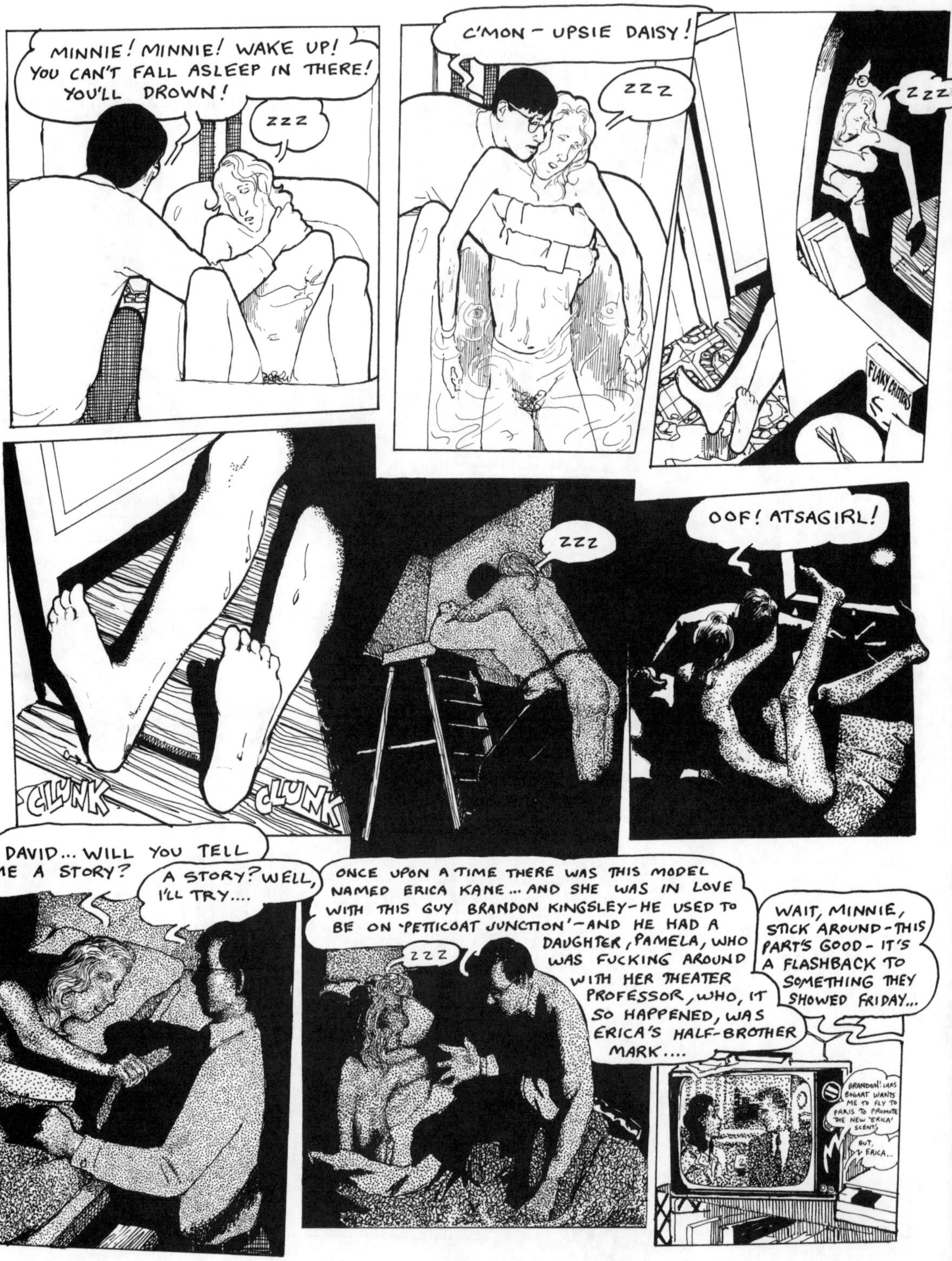
MINNIE! MINNIE! WAKE UP! YOU CAN'T FALL ASLEEP IN THERE! YOU'LL DROWN!
ZZZ
C'MON – UPSIE DAISY!
ZZZ
ZZZ
FLAKY CRITTERS
CLUNK
CLUNK
ZZZ
OOF! ATSAGIRL!
DAVID... WILL YOU TELL ME A STORY?
A STORY? WELL, I'LL TRY....
ONCE UPON A TIME THERE WAS THIS MODEL NAMED ERICA KANE... AND SHE WAS IN LOVE WITH THIS GUY BRANDON KINGSLEY–HE USED TO BE ON 'PETTICOAT JUNCTION'–AND HE HAD A DAUGHTER, PAMELA, WHO WAS FUCKING AROUND WITH HER THEATER PROFESSOR, WHO, IT SO HAPPENED, WAS ERICA'S HALF-BROTHER MARK....
ZZZ
WAIT, MINNIE, STICK AROUND–THIS PART'S GOOD– IT'S A FLASHBACK TO SOMETHING THEY SHOWED FRIDAY...
BRANDON! LARS BOGART WANTS ME TO FLY TO PARIS TO PROMOTE THE NEW 'ERICA' SCENT!
BUT, ERICA...

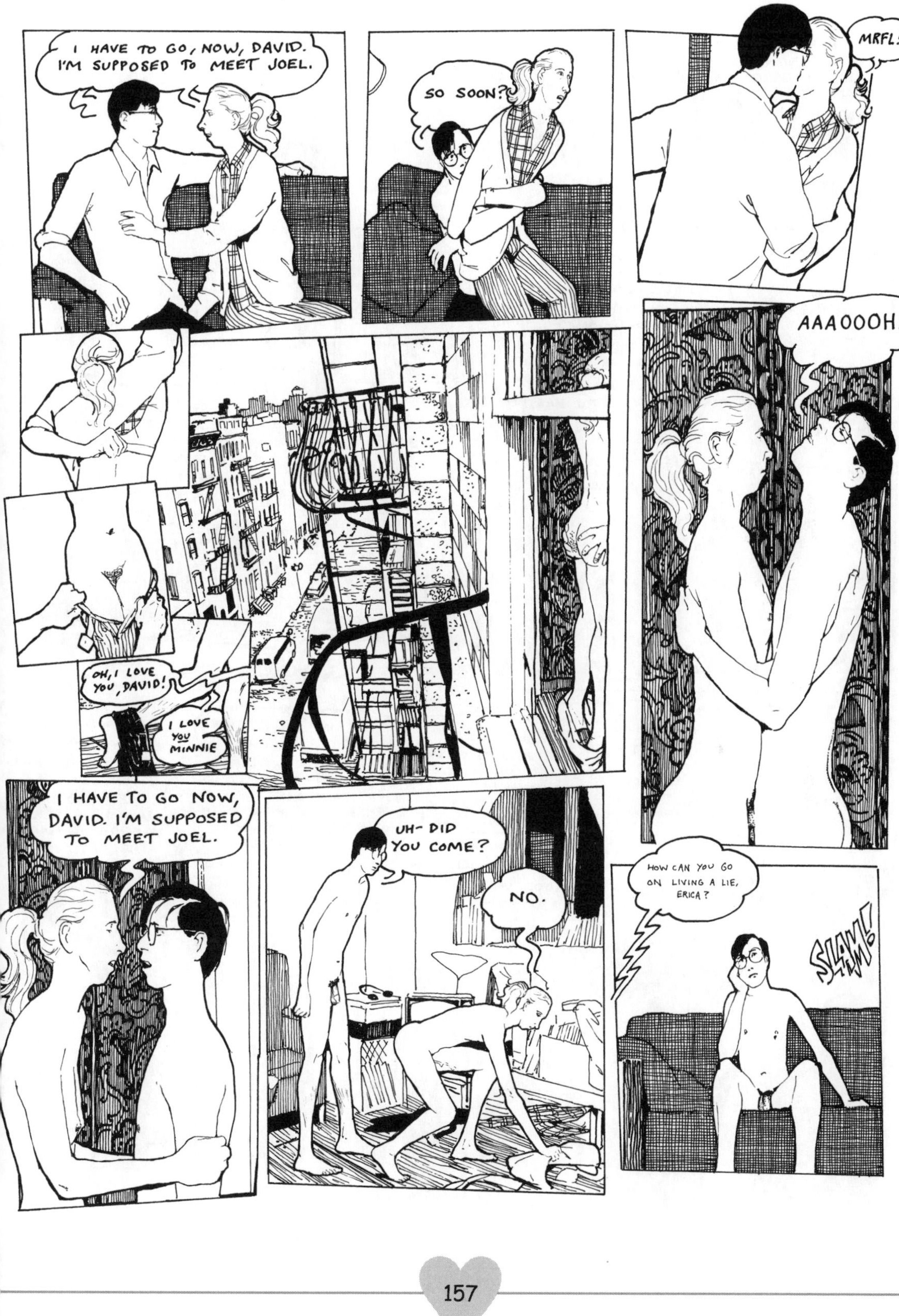
I HAVE TO GO, NOW, DAVID. I'M SUPPOSED TO MEET JOEL.
SO SOON?
MRFL!
AAAOOOH!!
OH, I LOVE YOU, DAVID!
I LOVE YOU MINNIE
I HAVE TO GO NOW, DAVID. I'M SUPPOSED TO MEET JOEL.
UH- DID YOU COME?
NO.
HOW CAN YOU GO ON LIVING A LIE, ERICA?
SLAM!

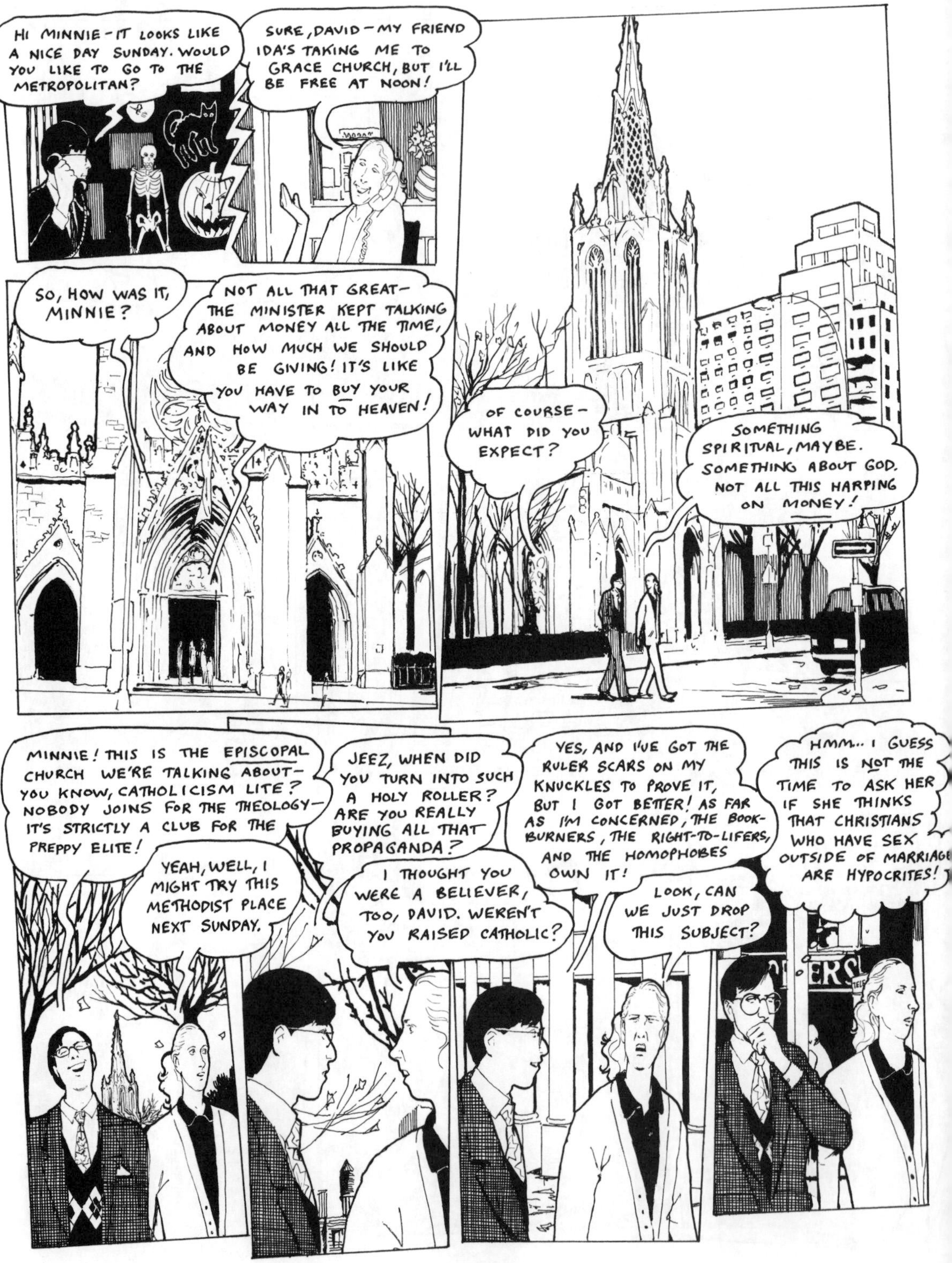
HI MINNIE - IT LOOKS LIKE A NICE DAY SUNDAY. WOULD YOU LIKE TO GO TO THE METROPOLITAN?
SURE, DAVID - MY FRIEND IDA'S TAKING ME TO GRACE CHURCH, BUT I'LL BE FREE AT NOON!
SO, HOW WAS IT, MINNIE?
NOT ALL THAT GREAT - THE MINISTER KEPT TALKING ABOUT MONEY ALL THE TIME, AND HOW MUCH WE SHOULD BE GIVING! IT'S LIKE YOU HAVE TO BUY YOUR WAY IN TO HEAVEN!
OF COURSE - WHAT DID YOU EXPECT?
SOMETHING SPIRITUAL, MAYBE. SOMETHING ABOUT GOD. NOT ALL THIS HARPING ON MONEY!
MINNIE! THIS IS THE EPISCOPAL CHURCH WE'RE TALKING ABOUT - YOU KNOW, CATHOLICISM LITE? NOBODY JOINS FOR THE THEOLOGY - IT'S STRICTLY A CLUB FOR THE PREPPY ELITE!
YEAH, WELL, I MIGHT TRY THIS METHODIST PLACE NEXT SUNDAY.
JEEZ, WHEN DID YOU TURN INTO SUCH A HOLY ROLLER? ARE YOU REALLY BUYING ALL THAT PROPAGANDA?
I THOUGHT YOU WERE A BELIEVER, TOO, DAVID. WEREN'T YOU RAISED CATHOLIC?
YES, AND I'VE GOT THE RULER SCARS ON MY KNUCKLES TO PROVE IT, BUT I GOT BETTER! AS FAR AS I'M CONCERNED, THE BOOK-BURNERS, THE RIGHT-TO-LIFERS, AND THE HOMOPHOBES OWN IT!
LOOK, CAN WE JUST DROP THIS SUBJECT?
HMM.. I GUESS THIS IS NOT THE TIME TO ASK HER IF SHE THINKS THAT CHRISTIANS WHO HAVE SEX OUTSIDE OF MARRIAGE ARE HYPOCRITES!

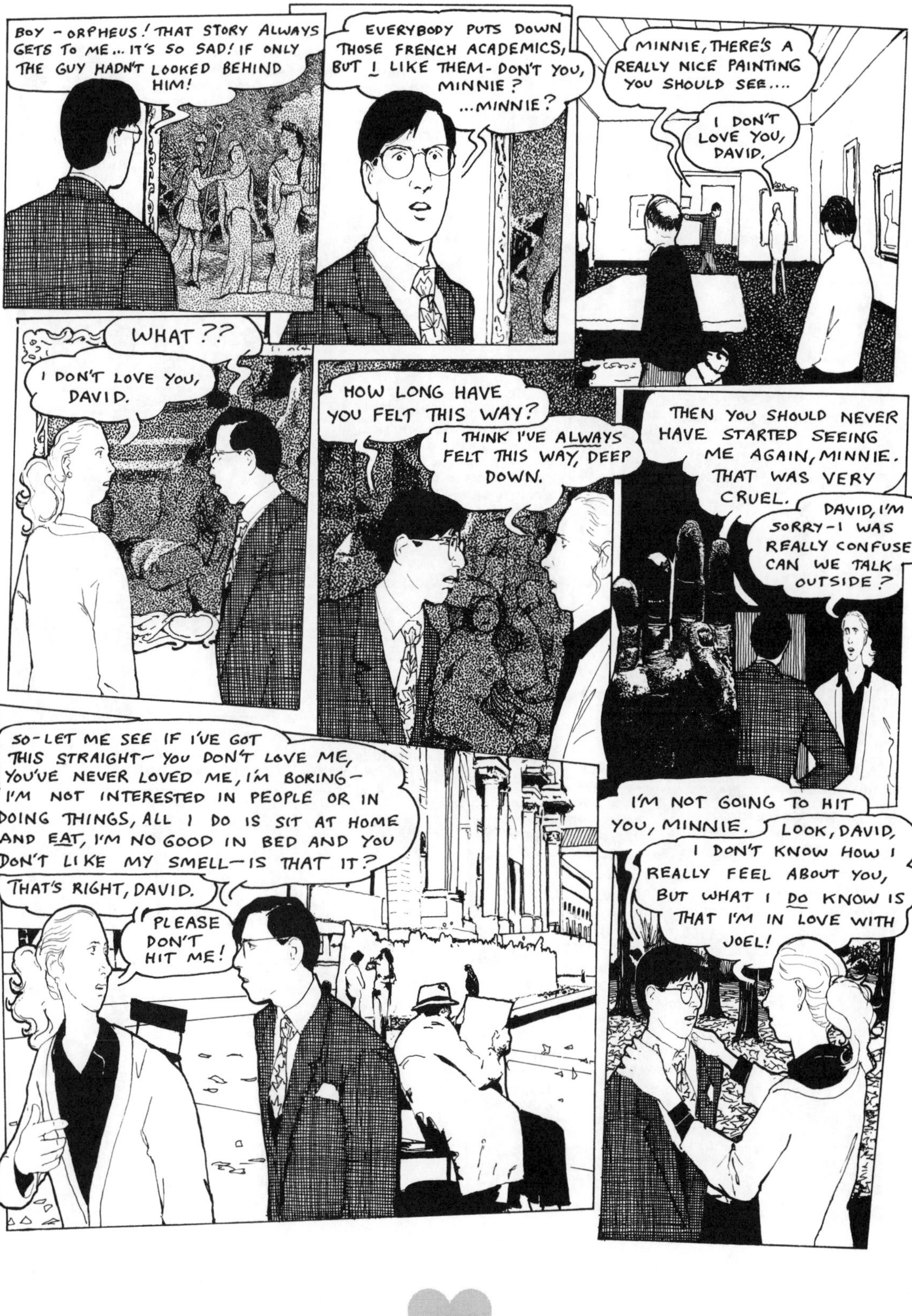
BOY - ORPHEUS! THAT STORY ALWAYS GETS TO ME... IT'S SO SAD! IF ONLY THE GUY HADN'T LOOKED BEHIND HIM!
EVERYBODY PUTS DOWN THOSE FRENCH ACADEMICS, BUT I LIKE THEM - DON'T YOU, MINNIE? ...MINNIE?
MINNIE, THERE'S A REALLY NICE PAINTING YOU SHOULD SEE....
I DON'T LOVE YOU, DAVID.
WHAT??
I DON'T LOVE YOU, DAVID.
HOW LONG HAVE YOU FELT THIS WAY?
I THINK I'VE ALWAYS FELT THIS WAY, DEEP DOWN.
THEN YOU SHOULD NEVER HAVE STARTED SEEING ME AGAIN, MINNIE. THAT WAS VERY CRUEL.
DAVID, I'M SORRY - I WAS REALLY CONFUSED! CAN WE TALK OUTSIDE?
SO - LET ME SEE IF I'VE GOT THIS STRAIGHT - YOU DON'T LOVE ME, YOU'VE NEVER LOVED ME, I'M BORING - I'M NOT INTERESTED IN PEOPLE OR IN DOING THINGS, ALL I DO IS SIT AT HOME AND EAT, I'M NO GOOD IN BED AND YOU DON'T LIKE MY SMELL - IS THAT IT?
THAT'S RIGHT, DAVID.
PLEASE DON'T HIT ME!
I'M NOT GOING TO HIT YOU, MINNIE.
LOOK, DAVID, I DON'T KNOW HOW I REALLY FEEL ABOUT YOU, BUT WHAT I DO KNOW IS THAT I'M IN LOVE WITH JOEL!

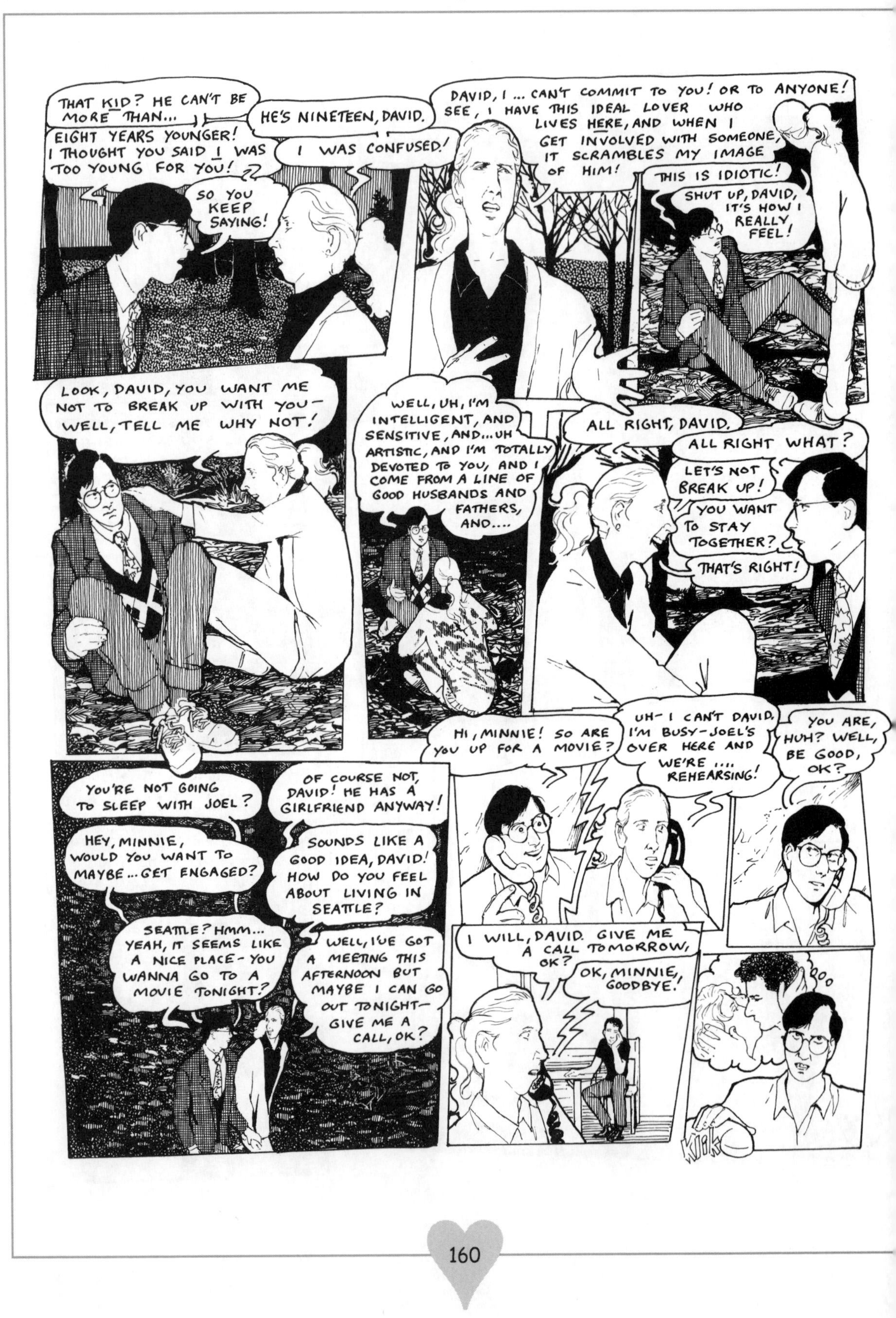
THAT KID? HE CAN'T BE MORE THAN...
HE'S NINETEEN, DAVID.
EIGHT YEARS YOUNGER! I THOUGHT YOU SAID I WAS TOO YOUNG FOR YOU!
I WAS CONFUSED!
SO YOU KEEP SAYING!
DAVID, I ... CAN'T COMMIT TO YOU! OR TO ANYONE! SEE, I HAVE THIS IDEAL LOVER WHO LIVES HERE, AND WHEN I GET INVOLVED WITH SOMEONE, IT SCRAMBLES MY IMAGE OF HIM!
THIS IS IDIOTIC!
SHUT UP, DAVID, IT'S HOW I REALLY FEEL!
LOOK, DAVID, YOU WANT ME NOT TO BREAK UP WITH YOU- WELL, TELL ME WHY NOT!
WELL, UH, I'M INTELLIGENT, AND SENSITIVE, AND...UH ARTISTIC, AND I'M TOTALLY DEVOTED TO YOU, AND I COME FROM A LINE OF GOOD HUSBANDS AND FATHERS, AND....
ALL RIGHT, DAVID.
ALL RIGHT WHAT?
LET'S NOT BREAK UP!
YOU WANT TO STAY TOGETHER?
THAT'S RIGHT!
YOU'RE NOT GOING TO SLEEP WITH JOEL?
OF COURSE NOT, DAVID! HE HAS A GIRLFRIEND ANYWAY!
HEY, MINNIE, WOULD YOU WANT TO MAYBE...GET ENGAGED?
SOUNDS LIKE A GOOD IDEA, DAVID! HOW DO YOU FEEL ABOUT LIVING IN SEATTLE?
SEATTLE? HMM... YEAH, IT SEEMS LIKE A NICE PLACE- YOU WANNA GO TO A MOVIE TONIGHT?
WELL, I'VE GOT A MEETING THIS AFTERNOON BUT MAYBE I CAN GO OUT TONIGHT- GIVE ME A CALL, OK?
HI, MINNIE! SO ARE YOU UP FOR A MOVIE?
UH- I CAN'T DAVID. I'M BUSY- JOEL'S OVER HERE AND WE'RE .... REHEARSING!
YOU ARE, HUH? WELL, BE GOOD, OK?
I WILL, DAVID. GIVE ME A CALL TOMORROW, OK?
OK, MINNIE, GOODBYE!
OOO
KLIK

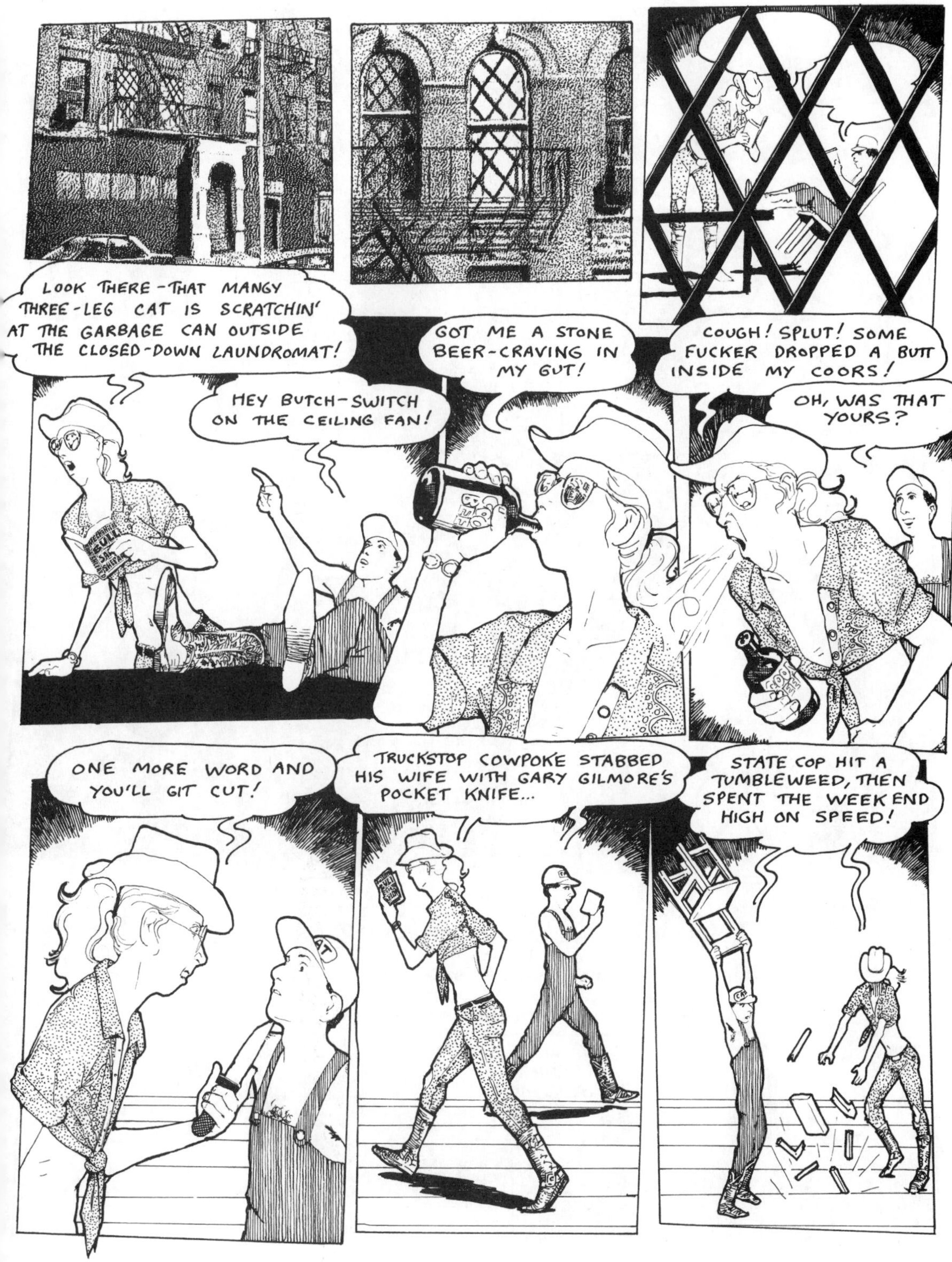
LOOK THERE - THAT MANGY THREE-LEG CAT IS SCRATCHIN' AT THE GARBAGE CAN OUTSIDE THE CLOSED-DOWN LAUNDROMAT!
HEY BUTCH-SWITCH ON THE CEILING FAN!
GOT ME A STONE BEER-CRAVING IN MY GUT!
COUGH! SPLUT! SOME FUCKER DROPPED A BUTT INSIDE MY COORS!
OH, WAS THAT YOURS?
ONE MORE WORD AND YOU'LL GIT CUT!
TRUCKSTOP COWPOKE STABBED HIS WIFE WITH GARY GILMORE'S POCKET KNIFE...
STATE COP HIT A TUMBLEWEED, THEN SPENT THE WEEK END HIGH ON SPEED!

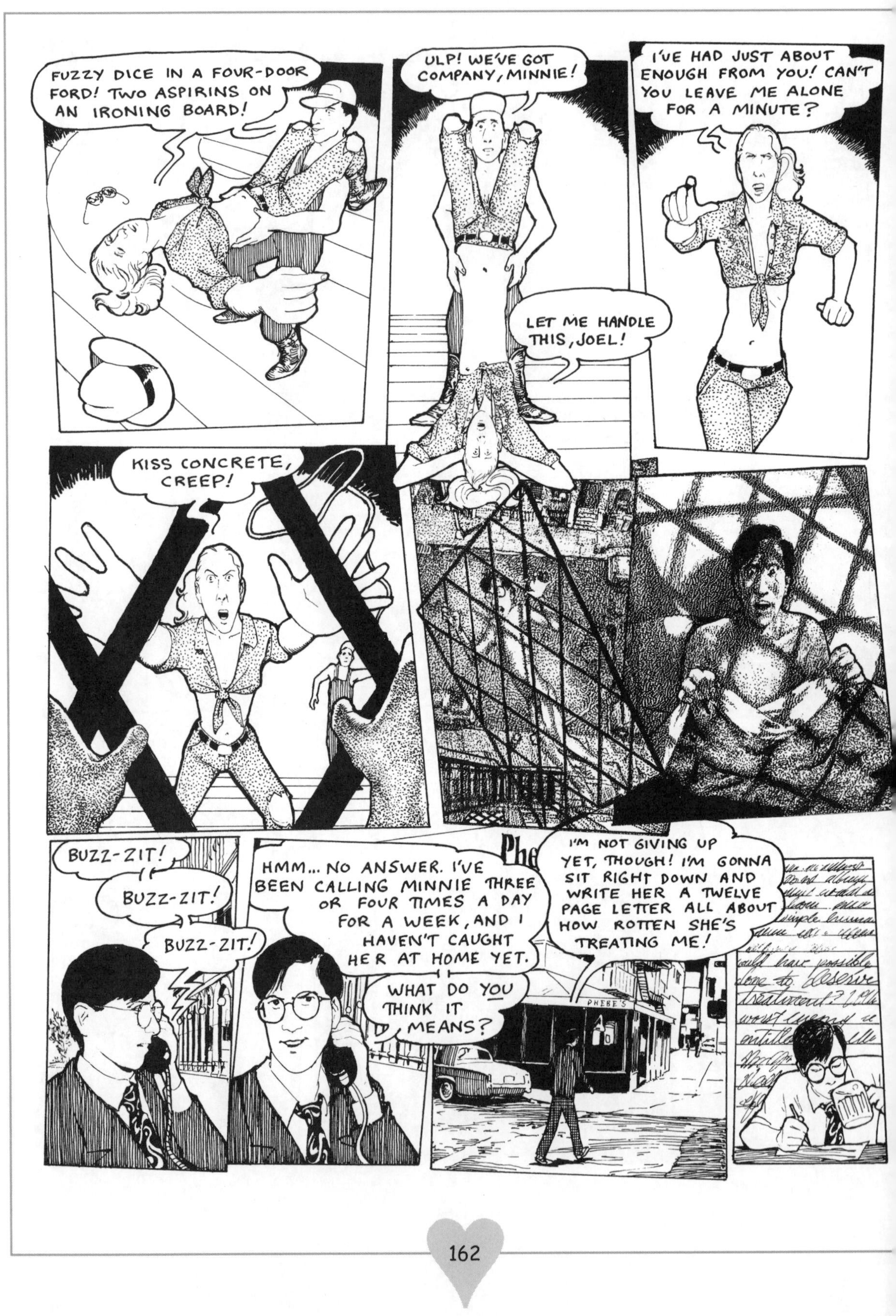
FUZZY DICE IN A FOUR-DOOR FORD! TWO ASPIRINS ON AN IRONING BOARD!
ULP! WE'VE GOT COMPANY, MINNIE!
LET ME HANDLE THIS, JOEL!
I'VE HAD JUST ABOUT ENOUGH FROM YOU! CAN'T YOU LEAVE ME ALONE FOR A MINUTE?
KISS CONCRETE, CREEP!
BUZZ-ZIT!
BUZZ-ZIT!
BUZZ-ZIT!
HMM... NO ANSWER. I'VE BEEN CALLING MINNIE THREE OR FOUR TIMES A DAY FOR A WEEK, AND I HAVEN'T CAUGHT HER AT HOME YET.
WHAT DO YOU THINK IT MEANS?
I'M NOT GIVING UP YET, THOUGH! I'M GONNA SIT RIGHT DOWN AND WRITE HER A TWELVE PAGE LETTER ALL ABOUT HOW ROTTEN SHE'S TREATING ME!
PHEBE'S

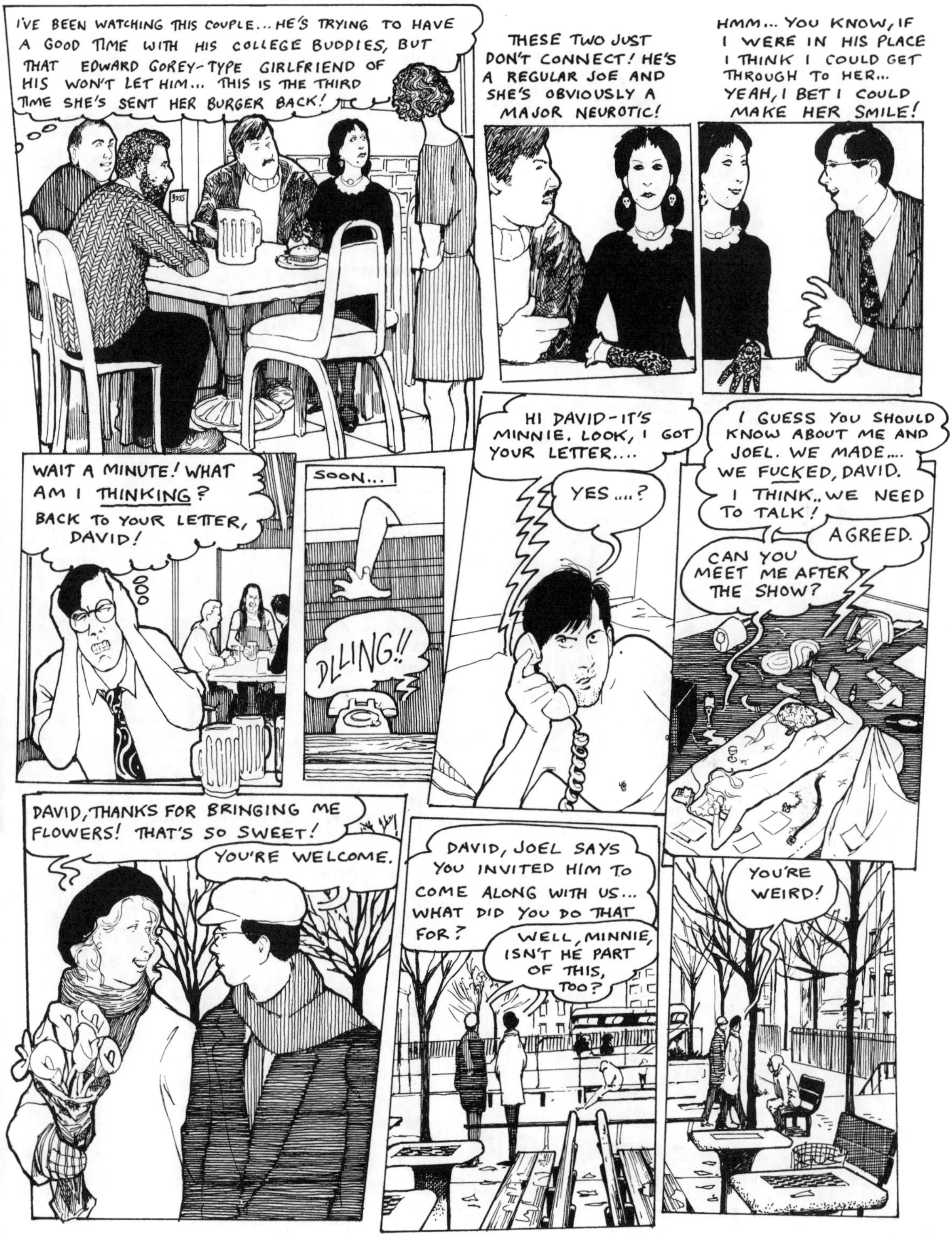
I'VE BEEN WATCHING THIS COUPLE... HE'S TRYING TO HAVE A GOOD TIME WITH HIS COLLEGE BUDDIES, BUT THAT EDWARD GOREY-TYPE GIRLFRIEND OF HIS WON'T LET HIM... THIS IS THE THIRD TIME SHE'S SENT HER BURGER BACK!
THESE TWO JUST DON'T CONNECT! HE'S A REGULAR JOE AND SHE'S OBVIOUSLY A MAJOR NEUROTIC!
HMM... YOU KNOW, IF I WERE IN HIS PLACE I THINK I COULD GET THROUGH TO HER... YEAH, I BET I COULD MAKE HER SMILE!
WAIT A MINUTE! WHAT AM I THINKING? BACK TO YOUR LETTER, DAVID!
SOON...
DLLING!!
HI DAVID-IT'S MINNIE. LOOK, I GOT YOUR LETTER....
YES....?
I GUESS YOU SHOULD KNOW ABOUT ME AND JOEL. WE MADE.... WE FUCKED, DAVID. I THINK.. WE NEED TO TALK!
AGREED.
CAN YOU MEET ME AFTER THE SHOW?
DAVID, THANKS FOR BRINGING ME FLOWERS! THAT'S SO SWEET!
YOU'RE WELCOME.
DAVID, JOEL SAYS YOU INVITED HIM TO COME ALONG WITH US... WHAT DID YOU DO THAT FOR?
WELL, MINNIE, ISN'T HE PART OF THIS, TOO?
YOU'RE WEIRD!

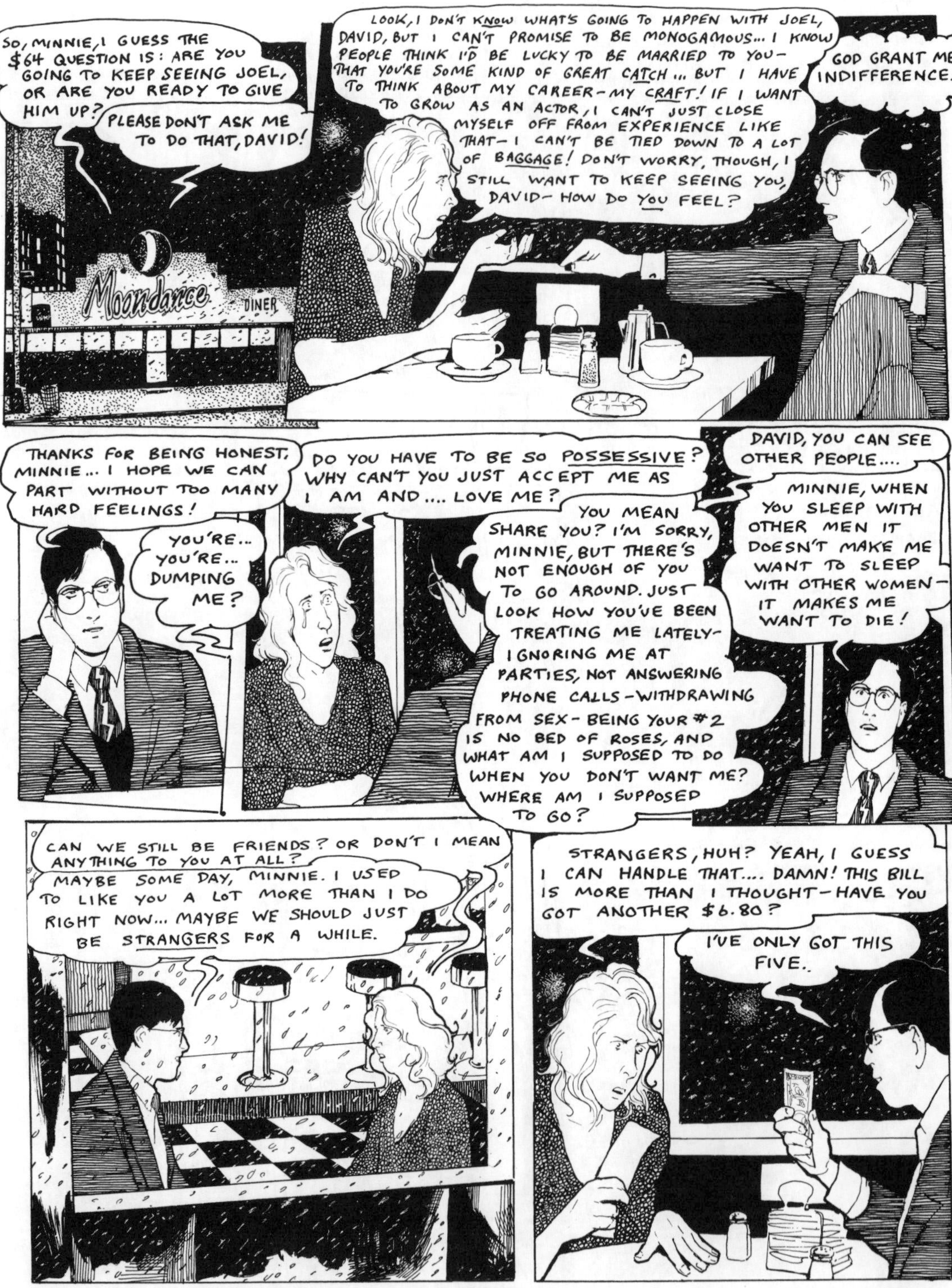

SO, MINNIE, I GUESS THE $64 QUESTION IS: ARE YOU GOING TO KEEP SEEING JOEL, OR ARE YOU READY TO GIVE HIM UP?
PLEASE DON'T ASK ME TO DO THAT, DAVID!
Moondance
DINER
LOOK, I DON'T KNOW WHAT'S GOING TO HAPPEN WITH JOEL, DAVID, BUT I CAN'T PROMISE TO BE MONOGAMOUS... I KNOW PEOPLE THINK I'D BE LUCKY TO BE MARRIED TO YOU- THAT YOU'RE SOME KIND OF GREAT CATCH ... BUT I HAVE TO THINK ABOUT MY CAREER- MY CRAFT! IF I WANT TO GROW AS AN ACTOR, I CAN'T JUST CLOSE MYSELF OFF FROM EXPERIENCE LIKE THAT- I CAN'T BE TIED DOWN TO A LOT OF BAGGAGE! DON'T WORRY, THOUGH, I STILL WANT TO KEEP SEEING YOU, DAVID- HOW DO YOU FEEL?
GOD GRANT ME INDIFFERENCE!
THANKS FOR BEING HONEST, MINNIE... I HOPE WE CAN PART WITHOUT TOO MANY HARD FEELINGS!
YOU'RE... YOU'RE... DUMPING ME?
DO YOU HAVE TO BE SO POSSESSIVE? WHY CAN'T YOU JUST ACCEPT ME AS I AM AND.... LOVE ME?
YOU MEAN SHARE YOU? I'M SORRY, MINNIE, BUT THERE'S NOT ENOUGH OF YOU TO GO AROUND. JUST LOOK HOW YOU'VE BEEN TREATING ME LATELY- IGNORING ME AT PARTIES, NOT ANSWERING PHONE CALLS- WITHDRAWING FROM SEX- BEING YOUR #2 IS NO BED OF ROSES, AND WHAT AM I SUPPOSED TO DO WHEN YOU DON'T WANT ME? WHERE AM I SUPPOSED TO GO?
DAVID, YOU CAN SEE OTHER PEOPLE....
MINNIE, WHEN YOU SLEEP WITH OTHER MEN IT DOESN'T MAKE ME WANT TO SLEEP WITH OTHER WOMEN- IT MAKES ME WANT TO DIE!
CAN WE STILL BE FRIENDS? OR DON'T I MEAN ANYTHING TO YOU AT ALL?
MAYBE SOME DAY, MINNIE. I USED TO LIKE YOU A LOT MORE THAN I DO RIGHT NOW... MAYBE WE SHOULD JUST BE STRANGERS FOR A WHILE.
STRANGERS, HUH? YEAH, I GUESS I CAN HANDLE THAT.... DAMN! THIS BILL IS MORE THAN I THOUGHT- HAVE YOU GOT ANOTHER $6.80?
I'VE ONLY GOT THIS FIVE.

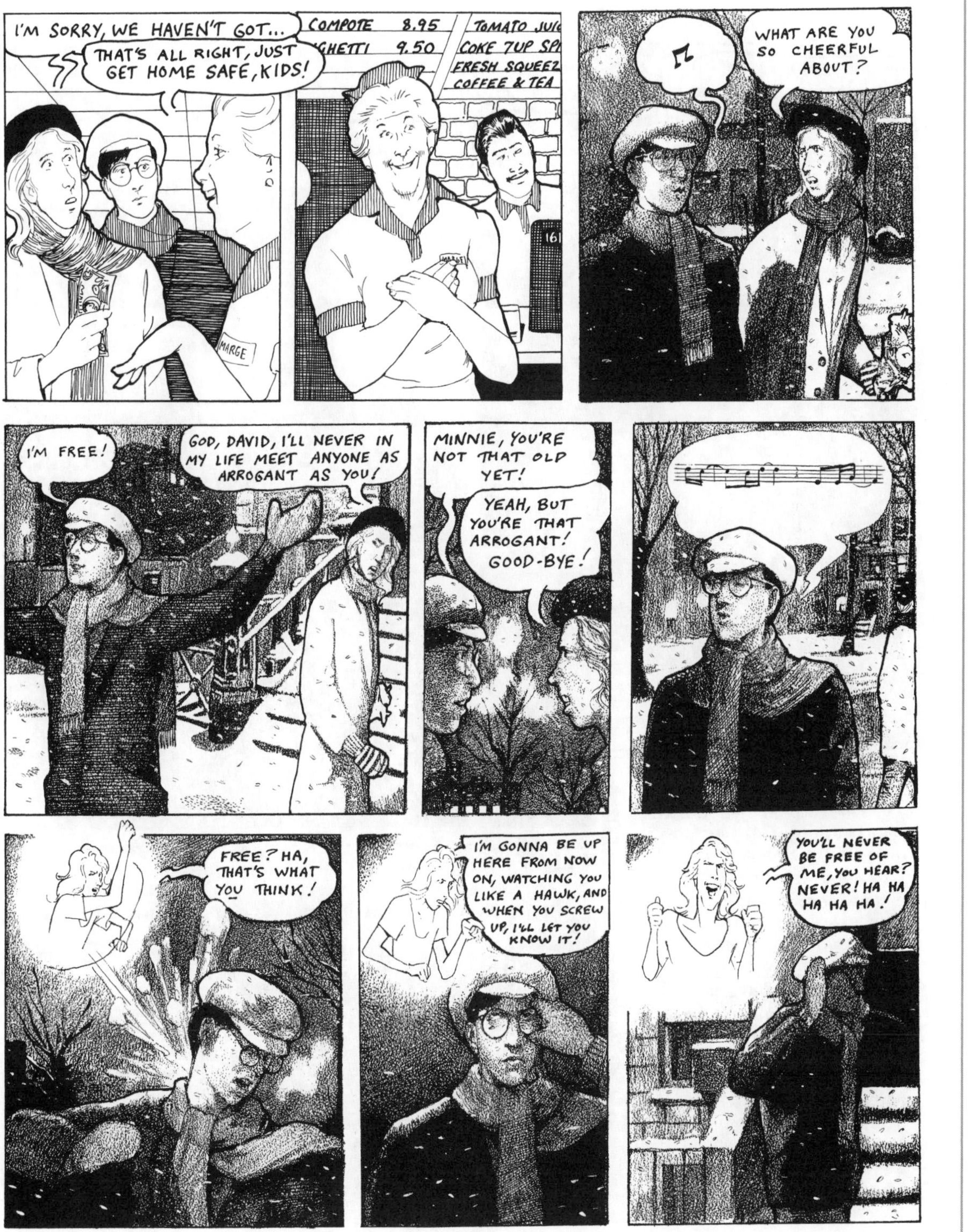
I'M SORRY, WE HAVEN'T GOT...
THAT'S ALL RIGHT, JUST GET HOME SAFE, KIDS!
MARGE
COMPOTE 8.95
GHETTI 9.50
TOMATO JUI
COKE 7UP SP
FRESH SQUEEZ
COFFEE & TEA
WHAT ARE YOU SO CHEERFUL ABOUT?
I'M FREE!
GOD, DAVID, I'LL NEVER IN MY LIFE MEET ANYONE AS ARROGANT AS YOU!
MINNIE, YOU'RE NOT THAT OLD YET!
YEAH, BUT YOU'RE THAT ARROGANT! GOOD-BYE!
FREE? HA, THAT'S WHAT YOU THINK!
I'M GONNA BE UP HERE FROM NOW ON, WATCHING YOU LIKE A HAWK, AND WHEN YOU SCREW UP, I'LL LET YOU KNOW IT!
YOU'LL NEVER BE FREE OF ME, YOU HEAR? NEVER! HA HA HA HA HA!

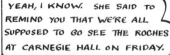

HEY, DAVID – MINNIE CALLED WHILE YOU WERE OUT.

WELL, I DON'T WANT TO TALK TO HER, WE JUST BROKE UP.

YEAH, I KNOW. SHE SAID TO REMIND YOU THAT WE'RE ALL SUPPOSED TO GO SEE THE ROCHES AT CARNEGIE HALL ON FRIDAY.

AAARGH!

SHE SAID YOU CAN BACK OUT IF YOU REALLY DON'T WANT TO SEE HER.

NO, IT'S ALL RIGHT.

I'VE GOT TO GET AWAY FROM YOOO ♪ YOU DON'T KNOW WHAT YOU PUT ME THROUGH... ♪

SWELL SEATS. THANKS FOR PICKING UP THE TICKETS, DAVID.

WE'RE FRIENDS AGAIN, AREN'T WE, DAVID?

SO, HOW'S JOEL?

JUST GREAT – WE'RE REALLY GETTING ALONG! BUT SOMETHING REALLY AWFUL HAPPENED TO US LAST WEEK.

WE HAD THESE PROPS FOR THIS SAM SHEPARD SCENE WE'RE WORKING ON, AND WE LEFT THEM IN A STORAGE CLOSET AND WHEN IT CAME TIME TO DO THE SCENE, THE PROPS WERE GONE – SOMEONE HAD TAKEN THEM! CAN YOU IMAGINE? WHO WOULD DO SUCH A THING?

GEE, MINNIE, THAT'S THE MOST TRAGIC THING I COULD POSSIBLY IMAGINE.

I WISH YOU WOULDN'T SIT SO CLOSE, DAVID. YOUR BREATH IS REALLY BAD.

IT IS?

JUST THOUGHT YOU'D LIKE TO KNOW.

CLAP CLAP CLAP

WHAT A GREAT CONCERT! I'M GOING TO GO OUT AND BUY ALL THEIR RECORDS!

ME TOO!

LET'S GO OUT FOR SOME ICE CREAM! THERE'S A HAAGEN DAZ DOWN THE BLOCK.

HEY, HOLD ON A MINUTE—WHERE'S DAVID?

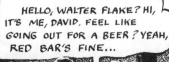

HELLO, WALTER FLAKE? HI, IT'S ME, DAVID, FEEL LIKE GOING OUT FOR A BEER? YEAH, RED BAR'S FINE...

Phone

...RIGHT IN THE MIDDLE OF CARNEGIE HALL! RUINED THE WHOLE CONCERT FOR ME! ALL I COULD THINK OF WAS GETTING OUT OF THERE! SAY, ARE YOU SURE YOU DON'T WANT SOME OF THIS PARSLEY? IT'S SUPPOSED TO BE DEATH ON BAD BREATH!

NAW, IT DOESN'T MIX WITH ROLLING ROCK!

I THOUGHT THAT NOW THAT WE'RE QUITS SHE COULDN'T HURT ME ANYMORE—WELL, IT'S NOT THE FIRST TIME I'VE BEEN WRONG ABOUT HER!

SHE SOUNDS LIKE PURE POISON. WAS THE SEX ANY GOOD?

NOT AFTER SHE GOT TO NEW YORK, BUT I DIDN'T THINK IT MATTERED...

SO WHAT WAS THE ATTRACTION, ANYWAY?

I DON'T KNOW—IT'S JUST... WELL, ONCE, BEFORE WE WERE INVOLVED, I SAW HER IN A PLAY. SHE WAS PLAYING A VIKING MAIDEN AND AT ONE POINT SHE STRUCK THIS POSE—AND SHE LOOKED SO FRAIL AND VULNERABLE, I KNEW AT THAT MOMENT THAT I WANTED HER. THE REASONS WHY CAME LATER.

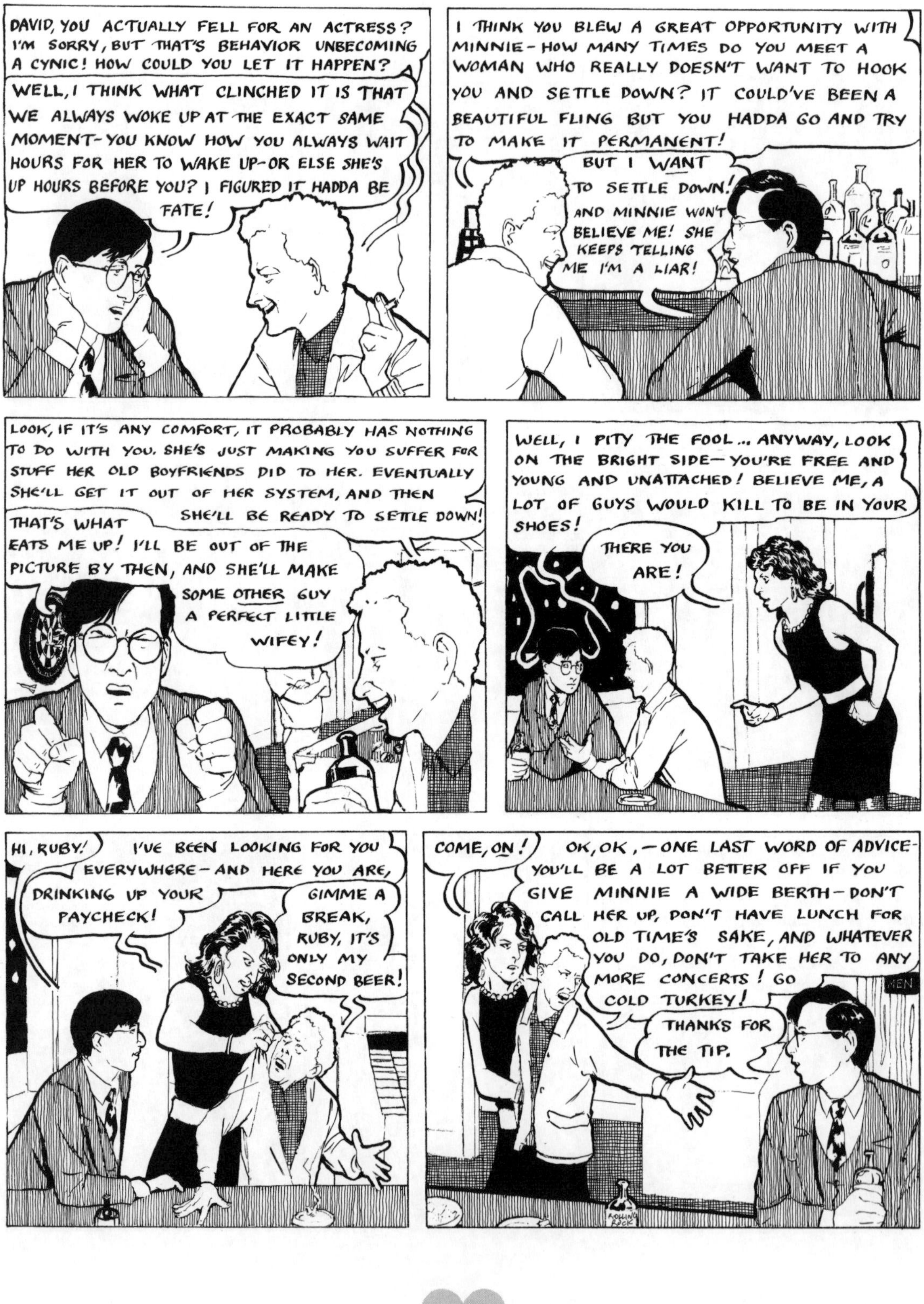
DAVID, YOU ACTUALLY FELL FOR AN ACTRESS? I'M SORRY, BUT THAT'S BEHAVIOR UNBECOMING A CYNIC! HOW COULD YOU LET IT HAPPEN?
WELL, I THINK WHAT CLINCHED IT IS THAT WE ALWAYS WOKE UP AT THE EXACT SAME MOMENT- YOU KNOW HOW YOU ALWAYS WAIT HOURS FOR HER TO WAKE UP-OR ELSE SHE'S UP HOURS BEFORE YOU? I FIGURED IT HADDA BE FATE!
I THINK YOU BLEW A GREAT OPPORTUNITY WITH MINNIE- HOW MANY TIMES DO YOU MEET A WOMAN WHO REALLY DOESN'T WANT TO HOOK YOU AND SETTLE DOWN? IT COULD'VE BEEN A BEAUTIFUL FLING BUT YOU HADDA GO AND TRY TO MAKE IT PERMANENT!
BUT I WANT TO SETTLE DOWN! AND MINNIE WON'T BELIEVE ME! SHE KEEPS TELLING ME I'M A LIAR!
LOOK, IF IT'S ANY COMFORT, IT PROBABLY HAS NOTHING TO DO WITH YOU. SHE'S JUST MAKING YOU SUFFER FOR STUFF HER OLD BOYFRIENDS DID TO HER. EVENTUALLY SHE'LL GET IT OUT OF HER SYSTEM, AND THEN SHE'LL BE READY TO SETTLE DOWN!
THAT'S WHAT EATS ME UP! I'LL BE OUT OF THE PICTURE BY THEN, AND SHE'LL MAKE SOME OTHER GUY A PERFECT LITTLE WIFEY!
WELL, I PITY THE FOOL... ANYWAY, LOOK ON THE BRIGHT SIDE— YOU'RE FREE AND YOUNG AND UNATTACHED! BELIEVE ME, A LOT OF GUYS WOULD KILL TO BE IN YOUR SHOES!
THERE YOU ARE!
HI, RUBY!
I'VE BEEN LOOKING FOR YOU EVERYWHERE— AND HERE YOU ARE, DRINKING UP YOUR PAYCHECK!
GIMME A BREAK, RUBY, IT'S ONLY MY SECOND BEER!
COME, ON!
OK, OK, —ONE LAST WORD OF ADVICE- YOU'LL BE A LOT BETTER OFF IF YOU GIVE MINNIE A WIDE BERTH—DON'T CALL HER UP, DON'T HAVE LUNCH FOR OLD TIME'S SAKE, AND WHATEVER YOU DO, DON'T TAKE HER TO ANY MORE CONCERTS! GO COLD TURKEY!
THANKS FOR THE TIP.
MEN
ROLLING ROCK

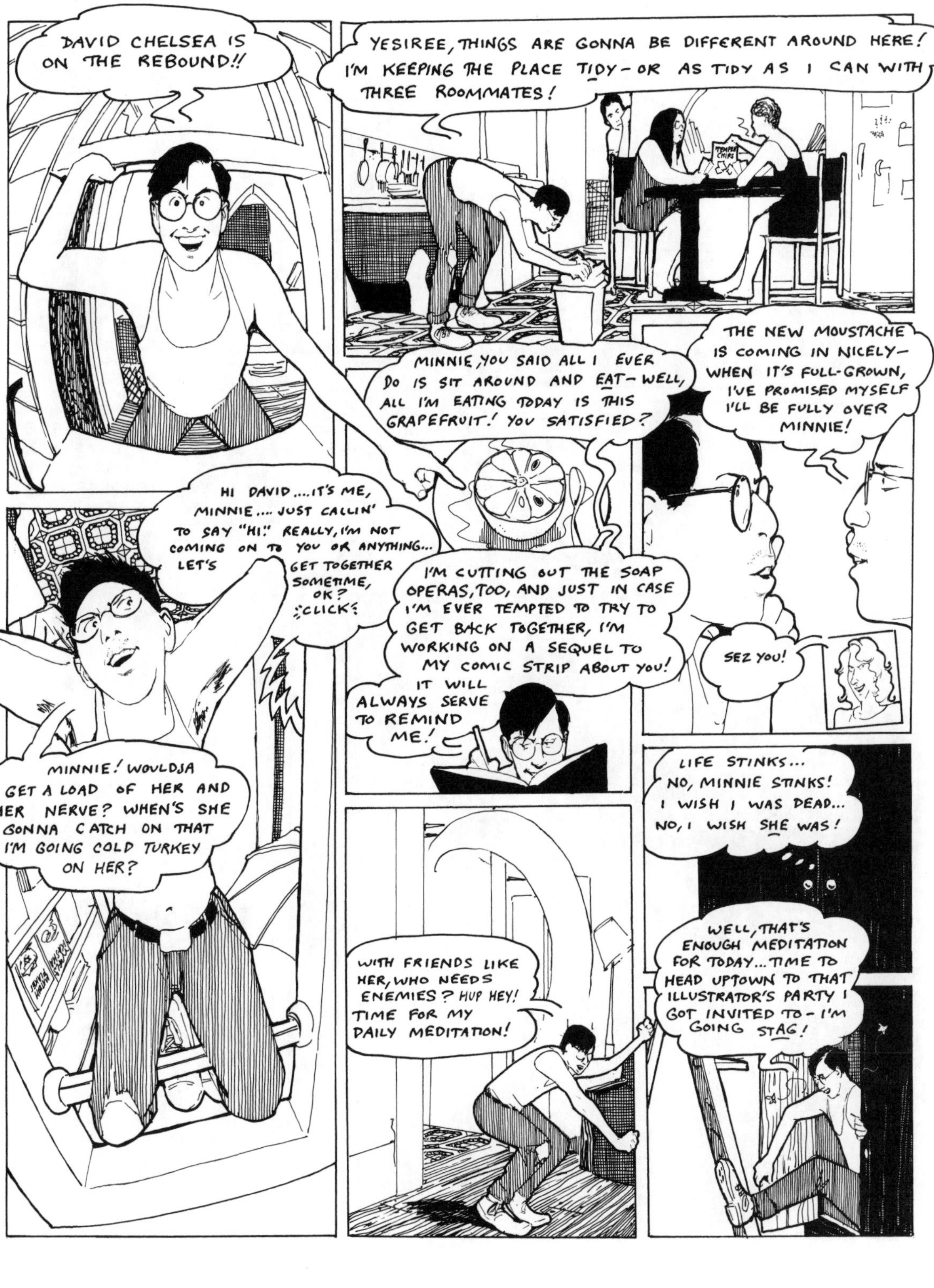
DAVID CHELSEA IS ON THE REBOUND!!
YESIREE, THINGS ARE GONNA BE DIFFERENT AROUND HERE! I'M KEEPING THE PLACE TIDY - OR AS TIDY AS I CAN WITH THREE ROOMMATES!
TEMPLE CHIPS
MINNIE, YOU SAID ALL I EVER DO IS SIT AROUND AND EAT - WELL, ALL I'M EATING TODAY IS THIS GRAPEFRUIT! YOU SATISFIED?
THE NEW MOUSTACHE IS COMING IN NICELY- WHEN IT'S FULL-GROWN, I'VE PROMISED MYSELF I'LL BE FULLY OVER MINNIE!
HI DAVID....IT'S ME, MINNIE.... JUST CALLIN' TO SAY "HI." REALLY, I'M NOT COMING ON TO YOU OR ANYTHING... LET'S GET TOGETHER SOMETIME, OK? :CLICK:
I'M CUTTING OUT THE SOAP OPERAS, TOO, AND JUST IN CASE I'M EVER TEMPTED TO TRY TO GET BACK TOGETHER, I'M WORKING ON A SEQUEL TO MY COMIC STRIP ABOUT YOU!
IT WILL ALWAYS SERVE TO REMIND ME!
SEZ YOU!
MINNIE! WOULDJA GET A LOAD OF HER AND HER NERVE? WHEN'S SHE GONNA CATCH ON THAT I'M GOING COLD TURKEY ON HER?
WITH FRIENDS LIKE HER, WHO NEEDS ENEMIES? HUP HEY! TIME FOR MY DAILY MEDITATION!
LIFE STINKS... NO, MINNIE STINKS! I WISH I WAS DEAD... NO, I WISH SHE WAS!
WELL, THAT'S ENOUGH MEDITATION FOR TODAY... TIME TO HEAD UPTOWN TO THAT ILLUSTRATOR'S PARTY I GOT INVITED TO - I'M GOING STAG!

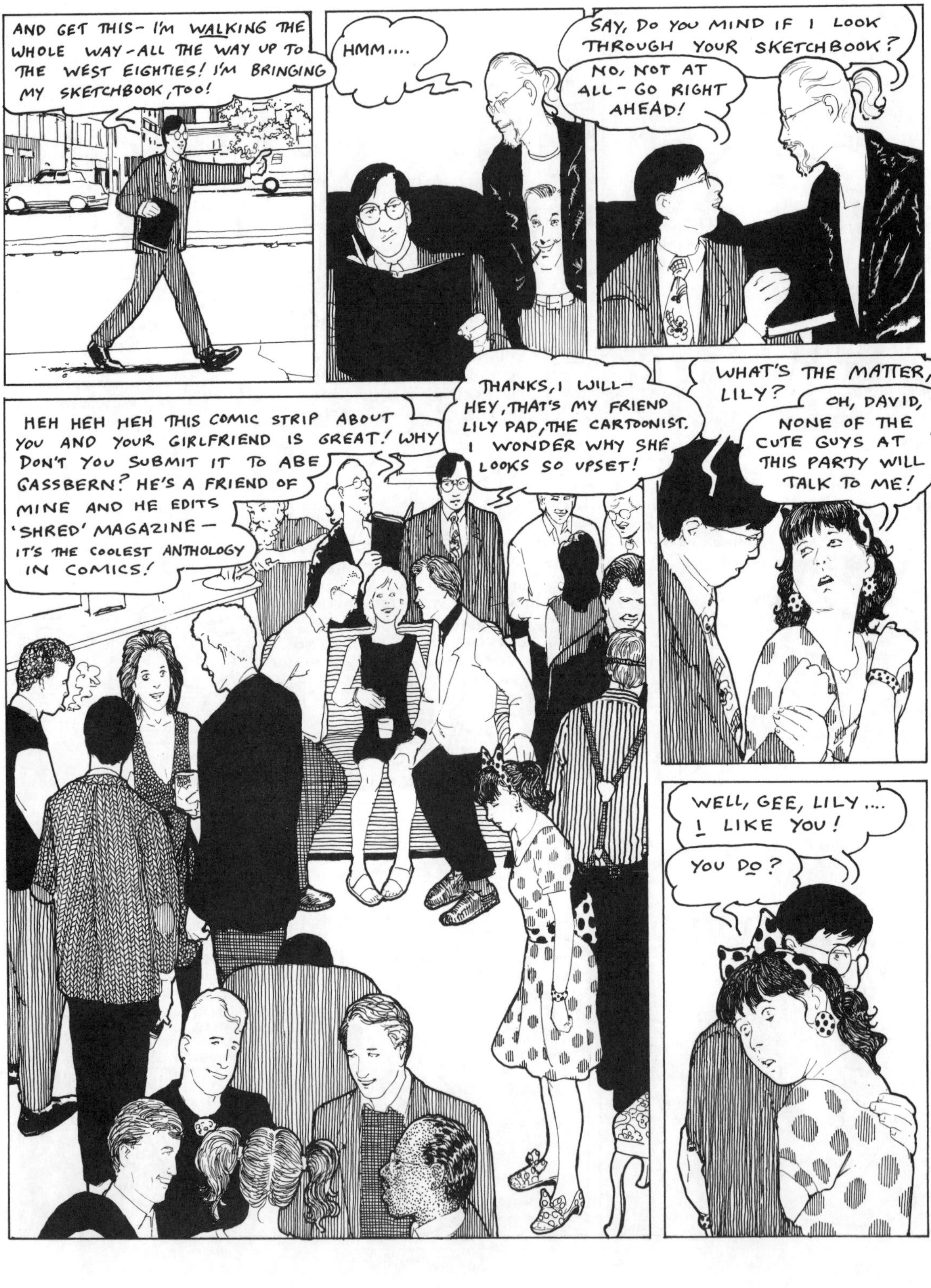
AND GET THIS- I'M WALKING THE WHOLE WAY-ALL THE WAY UP TO THE WEST EIGHTIES! I'M BRINGING MY SKETCHBOOK, TOO!
HMM....
SAY, DO YOU MIND IF I LOOK THROUGH YOUR SKETCHBOOK?
NO, NOT AT ALL- GO RIGHT AHEAD!
HEH HEH HEH THIS COMIC STRIP ABOUT YOU AND YOUR GIRLFRIEND IS GREAT! WHY DON'T YOU SUBMIT IT TO ABE GASSBERN? HE'S A FRIEND OF MINE AND HE EDITS 'SHRED' MAGAZINE— IT'S THE COOLEST ANTHOLOGY IN COMICS!
THANKS, I WILL- HEY, THAT'S MY FRIEND LILY PAD, THE CARTOONIST. I WONDER WHY SHE LOOKS SO UPSET!
WHAT'S THE MATTER, LILY?
OH, DAVID, NONE OF THE CUTE GUYS AT THIS PARTY WILL TALK TO ME!
WELL, GEE, LILY.... I LIKE YOU!
YOU DO?

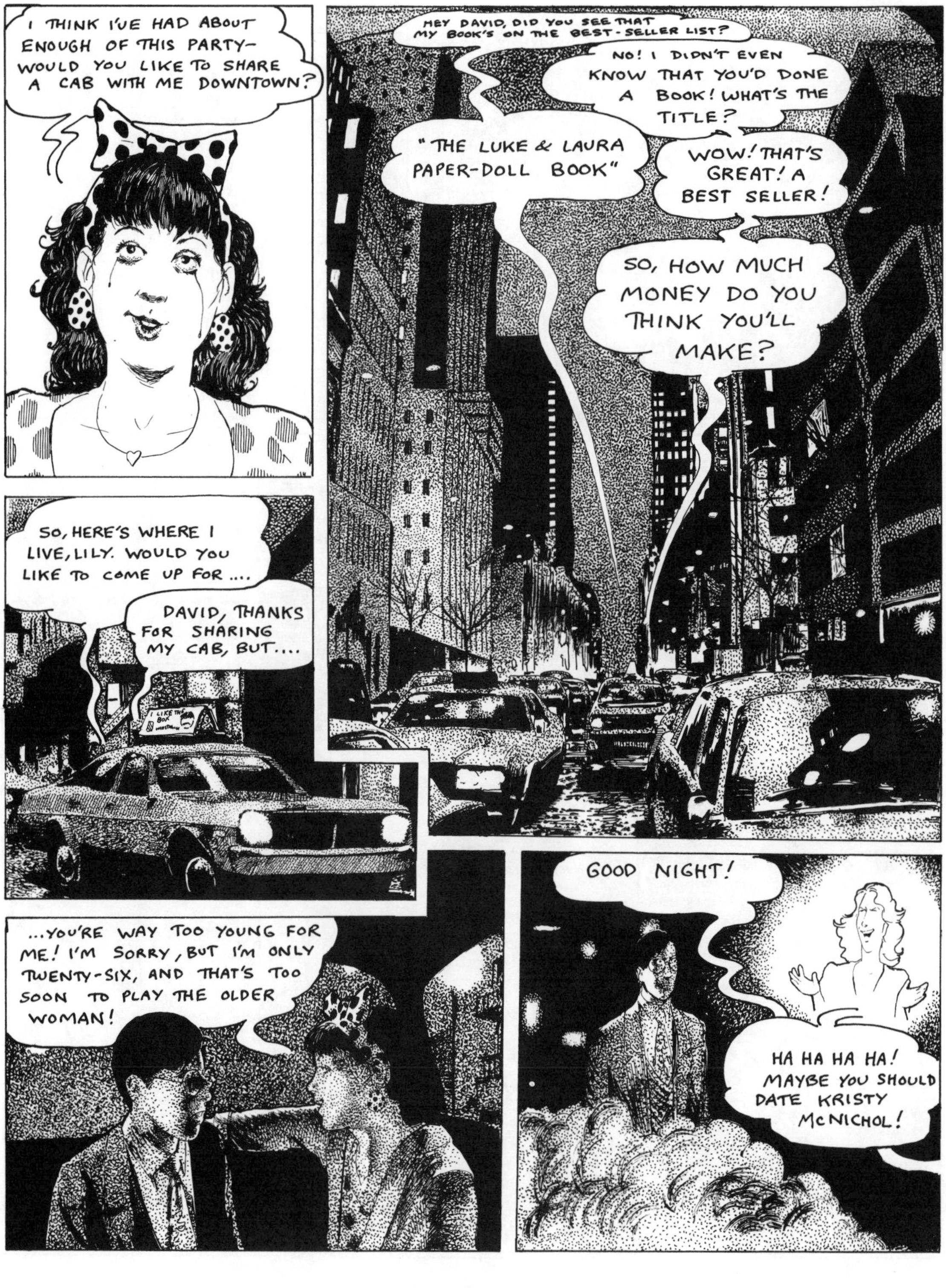
I THINK I'VE HAD ABOUT ENOUGH OF THIS PARTY- WOULD YOU LIKE TO SHARE A CAB WITH ME DOWNTOWN?
HEY DAVID, DID YOU SEE THAT MY BOOK'S ON THE BEST-SELLER LIST?
NO! I DIDN'T EVEN KNOW THAT YOU'D DONE A BOOK! WHAT'S THE TITLE?
"THE LUKE & LAURA PAPER-DOLL BOOK"
WOW! THAT'S GREAT! A BEST SELLER!
SO, HOW MUCH MONEY DO YOU THINK YOU'LL MAKE?
SO, HERE'S WHERE I LIVE, LILY. WOULD YOU LIKE TO COME UP FOR....
DAVID, THANKS FOR SHARING MY CAB, BUT....
...YOU'RE WAY TOO YOUNG FOR ME! I'M SORRY, BUT I'M ONLY TWENTY-SIX, AND THAT'S TOO SOON TO PLAY THE OLDER WOMAN!
GOOD NIGHT!
HA HA HA HA! MAYBE YOU SHOULD DATE KRISTY McNICHOL!

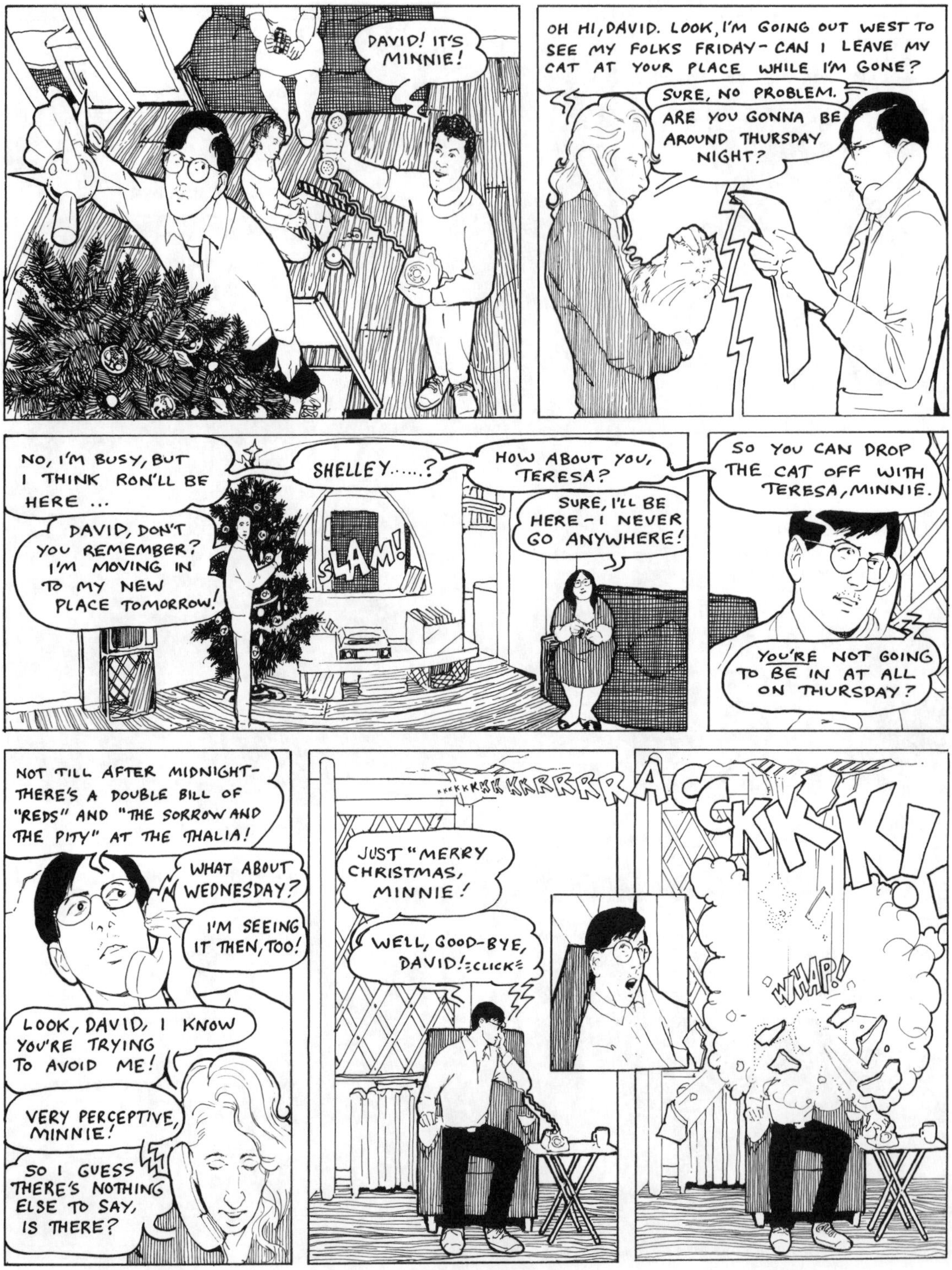
DAVID! IT'S MINNIE!
OH HI, DAVID. LOOK, I'M GOING OUT WEST TO SEE MY FOLKS FRIDAY - CAN I LEAVE MY CAT AT YOUR PLACE WHILE I'M GONE?
SURE, NO PROBLEM.
ARE YOU GONNA BE AROUND THURSDAY NIGHT?
NO, I'M BUSY, BUT I THINK RON'LL BE HERE ...
SHELLEY.....?
DAVID, DON'T YOU REMEMBER? I'M MOVING IN TO MY NEW PLACE TOMORROW!
SLAM!
HOW ABOUT YOU, TERESA?
SURE, I'LL BE HERE - I NEVER GO ANYWHERE!
SO YOU CAN DROP THE CAT OFF WITH TERESA, MINNIE.
YOU'RE NOT GOING TO BE IN AT ALL ON THURSDAY?
NOT TILL AFTER MIDNIGHT - THERE'S A DOUBLE BILL OF "REDS" AND "THE SORROW AND THE PITY" AT THE THALIA!
WHAT ABOUT WEDNESDAY?
I'M SEEING IT THEN, TOO!
LOOK, DAVID, I KNOW YOU'RE TRYING TO AVOID ME!
VERY PERCEPTIVE, MINNIE!
SO I GUESS THERE'S NOTHING ELSE TO SAY, IS THERE?
JUST "MERRY CHRISTMAS, MINNIE!
WELL, GOOD-BYE, DAVID! CLICK
KKKKKKKKKKRRRRRACCKKK!
WHAP!

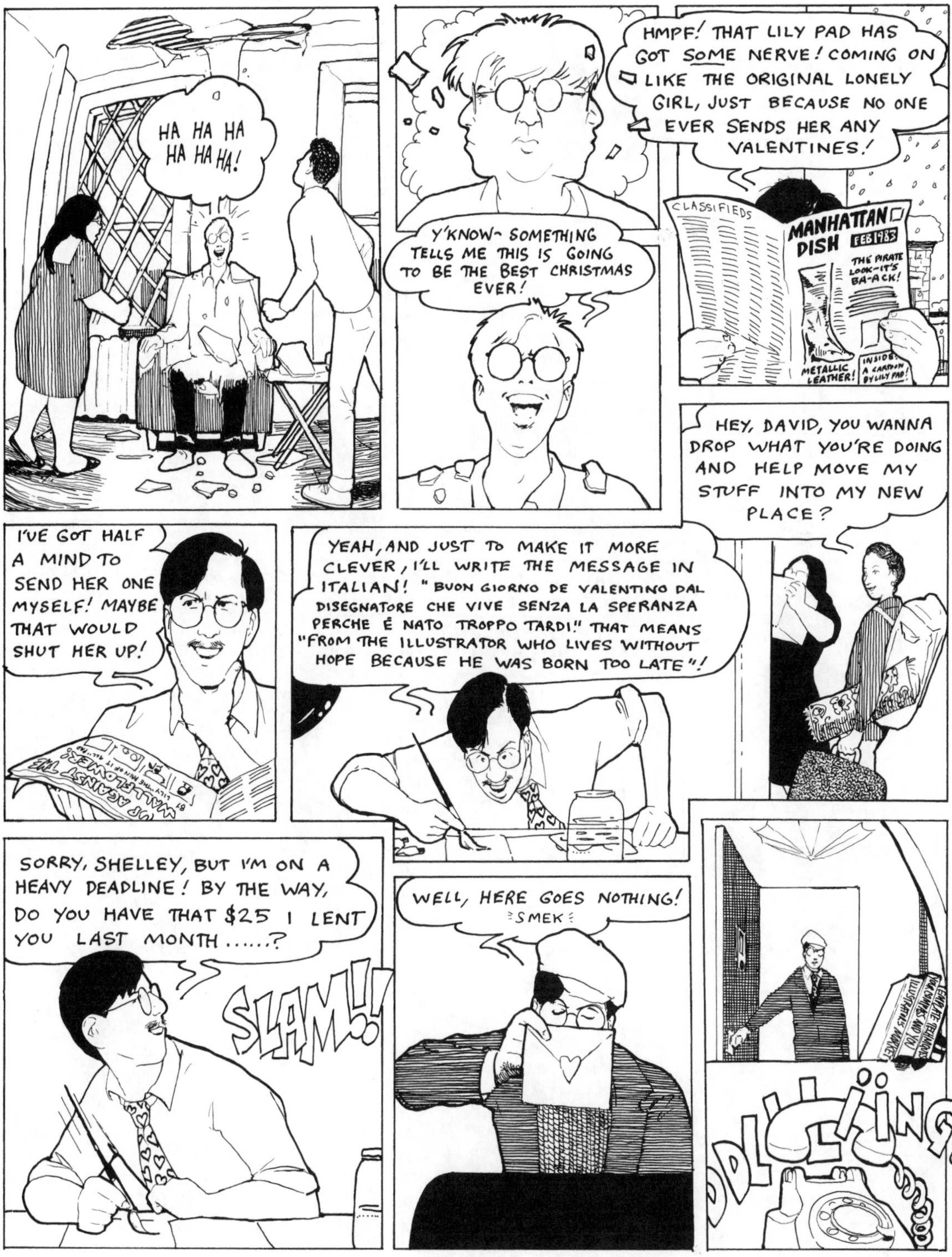
HA HA HA HA HA HA!
Y'KNOW~ SOMETHING TELLS ME THIS IS GOING TO BE THE BEST CHRISTMAS EVER!
HMPF! THAT LILY PAD HAS GOT SOME NERVE! COMING ON LIKE THE ORIGINAL LONELY GIRL, JUST BECAUSE NO ONE EVER SENDS HER ANY VALENTINES!
CLASSIFIEDS
MANHATTAN DISH
FEB 1983
THE PIRATE LOOK—IT'S BA-ACK!
METALLIC LEATHER!
INSIDE: A CARTOON BY LILY PAD!
I'VE GOT HALF A MIND TO SEND HER ONE MYSELF! MAYBE THAT WOULD SHUT HER UP!
YEAH, AND JUST TO MAKE IT MORE CLEVER, I'LL WRITE THE MESSAGE IN ITALIAN! "BUON GIORNO DE VALENTINO DAL DISEGNATORE CHE VIVE SENZA LA SPERANZA PERCHE È NATO TROPPO TARDI!" THAT MEANS "FROM THE ILLUSTRATOR WHO LIVES WITHOUT HOPE BECAUSE HE WAS BORN TOO LATE"!
HEY, DAVID, YOU WANNA DROP WHAT YOU'RE DOING AND HELP MOVE MY STUFF INTO MY NEW PLACE?
SORRY, SHELLEY, BUT I'M ON A HEAVY DEADLINE! BY THE WAY, DO YOU HAVE THAT $25 I LENT YOU LAST MONTH......?
SLAM!!
WELL, HERE GOES NOTHING!
SMEK
DDLLLLING!

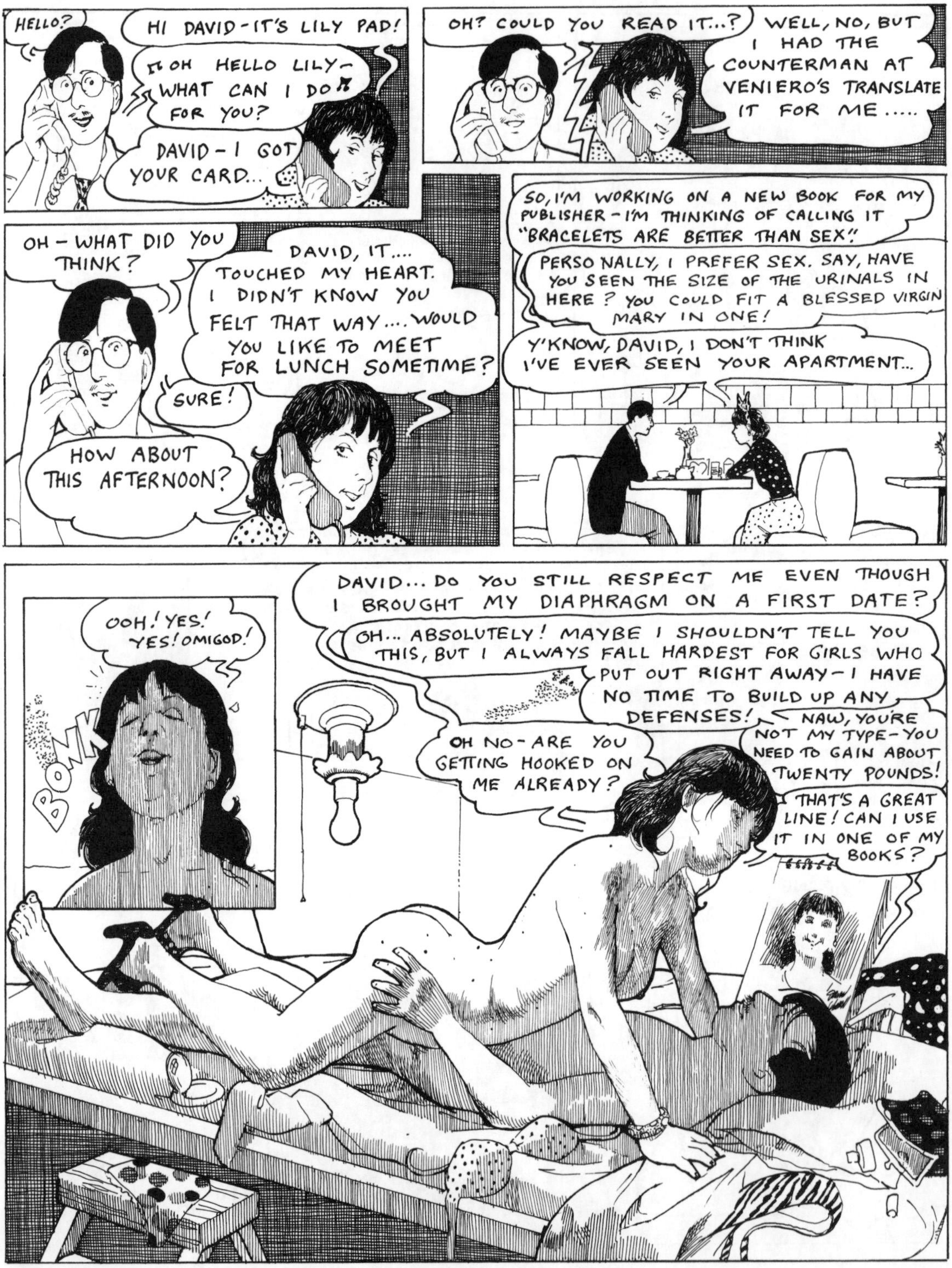
HELLO?
HI DAVID - IT'S LILY PAD!
OH HELLO LILY - WHAT CAN I DO FOR YOU?
DAVID - I GOT YOUR CARD...
OH? COULD YOU READ IT...?
WELL, NO, BUT I HAD THE COUNTERMAN AT VENIERO'S TRANSLATE IT FOR ME.....
OH - WHAT DID YOU THINK?
DAVID, IT.... TOUCHED MY HEART. I DIDN'T KNOW YOU FELT THAT WAY.... WOULD YOU LIKE TO MEET FOR LUNCH SOMETIME?
SURE!
HOW ABOUT THIS AFTERNOON?
SO, I'M WORKING ON A NEW BOOK FOR MY PUBLISHER - I'M THINKING OF CALLING IT "BRACELETS ARE BETTER THAN SEX!"
PERSONALLY, I PREFER SEX. SAY, HAVE YOU SEEN THE SIZE OF THE URINALS IN HERE? YOU COULD FIT A BLESSED VIRGIN MARY IN ONE!
Y'KNOW, DAVID, I DON'T THINK I'VE EVER SEEN YOUR APARTMENT...
OOH! YES! YES! OMIGOD!
BONK
DAVID... DO YOU STILL RESPECT ME EVEN THOUGH I BROUGHT MY DIAPHRAGM ON A FIRST DATE?
OH... ABSOLUTELY! MAYBE I SHOULDN'T TELL YOU THIS, BUT I ALWAYS FALL HARDEST FOR GIRLS WHO PUT OUT RIGHT AWAY - I HAVE NO TIME TO BUILD UP ANY DEFENSES!
OH NO - ARE YOU GETTING HOOKED ON ME ALREADY?
NAW, YOU'RE NOT MY TYPE - YOU NEED TO GAIN ABOUT TWENTY POUNDS!
THAT'S A GREAT LINE! CAN I USE IT IN ONE OF MY BOOKS?

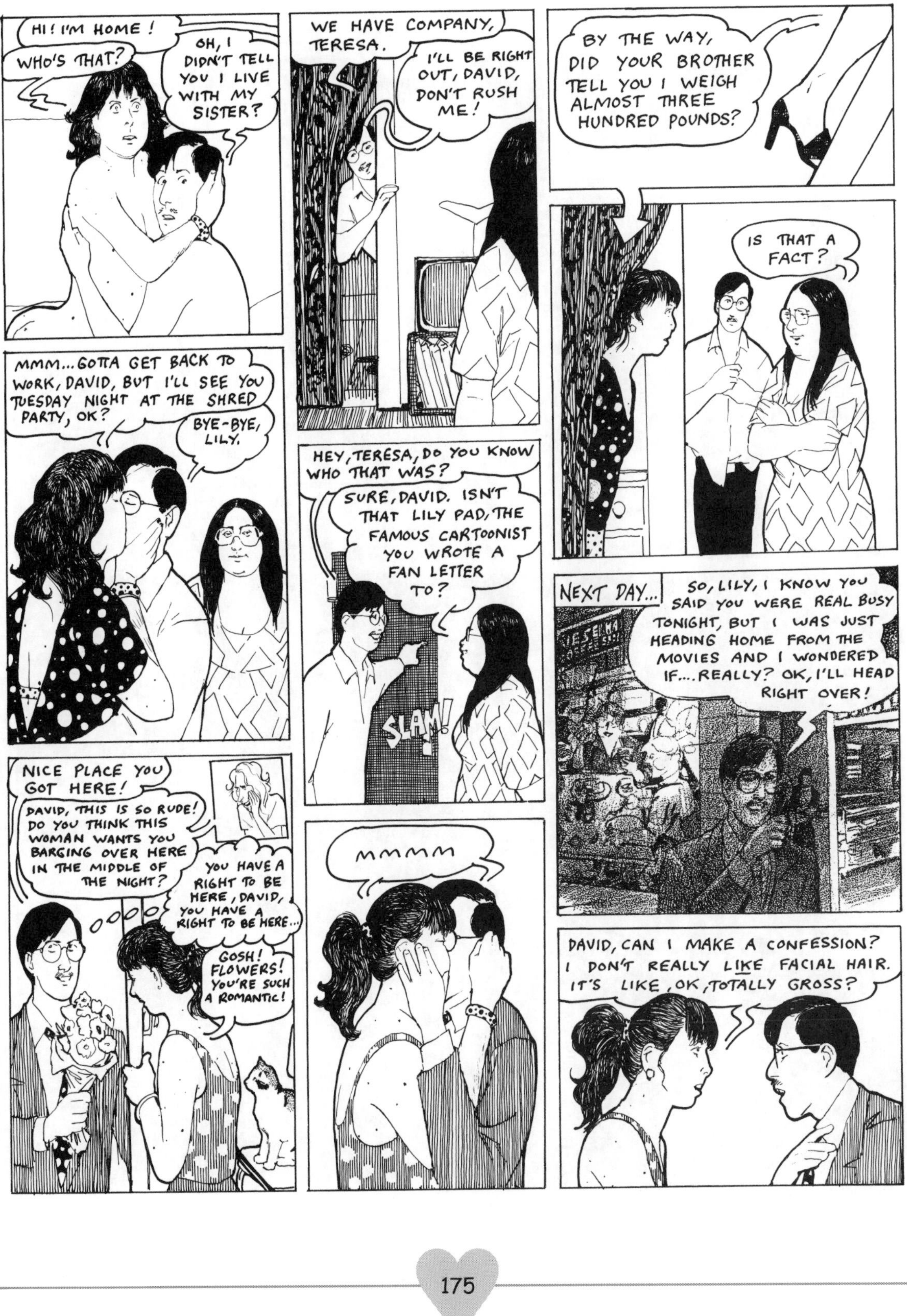
HI! I'M HOME!
WHO'S THAT?
OH, I DIDN'T TELL YOU I LIVE WITH MY SISTER?
WE HAVE COMPANY, TERESA.
I'LL BE RIGHT OUT, DAVID, DON'T RUSH ME!
BY THE WAY, DID YOUR BROTHER TELL YOU I WEIGH ALMOST THREE HUNDRED POUNDS?
IS THAT A FACT?
MMM... GOTTA GET BACK TO WORK, DAVID, BUT I'LL SEE YOU TUESDAY NIGHT AT THE SHRED PARTY, OK?
BYE-BYE, LILY.
HEY, TERESA, DO YOU KNOW WHO THAT WAS?
SURE, DAVID. ISN'T THAT LILY PAD, THE FAMOUS CARTOONIST YOU WROTE A FAN LETTER TO?
SLAM!
NEXT DAY...
SO, LILY, I KNOW YOU SAID YOU WERE REAL BUSY TONIGHT, BUT I WAS JUST HEADING HOME FROM THE MOVIES AND I WONDERED IF.... REALLY? OK, I'LL HEAD RIGHT OVER!
NICE PLACE YOU GOT HERE!
DAVID, THIS IS SO RUDE! DO YOU THINK THIS WOMAN WANTS YOU BARGING OVER HERE IN THE MIDDLE OF THE NIGHT?
YOU HAVE A RIGHT TO BE HERE, DAVID, YOU HAVE A RIGHT TO BE HERE...
OOOOO
GOSH! FLOWERS! YOU'RE SUCH A ROMANTIC!
MMMM
DAVID, CAN I MAKE A CONFESSION? I DON'T REALLY LIKE FACIAL HAIR. IT'S LIKE, OK, TOTALLY GROSS?

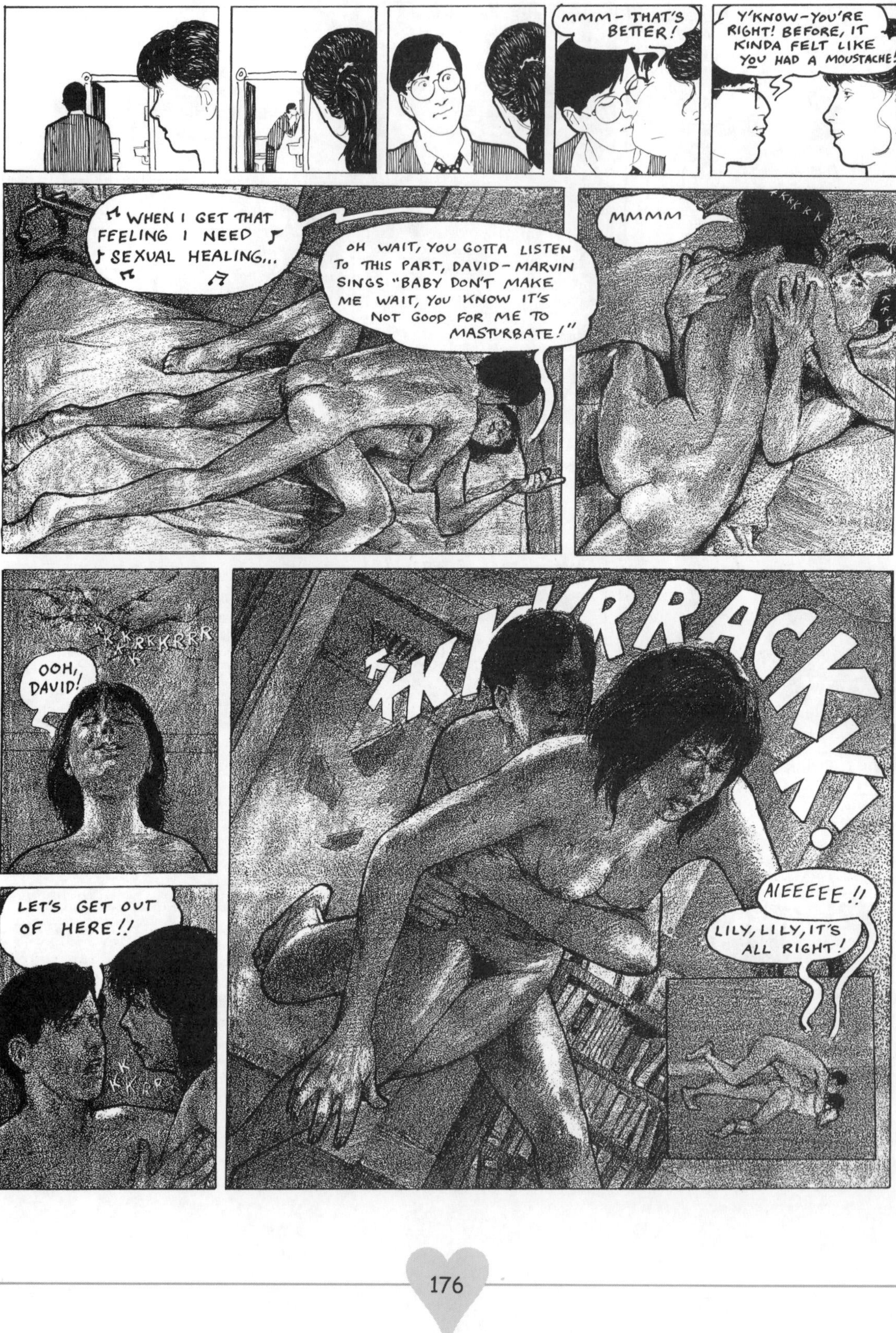
MMM- THAT'S BETTER!
Y'KNOW-YOU'RE RIGHT! BEFORE, IT KINDA FELT LIKE YOU HAD A MOUSTACHE!
WHEN I GET THAT FEELING I NEED SEXUAL HEALING...
OH WAIT, YOU GOTTA LISTEN TO THIS PART, DAVID- MARVIN SINGS "BABY DON'T MAKE ME WAIT, YOU KNOW IT'S NOT GOOD FOR ME TO MASTURBATE!"
MMMM
OOH, DAVID!
KKKRRACKK!
AIEEEEE!!
LILY, LILY, IT'S ALL RIGHT!
LET'S GET OUT OF HERE!!

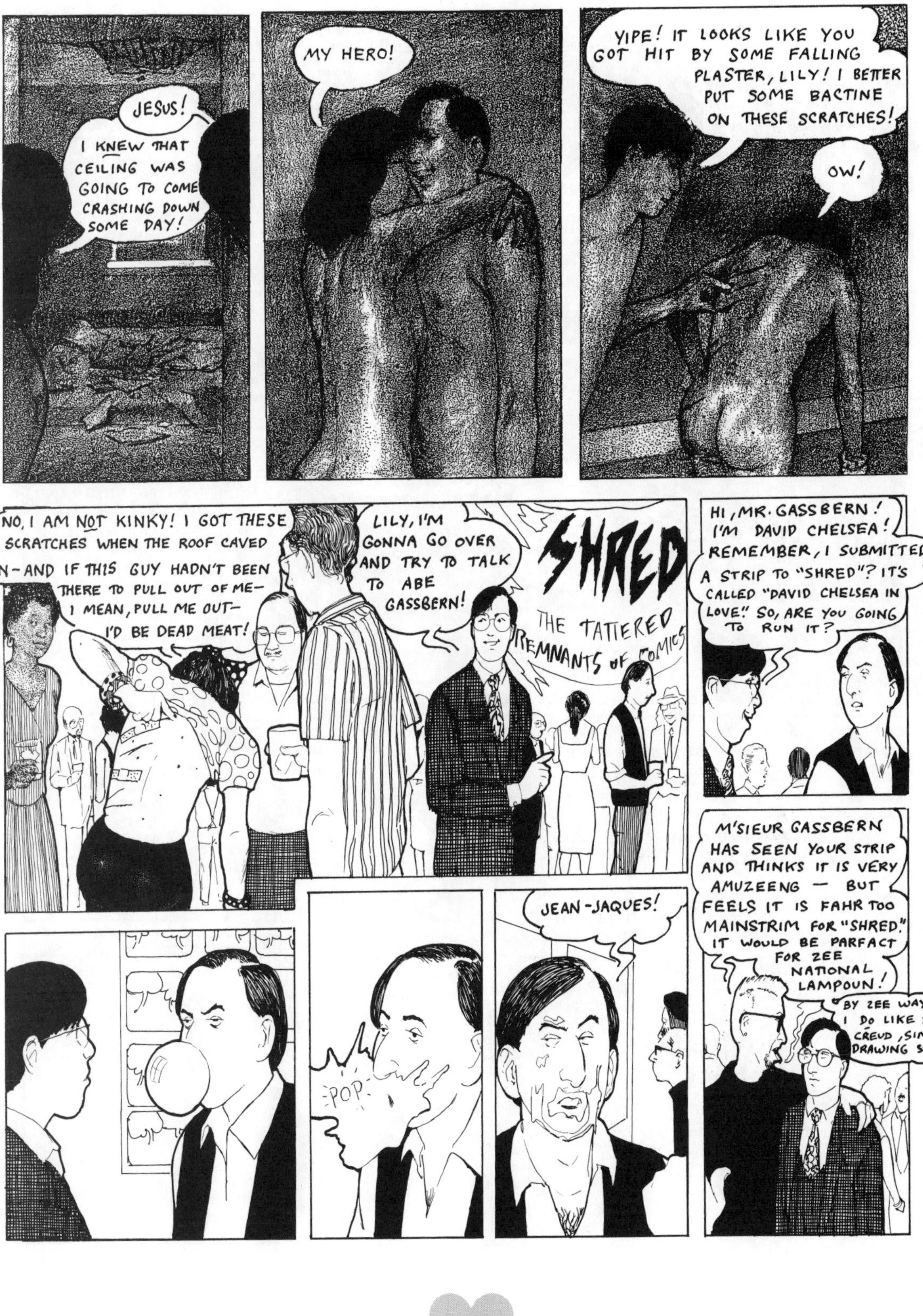
JESUS!
I KNEW THAT CEILING WAS GOING TO COME CRASHING DOWN SOME DAY!
MY HERO!
YIPE! IT LOOKS LIKE YOU GOT HIT BY SOME FALLING PLASTER, LILY! I BETTER PUT SOME BACTINE ON THESE SCRATCHES!
OW!
NO, I AM NOT KINKY! I GOT THESE SCRATCHES WHEN THE ROOF CAVED IN - AND IF THIS GUY HADN'T BEEN THERE TO PULL OUT OF ME - I MEAN, PULL ME OUT - I'D BE DEAD MEAT!
LILY, I'M GONNA GO OVER AND TRY TO TALK TO ABE GASSBERN!
SHRED
THE TATTERED REMNANTS OF COMICS
HI, MR. GASSBERN! I'M DAVID CHELSEA! REMEMBER, I SUBMITTED A STRIP TO "SHRED"? IT'S CALLED "DAVID CHELSEA IN LOVE." SO, ARE YOU GOING TO RUN IT?
POP
JEAN-JAQUES!
M'SIEUR GASSBERN HAS SEEN YOUR STRIP AND THINKS IT IS VERY AMUZEENG — BUT FEELS IT IS FAHR TOO MAINSTRIM FOR "SHRED." IT WOULD BE PARFACT FOR ZEE NATIONAL LAMPOUN!
BY ZEE WAY, I DO LIKE YOUR CREUD, SIMPLE DRAWING STYLE!

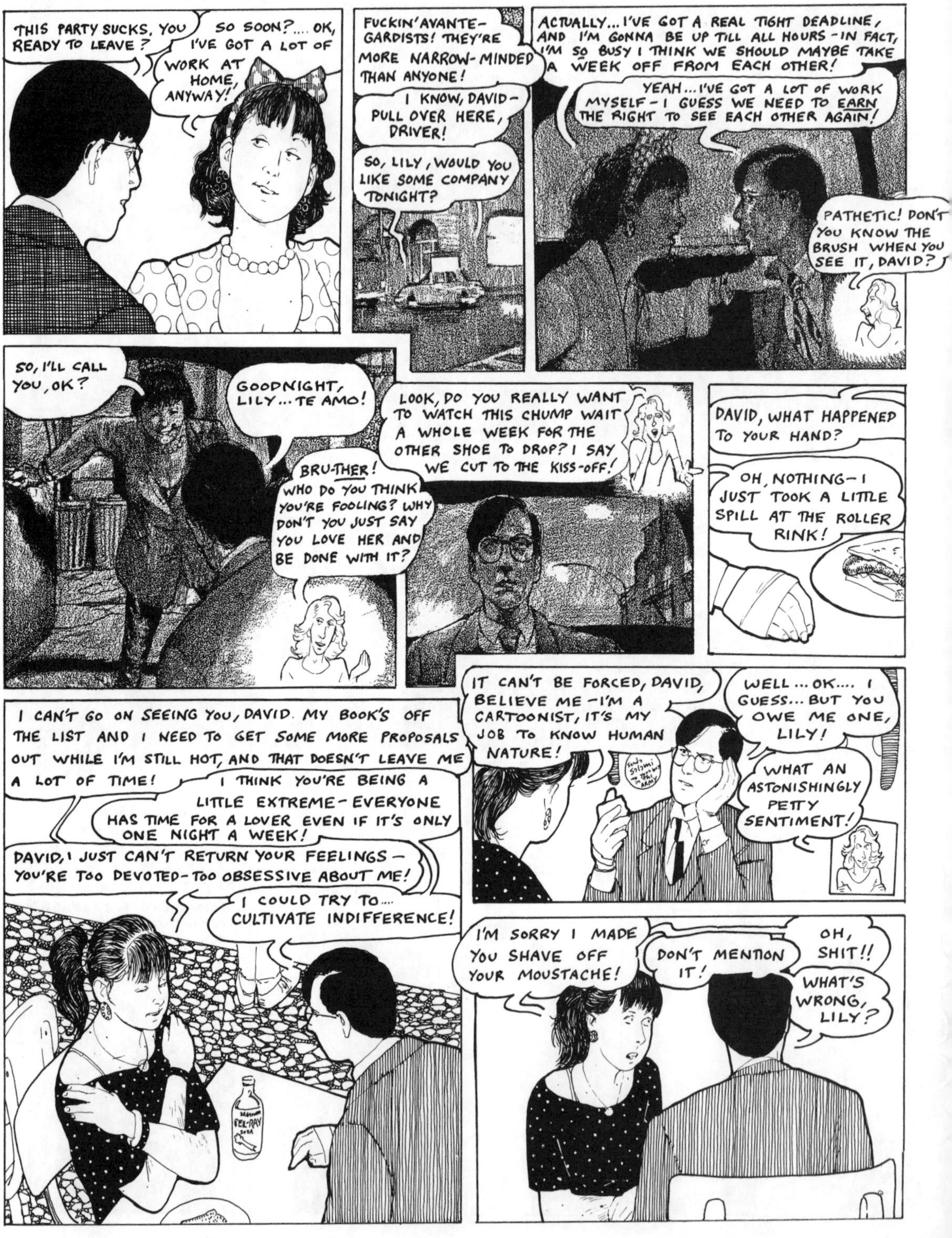
THIS PARTY SUCKS. YOU READY TO LEAVE?
SO SOON?.... OK, I'VE GOT A LOT OF WORK AT HOME, ANYWAY!
FUCKIN' AVANTE-GARDISTS! THEY'RE MORE NARROW-MINDED THAN ANYONE!
I KNOW, DAVID- PULL OVER HERE, DRIVER!
SO, LILY, WOULD YOU LIKE SOME COMPANY TONIGHT?
ACTUALLY... I'VE GOT A REAL TIGHT DEADLINE, AND I'M GONNA BE UP TILL ALL HOURS - IN FACT, I'M SO BUSY I THINK WE SHOULD MAYBE TAKE A WEEK OFF FROM EACH OTHER!
YEAH... I'VE GOT A LOT OF WORK MYSELF - I GUESS WE NEED TO EARN THE RIGHT TO SEE EACH OTHER AGAIN!
PATHETIC! DON'T YOU KNOW THE BRUSH WHEN YOU SEE IT, DAVID?
SO, I'LL CALL YOU, OK?
GOODNIGHT, LILY... TE AMO!
BRU-THER! WHO DO YOU THINK YOU'RE FOOLING? WHY DON'T YOU JUST SAY YOU LOVE HER AND BE DONE WITH IT?
LOOK, DO YOU REALLY WANT TO WATCH THIS CHUMP WAIT A WHOLE WEEK FOR THE OTHER SHOE TO DROP? I SAY WE CUT TO THE KISS-OFF!
DAVID, WHAT HAPPENED TO YOUR HAND?
OH, NOTHING - I JUST TOOK A LITTLE SPILL AT THE ROLLER RINK!
I CAN'T GO ON SEEING YOU, DAVID. MY BOOK'S OFF THE LIST AND I NEED TO GET SOME MORE PROPOSALS OUT WHILE I'M STILL HOT, AND THAT DOESN'T LEAVE ME A LOT OF TIME!
I THINK YOU'RE BEING A LITTLE EXTREME - EVERYONE HAS TIME FOR A LOVER EVEN IF IT'S ONLY ONE NIGHT A WEEK!
DAVID, I JUST CAN'T RETURN YOUR FEELINGS - YOU'RE TOO DEVOTED - TOO OBSESSIVE ABOUT ME!
I COULD TRY TO.... CULTIVATE INDIFFERENCE!
IT CAN'T BE FORCED, DAVID, BELIEVE ME - I'M A CARTOONIST, IT'S MY JOB TO KNOW HUMAN NATURE!
WELL... OK.... I GUESS... BUT YOU OWE ME ONE, LILY!
WHAT AN ASTONISHINGLY PETTY SENTIMENT!
I'M SORRY I MADE YOU SHAVE OFF YOUR MOUSTACHE!
DON'T MENTION IT!
OH, SHIT!!
WHAT'S WRONG, LILY?

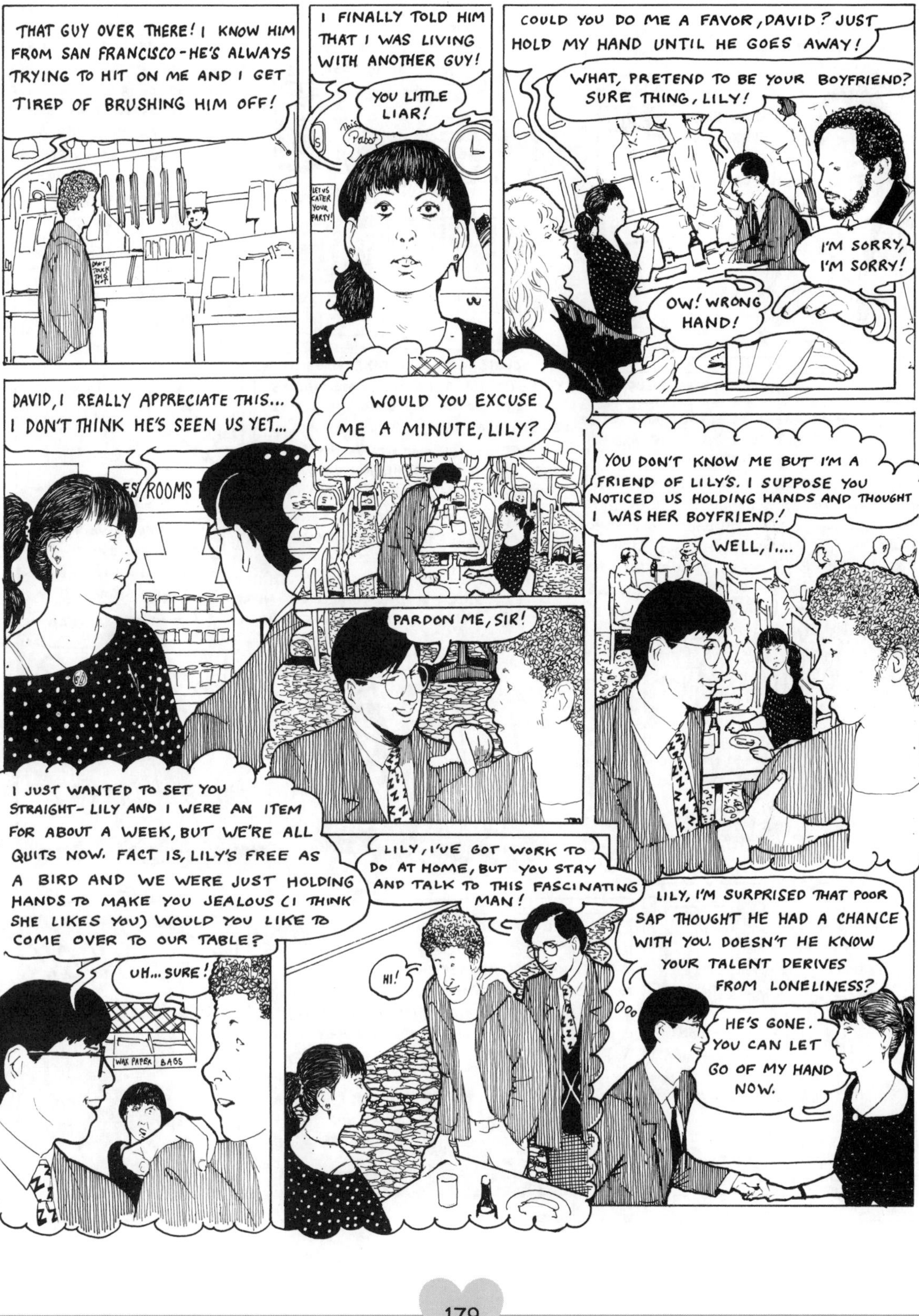
THAT GUY OVER THERE! I KNOW HIM FROM SAN FRANCISCO - HE'S ALWAYS TRYING TO HIT ON ME AND I GET TIRED OF BRUSHING HIM OFF!
I FINALLY TOLD HIM THAT I WAS LIVING WITH ANOTHER GUY!
YOU LITTLE LIAR!
LET US CATER YOUR PARTY!
COULD YOU DO ME A FAVOR, DAVID? JUST HOLD MY HAND UNTIL HE GOES AWAY!
WHAT, PRETEND TO BE YOUR BOYFRIEND? SURE THING, LILY!
I'M SORRY, I'M SORRY!
OW! WRONG HAND!
DAVID, I REALLY APPRECIATE THIS... I DON'T THINK HE'S SEEN US YET...
WOULD YOU EXCUSE ME A MINUTE, LILY?
PARDON ME, SIR!
YOU DON'T KNOW ME BUT I'M A FRIEND OF LILY'S. I SUPPOSE YOU NOTICED US HOLDING HANDS AND THOUGHT I WAS HER BOYFRIEND!
WELL, I....
I JUST WANTED TO SET YOU STRAIGHT- LILY AND I WERE AN ITEM FOR ABOUT A WEEK, BUT WE'RE ALL QUITS NOW. FACT IS, LILY'S FREE AS A BIRD AND WE WERE JUST HOLDING HANDS TO MAKE YOU JEALOUS (I THINK SHE LIKES YOU) WOULD YOU LIKE TO COME OVER TO OUR TABLE?
UH... SURE!
WAX PAPER BAGS
LILY, I'VE GOT WORK TO DO AT HOME, BUT YOU STAY AND TALK TO THIS FASCINATING MAN!
HI!
LILY, I'M SURPRISED THAT POOR SAP THOUGHT HE HAD A CHANCE WITH YOU. DOESN'T HE KNOW YOUR TALENT DERIVES FROM LONELINESS?
HE'S GONE. YOU CAN LET GO OF MY HAND NOW.

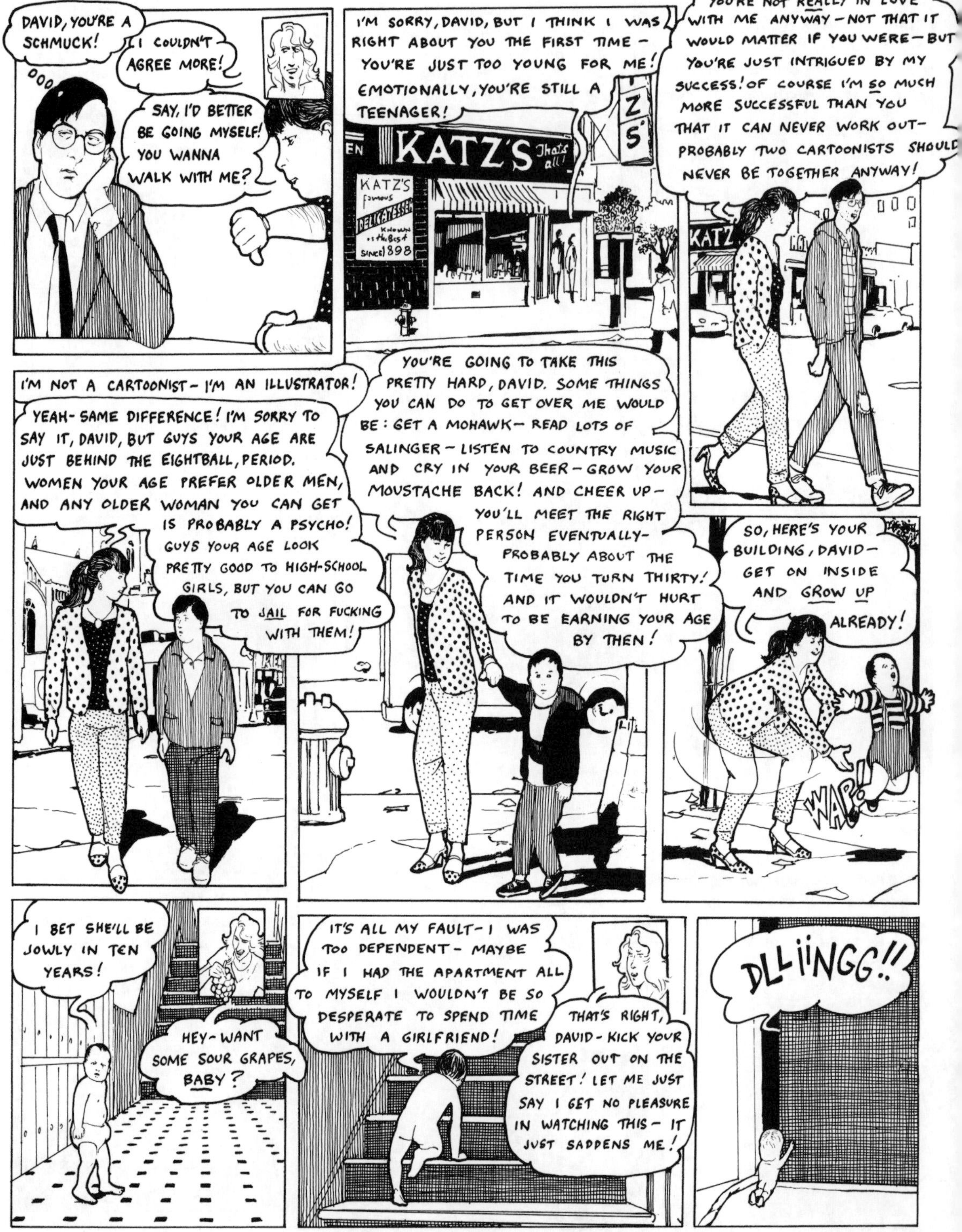

DAVID, YOU'RE A SCHMUCK!
I COULDN'T AGREE MORE!
SAY, I'D BETTER BE GOING MYSELF! YOU WANNA WALK WITH ME?
I'M SORRY, DAVID, BUT I THINK I WAS RIGHT ABOUT YOU THE FIRST TIME - YOU'RE JUST TOO YOUNG FOR ME! EMOTIONALLY, YOU'RE STILL A TEENAGER!
KATZ'S That's all!
KATZ'S famous DELICATESSEN Known as the Best SINCE 1898
YOU'RE NOT REALLY IN LOVE WITH ME ANYWAY - NOT THAT IT WOULD MATTER IF YOU WERE - BUT YOU'RE JUST INTRIGUED BY MY SUCCESS! OF COURSE I'M SO MUCH MORE SUCCESSFUL THAN YOU THAT IT CAN NEVER WORK OUT - PROBABLY TWO CARTOONISTS SHOULD NEVER BE TOGETHER ANYWAY!
I'M NOT A CARTOONIST - I'M AN ILLUSTRATOR!
YEAH - SAME DIFFERENCE! I'M SORRY TO SAY IT, DAVID, BUT GUYS YOUR AGE ARE JUST BEHIND THE EIGHTBALL, PERIOD. WOMEN YOUR AGE PREFER OLDER MEN, AND ANY OLDER WOMAN YOU CAN GET IS PROBABLY A PSYCHO! GUYS YOUR AGE LOOK PRETTY GOOD TO HIGH-SCHOOL GIRLS, BUT YOU CAN GO TO JAIL FOR FUCKING WITH THEM!
YOU'RE GOING TO TAKE THIS PRETTY HARD, DAVID. SOME THINGS YOU CAN DO TO GET OVER ME WOULD BE: GET A MOHAWK - READ LOTS OF SALINGER - LISTEN TO COUNTRY MUSIC AND CRY IN YOUR BEER - GROW YOUR MOUSTACHE BACK! AND CHEER UP - YOU'LL MEET THE RIGHT PERSON EVENTUALLY - PROBABLY ABOUT THE TIME YOU TURN THIRTY! AND IT WOULDN'T HURT TO BE EARNING YOUR AGE BY THEN!
SO, HERE'S YOUR BUILDING, DAVID - GET ON INSIDE AND GROW UP ALREADY!
WAP!
I BET SHE'LL BE JOWLY IN TEN YEARS!
HEY - WANT SOME SOUR GRAPES, BABY?
IT'S ALL MY FAULT - I WAS TOO DEPENDENT - MAYBE IF I HAD THE APARTMENT ALL TO MYSELF I WOULDN'T BE SO DESPERATE TO SPEND TIME WITH A GIRLFRIEND!
THAT'S RIGHT, DAVID - KICK YOUR SISTER OUT ON THE STREET! LET ME JUST SAY I GET NO PLEASURE IN WATCHING THIS - IT JUST SADDENS ME!
DLLiiNGG!!

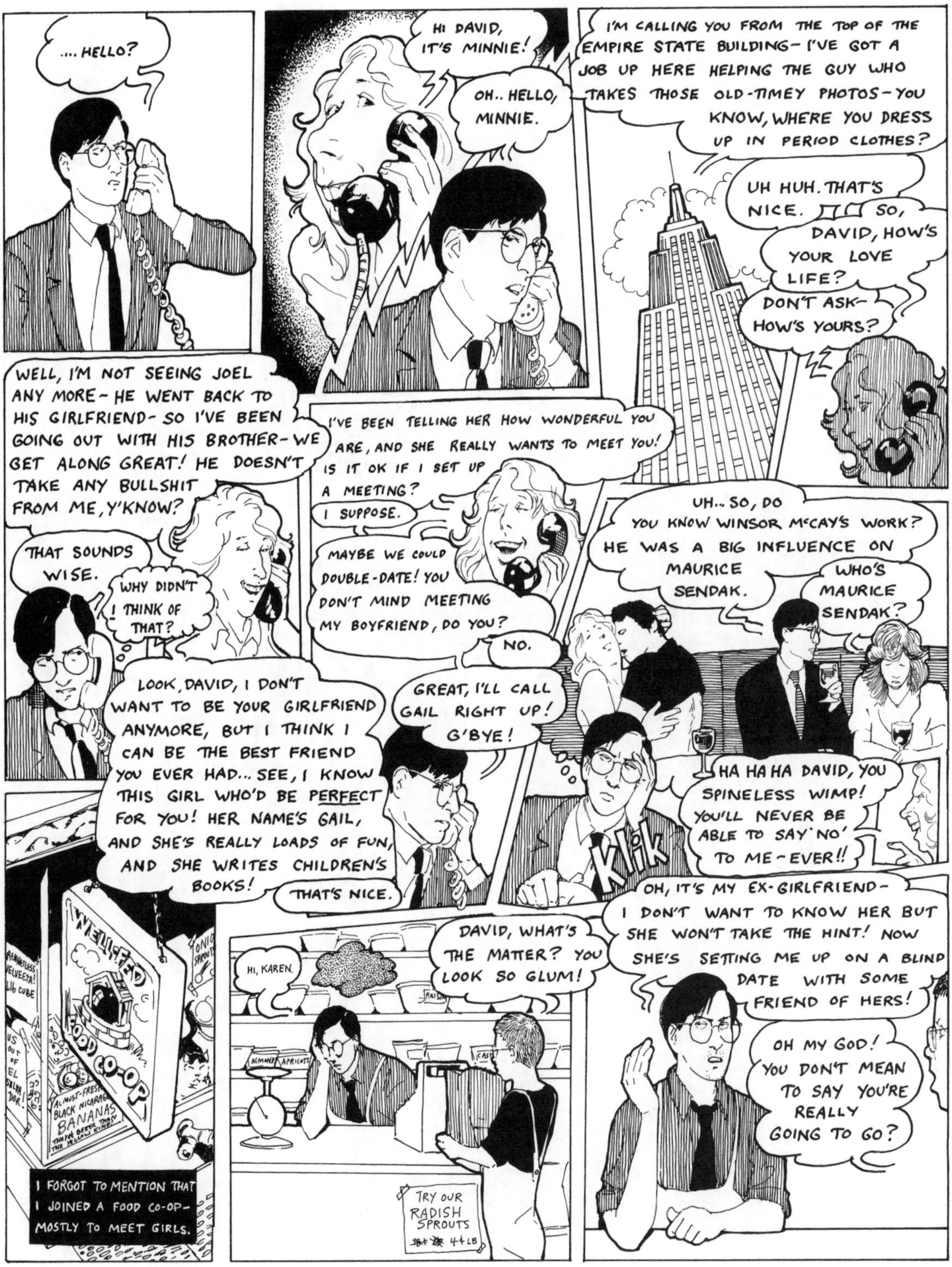
....HELLO?
HI DAVID, IT'S MINNIE!
OH.. HELLO, MINNIE.
I'M CALLING YOU FROM THE TOP OF THE EMPIRE STATE BUILDING- I'VE GOT A JOB UP HERE HELPING THE GUY WHO TAKES THOSE OLD-TIMEY PHOTOS- YOU KNOW, WHERE YOU DRESS UP IN PERIOD CLOTHES?
UH HUH. THAT'S NICE.
SO, DAVID, HOW'S YOUR LOVE LIFE?
DON'T ASK- HOW'S YOURS?
WELL, I'M NOT SEEING JOEL ANY MORE- HE WENT BACK TO HIS GIRLFRIEND- SO I'VE BEEN GOING OUT WITH HIS BROTHER- WE GET ALONG GREAT! HE DOESN'T TAKE ANY BULLSHIT FROM ME, Y'KNOW?
THAT SOUNDS WISE.
WHY DIDN'T I THINK OF THAT?
LOOK, DAVID, I DON'T WANT TO BE YOUR GIRLFRIEND ANYMORE, BUT I THINK I CAN BE THE BEST FRIEND YOU EVER HAD... SEE, I KNOW THIS GIRL WHO'D BE PERFECT FOR YOU! HER NAME'S GAIL, AND SHE'S REALLY LOADS OF FUN, AND SHE WRITES CHILDREN'S BOOKS!
THAT'S NICE.
I'VE BEEN TELLING HER HOW WONDERFUL YOU ARE, AND SHE REALLY WANTS TO MEET YOU! IS IT OK IF I SET UP A MEETING?
I SUPPOSE.
MAYBE WE COULD DOUBLE-DATE! YOU DON'T MIND MEETING MY BOYFRIEND, DO YOU?
NO.
GREAT, I'LL CALL GAIL RIGHT UP! G'BYE!
UH.. SO, DO YOU KNOW WINSOR McCAY'S WORK? HE WAS A BIG INFLUENCE ON MAURICE SENDAK.
WHO'S MAURICE SENDAK?
HA HA HA DAVID, YOU SPINELESS WIMP! YOU'LL NEVER BE ABLE TO SAY 'NO' TO ME- EVER!!
KLIK
WELLFED FOOD CO-OP
ALMOST-FRESH BLACK NICARAGUAN BANANAS
I FORGOT TO MENTION THAT I JOINED A FOOD CO-OP- MOSTLY TO MEET GIRLS.
HI, KAREN.
DAVID, WHAT'S THE MATTER? YOU LOOK SO GLUM!
ALMONDS
APRICOTS
TRY OUR RADISH SPROUTS
OH, IT'S MY EX-GIRLFRIEND- I DON'T WANT TO KNOW HER BUT SHE WON'T TAKE THE HINT! NOW SHE'S SETTING ME UP ON A BLIND DATE WITH SOME FRIEND OF HERS!
OH MY GOD! YOU DON'T MEAN TO SAY YOU'RE REALLY GOING TO GO?

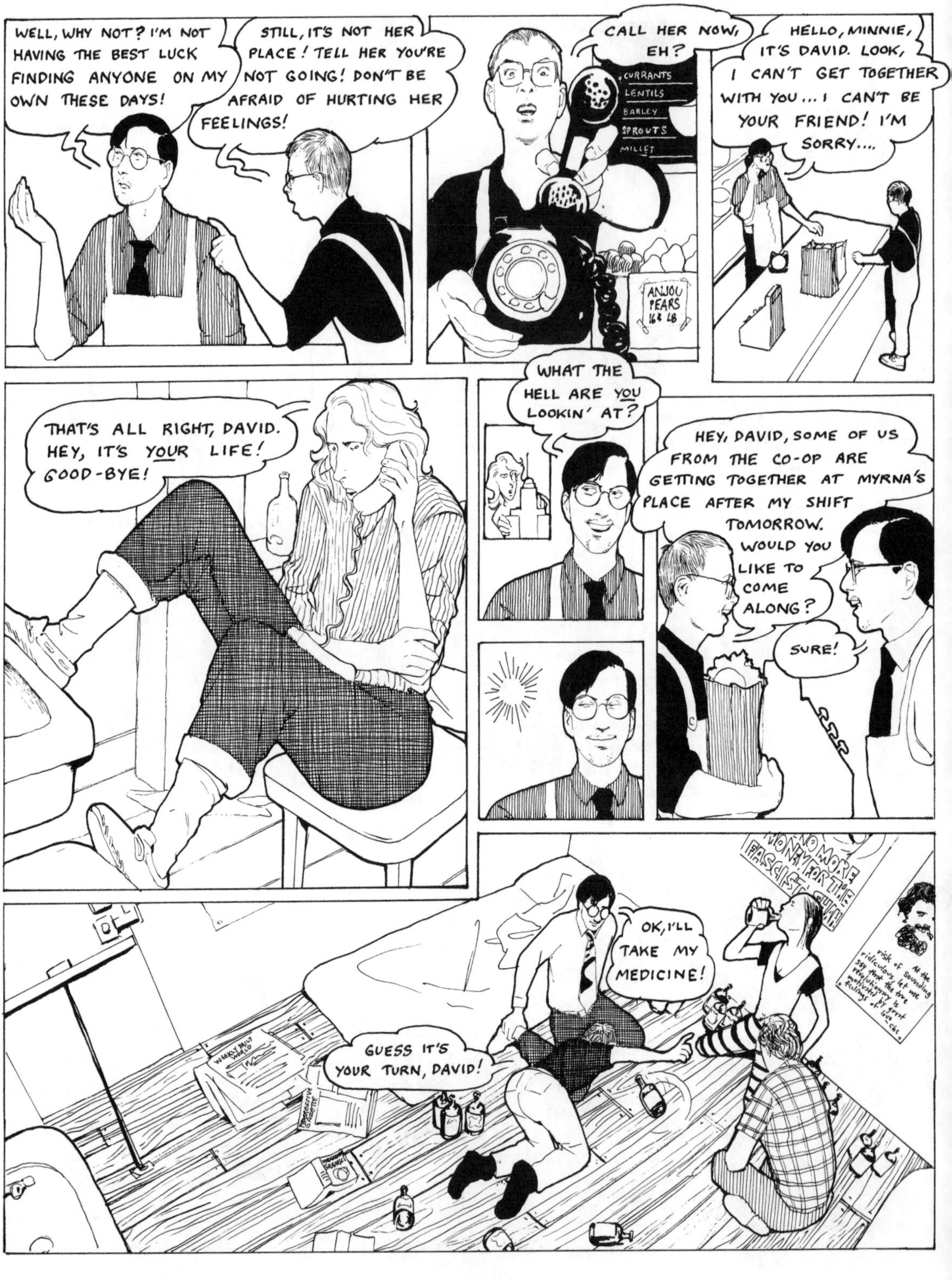
WELL, WHY NOT? I'M NOT HAVING THE BEST LUCK FINDING ANYONE ON MY OWN THESE DAYS!
STILL, IT'S NOT HER PLACE! TELL HER YOU'RE NOT GOING! DON'T BE AFRAID OF HURTING HER FEELINGS!
CALL HER NOW, EH?
CURRANTS
LENTILS
BARLEY
SPROUTS
MILLET
ANJOU PEARS 16¢ LB
HELLO, MINNIE, IT'S DAVID. LOOK, I CAN'T GET TOGETHER WITH YOU... I CAN'T BE YOUR FRIEND! I'M SORRY....
THAT'S ALL RIGHT, DAVID. HEY, IT'S YOUR LIFE! GOOD-BYE!
WHAT THE HELL ARE YOU LOOKIN' AT?
HEY, DAVID, SOME OF US FROM THE CO-OP ARE GETTING TOGETHER AT MYRNA'S PLACE AFTER MY SHIFT TOMORROW. WOULD YOU LIKE TO COME ALONG?
SURE!
NO MORE MONEY FOR THE FASCIST SHAH
At the risk of sounding ridiculous, let me say that the true revolutionary is motivated by great feelings of love. ~Che
OK, I'LL TAKE MY MEDICINE!
GUESS IT'S YOUR TURN, DAVID!
WEEKLY DAILY WORLD

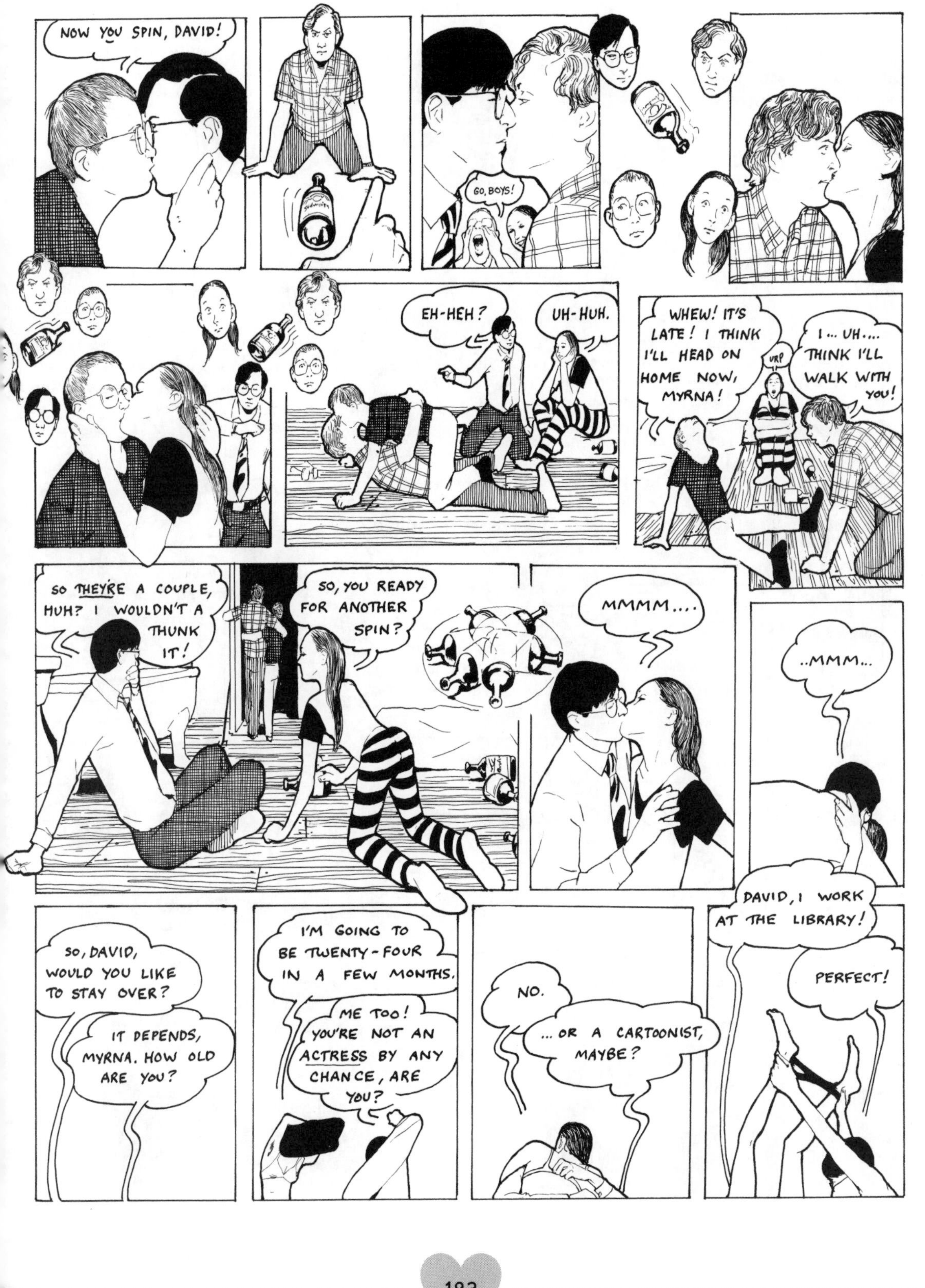
NOW YOU SPIN, DAVID!
GO, BOYS!
EH-HEH?
UH-HUH.
WHEW! IT'S LATE! I THINK I'LL HEAD ON HOME NOW, MYRNA!
URP
I... UH.... THINK I'LL WALK WITH YOU!
SO THEY'RE A COUPLE, HUH? I WOULDN'T A THUNK IT!
SO, YOU READY FOR ANOTHER SPIN?
MMMM....
..MMM...
SO, DAVID, WOULD YOU LIKE TO STAY OVER?
IT DEPENDS, MYRNA. HOW OLD ARE YOU?
I'M GOING TO BE TWENTY-FOUR IN A FEW MONTHS.
ME TOO! YOU'RE NOT AN ACTRESS BY ANY CHANCE, ARE YOU?
NO.
...OR A CARTOONIST, MAYBE?
DAVID, I WORK AT THE LIBRARY!
PERFECT!

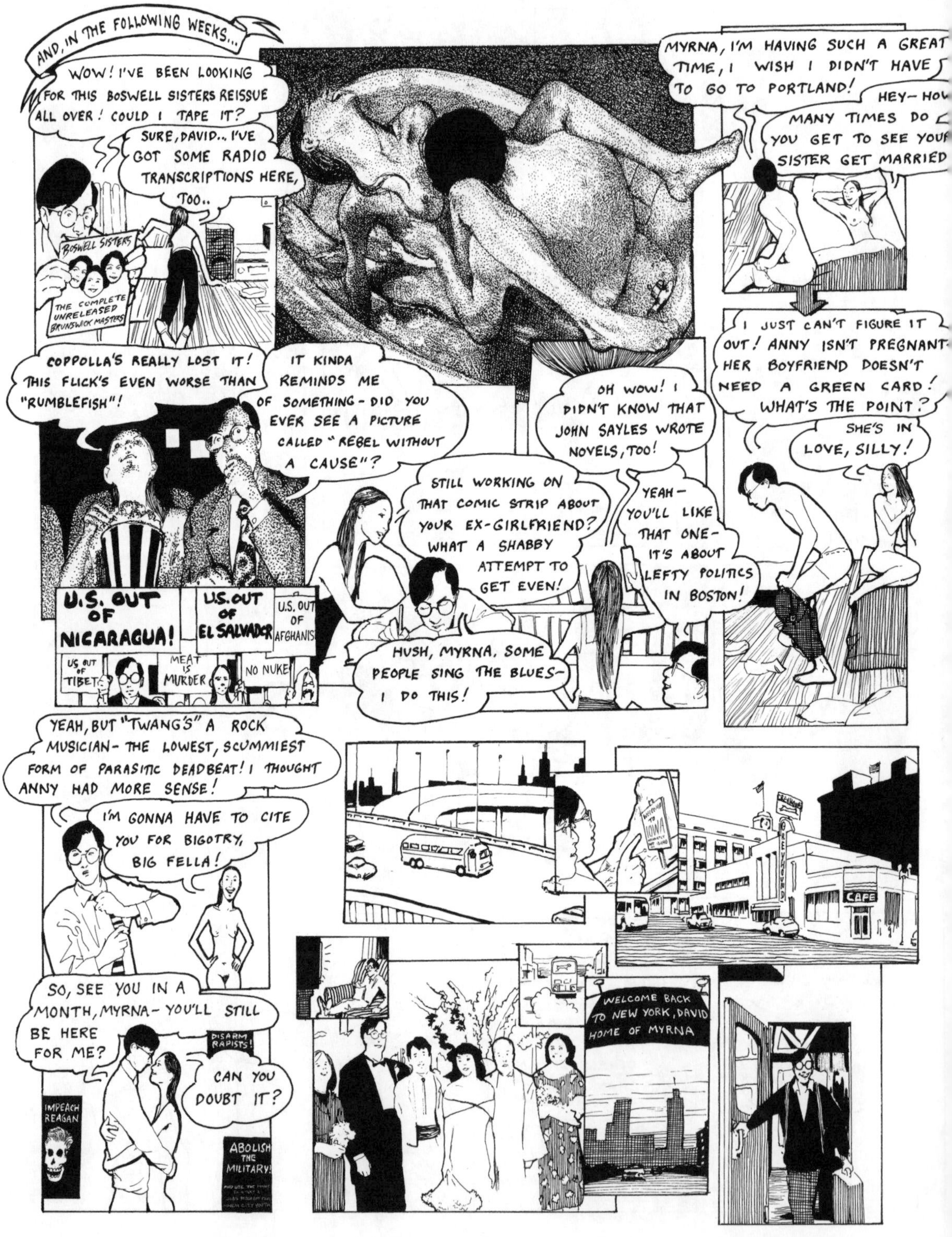

AND, IN THE FOLLOWING WEEKS...
WOW! I'VE BEEN LOOKING FOR THIS BOSWELL SISTERS REISSUE ALL OVER! COULD I TAPE IT?
SURE, DAVID.. I'VE GOT SOME RADIO TRANSCRIPTIONS HERE, TOO..
BOSWELL SISTERS
THE COMPLETE UNRELEASED BRUNSWICK MASTERS
MYRNA, I'M HAVING SUCH A GREAT TIME, I WISH I DIDN'T HAVE TO GO TO PORTLAND!
HEY- HOW MANY TIMES DO YOU GET TO SEE YOUR SISTER GET MARRIED
I JUST CAN'T FIGURE IT OUT! ANNY ISN'T PREGNANT- HER BOYFRIEND DOESN'T NEED A GREEN CARD! WHAT'S THE POINT?
SHE'S IN LOVE, SILLY!
COPPOLLA'S REALLY LOST IT! THIS FLICK'S EVEN WORSE THAN "RUMBLEFISH"!
IT KINDA REMINDS ME OF SOMETHING- DID YOU EVER SEE A PICTURE CALLED "REBEL WITHOUT A CAUSE"?
OH WOW! I DIDN'T KNOW THAT JOHN SAYLES WROTE NOVELS, TOO!
YEAH- YOU'LL LIKE THAT ONE- IT'S ABOUT LEFTY POLITICS IN BOSTON!
STILL WORKING ON THAT COMIC STRIP ABOUT YOUR EX-GIRLFRIEND? WHAT A SHABBY ATTEMPT TO GET EVEN!
HUSH, MYRNA. SOME PEOPLE SING THE BLUES- I DO THIS!
U.S. OUT OF NICARAGUA!
U.S. OUT OF EL SALVADOR
U.S. OUT OF AFGHANIS
US OUT OF TIBET
MEAT IS MURDER
NO NUKE
YEAH, BUT "TWANG'S" A ROCK MUSICIAN- THE LOWEST, SCUMMIEST FORM OF PARASITIC DEADBEAT! I THOUGHT ANNY HAD MORE SENSE!
I'M GONNA HAVE TO CITE YOU FOR BIGOTRY, BIG FELLA!
IOWA
GREYHOUND
CAFE
SO, SEE YOU IN A MONTH, MYRNA- YOU'LL STILL BE HERE FOR ME?
CAN YOU DOUBT IT?
DISARM RAPISTS!
IMPEACH REAGAN
ABOLISH THE MILITARY!
WELCOME BACK TO NEW YORK, DAVID HOME OF MYRNA

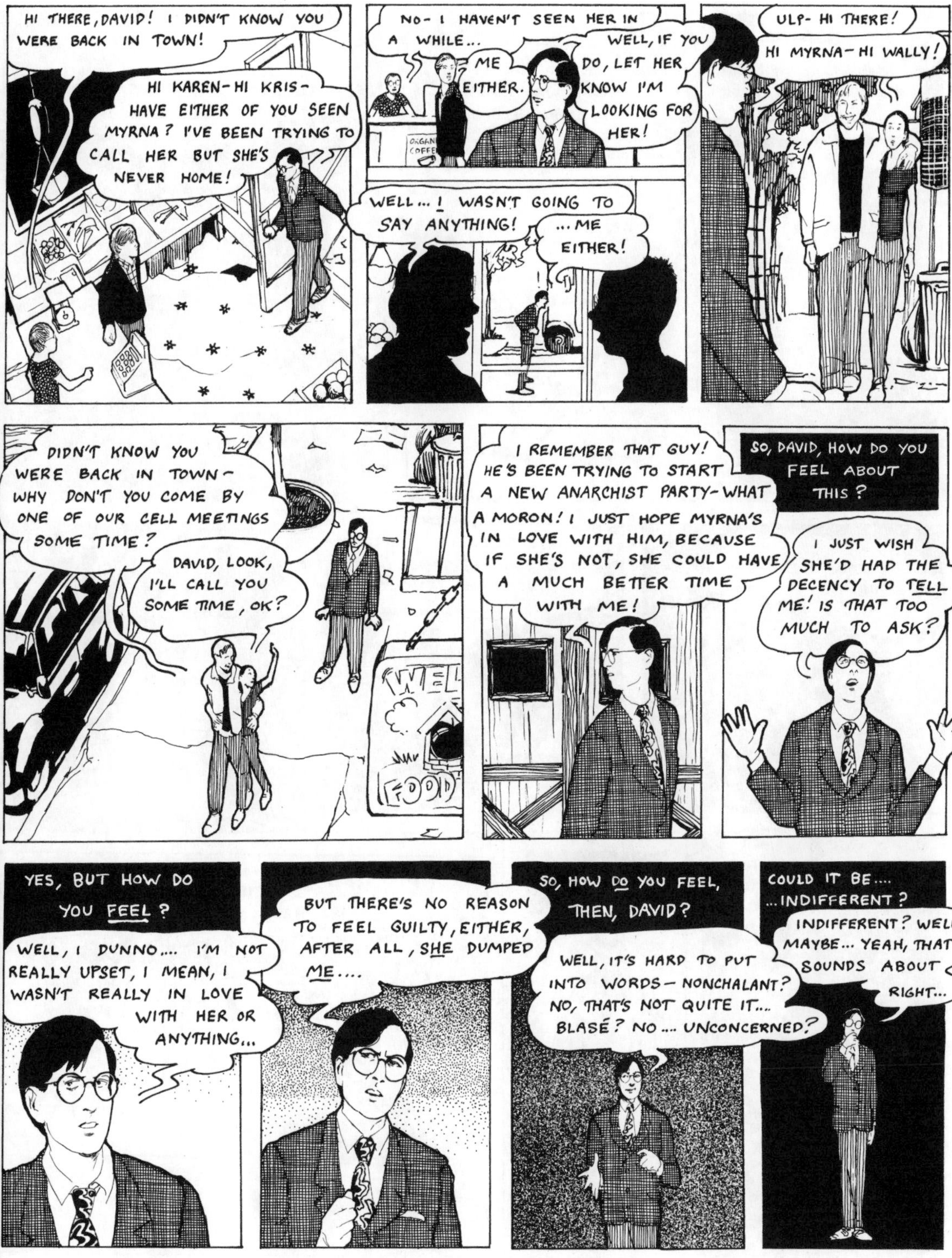
HI THERE, DAVID! I DIDN'T KNOW YOU WERE BACK IN TOWN!
HI KAREN-HI KRIS-HAVE EITHER OF YOU SEEN MYRNA? I'VE BEEN TRYING TO CALL HER BUT SHE'S NEVER HOME!
NO- I HAVEN'T SEEN HER IN A WHILE...
ME EITHER.
WELL, IF YOU DO, LET HER KNOW I'M LOOKING FOR HER!
WELL... I WASN'T GOING TO SAY ANYTHING!
...ME EITHER!
ULP- HI THERE!
HI MYRNA-HI WALLY!
DIDN'T KNOW YOU WERE BACK IN TOWN-WHY DON'T YOU COME BY ONE OF OUR CELL MEETINGS SOME TIME?
DAVID, LOOK, I'LL CALL YOU SOME TIME, OK?
I REMEMBER THAT GUY! HE'S BEEN TRYING TO START A NEW ANARCHIST PARTY-WHAT A MORON! I JUST HOPE MYRNA'S IN LOVE WITH HIM, BECAUSE IF SHE'S NOT, SHE COULD HAVE A MUCH BETTER TIME WITH ME!
SO, DAVID, HOW DO YOU FEEL ABOUT THIS?
I JUST WISH SHE'D HAD THE DECENCY TO TELL ME! IS THAT TOO MUCH TO ASK?
YES, BUT HOW DO YOU FEEL?
WELL, I DUNNO.... I'M NOT REALLY UPSET, I MEAN, I WASN'T REALLY IN LOVE WITH HER OR ANYTHING...
BUT THERE'S NO REASON TO FEEL GUILTY, EITHER, AFTER ALL, SHE DUMPED ME....
SO, HOW DO YOU FEEL, THEN, DAVID?
WELL, IT'S HARD TO PUT INTO WORDS- NONCHALANT? NO, THAT'S NOT QUITE IT.... BLASÉ? NO.... UNCONCERNED?
COULD IT BE.... ...INDIFFERENT?
INDIFFERENT? WELL, MAYBE... YEAH, THAT SOUNDS ABOUT RIGHT...

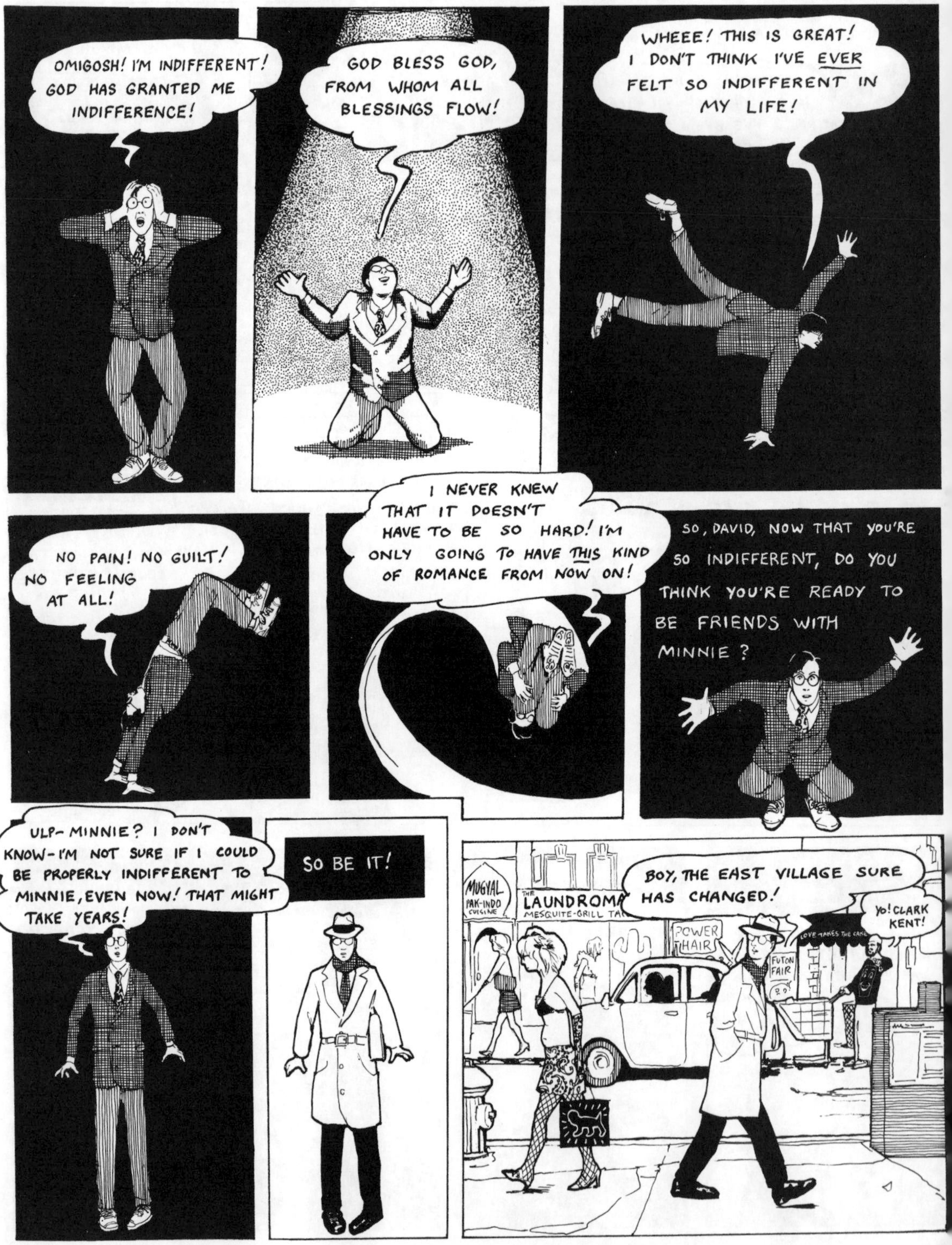
OMIGOSH! I'M INDIFFERENT! GOD HAS GRANTED ME INDIFFERENCE!
GOD BLESS GOD, FROM WHOM ALL BLESSINGS FLOW!
WHEEE! THIS IS GREAT! I DON'T THINK I'VE EVER FELT SO INDIFFERENT IN MY LIFE!
NO PAIN! NO GUILT! NO FEELING AT ALL!
I NEVER KNEW THAT IT DOESN'T HAVE TO BE SO HARD! I'M ONLY GOING TO HAVE THIS KIND OF ROMANCE FROM NOW ON!
SO, DAVID, NOW THAT YOU'RE SO INDIFFERENT, DO YOU THINK YOU'RE READY TO BE FRIENDS WITH MINNIE?
ULP- MINNIE? I DON'T KNOW- I'M NOT SURE IF I COULD BE PROPERLY INDIFFERENT TO MINNIE, EVEN NOW! THAT MIGHT TAKE YEARS!
SO BE IT!
MUGYAL PAK-INDO CUISINE
THE LAUNDROMA
MESQUITE-GRILL TA
BOY, THE EAST VILLAGE SURE HAS CHANGED!
POWER HAIR
FUTON FAIR
LOVE TAKES THE CAKE
YO! CLARK KENT!

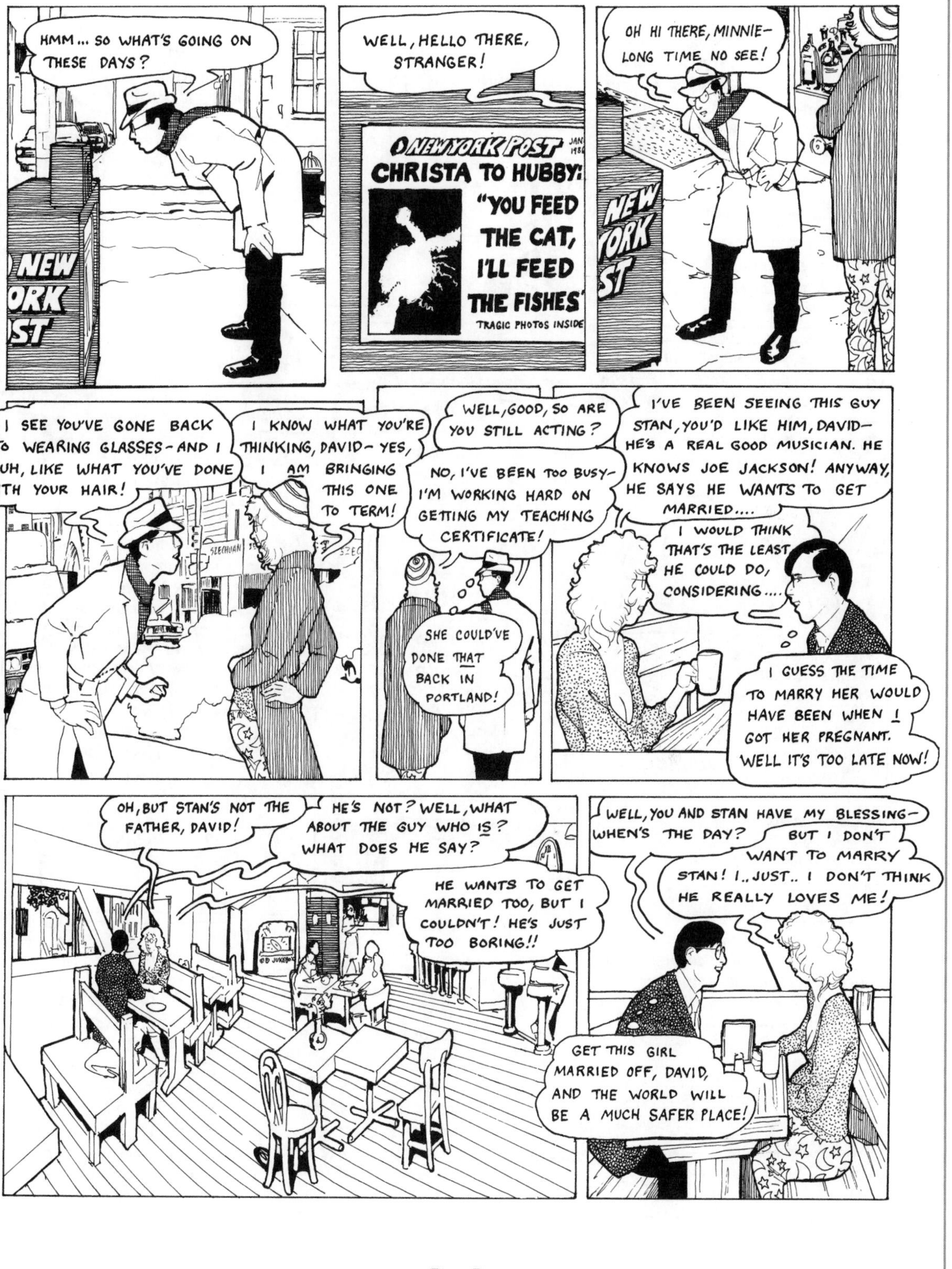
HMM... SO WHAT'S GOING ON THESE DAYS?
WELL, HELLO THERE, STRANGER!
NEW YORK POST
CHRISTA TO HUBBY: "YOU FEED THE CAT, I'LL FEED THE FISHES"
TRAGIC PHOTOS INSIDE
OH HI THERE, MINNIE- LONG TIME NO SEE!
NEW YORK POST
I SEE YOU'VE GONE BACK TO WEARING GLASSES- AND I UH, LIKE WHAT YOU'VE DONE WITH YOUR HAIR!
I KNOW WHAT YOU'RE THINKING, DAVID- YES, I AM BRINGING THIS ONE TO TERM!
SZECHUAN
WELL, GOOD, SO ARE YOU STILL ACTING?
NO, I'VE BEEN TOO BUSY- I'M WORKING HARD ON GETTING MY TEACHING CERTIFICATE!
SHE COULD'VE DONE THAT BACK IN PORTLAND!
I'VE BEEN SEEING THIS GUY STAN, YOU'D LIKE HIM, DAVID- HE'S A REAL GOOD MUSICIAN. HE KNOWS JOE JACKSON! ANYWAY, HE SAYS HE WANTS TO GET MARRIED....
I WOULD THINK THAT'S THE LEAST HE COULD DO, CONSIDERING....
I GUESS THE TIME TO MARRY HER WOULD HAVE BEEN WHEN I GOT HER PREGNANT. WELL IT'S TOO LATE NOW!
OH, BUT STAN'S NOT THE FATHER, DAVID!
HE'S NOT? WELL, WHAT ABOUT THE GUY WHO IS? WHAT DOES HE SAY?
HE WANTS TO GET MARRIED TOO, BUT I COULDN'T! HE'S JUST TOO BORING!!
JUKEBOX
WELL, YOU AND STAN HAVE MY BLESSING- WHEN'S THE DAY?
BUT I DON'T WANT TO MARRY STAN! I.. JUST.. I DON'T THINK HE REALLY LOVES ME!
GET THIS GIRL MARRIED OFF, DAVID, AND THE WORLD WILL BE A MUCH SAFER PLACE!

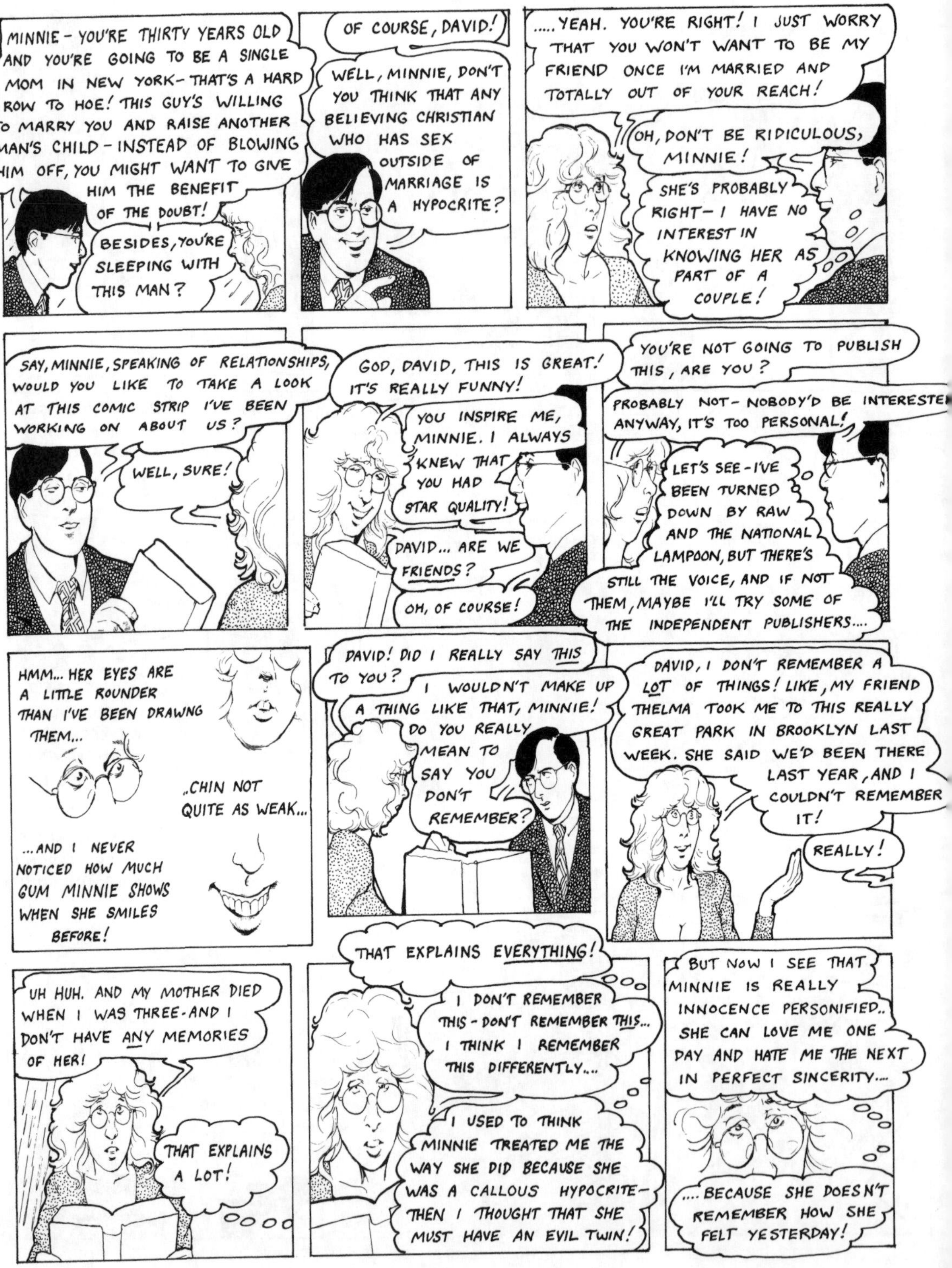
MINNIE - YOU'RE THIRTY YEARS OLD AND YOU'RE GOING TO BE A SINGLE MOM IN NEW YORK - THAT'S A HARD ROW TO HOE! THIS GUY'S WILLING TO MARRY YOU AND RAISE ANOTHER MAN'S CHILD - INSTEAD OF BLOWING HIM OFF, YOU MIGHT WANT TO GIVE HIM THE BENEFIT OF THE DOUBT!
BESIDES, YOU'RE SLEEPING WITH THIS MAN?
OF COURSE, DAVID!
WELL, MINNIE, DON'T YOU THINK THAT ANY BELIEVING CHRISTIAN WHO HAS SEX OUTSIDE OF MARRIAGE IS A HYPOCRITE?
.....YEAH. YOU'RE RIGHT! I JUST WORRY THAT YOU WON'T WANT TO BE MY FRIEND ONCE I'M MARRIED AND TOTALLY OUT OF YOUR REACH!
OH, DON'T BE RIDICULOUS, MINNIE!
SHE'S PROBABLY RIGHT- I HAVE NO INTEREST IN KNOWING HER AS PART OF A COUPLE!
SAY, MINNIE, SPEAKING OF RELATIONSHIPS, WOULD YOU LIKE TO TAKE A LOOK AT THIS COMIC STRIP I'VE BEEN WORKING ON ABOUT US?
WELL, SURE!
GOD, DAVID, THIS IS GREAT! IT'S REALLY FUNNY!
YOU INSPIRE ME, MINNIE. I ALWAYS KNEW THAT YOU HAD STAR QUALITY!
DAVID... ARE WE FRIENDS?
OH, OF COURSE!
YOU'RE NOT GOING TO PUBLISH THIS, ARE YOU?
PROBABLY NOT- NOBODY'D BE INTERESTE
ANYWAY, IT'S TOO PERSONAL!
LET'S SEE - I'VE BEEN TURNED DOWN BY RAW AND THE NATIONAL LAMPOON, BUT THERE'S STILL THE VOICE, AND IF NOT THEM, MAYBE I'LL TRY SOME OF THE INDEPENDENT PUBLISHERS....
HMM... HER EYES ARE A LITTLE ROUNDER THAN I'VE BEEN DRAWNG THEM...
..CHIN NOT QUITE AS WEAK...
...AND I NEVER NOTICED HOW MUCH GUM MINNIE SHOWS WHEN SHE SMILES BEFORE!
DAVID! DID I REALLY SAY THIS TO YOU?
I WOULDN'T MAKE UP A THING LIKE THAT, MINNIE!
DO YOU REALLY MEAN TO SAY YOU DON'T REMEMBER?
DAVID, I DON'T REMEMBER A LOT OF THINGS! LIKE, MY FRIEND THELMA TOOK ME TO THIS REALLY GREAT PARK IN BROOKLYN LAST WEEK. SHE SAID WE'D BEEN THERE LAST YEAR, AND I COULDN'T REMEMBER IT!
REALLY!
UH HUH. AND MY MOTHER DIED WHEN I WAS THREE - AND I DON'T HAVE ANY MEMORIES OF HER!
THAT EXPLAINS A LOT!
THAT EXPLAINS EVERYTHING!
I DON'T REMEMBER THIS - DON'T REMEMBER THIS... I THINK I REMEMBER THIS DIFFERENTLY....
I USED TO THINK MINNIE TREATED ME THE WAY SHE DID BECAUSE SHE WAS A CALLOUS HYPOCRITE - THEN I THOUGHT THAT SHE MUST HAVE AN EVIL TWIN!
BUT NOW I SEE THAT MINNIE IS REALLY INNOCENCE PERSONIFIED.. SHE CAN LOVE ME ONE DAY AND HATE ME THE NEXT IN PERFECT SINCERITY....
.... BECAUSE SHE DOESN'T REMEMBER HOW SHE FELT YESTERDAY!

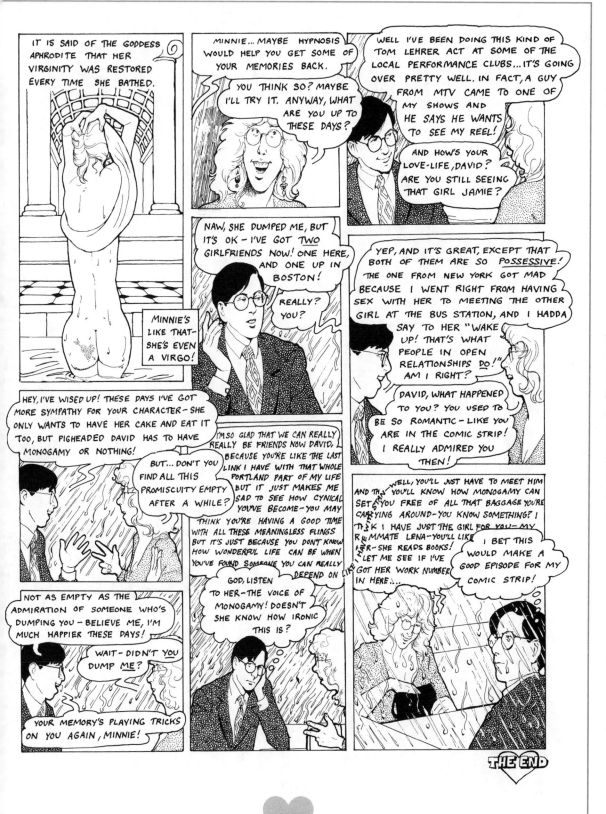

IT IS SAID OF THE GODDESS APHRODITE THAT HER VIRGINITY WAS RESTORED EVERY TIME SHE BATHED.

MINNIE... MAYBE HYPNOSIS WOULD HELP YOU GET SOME OF YOUR MEMORIES BACK.

YOU THINK SO? MAYBE I'LL TRY IT. ANYWAY, WHAT ARE YOU UP TO THESE DAYS?

WELL I'VE BEEN DOING THIS KIND OF TOM LEHRER ACT AT SOME OF THE LOCAL PERFORMANCE CLUBS...IT'S GOING OVER PRETTY WELL. IN FACT, A GUY FROM MTV CAME TO ONE OF MY SHOWS AND HE SAYS HE WANTS TO SEE MY REEL!

AND HOW'S YOUR LOVE-LIFE, DAVID? ARE YOU STILL SEEING THAT GIRL JAMIE?

NAW, SHE DUMPED ME, BUT IT'S OK — I'VE GOT TWO GIRLFRIENDS NOW! ONE HERE, AND ONE UP IN BOSTON!

REALLY? YOU?

MINNIE'S LIKE THAT-SHE'S EVEN A VIRGO!

YEP, AND IT'S GREAT, EXCEPT THAT BOTH OF THEM ARE SO POSSESSIVE! THE ONE FROM NEW YORK GOT MAD BECAUSE I WENT RIGHT FROM HAVING SEX WITH HER TO MEETING THE OTHER GIRL AT THE BUS STATION, AND I HADDA SAY TO HER "WAKE UP! THAT'S WHAT PEOPLE IN OPEN RELATIONSHIPS DO!" AM I RIGHT?

DAVID, WHAT HAPPENED TO YOU? YOU USED TO BE SO ROMANTIC - LIKE YOU ARE IN THE COMIC STRIP! I REALLY ADMIRED YOU THEN!

HEY, I'VE WISED UP! THESE DAYS I'VE GOT MORE SYMPATHY FOR YOUR CHARACTER - SHE ONLY WANTS TO HAVE HER CAKE AND EAT IT TOO, BUT PIGHEADED DAVID HAS TO HAVE MONOGAMY OR NOTHING!

BUT... DON'T YOU FIND ALL THIS PROMISCUITY EMPTY AFTER A WHILE?

I'M SO GLAD THAT WE CAN REALLY REALLY BE FRIENDS NOW DAVID, BECAUSE YOU'RE LIKE THE LAST LINK I HAVE WITH THAT WHOLE PORTLAND PART OF MY LIFE BUT IT JUST MAKES ME SAD TO SEE HOW CYNICAL YOU'VE BECOME - YOU MAY THINK YOU'RE HAVING A GOOD TIME WITH ALL THESE MEANINGLESS FLINGS BUT IT'S JUST BECAUSE YOU DON'T KNOW HOW WONDERFUL LIFE CAN BE WHEN YOU'VE FOUND SOMEONE YOU CAN REALLY DEPEND ON...

GOD, LISTEN TO HER - THE VOICE OF MONOGAMY! DOESN'T SHE KNOW HOW IRONIC THIS IS?

WELL, YOU'LL JUST HAVE TO MEET HIM AND THEN YOU'LL KNOW HOW MONOGAMY CAN SET YOU FREE OF ALL THAT BAGGAGE YOU'RE CARRYING AROUND - YOU KNOW SOMETHING? I THINK I HAVE JUST THE GIRL FOR YOU— MY ROOMMATE LENA-YOU'LL LIKE HER-SHE READS BOOKS! LET ME SEE IF I'VE GOT HER WORK NUMBER IN HERE...

I BET THIS WOULD MAKE A GOOD EPISODE FOR MY COMIC STRIP!

NOT AS EMPTY AS THE ADMIRATION OF SOMEONE WHO'S DUMPING YOU - BELIEVE ME, I'M MUCH HAPPIER THESE DAYS!

WAIT- DIDN'T YOU DUMP ME?

YOUR MEMORY'S PLAYING TRICKS ON YOU AGAIN, MINNIE!

THE END

189

Update

while the information on the previous two pages was accurate- except for the stuff I made up- when this book was first published ten years ago, a lot has happened in the years since. I've lost touch with a lot of people, but here's some of what I do know:

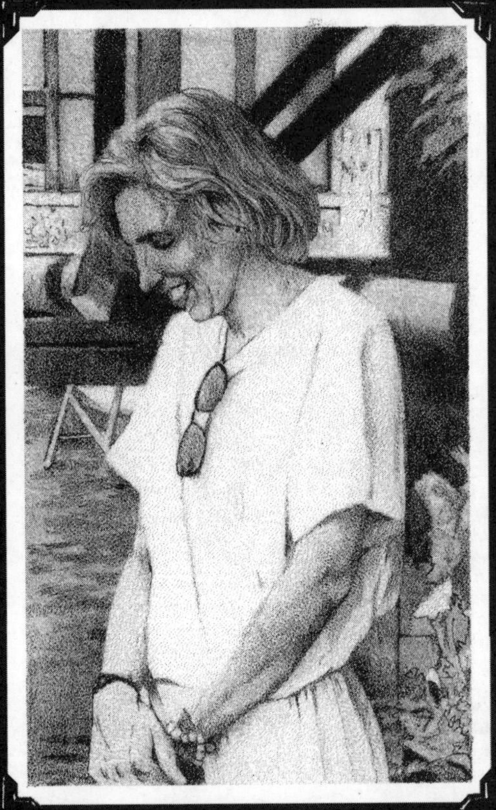

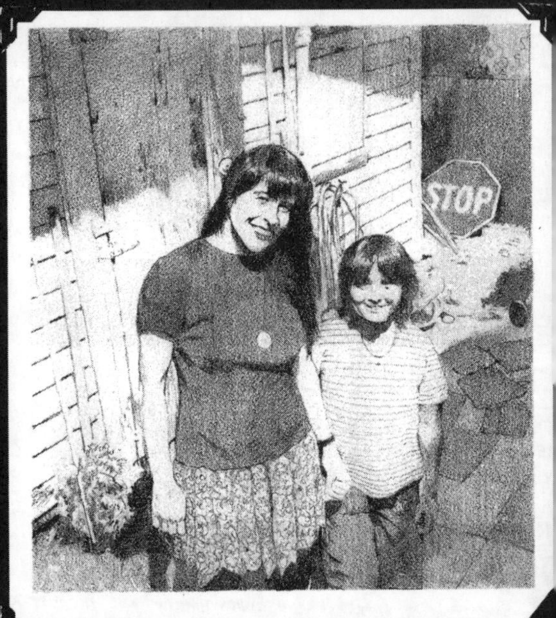

STOP

Anny is divorced and living in Los Angeles with her son. She'd like to quit her day job at Trader Joe's to do m full time. You can help by buying a copy of her lates at: www.cdbaby.com/cd/annycelsi

Teresa lives in Portland and does freelance writing as we teaching a class in water aerobics at the Matt Dishman

Minnie has remarried and now lives with her husband and two children in a Minneapolis suburb.

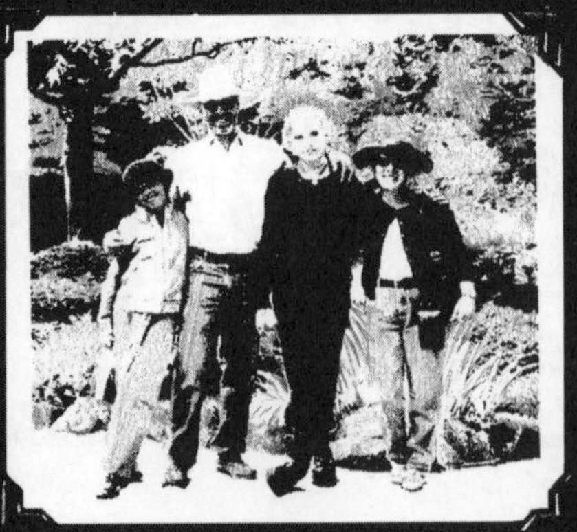

Paprika lives in Portland with her husband and two daughters (yeah, I made one of her kids a boy in the book just so I could throw in a cheesy Michael Jackson joke). Until recently, she worked at an agency booking extras for movie productions shooting in Portland, and even recommended me for a job as Keanu Reeves' stand-in (I didn't get it).

Jim is a carpenter and part-time singer-songwriter who has put out two of his own CD's. He lives in Brooklyn.

Shelley is married to a German who works at the U.N. They live in Brooklyn and are expecting their first child in the fall. She is studying to be something called a "family constellation facilitator" (don't ask).

Ron is now a technical writer for medical publications, and acts only occasionally. After living for seven years in the New York City loft that Eve and I moved out of, Ron and his partner recently bought a house in southeast Portland.

Rhonda is still married, as far as I know, and practices therapy in a city on the west coast.

Eight years ago Eve and I left New York and moved to my old family home in Portland (the very one which is a frequent locale in the book). It was a natural step—we were itching for more space than our loft afforded and ready to start a family.

Here is the family we started. Ben was born in 1996 and Rebecca in 2000.

There's not much to say beyond that. "David Chelsea In Love" is already a story from another century. I've been single and I've been coupled, and I like coupled better even if it lacks the drama of a good graphic novel.

— David Chelsea,
September 2003

191

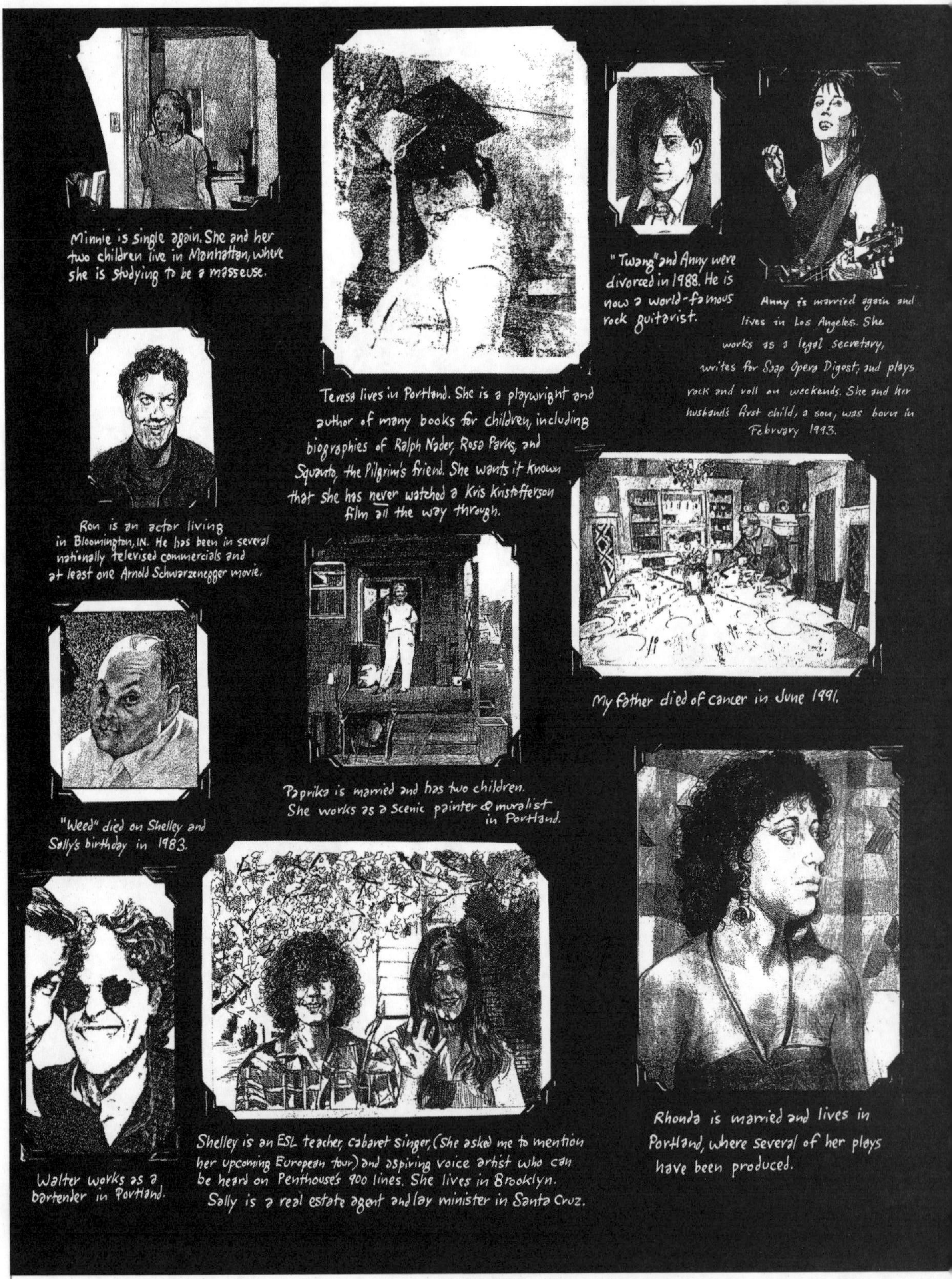
Minnie is single again. She and her two children live in Manhattan, where she is studying to be a masseuse.
Teresa lives in Portland. She is a playwright and author of many books for children, including biographies of Ralph Nader, Rosa Parks, and Squanto, the Pilgrim's friend. She wants it known that she has never watched a Kris Kristofferson film all the way through.
"Twang" and Anny were divorced in 1988. He is now a world-famous rock guitarist.
Anny is married again and lives in Los Angeles. She works as a legal secretary, writes for Soap Opera Digest, and plays rock and roll on weekends. She and her husband's first child, a son, was born in February 1993.
Ron is an actor living in Bloomington, IN. He has been in several nationally televised commercials and at least one Arnold Schwarzenegger movie.
My father died of cancer in June 1991.
"Weed" died on Shelley and Sally's birthday in 1983.
Paprika is married and has two children. She works as a scenic painter & muralist in Portland.
Walter works as a bartender in Portland.
Shelley is an ESL teacher, cabaret singer, (She asked me to mention her upcoming European tour) and aspiring voice artist who can be heard on Penthouse's 900 lines. She lives in Brooklyn.
Sally is a real estate agent and lay minister in Santa Cruz.
Rhonda is married and lives in Portland, where several of her plays have been produced.